WRITING AND AFRICA

Crosscurrents

General Editors:
Professor J B Bullen, University of Reading
Dr Neil Sammells, Bath College of Higher Education
Dr Paul Hyland, Bath College of Higher Education

Addison Wesley Longman Limited
Edinburgh Gate, Harlow
Essex CM2O 2JE, England
and Associated Companies throughout the world.

Published in the United States of America
by Addison Wesley Longman Inc., New York.

© Addison Wesley Longman Limited 1997

First published 1997

ISBN 0 582 21419 X CSD
ISBN 0 582 21418 1 PPR

British Library Cataloguing-in-Publication Data

A catalogue record of this book is
available from the British Library

Library of Congress Cataloging-in-Publication Data

A catalog entry for this title is available
from the Library of Congress

Set by 7 in 10/12 sabon
Produced by Longman Singapore Publishers (Pte) Ltd
Printed in Singapore

Contents

Notes on contributors

Jane Bryce-Okunlola lectures in the Department of English at the University of the West Indies, Cave Hill Campus, Barbados. Her recent publications include essays in *Motherlands: Black Women's Writing from Africa, the Caribbean and South Asia*, ed. S. Nasta (1991), *Unbecoming Daughters of Empire*, ed. S. Chew and A. Rutherford (1993) and *Readings in African Popular Culture*, ed. K. Barber (forthcoming).

Michael Green is a Professor in the Department of English, University of Natal, Durban. Recent publications include essays in *Critical Arts*, *World Literature Written in English*, *Wasafiri*, *English in Africa*, *Researches in African Literature* and the *Journal of Literary Studies*. He is the author of two forthcoming books: a study of the uses of history in South African fiction, and a work of historical fiction entitled *Sinking*.

Gareth Griffiths is Professor and Head of English at the University of Western Australia, Perth, Australia. In addition to numerous articles in journals and collections, he is the author of *A Double Exile: African and West Indian Writing Between Two Cultures* (1978) and one of the authors of *The Empire Writes Back: Theory and Practice in Post-Colonial Literatures* (1989) and co-editor of *The Post-Colonial-Studies Reader* (1995).

Lyn Innes is Professor of Post-Colonial Literatures at the University of Kent, Canterbury, England. Her recent books include *The Devil's Own Mirror: The Irishman and the African in Modern Literature* (1990), *Chinua Achebe* (1990), and *Woman and Nation in Irish Literature and Society* (1993).

Kadiatu Kanneh is a Lecturer in the School of English at the University of Birmingham. Her work has appeared in, among others, *The Oxford Literary Review*, *Women* and most recently in *The Post-Colonial-Studies Reader* (1995).

Kwaku Larbi Korang is a member of the Department of English at the University of Ghana. He is currently enrolled in the PhD programme in English at the University of Alberta, Canada. His work has appeared in *Kunapipi* and *World Literature Written in English*.

Robin Law is Professor of History at Stirling University. His many publications include *Early Yoruba Historiography* (1976), *The Horse in West Africa* (1980), *The Oyo Empire c. 1600 – c. 1836: A West African Imperialism in the Era of Atlantic Slave Trade* (1977) and *The Slave Coast of West Africa: The Impact of the Slave Trade on African Society* (1991).

Adewale Maja-Pearce is the Africa Editor of *Index On Censorship* and the Series Editor of the Heinemann African Writers Series. His publications include *Loyalties and Other Stories* (1986), *In My Father's Country* (1987), *How Many Miles to Babylon* (1990) and, most recently, *Nigerian Novelists of the Eighties* (1992)

Jack Mapanje is a Professorial Fellow in the School of English at Leeds University and was the Head of the English Department at the University of Malawi prior to his incarceration in 1987 by the Banda regime. His two anthologies of poetry, *Of Chameleons and Gods* (1981) and *The Chattering Wagtails of Mikuyu Prison* (1993) have received international critical acclaim. He is also co-editor of *Oral Poetry from Africa: An Anthology* (1983), and *Summer Fires: An Anthology of Modern African Poetry* (1983).

Ed Marum is Principal Lecturer and Head of the Division of Humanities at the University of Derby. He is currently engaged in researching the role of narrative in learning, with particular reference to twentieth-century African, Caribbean, Indian and European fiction.

Mpalive-Hangson Msiska is a Lecturer in English and Course Director for the BA Humanities at Birkbeck College, University of London, having previously taught at Bath College of Higher Education and the Universities of Malawi and Stirling. He is co-author of *The Quiet Chameleon: Modern Poetry from Central Africa* (1992).

Terence Rodgers is a Principal Lecturer in History and Assistant Dean of Humanities at Bath College of Higher Education. He has published on labour history and social history and on the politics of popular fiction. He is currently engaged in research on Rider Haggard and colonial fiction.

Caroline Rooney is a Lecturer in English and Post-Colonial Literatures at the University of Kent, Canterbury, England. She has held lectureships at Oxford University and the University of Capetown. Recent publications include essays in *Motherlands: Black Women's Writing from Africa, the Caribbean and South Asia*, ed. S. Nasta (1991) and *Essays on African Writing*, ed. A. Gurnah (1995). Her book on 'The Androgyne and the Double' will shortly be published by Routledge.

Stephen Slemon teaches post-colonial literatures and literary theory at the University of Alberta, Canada. His work on post-colonial theory has appeared in a number of journals and critical collections. He has edited, with Helen Tiffin, *After Europe: Critical Theory and Post-Colonial Writing* (1989) and is currently writing a book on post-colonial theory.

Anissa Talahite is a Lecturer in French in the Department of Languages at Manchester Metropolitan University. Her interests include post-colonial writing and, in particular, Maghrebian francophone literature. She has researched questions of race and gender in literature by Southern African women writers, and has published articles on gender, race and representation.

Patrick Williams is a Reader in Critical and Cultural Theory at Nottingham Trent University. He has published widely on colonial and post-colonial topics, including essays on Rudyard Kipling and Orientalism and the relationship between theory and poetry. His publications include *Colonial Discourse and Post-Colonial Theory: A Reader* (1991), co-edited with Laura Chrisman and *An Introduction to Post-Colonial Theory* (1996), co-authored with Peter Childs.

General Editors' Preface

Crosscurrents is an interdisciplinary series which explores simultaneously the new terrain revealed by recently developed methodologies while offering fresh insights into more familiar and established subject areas. In order to foster the cross-fertilisation of ideas and methods the topic broached by each volume is rich and substantial and ranges from issues developed in culture and gender studies to the re-examination of aspects of English studies, history and politics. Within each of the volumes, however, the sharpness of focus is provided by a series of essays which is directed to examining that topic from a variety of perspectives. There is no intention that these essays, either individually or collectively, should offer the last word on the subject – on the contrary. They are intended to be stimulating rather than definitive, open-ended rather than conclusive, and it is hoped that each of them will be pithy, and thought-provoking.

Each volume has a general introduction setting out the scope of the topic, the various modes in which it has been developed and which places the volume as a whole in the context of other work in the field. Everywhere, from the introduction to the bibliographies, pointers will be given on how and where the ideas suggested in the volumes might be developed in different ways and different directions, and how the insights and methods of various disciplines might be brought to bear to yield new approaches to questions in hand. The stress throughout the books will be on crossing traditional boundaries, linking ideas and bringing together concepts in ways which offer a challenge to previously compartmentalised modes of thinking.

Some of the essays will deal with literary or visual texts which are well-known and in general circulation. Many touch on primary material which is not easily accessible outside major library collections, and where appropriate, that material has been placed in a portfolio of documents collected at the end of each volume. Here again, it is hoped that this will provide a stimulus to discussion; it will give readers who are curious to explore further the implications of the arguments an opportunity to develop their own initiatives and to broaden the spectrum of their reading.

The authors of these essays range from international writers who are established in their respective fields to younger scholars who are bringing fresh ideas to the subjects. This means that the styles of the chapters are as various as their approaches, but in each case the essays have been selected by the general editors for their high level of critical acumen.

Professor Barrie Bullen
Dr Paul Hyland
Dr Neil Sammells

Acknowledgements

The publishers are grateful to the author, Freedom Nyambaya, for permission to reproduce her poem 'Of Course, it's not the same' from *On The Road Again* (1986).

Introduction

Mpalive-Hangson Msiska

The essays gathered here represent a variety of critical positions and constitute a re-examination of some of the central issues in the analysis of the production, distribution or mediation and reception of African writing. Without implying that the contributions are easily reducible to some common theme, one can, nevertheless, highlight some questions which appear most frequently in the collection. Rereading the essays, I am struck by the degree to which all contributions, in one way or another, focus on the problem of identity and difference as articulated, mapped out and inscribed in writing, politics and history.

The principal aim of the first section of the collection is to delineate the historical development of the literature of each of the major regions of the continent.. Clearly, the regions should not be regarded as absolute and discrete cultural units, but as ideologically determined constructs, some of which have their origins in colonial as well as post-colonial histories, and others in the more mundane editorial need to focus on particular supranational geo-cultural units. The three essays in this section collectively foreground the degree to which the historical frames, within which the respective literatures evolved, vary in both content and form as well as in terms of the specific character and intensity of the determining cultural and political forces. Anissa Talahite's essay presents the complex history of North African writing, detailing, among other things, the development of modern poetry from its emergence as a radical break with classical Arabic aesthetics in the nineteenth century through the early twentieth century when, under the influence of exile poets such as Kahil Gibran, it adopted elements of Romanticism, to the most recent period when, following the 1948 forced dispersal of the Palestinians, the poetry was dominated by gloom. Whether it is in poetry or prose, the defining feature of North

African literature, which is shared by other regions of the continent, is the quest to specify a space of cultural identity outside the trace of the hegemony of the past and the simple binarism of authenticity and hybridity. Thus, the need to preserve a distinct cultural identity has always been accompanied by the simultaneous incorporation and rejection of a colonising alterity or modernity. This has particularly been the case with regard to novelists, who have not only imaginatively adapted European aesthetic forms to local political and cultural needs, but also, as in the case of the Algerian writer Rachid Boudjedra, counterbalanced identification with disidentification. In a gesture similar to Ngugi wa Thiong'o's, in the 1980s Boudjedra switched from writing predominantly in French to writing solely in Arabic.

From Patrick Williams's account of the development of West African writing, we are reminded of the critical role of the African diaspora in the emergence of the literature of that region. For eighteenth-century writers such as Ouladah Equiano, who had had first-hand experience of slavery and slave trade, writing provided the means by which the Manichean dichotomy which underpinned and legitimised slavery could be interrogated as well as employed to highlight what Hélène Cixous has called, the annihilating logic of discourses of difference in which difference itself is frozen into an absolute defining sign of the relationship between Self and Other.[1] In some ways the political and historical problematic which structures Equiano's text is similarly at work in the writing of later writers such as Chinua Achebe and Wole Soyinka, especially in their critique of colonial cultural ideologies as well as in the use of writing as a vehicle for self-representation. Williams notes how the question of self-representation is not confined to the colonial relationship, but encompasses gender as well. Another opposition discernible in West African writing, according to Williams, is the tension between universalism and indigenity in creative practices as well as critical discourses, a problem that is explored further in the collection, particularly in contributions by Kwaku Larbi Korang and Stephen Slemon as well as Kadiatu Kanneh.

In the essay on East and Central African writing, in addition to reviewing the development of the literature of the region, I attempt a problematisation of the concept of African literary history. Given a certain repetition of events and ideas in the history of East African writing, we need to adopt a dialectical model of history which moves between teleology and iteration, totalisation and detotalisation – a model that approximates Gaston Bachelard's notion of differential history in which, apart from the dominant concept of time, other temporalities are regarded not only as conceivable, but also as constituting a permanent reminder of the provisional status of every determination of the historicity of experience.[2]

The link between history and writing features strongly in a number of essays in the second section of the book, which focuses on significant topics in debates about writing and culture in Africa. Michael Green's essay examines the relationship between fiction and history in South Africa, exploring the ways in which history is plotted and structured as an expression of a particular relation between time and ideology. Most importantly, Green contests the opposition between history and literature and argues that through Fredric Jameson's concept of historicising form 'we can approach uses of history in fiction without making the fictional simply evidence for the historical, or the historical merely something subsumed in the fictional' (p. 98). The desire to rethink the boundary between history and literature is shared by historians such as Hayden White who argue that 'the very distinction between imaginative and realistic writing and fictional and factual discourse, on the basis of which historiographical writing had been analyzed since its disengagement from rhetoric in the nineteenth century [needs] to be reassessed and reconceptualised'.[3] Furthermore, despite differences in procedures employed in the writing of history and of fiction, they are both, nevertheless, a site of a differential distribution of power, and thus always open to contestation, particularly in a place like South Africa where histories and literatures or fictions of different communities may overlap, but not always as scripts of a shared story, but of polarising difference.

It is an instance of a univocal narrativisation of otherness that Terence Rodgers provides in his study of Haggard's fiction about Africa. Avoiding an Orientalist reading and moving closer to critical colonial discourse analysis such as represented by Homi Bhabha, Rodgers argues that Haggard's figuration of Africa is less of a coherent presentation of the relationship between Self and Other, and more of an ambivalent display of a sort of Lacanian play of desire and lack.[4] Thus Haggard's texts are not simply a fulfilment of his authorial ideological intentions, but are subject to a certain logic of displacement in which the Self finds itself located at the very place it had reserved for the Other. According to Rodgers, this takes the form of a vacillation between Africa's supposed primitiveness and its possible educational value – between Africa as a subject of romance or desire and as a subject of a *bildungsroman* or a project of subject formation.

The articulation of power with history in the domain of writing and reading within the colonial formation is one of the problems Gareth Griffiths examines in his essay 'Writing, literacy and history'. He argues that writing was the means by which imperial and colonial projects in Africa were legitimated and entrenched. The cooption of Africans in external modes of writing such as Arabic or European languages ensured the continued production of the very terms of alienation and selective access to dominant and valorised cultures accompanying the imposition of forms of writing. Griffiths further notes that the privileging of writing over orature has continued to inform the allocation of cultural value in the continent, since the new African elite are themselves products of a history and an experience which has always associated writing with civilisation and orature with primitivism. In this way, writing serves as one of the many visible forms of the differential access to cultural capital, or, as Jacques Derrida would put it, here writing functions as one of those 'ethnocentric misconceptions of writing, "in the name of which we have long spoken of a people without writing and without history" '.[5] The interrogation of the relationship between writing and history in Griffiths's essay suggests that we can no longer safely operate with a calibration of African history in terms of the familiar designations such as pre-colonial, colonial and post-colonial, for they mask the extent to which processes of cultural and ideological production are repeated or indeed re-presented at different historical moments.

The dearth, if not virtual absence, of written records for pre-colonial African history has ensured an important role for oral tradition in African history. Robin Law presents the history of the methodology of oral tradition in African historiography, noting that influential models of interpreting and organising oral traditions, such as Jan Vansina's, are based on the idea that oral traditions are similar to the written text. Law regards it as erroneous to take oral traditions as a record of the past and suggests that they should rather be seen as interpretations of the historical moments they refer to and those in which they are recounted. One major implication of Law's remarks on the relationship between oral tradition and literature is that advocating a return to the use of oral traditions, as countless African critics and writers do, in the belief that this secures a pure alterity of writing, is mistaken, for there are no unmediated oral traditions, as all traditions bear the imprint of the moment of their production, the history of transmission and the moment of usage. Moreover, oral traditions, like written texts, are inscribed in the politics of meaning and interpretation of a given social formation.

Nowhere is writing's articulation of difference more evident than in relation to gender ideology. As Lyn Innes and Caroline Rooney explain, the privileging of writing in Africa is perhaps simultaneously a privileging of a masculine concept of writing in which women mostly feature either as absence or alterity. It is in the work of women writers, for instance Flora Nwapa, Ama Ata Aidoo and Tsitsi Dangarembga, that a more complex concept of female subjectivity is presented. Innes and Rooney also observe that women writers in Africa have sought distinctive ways of inscribing their being in writing, recording the various accents and inflections of being a woman in Africa. The interrogation of the distinction between speech and writing forms an important part of women writers' attempt to depart from traditional modes of representation and writing. According to the two authors, Ama Ata Aidoo, whom they describe as employing a 'spoken writing', is a good example of women's effort to radicalise both the content and form of African writing. The disruption of the dividing line between speech and writing represents a way of robbing writing of its association with gendered authority.

It is a margin within the economy of writing itself that Jane Bryce-Okunlola's essay addresses. She argues that there is need to pay greater attention to African popular literature. In her view, it is an important political and cultural area, one in which the Bakhtinian carnivalesque undermines the tendency towards unitary writing embodied in official discourse.[6] In this instance, it is the opening up and even the preservation of difference within African writing that becomes politically desirable, as the suppression of the play of difference is shown to simulate some more serious forms of political closure.

Drawing on his own and other writers' personal experiences, in his essay 'The changing fortunes of the writer in Africa?', the Malawian poet and critic Jack Mapanje charts the history of the politics of writing in Africa, in particular, the relationship between writers and the colonial and post-colonial state. He notes, for example, that the artist in traditional Africa seems to have had less constraints placed on him by political authority than his modern counterpart. However, such a comparison must not lead to an uncritical valorisation of the past. Even so, the writer will continue to have an important social and political role in Africa, even where visible forms of political oppression have been swept away. As Mapanje puts it, the writer will 'continue to become the memory of the nation. The writer, the musician and the painter [will] sing the song of reparation of the names of those heroes and heroines that our despotic regime[s] [have] obliterated from our history' (p. 230). Such a role, however, requires constant adaptation of strategies of subversion, since dictators show a remarkable resourcefulness, not least in seeking the assistance of fellow dictators if need be. Mapanje calls for the sort of strategic subterraneanity that is evident in his poetry, in which subversive agency relocates itself frequently in order to disable the mechanisms of censorship.[7]

The role of the writer in Africa is further explored in Adewale Maja-Pearce's analysis of the press. Maja-Pearce identifies institutional constraints which impede the effective functioning of the press in Africa. Like Mapanje, he underlines the effect of censorship on the press, but also demonstrates how international capital is implicated in the suppression of the freedom of the press in Africa. In other words, the conventional comparison between the local and international media in terms of their relative autonomy from political influence may in fact elide a more general connection between international capital and the media which may not be unique to a particular country, region or continent. In the light of this, Maja-Pearce argues that those who call for an independent press in Africa fail to recognise that such a situation could merely replace government ideological control of the press with that of private business. Already, in some countries, private business has demonstrated a marked tendency to employ the press and the media in general for particular partisan interests. This does not augur well for the maintenance of high journalistic standards in the continent. He concludes that Africa needs a combination of private and public control of the media if the excesses to which either form of ownership is prone are to be curbed.

In this context, Ed Marum's contribution, focusing on the role of African writing in resisting forms of ideological hegemony, is especially relevant. In his view, it is important to re-examine the work of early writers such as Edward Blyden, if only to appreciate the history of the problematic within which later writers were and are still operating. The discourse of cultural authenticity articulated by writers such as Chinua Achebe and Ngugi wa Thiong'o bears close resemblance to the work of earlier writers. In addition, Marum insists on the radical quality of Negritude, showing that in its immediate historical context, it represented a profound questioning of the terms of differentiation between Self and Other within colonialist ideology and discourse. Thus, for Marum, it is African literature's historical capacity to write back to the centre within and without that accounts for its principal functional distinctiveness.

Finally, the collection's examination of the question of language needs to be highlighted, not only because several of the contributors refer to it, but also because it is one of the most thorny problems in the debates about African literature and culture. For Chinua Achebe, for instance, the use of a colonial language does not necessarily dilute the ideological content or impact of African writing, but rather the question to be considered is how well a writer has adapted a particular European language to his world view.[8] Elsewhere Achebe regards the English language as a legitimate part of his local cultural resources rather than simply an aspect of colonial history and a neo-colonial cultural imperialism. He declares unapologetically: 'For me there is no other choice. I have been given the language and I intend to use it.'[9] Nevertheless, there has always been the suspicion that the continued use of European languages in African writing amounts to an acceptance of neo-colonial cultural relations. Ngugi's position is a Marxist reworking of Obi Wali's purely nationalist argument and a valorisation of the view articulated by some Negritudists such as David Diop that language is the essence of African specificity of being.[10]

A second but equally important aspect of the problem of language in African writing relates to the very language of cultural and critical interpretation. Wole Soyinka was perhaps the first writer to foreground the possibility of a colonialism of critical discourse.[11] It is ironic that Soyinka, the defender of local forms of knowledge, should himself be accused by Chinweizu and his colleagues as one of the misguided purveyors of Eurocentric values.[12] This debate has recently resurfaced in terms of the use of contemporary critical theory in African writing and post-colonial literatures in general.[13] Kwaku Larbi Korang and Stephen Slemon's essay intervenes in the debate about language in post-colonial Africa, reviewing some of the major positions on the matter and taking the problem of language beyond the politics of decolonisation to the unequal social relations of production underpinning both the colonial and post-colonial economy in most of the continent. They support the idea that the status of English in South Africa, for example, 'despite its many poses of political innocence, is inevitably the carrier of social perceptions, attitudes and goals that perpetuate unequal relations in race and class, and is functionally bound to social mechanisms for the manufacture of consent to oppression' (p. 258). Additionally, the essay clarifies and engages with the meaning of the term 'post-colonialism', itself.

It is critical discourse about African writing and culture that Kadiatu Kanneh's essay, 'What is African literature?: ethnography and criticism', examines. Kanneh's is a critique of the anthropology of African writing which she argues is always in danger of 'removing African literature into the realm of *cultural difference* away from the literature itself' (p. 73). Such cultural difference is a function of the use of a frame of temporality that has less to do with African literature and culture as such than with anthropology's commitment to particular notions of time and subjectivity rooted in Social Darwinism. No wonder that Afrocentric criticism, such as Chinweizu's, founds its critique of Eurocentricism on the concept of autochthonous time as disclosed by orature and other indigenous cultural forms. Nevertheless, as Kanneh demonstrates, Afrocentric critics fall into the same trap as their opponents, since they too conflate 'culture' and 'race'. She concludes the essay by highlighting the troubled relationship between critical, textual as well as political practice, arguing that: 'The most difficult point to accept, for Western literary criticism, might still be that Africa is not always thinking of, or speaking to the West, and that, at moments, it escapes.' (p 83).

Evidently the places to which Africa escapes are numerous, as are the spaces in which it makes itself visible. So it would be giving a false impression to claim that this collection offers a comprehensive coverage of the continent's writing. There are obvious gaps: for example, no general survey on Southern African writing has been included for the reason that an essay on the topic we commissioned was not submitted, but aspects of the literature of the region have been covered in a number of contributions, including Michael Green's extensive discussion of history and its uses in South Africa and Jack Mapanje's discussion of the politics of being a writer in Africa. However, readers needing a more detailed survey of the literatures of the region would profit greatly from Michael Chapman's *Southern African Literatures* (1995).

Nevertheless, we hope we have brought together a collection of essays which offers fresh historical and critical perspectives on African writing, giving an accessible analysis of the development of writing in

the continent while taking into account some of the ma
the literary and cultural criticism of African writing, esp
brought about by the use of contemporary critical
pedagogical reasons, specifically in order to illustrate topics
covered by the book, we have included a Document Section
of the collection containing long excerpts taken from key   ⌐s on
African writing and culture.

Notes

1. Hélène Cixous and Catherine Clement, *The Newly Born Woman* (Manchester, 1986), pp. 79–81.
2. See Robert Young, *White Mythologies* (London, 1990), pp. 69–90.
3. Hayden White, ' "Figuring the nature of the times deceased": Literary Theory and Historical Writing', in Ralph Cohen (ed.), *The Future of Literary Theory* (London, 1990), p. 23.
4. See Homi Bhabha, *The Location of Culture* (London, 1994); and Jacques Lacan, *Ecrits*, trans. Alan Sheridan (London, 1977).
5. Jacques Derrida, *Of Grammatology*, trans. Gayatri Chakravorty Spivak (London and Baltimore, 1974), pp. 27, 109.
6. Mikhail Bakhtin, *The Dialogic Imagination*, trans. Michael Holoquist (Austin, 1981).
7. See Mpalive-Hangson Msiska, 'Geopoetics: Subterraneanity and Subversion in Malawian Poetry', in Abdulrazak Gurnah (ed.), *Essays on African Writing: Contemporary Literature* (London, 1995), pp. 73–99.
8. Chinua Achebe, 'The African Writer and the English Language', *Morning Yet On Creation Day: Essays* (New York, 1975), p. 103.
9. Ibid., p. 102.
10. See Obi Wali, 'The Dead-End of African Literature?', *Transition*, vol. 10 (September, 1963), pp. 13–15; and for a summary of Diop's ideas, see Ngugi wa Thiong'o, *Decolonising the Mind: The Politics of Language* (London, 1986), p. 25.
11. Wole Soyinka, *Myth, Literature and the African World* (Cambridge, 1976), p. xii.
12. See Chinweizu, Onwuchekwa Jemie and Ihechukwu Madubuike, *Toward the Decolonization of African Writing* (Enugu, Nigeria, 1980).
13. See, for example, Diana Brydon, 'Commonwealth or Common Poverty?: The New Literatures in English and the New Discourse of Marginality', in Stephen Slemon and Helen Tiffin (eds), *After Europe* (Coventry, 1989), pp. 1–16.

Part I
Writing and History: A Survey

1 *North African Writing*

Anissa Talahite

North African writing offers a perspective that cannot be strictly confined within the geographical boundaries of North Africa. From a linguistic and cultural point of view, it is part of Arabic literature, a category that includes the literature from the countries both of North Africa and the Middle East. North African writing is therefore determined by the sense of belonging to an Arab nation which shares the same language and culture, and to a certain extent, the same religion. Since North Africa became part of the Arab Muslim empire in the eighth century, the Arabic language and the Muslim religion have symbolised the force bringing the Arab people together in a common destiny. Today, North African writing is largely informed by this common Arab heritage which represents not only a way of connecting with the cultural tradition but also a way of understanding the present. Beyond their denomination as Arab and Muslim, North African countries are also shaped by the Berber culture and language, a tradition that preceded the introduction of Arab culture. In Morocco, for instance, Berber is the mother tongue of nearly half of the population.[1] The Berber oral tradition is an important component of North African culture despite the fact that it has been overshadowed by the dominant position occupied by the written languages. It has, however, recently been the focus of writers who have attempted to give Berber folk stories, songs and poems a more significant place within North African literature.[2]

The more recent history of North Africa saw the birth of a new literature that originated from the experience of French colonialism in the former colonies of the Maghreb (namely Morocco, Algeria and Tunisia). After some timid attempts to address the 'native question' in articles often published in colonial journals in the late nineteenth and early twentieth centuries, North African writing in French acquired a more definite shape in the 1950s with the emergence of a greater national consciousness. The French language became a channel through which writers could confront colonial authority. Thus, North African writers started experimenting with narratives and with poetic language as a way of forging a distinct identity. For North African writers, writing in French means reflecting on the relationships between European and indigenous cultures in order to construct a North African voice which would integrate the different cultures inherited from the past.

The North African literary scene shows that it is difficult to regard North African writing as singular and homogeneous. Instead, it seems more appropriate to speak of North African *literatures* rather than of one literature: a literature in Arabic which extends beyond the confines of North Africa; an age-old Berber oral literature which has survived in certain areas; and a literature in French in the countries that were part of the former French empire. Given the range of North African writing, this survey concentrates only on the written literatures and on particular authors and texts that exemplify the main developments. Arabic and francophone literatures are dealt with in separate sections in order to highlight the importance of language in shaping modern literary forms.

Writing in Arabic

The countries of North Africa, from Morocco to Egypt, share the collective memory of their common Muslim Arab past, which survives today in their language and literature and which plays an important part in the shaping of an Arab identity. Although each country speaks its own variation of Arabic, the Arab world shares one official language (used in schools, the media, etc.) which is distinct from the spoken forms. This language, called 'fusha' in Arabic, but which in English is referred to as classical or sometimes literary Arabic, represents the crucible of Arab culture since it brings the Arab nation together as did Arab civilisation in the past. As far as writers are concerned, one of the great advantages of using classical Arabic is that it gives them access to a readership throughout the Arab world. However, modern writers have been increasingly confronted with the issue of bridging the gap between this higher form of Arabic, used by the educated minority, and the 'dialects' spoken by the majority.

The transformations of Arab society in the modern period brought about major changes in its literary expression. Arab societies at the beginning of the nineteenth century were faced with the need to reassess the heritage of Arab culture, incorporating technological and social change as well as making sense of the increasing contact of Arab culture with the West. A generation of writers, scholars and politicians started to formulate a debate on their society by exploring the intricacies of cultural transformation, the significance of religion in the face of scientific development and the political implications of social change. Their response to the increasing cultural and political impact of Europe on the Arab world was to redefine Arab culture and to create new forms of self-expression.

In Egypt, the cultural renaissance of the *Nahdah* in the late 1880s and the early 1900s was significant in shaping modern Arabic thinking as well as in influencing the development of literary forms. The *Nahdah* originated as an aesthetic movement in Lebanon but took on a political dimension in Egypt because of the particular historical circumstances brought about by the presence of European colonial powers. The invasion of Egypt by Napoleon in 1798 is seen as a crucial point in the modern history of the Arab world as it marks the beginning of increasing contacts between the East and the West. These contacts took the form of a military and cultural hegemony over Egypt and the rest of the Arab world. The military presence of European powers was accompanied by a particular interest in Arab culture: Orientalist scholars, archaeologists and painters identified with an exotic image of the 'Orient' which bore little in common with reality but which served to assert the supremacy of the West over Arab civilisation.[3] As a result of the increasing impact of European culture on the Arab way of life through the presence of traders, explorers, technicians and educationalists, a new class of Egyptians emerged, most having received an education in the schools set up by the colonial authorities. The writers who contributed to the cultural awakening of the *Nahdah* were scholars who were in close contact with European ideas and who had studied in European universities where they had become acquainted with European philosophy and literature. Rifa ah Rafi at-Tahtawi was one of the first modern Egyptian writers to write about European society.

At-Tahtawi and many of his contemporaries saw Europe's technological advance as a model of development for Arab societies. This idea, however, was not unambiguous and clashed with the Arab image of the past which symbolised, in many respects, civilisational progress. One of the ways in which some thinkers came to terms with this contradiction was to look at technological progress as distinct from moral superiority: the first an attribute of Europe; the second of the Arab world. Some writers tried to go beyond this dichotomy by analysing the changes that were affecting Islamic societies. The Tunisian politician and writer, Khayr ad-Din at-Tunisi provided an argument in favour of cultural borrowing from Europe. In his book, *Muqaddima*, he advocated a reform of Islamic institutions by arguing that Arab societies should learn from the experiences of European societies, mainly from the Industrial Revolution and from the democratic forms of political representation. His main contention was that, in the same way as the West had benefited from the scientific progress of the Arab world in the Middle Ages, it was now time for the Arabs to acquire knowledge from Europe. Others took a more nationalistic stand against European influence on the Islamic way of life. Although also calling for the need to adapt Islam to the demands of modern life, the leader of the Islamic Reformist movement, the Egyptian writer Jamal ad-Din al-Afghani, and later his follower, Muhammad Abduh, stressed the importance of religion in the spiritual life of a nation and the necessity to find strength in one's own cultural and spiritual heritage. Speaking against the cultural alienation threatening Arab societies, al-Afghani argued that reforms could only come from Islamic roots and not from a superficial imitation of European ways. In the same line of thought, another follower of the Reformist movement, Qasim Amin, suggested that one had to look at Islam itself in order to find a solution to gender inequalities. Arab women, according to him, had no status, not because of religion, but because autocratic rulers had determined a hierarchy whereby women were relegated to the lowest rank. Today, Qasim Amin's analysis seems to lack the depth of some of the more recent writings on gender in Arab societies by feminist authors, such as Nawal el-Saadawi and Fatima Mernissi. However, his position is to be interpreted in context: Qasim Amin's prime concern was not to analyse the question of gender but to formulate a critique of the social and symbolic structures in Arab society at a time of transition. The demands created by the economic, technological, social and political changes that were taking place at a very rapid pace forced writers to rethink their own cultural categories. This is clearly reflected in the literary production that has emerged since the *Nahdah*. The increasing contact with European culture and the internal dynamics of change that Arab societies were experiencing at the beginning of the century resulted in two main developments: the departure from classical poetry and the emergence of new narrative forms.

Arabic poetry, which pre-dates Islam, is the genre *par excellence* of classical Arabic literature. During the golden years of Arab Muslim civilisation, particularly under the Umayyad dynasty (660 AD), poetry reached the peak of its development and became a central element in the life of the Arabs. It was a means of recording history and celebrating battles and chivalrous rulers. Poetry played an important part in creating a sense of Arab national identity throughout the Arab world. The decline of this poetry in the nineteenth century coincided with the domination by the Ottoman empire and the stifling of Arab culture that resulted from it. One has to wait for the *Nahdah* in the early twentieth century to see a poetic revival in Arabic literature. The Egyptian poet Ahmad Shawqi symbolises the new spirit of the beginning of the century and is considered as the first poet who rescued Arabic poetry from decline. In line with the classical tradition of the *qasida* (the traditional ode with one rhyme), Shawqi's poetry recreates a harmonious world where the past and the present are one. Although celebrated as the 'Prince of Poets', Ahmad Shawqi was soon to be seen as failing to express the turmoil and the sense of displacement brought about by the deep transformations that the Arab world was experiencing. Still relying on the aesthetic conventions of the past, his poetry seemed unable to convey the urgency of the present.

The demands of the new era meant that poets had to find alternative poetic forms to express the deep transformations of Arab societies. The first generation of poets who broke away from the past found their inspiration in the European Romantic poets; but the main impulse came from those Arab poets who had emigrated to North America, the most celebrated of whom is probably the Lebanese-American Gibran Kahlil Gibran. The main contribution of the *Mahjar*, the literature in exile, was to introduce new techniques into Arabic poetry; namely, prose poems and free verse. The influence of the Mahjar poets was considerable, as in the case of the Tunisian, Abu al-Qasim al-Shabbi, a prominent figure of avant-garde Arabic poetry in the 1920s, whose romantic lyricism is the expression of a deeper yearning for freedom:

> O death, O fate that has no eyes,
> Stop where you are! Or turn aside,
> Let love and dream sing out for us[4]

Like his contemporaries, al-Shabbi is inspired by a desire to bring change and renewal to the old world. The poetic free flow of emotions is the expression of a need to break free from the constraints of classical poetry. This is made easier by the fact that the aesthetic conventions of Romantic poetry were borrowed from another tradition and therefore did not carry the weight of the Arabic past. Poets could therefore express themselves outside the social, political and aesthetic constraints of their culture.

Whether Arabic poetry in the first half of this century drew heavily on European romanticism, symbolism, or surrealism, it remained rooted in the Arab experience of a rapidly changing world. Technological and cultural changes brought about uncertainties which were to accentuate in the second half of the century with a series of events that affected the Arab world in a major way. The 1948 Palestine conflict, the creation of the state of Israel and the subsequent physical and symbolic displacement of the Palestinian people shattered the consciousness of Arab writers and marked a new turn in the way in which they perceived their place in the modern world. Disillusioned, they could no longer identify with the Romantic mood of the previous generation. Instead, they found an echo of their own gloom in the voices of poets in other parts of the world where people were experiencing similar situations of displacement, such as in the poetry of Pound, Eliot, Yeats, Aragon, Lorca, Neruda, and Hikmat.

After the 1950s, Arabic poetry took on a more vehement tone, denouncing injustice and oppression. This is shown in the writing by the Sudanese-Libyan poet Muhammad al-Faituri which reveals the evil of colonialism and racism by focusing on an image of Africa constructed around the idea of the struggle for freedom and dignity. In his later poems, al-Faituri uses the mythical figures of Bidpai and Dabshalim, taken from the Indian folk stories *Kalila wa Dimna*, which are also part of the Arabic folklore, to comment on the political situation in the Arab world following the defeat of 1967. Al-Faituri's work reflects the two-fold nature of Arabic poetry after the 1950s, as it moves between the outer world of politics on the one hand, and the inner world of the poet's dreams and aspirations, on the other. These dreams are often expressed through myths of resurrection which show, as Badawi put it, 'how deeply, and even tragically, concerned many of these poets are about the need to revive Arab culture and society, and drag it into the context of the fast-moving civilized western world'.[5]

The emergence of fiction in Arabic literature in the twentieth century also reflects the transition between the old world and the new age. Whether fiction and drama were part of Arabic literature prior to the introduction of European culture is an ongoing debate. Nevertheless, one could argue that they are new in the modern sense that is attributed to them today. Apart from the *maqama*, the traditional Arabic folk narrative which attracted writers as long ago as the tenth century, traditional folk stories were generally regarded as outside the literary canons which prevailed in the classical period. They did not generate any real interest among writers, who considered them as futile and as 'lower' forms of literature.[6]

Some critics have argued that the tradition of classical literature did not provide any framework for the development of narrative form and was even antagonistic to it. Bencheikh, for example, explained that classical Arabic literature 'neglected the individual for the benefit of the collective ideology . . . and privileged unifying abstractions to the expense of difference and reality.[7] Thus, according to this view, as genres that place the individual at their centre, fiction and drama could not have originated from the tradition of classical Arabic literature. It seems that what constituted the main impulse for the development of narrative genres was the influence of European fiction as well as the emergence of new concepts of history and human destiny in the modern period.

European works of fiction (mainly in French and in English) were first introduced to the Arabic-speaking public through translations but also in the original as, with the growing influence of European powers, the number of educated people who could read French and English was rising. Translations were part of the attempt to understand European culture, since the latter was becoming a model of technological as well as cultural progress. An important aspect of translation is the question that it raises about the difficulty of defining European concepts in Arabic and the necessity of adapting and transforming the original texts to comply with the specificities of Arab culture. The playwright Tawfiq al-Hakim, for example, describes how plots had to be altered when adapting European plays to the stage. At a time when tradition did not allow an Egyptian woman to appear unveiled in front of a person not related to her, translators had to change the plot so that male and female characters were related. As al-Hakim states, 'the alterations of social relations in accordance with the demands of our milieu in turn necessitated changes in the dialogue, the characterization and some of the situations of the play, adding up to considerable departures from the original'.[8] Thus, translations played an important part in introducing new ways of writing into Arabic literature.

The period of translation and adaptation of European texts was followed by the first attempts to write authentic Arabic narratives. The year 1923 saw the publication of what critics call the first significant novel in Arabic. Muhammad Husayn Haykal's *Zaynab* is the story of an Egyptian peasant forced to marry a man whom she does not love. Beyond the apparent simplicity of its theme, *Zaynab* addresses some important questions about Egyptian society which were not usually approached in literature, such as the life of the peasantry and the position of women. The novel is also innovative in its use of language as it attempts to break the barriers between high and low forms of Arabic by inserting colloquial patterns of speech into the dialogues. *Zaynab* marks the beginning of a search for authentic ways of translating the experiences of Arab people into narrative form.

The first novels to appear on the literary scene have a strong autobiographical flavour. Taha Husayn's *An Egyptian Childhood*, for example, portrays life in rural Egypt at the beginning of the century through the experiences of a boy who, struck by blindness in his early childhood (like the author himself), finds refuge in his thirst for learning. The novel uses the distance of the third-person narrative but at the same time tries to recreate the immediacy of the personal experiences. Like many of his contemporaries, Taha Husayn saw his individual life-story as part of the collective destiny of his people and, therefore, as a suitable subject for literature. The role of the novel in this early period was essentially to provide a framework for dealing with the individual experience as part of the wider social and historical changes that were happening in Arab society.

In the second half of the century, writers continued the experiments of the early novelists in a way more challenging and thematically diverse. The most prominent figure of this period is undoubtedly Naguib Mahfuz. It is interesting that Mahfuz's first novels attempt to resurrect history; not the history of the past Arab civilisation, but the ancient Pharaonic past. Set in Ancient Egypt, the novels are in fact a covert criticism of modern society. Evading censorship, Mahfuz uses the allegory of Ancient Egyptian history to make a critical comment about King Faruk's rule and the British protectorate. In his first novels, Mahfuz reinterprets the ancient past in order to analyse the present and establish historical continuity between the two. In his later novels, the Cairo trilogy, which is considered as his masterpiece, Mahfuz explores the recent past of Egyptian society by tracing the history of a Cairene family over several generations. This family is in many respects a microcosm of Egyptian society, and humanity in general. Beside being precisely located in time, the trilogy has a strong sense of place. The trilogy (each one named after a district of the old Cairo) focuses on the street as a social space, with its merchants, musicians and cafés. Critics have traditionally compared Mahfuz's realist descriptions with Dickens's London and Zola's Paris, emphasising the writer's debt to nineteenth-century European Realism. However, Mahfuz prefers to see his novels as part of a larger tradition, one that includes authors such as Dostoievsky, Tolstoi, Tchekhov, Maupassant, Shakespeare and Gide.[9]

European Realism has had a particular influence on Mahfuz and his contemporaries. It offered them a means of portraying the transformations of Arab society and the conflict between tradition and modernity by focusing on ordinary people: workers, shopkeepers, craftsmen, peasants, clerks, students. In Mahfuz's trilogy, the characters represent different stages in the life of the nation. The central figure, Kamal Abdel Jawad, a largely autobiographical character, embodies the tensions between the old and the new. Kamal struggles to come to grips with the contradictions between Arab traditional culture and a modernity that is, in many respects, an 'imported' concept. Like his character, Mahfuz, as a writer using the novel form, is involved in a similar process: the novel for him is a way of exploring new ways of perceiving reality. The classical language of literature is modified through the play between high and low forms of Arabic. Mahfuz's metaphors also show a desire to innovate; the presence of similes referring to science, technology and modern communication suggests, Somekh observes, that the novelist is attempting to create 'a language striving to become one which befits a modern urban writer'.[10] As one of Mahfuz's characters remarks, religion used to be a way of asserting truths, but now there is 'a new language, which is Science, and there is no way of asserting truths, great or small alike, except in this language'.[11] Science, often equated with modernity, is seen as the embodiment of the new era, an era where old ways of thinking have no place.

Realism in Arabic fiction was largely a reflection of the scientific and technological age where the writer saw him/herself as the rational voice interpreting reality. Thus, the novel provided the framework for expressing the ideas of progress and change that characterise the modern era. With the period of gloom following the 1967 Arab defeat, fiction started to offer a fragmented vision of reality that emphasised its contradictions rather than tried to resolve them. Like Romanticism in poetry, Realism lost its impact, and novelists started to search for other forms of writing. They often turned to psychological experience as a way of understanding reality. *Season of Migration to the North* (1966), by the Sudanese novelist al-Tayyib Salih, explores the violence of the inner conflicts brought about by the confrontation between the West and the East through the theme of the relationship between a European woman and an Arab emigrant, a theme explored by more than one writer.[12] More critical than the previous generation of the *Nahdah* about the civilising mission of Europe, writers like al-Tayyib turned inwards to interpret their own experience.[13]

The novel occupies an important place in the search for ways of redefining the individual's relation to the past. New perceptions of reality as well as influences from other literatures, particularly from Latin American writers, have led Arabic fiction away from Realism. Writers, such as the Egyptian novelist Yusuf Idris, have also found in the short story a way of portraying the fragmentation of today's world.

The development of North African writing in Arabic reflects the need to go beyond the duality between the old and the new, the East and the West, in order to create an authentic language. As it has been suggested, this 'new language' was born of a reappraisal of the Arabic classical tradition and the introduction of new forms of writing borrowed from other literatures and adapted to the North African context. In the French-speaking former colonies of North Africa, a similar process can be observed. Francophone Maghrebian writers deal with the contradictions and dualities of modern Arab societies by adapting the French language to their own world view.

Writing in French

North African literature in French has a relatively short history. In the period following the Second World War, writers from the North African French colonies (namely Morocco, Algeria and Tunisia) started to use fictional modes to describe their condition and their aspirations as colonised people. The collapse of the structures of pre-colonial society and the devalued (or non-existent) status which the Arabic language and culture occupied in this region meant that, for these writers, using the French language was the only way of making their voices heard. The French presence in the Maghreb resulted in an 'acculturation' whereby the French language was imposed at all levels of society, excluding all other languages and cultures. This was clearly reflected in the French policy of cultural *assimilation* – carried out mainly through the educational system – which meant that North Africans had to accept French culture and language as their own and deny their Arab Berber heritage. This does not mean that the indigenous traditions died out completely. The Berber culture was handed down from generation to generation through oral tradition, while the Muslim Arab tradition was kept alive, particularly by the Ulema, the religious scholars whose movement played an important role in shaping the nationalist consciousness that led to the independence of North Africa. A literature in Arabic and a literature in French, the products of different traditions, have developed side by side in the Maghreb as writers have been concerned with finding a voice of their own. In the case of the literature in French, this search has taken the form of an exploration and an alteration of the French language to make it suit the reality of North Africa.

With the exception of French colonial writers such as Albert Camus, whose writing, although set in Algeria, has very little to say about its people, North African writing started as a description of the life of the Arab Berber population, their humanity and their suffering under colonial rule. This literature of the 'unveiling' (*littérature du dévoilement*) was directed particularly at the French readership, especially as literacy among the colonised population was very limited.[14] In *Le Fils du Pauvre* (1950), Mouloud Feraoun described the hardship of life in the poverty-striken rural area of Kabylia in Algeria through the autobiographical character of Fouroulou (anagram of the author's name) who struggles to acquire an education. As he gradually moves away from his village towards the 'other world' of the city where he acquires another identity, Fouroulou feels increasingly alienated from himself. This sense of alienation is reflected in the writing which contains a certain restraint, which as Christiane Achour described, 'denounces, at a second reading, an impossible assimilation which would enable the individual to fully express himself or herself'.[15]

The suppressed voice that can be heard faintly in Feraoun's novels and that epitomises the difficulty of expressing oneself in the colonial language starts to gain confidence over the years. In Mohammed Dib's trilogy, it takes on a political tone. In the same realist vein as Feraoun, and with the same concern for unveiling the real life of the 'indigenes' (people who had no identity other than being 'natives'), Dib tells the story of Omar's childhood in the traditional household shared with other families. Through the eyes of the child, the novelist draws a picture of colonial society: the poverty, the hunger, the police intrusion into private life, the hypocrisy of the moralistic teaching at the French school. With a sense of urgency, we follow Omar through the events that herald the beginning of the Algerian liberation struggle in November 1954. The tensions preceding the revolution are felt through the poetic quality of the writing. Poems are directly inserted in the prose to express the despair and the suppressed dreams of the community.

From 1954, poetry seems to be the privileged form for conveying the suffering and repression of the years of struggle against French colonialism, particularly in Algeria where the fight was most violent. Such poetry, written in the heat of struggle, tries to capture the historical moment in images that speak of suffering and torture, but also of unremitting hope. Poets like Jean Senac, Djamal Amrani, Anna Greki and Bachir Hadj Ali denounced the atrocities perpetrated on the Algerian people. Some of the poetic intensity of their texts can also be found in the work of Frantz Fanon who, instead of poetry, used the essay genre in order to express the sense of urgency so characteristic of this period.

The dream of a new and liberated Algeria is a dominant theme in the writing that preceded and followed independence. In what is considered today the masterpiece of North African literature in French, the Algerian novelist Kateb Yacine gave a symbolic dimension to the dreams of independence. Published two years after the beginning of the war, *Nedjma* is a statement not only about French colonialism but also about the newly emerging nation in search of its deep psychic roots. The story revolves around four characters obsessed with their impossible love for one woman, Nedjma, a figure whose identity is never clearly defined. The unknown origin of her birth creates the tension in the novel: the daughter of a French woman and of a father who remains unknown, Nedjma is perhaps the sister of one of the four men in love with her. It is clear that Nedjma is a symbol of Algeria: a symbol that remains undefined and 'unfathered'.

In many respects, *Nedjma* is a novel that has confused its readers by its unconventional nature. While the non-linear structure of the plot has been attributed to a non-Western concept of time, critics have also compared the novel with the works of Faulkner and Joyce. Yet, parallels with other North African narratives can be drawn. Dib's later novel *Who Remembers the Sea* (1962) also explores the collective history of the nation by appealing to the collective unconscious. In a postscript to the book, Dib compares his novel with Picasso's *Guernica*, a painting where no horrific element can be found, but where horror is omnipresent. The departure from the Realism so characteristic of the early writing in French means that writers are no longer producing 'neatly written' autobiographies to fit into the world of the coloniser, but are transforming the dominant language to make it fit *their* reality.

Algerian writing in the 1950s has been described as a 'literature of crisis' because of the political tensions that dominated the period. However, politics did not create as great demands on Moroccan and Tunisian writers who, in this period, were less prolific than their Algerian counterparts. Tunisia and Morocco obtained their independence from French rule in 1956, while Algeria struggled through seven years of war until independence in 1962. In addition, the policy of cultural assimilation had particularly devastating effects in Algeria, a country considered during colonisation as a department of France. This accounts for the early writings in French by Algerian authors. Their focus is often on the colonial conflict, while, on the other hand, Moroccan and Tunisian writers could deal more easily with the internal conflicts of their society. In 1954, Driss Chraibi's virulent and uncompromising attack on Moroccan traditional society in *The Simple Past* shocked many readers. The novel revolves around the central image of the father; a symbol of the patriarchy which is seen as the basis of the repressive social order where authority and religion cannot be questioned. As in *The Pillar of Salt* (1953), a novel by the Tunisian author Albert Memmi, the story is strongly auto-biographical. In both novels, the experience of childhood is explored as an insight into the hierarchical structures of society, as the revolt against the father represents a revolt against the dominant order. In his later novel, *The Butts* (1955), Chraibi focuses on the world of North African immigrants in France in order to articulate a critique of Western civilisation.

The 1960s mark a turning point in North African writing in French, as writers start to 'scratch the surface' of the newly acquired independence to reveal the uncertainties of the present. Considered as the *enfant terrible* of Maghrebian francophone literature, the Algerian novelist Rachid Boudjedra first appeared on the literary scene in 1969 with *La Répudiation*; a controversial novel, not only because it deals with the taboos of religion and patriarchy, but also because of its style. *La Répudiation* was to revolutionise Maghrebian literature in French by its unembellished style and the proliferation of hallucinating images. The novel describes the traumatic experience of childhood in a house dominated by the powerful presence of a God-like father and the violence of male sexuality. Through a series of narratives, it unfolds the memories of childhood and adolescence which are haunted by the repudiation of the mother and the narrator's incestuous desire for his father's new wife. The stories are prompted by the narrator's lover, Celine, a French woman who acts as a mirror for his fantasies. Named after the French writer who influenced Boudjedra, Celine represents the 'other', through whom the narrator can reflect on his own culture.

Like his predecessors, Boudjedra is not simply writing a testimony of his childhood in a repressive society. His novels also bring together different traditions. In *Les 1001 Années de la Nostalgie* (1979), the author combines the Arab tradition of storytelling and the magical Realism of Gabriel García Márquez exemplified in his *One Hundred Years of Solitude* (1967), in order to rewrite the history of Algeria. The story breaks away from conventional notions of historical time by bringing together in one plot the fourteenth-century North African writer and historian Ibn Khaldun, a crew of American film-makers, and a character, Mohamed SNP, an anti-hero who symbolises the loss of identity. Boudjedra has undoubtedly played a significant role in shaping the French language to articulate a new vision, one that explodes the taboos of both the East and the West to reveal the other side of reality. His switching to writing in Arabic in the 1980s has puzzled and sometimes saddened his critics who saw in him a major figure of Maghrebian francophone literature. Yet, it seems that, for Boudjedra, moving between languages and cultures has not altered the defiant tone of his writing.

Women writers have also made a significant contribution to the critique of power within traditional and modern society and have highlighted the link between patriarchy and colonialism. The important role played by women in the fight against colonial rule and the difficult position they occupy today in post-independent society have made them particularly sensitive to social issues. Women started to write well before independence, but it is only recently that their voices have been acknowledged as a tradition in its own right. Assia Djebar is one of the early novelists who has contributed to that tradition. Her first three novels, published in the late 1950s and 1960s, deal with the issue of female emancipation through political involvement and personal experience. Through the young female heroine of Djebar's early novels, one can hear the *female voice* that was to become so characteristic of Djebar's later fiction.

In 1980, Djebar published a collection of texts written over a period of twenty years, all organised around a central theme: Delacroix's painting, *Women of Algiers in their Apartment* (from which the collection takes its title). The texts are in dialogue with Delacroix's work by presenting *the other side* of the Orientalist painting: the world of women; their relationships with one another, their inner world, their dreams and their uncertainties. The female voice is the plural voice of these women who try to reconstruct history away from colonial and male-centred perspectives. Djebar's later fiction combines auto-biography and the historical genre to present the reader with a view of history that brings women to the centre. *Loin de Médine* (1991), for example, explores religious history in order to analyse the position women occupied in society at the time of the prophet.

It is significant that, for North African writers, attempting a critique of their society means reassessing the ways in which it has traditionally been portrayed, often by breaking the conventional literary canons and mixing different genres (poetry, fictionalised histories, folk literature), different traditions of literature, and sometimes different languages. This tendency has intensified in recent decades. In Morocco, a generation of young writers who emerged in the 1960s, such as Mohammed Khair Eddine, Abdellatif Laabi, Abdelkebir Khatibi and Tahar Ben Jelloun, have remodelled the structure of French to create a poetic language that transcends the traditional divisions between genres. Laabi sees his novels as 'itineraries', a genre that he has invented and which is a fusion between the European novel and the old Arabic narratives, namely the *Rihla* and the *Maqama*. Laabi founded the literary journal *Souffles*, bringing together both francophone and Arabic writers in order to create a poetic language 'in the midst of linguistic chaos'.[16] For this new generation, language and change are part of the same process. The French language is not only a medium of expression, but material that can be altered, transformed and regenerated. As in the novels of Boudjedra, the violence of the metaphor expresses the desire to explode and invigorate the old colonial language.

The Tunisian novelist Abdelwahab Meddeb adopts a more dispassionate position. For him, writing in French is a source of creative inspiration that enables him to explore the plurality of poetic language. Meddeb is part of the Arabic classical tradition, particularly the Sufi tradition, in terms of his cultural and linguistic references. Like Laabi, he has translated Arabic texts into French, such as al-Tayyib Salih's *A Season of Migration to the North* (1966). Nevertheless, Meddeb chooses to write his novels in French, a language through which he expresses his double heritage. Yet, the presence of the Arabic language can be felt behind the text and sometimes it even emerges at the surface of the novel, as in *Phantasia* (1986), where words and sometimes sentences in Arabic graphic form are inserted. The plurality of forms, voices, languages and perceptions that characterises North African writing in French today, reflects the need to come to terms with a language that has for a long time occupied a dominant position. From '*une littérature d'expression française*', that is a literature which uses French as a form of expression, North African writing has now evolved to become '*une littérature de langue française*', a literature that makes the French language a stylistic device that can be adapted, transformed and reconstructed.

Conclusion

This survey has revealed some important issues about the way in which writers have dealt with the profound transformations of North African society in the modern period. The dominant themes seem to have been the duality between tradition and modernity and the conflict of cultures. Yet, these antagonisms have often been the outer expression of an inner and deeper division in the consciousness of North African writers. In the face of intense historical changes, the quest for an identity has become the prime preoccupation. Looking for an identity often means recreating a continuity with the past by exploring collective images and reconstructing an historical archetype.

North African writers have turned to the past and have revitalised the classical tradition of Arabic literature in order to shape a modern discourse. They have also looked for sources of inspiration outside their culture. In this respect, the influence of European aesthetics has played a significant role. However, North African writers have not merely borrowed Western forms of writing; they have shaped a literature that uses European culture as a mirror rather than as a model. Writers using the Arabic language have adapted European aesthetic conventions in order to regenerate the Arabic language, while, on the other hand, francophone writing has translated the North African experience into the French language itself. The implications of linguistic and cultural borrowing are, of course, greater for francophone writers. Yet, whether they are using French or Arabic, North African writers are part of a dialogue that goes beyond the dualities of the West and the East.

Notes

1. Magali Morsy, *North Africa 1800–1900: A Survey from the Nile Valley to the Atlantic* (London, 1984), p. 15.
2. See, for example, Mouloud Mammeri, *Poèmes Kabyles Ancients* (Paris, 1980).
3. For a detailed analysis of this period, see Edward Said, *Orientalism: Western Conceptions of the Orient* (London, 1978).
4. Salma Khadra Jayyusi, *Modern Arabic Poetry* (New York, 1987), p. 99.
5. M.M. Badawi, *A Critical Introduction to Modern Arabic Poetry* (Cambridge, 1975), p. 260.
6. It is interesting to note that *The Arabian Nights*, which is believed to have originated in Egyptian folk literature, never achieved as great a success in the Arab world as it did in the West.
7. *Encyclopedia Universalis* (Paris, 1985), p. 431. Author's translation.
8. Tawfiq al-Hakim, *Hayati*, as quoted in Pierre Cachia, *An Overview of Modern Arabic Literature* (Edinburgh, 1990), p. 37.
9. Naguib Mahfuz, 'En creusant sa propre réalité on Débouche sur l'universel', in *Arabies, Mensuel du Monde Arabe et de la Francophonie*, no. 24 (1988), p. 75.
10. Sasson Somekh, *The Changing Rhythm* (Leiden, 1973), p. 136.
11. As quoted in P. Cachia, *An Overview of Modern Arabic Literature*, p. 120.
12. Titles are given in English whenever a translation is available; the date in brackets, however, refers to the year of publication of the original text.
13. See also writers such as Tawfiq al-Hakim and Yusuf Idris.
14. In 1960, 75 per cent of the indigenous adult population in Tunisia, 88 per cent in Algeria and 89 per cent in Morocco were illiterate: *Encyclopedia Universalis* (Paris, 1985), p. 471.

15. Christiane Achour, *Anthologie de la Littérature Algérienne de Langue Française* (Paris, 1990), p. 55. Author's translation.
16. *Souffles*, no. 1, as quoted in Jacqueline Arnaud, *La Littérature Maghrébine de Langue Française* (Paris, 1986), p. 121. Author's translation.

2 West African Writing

Patrick Williams

The field of cultural production encompassed by the seemingly simple title 'West Africa' is a particularly rich and diverse one, and as such, well beyond the scope of this chapter to cover in depth. I have not attempted any coverage of writing in indigenous languages – even though the Kenyan novelist Ngugi wa Thiong'o has frequently argued that this is where the future of properly African literature must lie[1] – nor have I addressed the other major corpus of texts in one of the former colonial languages, in this case, French. Francophone West Africa has produced major writers, from Leopold Senghor and Camara Laye in the Negritude movement, to contemporary poets like Mongo Beti, or the remarkable Sembene Ousmane, novelist and film-maker, and the reader is encouraged to become acquainted with these very different but important bodies of writing. This chapter is concerned with writing in English, concentrating on a number of key moments and figures.

Early writing in English

In most accounts of African literature, contemporary figures such as Soyinka and Achebe assume such proportions that it is easy to imagine that West African writing began with them in the period of decolonisation. There have, however, been people from West Africa writing in English since the eighteenth century. The best-known of these early works (and the most important in terms of political impact), was *The Interesting Narrative of the Life of Olaudah Equiano, or Gustavus Vassa the African*, published in London in 1789. Its subtitle, 'Written by Himself', is noteworthy for several reasons: it challenges the widely held view that Africans were incapable of writing anything worth publishing; it signals that the work is not co-authored or ghost-written, like some earlier books, such as Ukawsaw Gronniosaw's *Narrative of the Most Remarkable Particulars in the Life of James Albert Ukawsaw Gronniosaw, an African Prince* (1770), or Ottobah Cuguano's *Thoughts and Sentiments on the Evil and Wicked Traffic of the Slavery and Commerce of the Human Species* (1787); and it indicates a victory for at least one black slave in the face of determined attempts by white people to deny slaves access to literacy and education.

These works by people of West African origin – Gronniosaw from northern Nigeria, Cuguano from Ghana, and Equiano from the Onitsha area of eastern Nigeria – are important for their role in helping to establish a tradition of black writing in English and, more specifically in the case of Cuguano and Equiano, in furthering the emancipation of black people. Equiano was one of the first political leaders of the black community in Britain, and his book, journalism, speeches and lecture tours were influential in the campaign to abolish slavery. The use of narrative, autobiography and polemic as means of political protest or resistance to oppression has remained a significant aspect of black writing ever since. Equally importantly, Cuguano and Equiano articulated ideas which, a century later, became the basis for the Pan-African movement which, in turn, provided a focus and forum for many who would eventually lead or help to lead their countries to freedom from colonial rule.

The development towards Pan-Africanism was continued in the nineteenth century, during the high period of colonialism, by writers such as Edward Wilmot Blyden, Liberian ambassador to Britain in the 1870s, and James Africanus Horton, born in Sierra Leone of Ibo parents and educated at London and Edinburgh universities. Horton's *West African Countries and Peoples: A Vindication of the African Race* (1868), was a particularly remarkable book which attacked the (so-called) scientific race theories that had been gaining ground in the previous decades, and advanced the sounder – and more scientific – proposition that race was not an immutable category, as well as the more enlightened view that all races were equal. Horton wanted to demonstrate that Africans were fit for the self-government for which he was calling. He also advocated the use of aspects of Western culture: industrialisation, railways, banks, hospitals, schools and universities were all to be introduced. This was by no means an unthinking importation of Western civilisation, however, since it was to take place within a context of autonomy (preferably self-government), and these institutions were to be run by Africans for the benefit of Africans – all Africans, since, for example, education was specifically to include women.

The same polymath spirit and multi-discursive context which gave rise to Horton's book also produced Joseph Caseley-Heyford's *Ethiopia Unbound: Studies in Race Emancipation* (1911), both novel and treatise on an early version of Negritude: Ethiopianism. Like the works of Blyden and Horton, Caseley-Heyford's book is erudite and polemical, deploying Western discourses such as history and philosophy, but in order to resist what the West was doing in Africa. It uses an early form of the stock figure of later twentieth-century African fiction, the 'been-to', the (usually intellectual) individual who goes to Europe and returns – often alienated. In this case, however, the alienation or cultural dislocation becomes the occasion for a call for national and regional unity and transformation – West Africa is to unite and improve itself, a call which in some senses prefigures the internationalist position of writers like Fanon in *The Wretched of the Earth* half a century later: 'The native intellectual who decides to give battle to colonial lies fights on the field of the whole continent. The past is given back its value. Culture, extracted from the past to be displayed in all its splendour, is not necessarily that of his own country.'[2]

The emergence of modern West African literature

Published in 1958, just three years before Fanon's classic text, Chinua Achebe's first novel, *Things Fall Apart*, marks an epoch of its own. The effort to have the value of African people and culture acknowledged, which constitutes much of the driving force behind the works of Horton or Caseley-Heyford, also forms the motivation for Achebe's book. Although Achebe was not the first contemporary West African novelist in English (Cyprian Ekwensi, for example, was already writing in the 1940s), nor even the first novelist to have his work enthusiastically reviewed in the West (Amos Tutuola's *The Palm Wine Drinkard* was praised in the *Observer* by Dylan Thomas on its publication in 1952), Achebe's position in the history and development of the African novel is probably unparalleled, spanning over thirty years of the colonial and post-colonial periods. The publication of *Things Fall Apart* irrevocably changed the perception and status of African literature in English, both in Africa and in the rest of the world. (Its pre-eminence is such that in 1993 it is still the only African text on Kenyan secondary school syllabuses.) Ironically, an early review in the recently founded Nigerian journal *Black Orpheus* aligned *Things Fall Apart* with Joyce Cary's *Mister Johnson* (1939) as showing 'love and warmth' for its African subject matter – ironically, because, as Achebe later pointed out, it was the limited, ideologically blinkered, patronising representation of Africans, and 'Mister Johnson' in particular, which prompted him to become a writer in the first place, in order to present an image of Africa which was nearer the truth. This was not a question of accuracy for accuracy's sake, but rather one of the psychological damage which results from relentlessly negative images. This was particularly relevant since, with the exception of newly independent Ghana, and soon-to-be-independent Guinea, West Africa was still very much a colonised space, and all the more exposed, therefore, to those images of Africa and Africans produced in the West. The deliberate revisionist strategy adopted by Achebe, of answering back, is an example of how – in Salman Rushdie's now well-known phrase – 'The empire writes back to the centre', and indeed, for some critics is one of the defining features of all properly post-colonial writing. For Achebe, setting the historical record straight involves writing about both the past and the present of Nigeria, and his first four novels alternate between the colonial past (*Things Fall Apart* and *Arrow of God* (1964)), and the post-colonial present (*No Longer At Ease* (1960) and *A Man of the People* (1966)).

Like many of his contemporaries, Achebe is much concerned with the social function of culture and with the role of the producer of culture. However, whereas someone like Ousmane would take that to imply the necessity for a very active, even revolutionary, political involvement, Achebe's vision is more low-key and gradualist.[3] Part of that pedagogic purpose has involved a close scrutiny of Nigeria – what Fanon calls 'dissecting the heart of his people'. An important aspect of this has been the chronicling of the rise, from the late nineteenth century onwards, of what Achebe has dubbed the 'messenger class', that group which achieved some power and status as functionaries of the colonialists (in *Things Fall Apart*) and consolidated it by becoming the ruling elite in the independent African nations (depicted in *A Man of the People* and *Anthills of the Savannah* (1987)). If the nascent messenger class under colonialism can look rather pathetic – in the figure of the 'ashy buttocks' court messenger in *Things Fall Apart*, for instance – in the post-independence world it has become much more menacing, preserving its illegitimate hold on power by violence, as in the case of Chief Nanga's armed thugs in *A Man of the People*, or the full panoply of (misused) state power in *Anthills of the Savannah*. In the latter novel it is the messenger class in its military mode which rules, in the shape of Sandhurst-educated Sam. The messenger class in government exhibits all the negative characteristics identified by Fanon in his study of the black national bourgeoisies – self-interested, greedy, parasitic, unscrupulous, cynical and, above all, unproductive.[4]

The possibility of starting again or continuing differently is intimated at the end of *Anthills of the Savannah*, where a heterogeneous, and heterodox, group forms. Made up of all elements of Nigerian society – women and men, young and old, workers and intellectuals, soldiers and civilians, Christians and Muslims – the group transgresses normal divisions and binary oppositions by being led and organised by women and, in its most explicitly symbolic move, by giving Elewa's new-born baby daughter – the image of, and hope for, a better future – a boy's name. Its choice of a collective name and identity – 'All of Us' – is also important in signalling where the hope for change lies.

Achebe's anger and disappointment at the behaviour of the neo-colonial black elite is something he shares with probably the majority of African writers, so much so that some critics have described post-colonial African literature as a 'literature of disillusionment', and a glance at titles, particularly from the 1960s and early 1970s, would seem to confirm such an analysis: Achebe's *No Longer at Ease* (1960), Soyinka's *Season of Anomy* (1973), Ayi Kwei Armah's *Fragments* (1970) and *The Beautiful Ones Are Not Yet Born* (1968) are only the best-known; the loss of the opportunities represented by independence and the possibility of nation-building is especially hard to accept. In a novel like *The Beautiful Ones Are Not Yet Born* the political and moral decay is so all-pervasive that it even extends to the physical world.[5]

If there is something resembling a shared mood of bitterness and disappointment among writers, there is disagreement, however, over where to place the blame for the betrayal of the hopes embodied in independence. For Achebe, it is very much a case of personal failing, partly of ordinary people, but particularly at the level of the black leadership: 'Nigerians are what they are only because their leaders are not what they should be.'[6] For others, such as Ngugi, the problem is a systemic rather than a personal one, and belongs to the realm of political economy rather than morality or individual psychology. For Ngugi, it is the economic imperialism of the West and the continued subservience of African nations in their neo-colonial roles (though aided and abetted, it must be said, by a corrupt black bourgeoisie), which has made it impossible to realise the potential represented by independence.

There is, however, a school of thought which argues that independence in the form in which it was offered could not have achieved the things on which hopes were pinned. In the view of Fanon, once again, it is the transfer of power to a national bourgeoisie, functioning as the imitators and parasites of the Western bourgeoisie, which means that independence of this kind is a dead end. For critic Neil Lazarus, following the argument of historian Basil Davidson, it is the structural problems which African countries inherited from the colonial powers which ensured that 'the expectations of independence that were current at the time of decolonisation and that continued, negatively, to inform the problematic of postcolonialism for at least a decade, were unrealistic from the very beginning, even as they were first being articulated. It is impossible to overemphasise the significance of this point.'[7]

The Nigerian civil war

Achebe's *A Man of the People* provides a bitter picture of post-independence political life. It also marks a kind of terminus, historically and in terms of Achebe's artistic output. At the end of the novel, the politicians' corruption, squabbles and divisions result in an army coup. This resolution of the narrative has earned a type of prophetic status for the book, since a military coup did in fact take place in Nigeria not many months after the publication of the novel in 1966, ushering in perhaps the major historical event in terms of contemporary West African literature: the Nigerian civil war.

Although it was relatively short-lived in comparison to the continuing problems caused by the behaviour of the national leadership in the post-independence period, the civil war was a trauma whose repercussions in the cultural life of the nation continue to be felt. The artistic response to the war was so great that the critic Chidi Amuta has argued that it is the dominant and recurrent area of concern in contemporary Nigerian literature, as well as 'the single most [frequently] imaginatively recreated historical experience in Africa so far'. [8] Few writers did not respond in some way, and attempt to come to terms with it in their writing. Not all of them managed the response they would have wished; in Achebe's case, the response was almost to stop writing altogether. Unable to turn the experience into his preferred form, the novel, he did eventually produce a collection of poems, *Beware Soul Brother* (1972), and a volume of short stories, *Girls at War* (1972).

Responses to the civil war encompass many forms of writing: drama, such as Soyinka's *Madmen and Specialists* (1971); novels and short stories, such as Festus Iyayi's *Heroes* (1986), Elechi Amadi's *Sunset in Biafra* (1973), Buchi Emecheta's *Destination Biafra* (1981) or Iroh's *Forty Eight Guns for the General* (1976); poetry such as J.P. Clark's *Casualties* (1970) or Achebe's *Beware Soul Brother*; and prison memoirs like Soyinka's *The Man Died* (1972). The chronological span of works touched by the war is considerable, from those written before it began but which prefigure it, such as some of the later poems of Christopher Okigbo, to those written almost a generation later but which are nevertheless profoundly marked by it, such as Odia Ofeimun's *The Poet Lied* (1981). Okigbo's last sequence of poems, 'Path of Thunder: Poems Prophesying War', was written between the army coup of January 1966 and his death in August 1967 in the war which his poems prophesied, and is couched in language more reminiscent of Yeats's 'The Second Coming', than the T.S. Eliot who was such an influence on his early work:

> The smell of blood already floats in the lavender mist of the afternoon.
> The death sentence lies in ambush along the corridors of power;
> And a great fearful thing already tugs at the cables of the open air,
> A nebula immense and immeasurable, a night of deep waters –
> An iron dream unnamed and unprintable, a path of stone.
> . . .
> And the secret thing with its heaving
> Threatens with iron mask
> The last lighted torch of the century. [9]

The sense of prophesy extends even to his own death:

> If I don't learn to shut my mouth I'll soon go to hell,
> I, Okigbo, town crier, together with my iron bell. [10]

In *The Poet Lied*, Ofeimun offers a tribute to Okigbo in a poem whose language of drums, thunder and elephants consciously echoes Okigbo's own, but his more controversial engagement with an earlier poet comes in the title poem of the collection. The portrait of a shallow poet who

> meant to escape the acute fever
> the immoderacy of the rabble
> the learned folly of his drunk ex-comrades
> who strutted about in prison dungeons
> in malarial forests, refugee camps[11]

was taken by one of Nigeria's most famous poets, J.P. Clark, as a reference to himself, which led him to pressurise Longman into withdrawing the book from sale in Nigeria. Ofeimun has since said that his attack was principally aimed at 'manipulators of symbols' who misuse their power: 'All people who manipulate symbols are legislators. A politician, writer or public figure who makes a statement is providing images with which to live a life.'[12]

The title poem of Clark's own collection, *Casualties* is his best-known statement about the war:

> The casualties are not only those who are dead;
> They are well out of it.
> The casualties are not only those who are wounded;
> Though they await burial by instalment
> . . .
> We are all casualties,
> All sagging as are
> The cases celebrated for kwashiorkor,
> The unforeseen camp-follower of not just our war.[13]

For some, the poem's strategy of generalising the problems and suffering caused by the war is entirely laudable, a sort of equivalent of John Donne's sermon 'No man is an island', where any person's death diminishes all. Others regard such a stance less charitably, as an example of the problematic universalist–individualist approach which Chinweizu and his colleagues see as part of the 'Euro-modernism' foisted on African writers.[14] For others, and this would presumably include Ofeimun, such generalising represents an unacceptable watering down of the precise problems and issues of the civil war, a kind of disengagement from the historical specificities of the period.

Although it could not be accused of disengagement in terms of minimising horrors, Soyinka's *Madmen and Specialists* certainly avoids direct confrontation with the historical reality of the war. In the nightmarish world of 'specialist' Dr Bero, historical and geographical precision disappear as the regime of sadistic practices – amputations, executions – represents a wider condition in the mythic-symbolic manner beloved of Soyinka. Even his prison memoir, *The Man Died*, the account of his arrest and two-year imprisonment without trial during the war, deliberately takes on mythic overtones as Soyinka compares himself with Prometheus ('My liver is mended. I await the vultures for there are no eagles here.') while positioning himself within a tradition of misunderstood individuals who struggle and suffer for their people.

In later years, Soyinka may well have felt both more and less understood: the award of the 1986 Nobel Prize for Literature would suggest that, in certain quarters at least, he has been heard, while a series of protracted and sometimes bitter polemics with other writers and academics indicates a lack of agreement with, or, as Soyinka sees it, comprehension of, his position. Although Soyinka accepted the prize in the name of his people and of the tradition of African literature, it obviously represents the acknowledgement of a remarkable personal output: plays first and foremost, of course, including those like *Death and the King's Horseman* (1975), which were singled out for special mention by the Nobel committee, but also various collections of poetry and two influential novels, not to mention literary and cultural criticism, biography and translation. At the same time, Soyinka has always been outspoken, his early targets ranging from the Negritude movement (dismissed in his famous one-liner: 'The tiger does not proclaim his tigritude, he pounces.'), to the military regime denounced in *The Man Died*. More recently, he has attacked different critical or theoretical approaches to the nature of African culture, most notably the nativism of Chinweizu, Jemie and Madubuike, ridiculed by Soyinka as 'neo-Tarzanism', and African Marxism, its proponents variously labelled 'radical chic-ists' or 'leftocrats'. They, in turn, have accused him of pointless obscurantism and 'Euro-modernism' (Chinweizu), or of promoting, via his recurrent use of myth, an essentialist and de-historicised vision of society (Marxists).

While *Madmen and Specialists* would see the problem underlying the civil war as located within a generalised and ever-present evil, a novel like Festus Iyayi's *Heroes* argues strongly that it is historical and social circumstances, rather than 'natural' or metaphysical categories, which produce forms of behaviour. The latter constitutes one of the major realisations of the novel's central character, the journalist Osime, on his painful journey from home town to war zone:

> All along, he said, right up to this moment, I had assumed that the callousness and the viciousness and the wildness and brutality were natural to the men, that the men in uniform were natural rapists even in times of peace. All that is wrong, he acknowledged now. People are decent deep down and want to remain decent all their lives. But a bitter and spiteful war comes along and turns ordinary decent men into rapists, into animals, into something hateful even to themselves.[15]

Hand in hand with this new understanding of ordinary people goes a faith in them as the way out of the problems facing the country, a belief that the mass of his fellow countrymen can learn from their manipulation and betrayal by their rulers and come together to form a 'third army'. If Soyinka's analysis makes any solution difficult to imagine, Iyayi's – however utopian it may seem – attempts to offer both a solution and the grounds for future hope.

> "There are only two sides," Jato said quickly. "The Nigerian and the Biafran."
> "And you are wrong there," Osime argued. "There is a third side. The people's side. The side of the working Ibo, the side of the working Hausa, the side of the working Yoruba, in short – the side of the working Nigerian man and woman."[16]

Interestingly, given the apparent distance separating this from *Madmen and Specialists*, Soyinka has since said that during the war he was working towards the creation of a 'third movement' as a way out of the mess, but did not make clear of what such a movement might have consisted.

Women's writing

If an important dimension of the emergence of modern African literature as a whole has been the problem of representation – the dissatisfaction, as exemplified in Achebe, with white-authored versions of African culture and people – then an analogous movement may be seen in the emergence of African women's writing. While acknowledging the achievements of their male colleagues, many African women writers have complained that men's texts marginalise women, and portray them in negative, stereotypical and ideologically unacceptable ways: an exact counterpart to the accusation levelled against European writers. This does not indicate a desire for artificially created, improved positive images to enable women to feel better about themselves, but rather asks for women to be portrayed as they really are, without refracting such an image through the distorting lens of patriarchal ideology. As the novelist, poet and playwright, Ama Ata Aidoo says,

> If I write about strong women, it means that I see them to be around. People.have always assumed that to be feminine is silly and to be sweet. But I disagree. I hope that in being a woman writer, I have been faithful to the image of women as I see them around, strong women, women who are viable in their own right.[17]

For some, the negative representation of women is just one of the many unpleasant effects of Western influence. The dramatist Zulu Sofola has argued, for example, that Soyinka in *Death and the King's Horseman* allows Elesin Oba a dominance over Iyaloja which in reality he would not have possessed, and that this is the result of a Europeanised perception of male and female roles and characters. This will no doubt seem an idiosyncratic reading to many, given the fact that *Death and the King's Horseman* is usually seen as conveying a deeply traditional message, not to mention the fact that Iyaloja is generally regarded as Soyinka's strongest female character.

Representation, as Said pointed out in *Orientalism* (1978), and many have subsequently reiterated, carries the additional meaning of standing-in for, or speaking on behalf of, as in parliamentary representation, and just as African writers objected to being spoken for by Europeans, so many women are not happy about having their role as speaking subject usurped by men.[18] Certainly, such unlooked-for ventriloquising is only one of the problems African women writers have to face, and many of them point to the range of material and ideological constraints as the principal reason for the fact that women's writing in Africa was late in appearing and relatively slow in developing. The first works by West African women were published in the mid-1960s – the Ghanaian Ama Ata Aidoo's play, *The Dilemma of a Ghost* (1965) and the Nigerian Flora Nwapa's novel *Efuru* (1966)

– and progress since then, even among the pioneers, has generally been steady rather than startling.

The development of African women's writing has also resulted in a shift in criticism not unlike that in European and American feminist criticism indicated by Elaine Showalter. In 'Feminist Criticism in the Wilderness' and elsewhere, Showalter charts the move in feminist criticism from a concern with representation – the problem of the way men portray women; women as object, in a sense – to a focus on women as writers – women as subjects, rather than objects. These two moments are labelled, respectively, feminist critique, and gynocritics. Although African criticism by or about women is not necessarily feminist, the centre of interest around women has nevertheless moved in a manner similar to that outlined by Showalter. That such a shift should not be marked in an overtly feminist way is indicative of the difficult relation of African women to Western feminism. Nwapa is typical of many writers when she borrows Alice Walker's term and declares herself to be a 'womanist' rather than a feminist. Womanism is more openly accommodationist than feminism is perceived to be, and Nwapa's novels such as *Idu* (1970) and *Efuru* concentrate on central female characters who are simultaneously out-of-the-ordinary and part of their communities; striving for self-determination in (relatively) non-confrontational ways, yet doing so – spectacularly in the case of Idu – in relation to, or in partnership with men. Clearly, the idea of womanism as a black feminism is appealing, but the debate has undoubtedly suffered from a rather impoverished image of Western feminism as inherently radical, man-hating, separatist and individualistic. The latter is not just an African perception encouraged by the increasingly individualistic nature of Western society in general, it is also unhelpfully fostered by Western critics. In 'Feminist Criticism and the African Novel', for example, Katherine Frank argues: 'Feminism, by definition, is a profoundly individualistic philosophy: it values personal growth and individual fulfilment over any larger communal needs or good.'[19]

One of the writers who has most openly tried to reach an accommodation with Western feminism is the Nigerian novelist Buchi Emecheta. Among the most prolific of West African authors, and one of the best known world-wide, Emecheta has lived in Britain since the 1960s. Although her earliest and most recent works, *In the Ditch* (1972), *Second Class Citizen* (1974) and *Gwendolyn* (1991), are set in Britain, the eight written between 1976 and 1986 all have African settings, and, as titles such as *The Bride Price* (1976), *The Slave Girl* (1977) and *The Joys of Motherhood* (1979) suggest, are very much female-centred. In *The Joys of Motherhood*, Emecheta works on two levels to get her feminist message across. The central character, Nnu Ego, is considered to be the reincarnation of a sacrificed slave girl, and this obviously establishes the possibility of reading her life-story as one of slavery, ending with a death which, while it is much less violent than the slave girl's, may be no less unsatisfactory. An interpretation which simply followed the mythical/spiritual lead offered would perhaps suggest that events of this nature, while not ideal, are nevertheless acceptable, or must be endured, because they are part of a pattern much larger than the human. At the same time, the novel shows in great detail how Nnu Ego's 'enslavement' is the result of social restrictions, patriarchal norms – and women's collusion with the system that oppresses them. The fact that slavery is not an inevitable state is demonstrated by Nnu's younger co-wife, Adaku, who achieves a considerable amount of personal and economic freedom for herself and her children.

Younger novelists like Zaynab Alkali are often as wary of feminism as many of their predecessors, though often for different reasons. Alkali, for example, has denied that the women's movement has brought anything of substance to Africa, and regards it rather as a hindrance for women who are trying to write. Her interesting first novel, *The Stillborn* (1984), charts the long and difficult passage of the heroine Li to a kind of independence from the pressures of social stigma, from control by family or men, and towards becoming a person in her own right. Having achieved this, however, she then, in the space of a few lines at the end of the novel, unaccountably decides to return both to the city against which she has so strongly warned her sister, and to the husband who made life so difficult for her.

The contemporary

The contemporary situation is, among other things, typified by a number of contradictions: on the one hand, West African writing is flourishing more than at any time in the past, being more extensively taught and, one would hope, more sensitively studied; on the other hand, publishing and bookselling are in a state of crisis in the region, with materials scarce and rising prices putting many books beyond the purchasing power of the majority of the population, leaving African literature as much as ever at the mercy of the whims of Western publishers. Prior to this, encouraging changes had been taking place: publishers such as Ethiope and Onibonoje had been expanding, Flora Nwapa had started her own publishing company, Tana (as Emecheta had done in Britain), and some writers, like the novelist Kole Omotoso, had changed from Western publishers (in his case, Heinemann) to local ones. Another, and related, contradiction is between the large number of young writers appearing (or older ones continuing) and the few who become accepted or fêted in Western literary or academic circles: someone like Odia Ofeimun has achieved his degree of fame in the West more because of the controversy mentioned earlier than as a result of his undoubted talent, while other excellent young poets like Harry Garuba remain undeservedly unknown outside Nigeria.

One writer who has been conspicuously successful is the novelist and poet Ben Okri. Okri had lived in Britain since the late 1970s, published two novels and two collections of short stories, and alternated winning prizes and scholarships with periods of poverty, before his novel *The Famished Road* won the Booker Prize in 1991. If Achebe had made African religious ritual and spirituality part of the validated content of *Things Fall Apart*, Okri makes them as much part of the form of *The Famished Road* and its sequel *Songs of Enchantment* (1993). In *Things Fall Apart*, the notion that Ezinma is an *ogbanje* – a child who is repeatedly born to the same mother, only to die soon afterwards – is real, in that it forms part of the community's belief-system. In *The Famished Road* the reality of the concept is increased, in that the *abiku* (the Yoruba version of *ogbanje*), Azaro, is the narrator/focaliser of the whole novel, and the spirit world he half inhabits is made correspondingly more present to the reader. The heightened language and more than merely realistic events of the narrative, already seen in stories such as 'Worlds That Flourish' in *Stars of the New Curfew* (1988), meant that Okri's work was readily, if wrongly, assimilable to magic realism (which still unfortunately functions as an index of 'good writing from the Third World' in the minds of many critics), whereas it has more in common with other West African works such as Tutuola's *The Palm Wine Drinkard*, or the Yoruba writer D.O. Fagunwa's *The Forest of a Thousand Demons* (1968). The review of *The Famished Road* in *The Times* also repeated ideas which have dogged African literature in the forty years since the appearance of Tutuola's novel: 'unlike anything you have read before' 'the message is universal'.[20] Curious novelty; asserted universality . . .

it would appear that it is not only *abiku*s and *ogbanje*s who go thr
cycles of eternal return. It is perhaps time for more critics to put
practice the idea from Fanon and Achebe that one can, at le
continue differently, if not start again.

Notes

1. Ngugi wa Thiong'o, *Decolonising the Mind: The Politics of Language in African Literature* (London, 1986).
2. Frantz Fanon, *The Wretched of the Earth*, trans. Constance Farrington (Harmondsworth, 1967), p. 170.
3. Chinua Achebe, 'The Novelist as Teacher', in *Hopes and Impediments: Selected Essays 1965–87* (London, 1988), p. 30.
4. F. Fanon, *The Wretched of the Earth*, p. 142.
5. Ayi Kwei Armah, *The Beautyful Ones Are Not Yet Born* (London, 1967), pp. 11–12.
6. Chinua Achebe, *The Trouble With Nigeria* (London, 1984), p. 70.
7. Neil Lazarus, *Resistance in Postcolonial African Fiction* (New Haven, 1990), p. 23.
8. Chidi Amuta, 'Literature of the Nigerian Civil War', in Yemi Ogunbiyi (ed.), *Perspectives on Nigerian Literature* vol. 1 (Lagos, 1988), p. 85.
9. Christopher Okigbo, 'Come Thunder', in *Collected Poems* (London, 1986), pp. 92–3.
10. Ibid., p. 94.
11. Odia Ofeimun, 'The Poet Lied', in Adewale Maja-Pearce (ed.), *The Heinemann Book of African Poetry in English* (London, 1990), p. 188.
12. Odia Ofeimun, in Jane Wilkinson (ed.), *Talking with African Writers* (London, 1992), p. 67.
13. J.P. Clark, 'Casualties', in A. Maja-Pearce (ed.), *The Heinemann Book of African Poetry in English*, pp. 60–1.
14. Chinweizu, Onwachekwa Jemie and Ihechukwu Madubuike, *Toward the Decolonisation of African Literature*. Vol. 1: African Fiction and Poetry and their Critics (Washington DC, 1983).
15. Festus Iyayi, *Heroes* (Harlow, 1986), pp. 244–5.
16. Ibid., p. 169.
17. Ama Ata Aidoo, in Adeola James (ed.), *In Their Own Voices: African Women Writers Talk* (London, 1990), p. 12.
18. Adeola James and Molara Ogundipe Leslie, in A. James (ed.), *In Their Own Voices*, p. 72.
19. Katherine Frank, 'Feminist Criticism and the African Novel', in E.D. Jones (ed.), *African Literature Today*, no. 14 (London, 1984), p. 45.
20. Philip Howard, *The Times* review, quoted in the book.

3 East and Central African writing

Mpalive-Hangson Msiska

This chapter presents an outline of the development of literature written in English from the former East African Community (Kenya, Tanzania and Uganda) and what used to be known as The Federation of Rhodesia and Nyasaland (Malawi, Zambia and Zimbabwe). The literature of the region followed the same pattern of development as other post-colonial literatures. In their book, *The Empire Writes Back*, Bill Ashcroft, Gareth Griffiths and Helen Tiffin, have argued that post-colonial literatures generally pass through three phases.[1] Initially, most of the literature in the colony is produced by writers of European origin. There are several examples of this type of literature in East and Central Africa, of which Karen Blixen's *Out of Africa* and Elizabeth Huxley's *Red Strangers*, both set in Kenya, and Gertrude Page's and Cynthia Stockley's novels about Zimbabwe are better known. This literature is part of colonial discourse in which, according to Edward Said, the colonised is solely configured within the cultural and political terms of the coloniser.[2]

In the second phase, which in East and Central Africa stretches from the 1920s to the early 1960s, there is usually a measure of local participation in literary production, but, as Ashcroft and company point out, it 'is under the direct control of the imperial ruling class who alone license the acceptable form and permit the publication and distribution of the resulting work'.[3] In the region under consideration, literary output was limited to didactic school-readers published by missionary presses and government publication bureaux. The last phase describes a period when local writers disengage from imperial patronage and appropriate European languages and writing practices for a local political and aesthetic project.[4] The literature produced during this stage essentially seeks to undermine the colonial representation of African culture and history by 'restori[ng] the African character to history'.[5] In the case of East and Central Africa, this took place during the last stages of decolonisation in the early 1960s. However, in Zimbabwe, this stage extended well into the 1970s, as the process of decolonisation was derailed by the unilateral declaration of independence (UDI) in 1964 by the settlers.

With regard to Africa, and in particular East and Central Africa, one needs to add a further stage to the list offered by Ashcroft and company. Subsequent to the nationalist phase, there emerges a literature which goes beyond writing back to the centre, by including in its critique the production of social and economic difference within the new national formations, as the writer who had once celebrated the value of traditional African culture and history begins to realise, in the words of the Ugandan writer, Taban Lo Liyong that, 'our intellectual leadership has been left to the politicians'.[6] This awareness is also accompanied by the feeling that the writer himself is implicated in the betrayal of the ideals of nationalism and the acknowledgment of the fact that there has been a 'great betrayal of the vast majority of our people by we who are here, by us who are ruling in universities, in government and everywhere'.[7]

However, the disadvantage of linear descriptions of literary change such as the one presented above is that they are based on a teleological conception of history in which post-colonial literatures are seen as progressively moving from an initial moment of absolute colonial control over literary production to one of absolute autonomy in the post-colonial era. Evidently, this is not true of the literary history of East and Central Africa where each period is characterised more by aporia than ideological coherence or consistency and where instances of regression to issues and concerns of earlier periods are not uncommon.

Clearly, one cannot compress the vast and diverse literature of the region in a short essay such as this, without some measure of simplification. There are important historical and cultural differences among the countries of the region, which account for the distinctiveness of each national and sub-regional literature. For instance, linguistically, East Africa is much more homogeneous than Central Africa, having Kiswahili as its local lingua franca in addition to English. In contrast, the countries of Central Africa do not have a common language apart from English. Thus the literatures of East Africa have influenced each other much more than those of Central

Africa. Moreover, as a consequence of greater access to higher education in East Africa during the colonial period, the sub-region embarked on writing in English much earlier than Central Africa.

There are significant national differences even within each sub-region. For example, Kenya has produced more literature in English than either Uganda or Tanzania. With regard to Tanzania, where the policy of Ujamaa or African socialism introduced in the 1960s privileged Kiswahili over English as a language of cultural expression, the volume of literature written in English has always lagged behind that of Kenya and Uganda.[8] There are also thematic differences among the various literatures of the region.[9] National differences can be detected in the literature of Central Africa as well. To a large extent, Zimbabwean literature has been shaped by the war of liberation and its aftermath, just as Malawian literature has been determined by the constraints of operating within a post-colonial dictatorship.

Nevertheless, however useful the national approach to literary classification is, it can often underestimate the extent to which writers in a given country are influenced by and respond to debates and ideas from outside their immediate environment. This is even more true of East and Central Africa where historically the intellectual elite have moved easily between countries. For instance, the former Malawian cabinet minister, the journalist Kanyama Chiume, is regarded as both a Tanzanian and Malawian writer, having written in Kiswahili, Chitumbuka and English.[10] David Rubadiri is another case in point: a former Malawian diplomat and University of Makerere student and lecturer, Rubadiri has been at the centre of literary developments in East Africa.[11] Furthermore, the Kenyan writer Ngugi wa Thiong'o wrote his first two novels, *Weep Not Child* (1964) and *The River Between* (1965) while a student in Uganda. Evidently, in a situation of immense cross-national cultural exchange such as East and Central Africa, tethering writers to the flagstaffs of their nations unnecessarily confines them within boundaries which correspond more to an imaginary solidity of national identity than to the more fluid cultural universe in which the writers move and work. Moreover, when one looks at the development of writing in the region, it is evident that right from the beginning of colonialism in the late nineteenth century up to the period of decolonisation in the early 1960s, the area had similar institutions of literary production and distribution, mostly missionary-owned presses and government-controlled publication bureaux.

In the late 1920s, missionary and scholarly organisations in the United Kingdom realised that the provision of local reading material would enable African pupils to cultivate the habit of reading. It was in this context that the International African Institute for Languages and Literature launched an annual creative writing competition around 1926. Some of the winning entries were later translated into English; for instance, the novel *Man of Africa* by the Malawian writer Samuel Ntara which won the 1933 Chinyanja prize.[12] The protagonist of the novel starts off as a criminal, but later converts to Christianity and becomes the chief of his village. Ntara's novel is typical of the literature produced during the period, most of which was no more than Christian propaganda. The quality of writing does not seem to have improved much with the introduction of the government-controlled literature bureaux after the Second World War.[13]

However, to regard the writers, the texts and the literary institutions of the period simply as effects of ideology is to accept uncritically that colonial ideological intentionality was always true of colonial ideological practice, which was never the case. For instance, Ngugi wa Thiong'o's first novel *The River Between* (1965) which, among other things, portrays the destructiveness of Christianity, was written for the 1961 competition organised by the East African Literature Bureau.[14] Of course, Ngugi admits to having been influenced by Christian belief in writing the novel.[15] It is possible to argue that sediments of Christianity, which a number of critics have found in most of Ngugi's work, originate in his early contacts with a literary value system in which Christianity was a dominant literary subject.[16] However, no one, let alone Ngugi, would claim that his earliest novel, which is patently secular, bears the imprint of a high-handed official of the East African Bureau or that of an over-zealous missionary. In fact, what Ngugi's case suggests is that the colonial institutions of literary production may not always have succeeded in determining and policing the content of their publications, which implies the availability of a space within the prevailing ideology for an alternative voice such as Ngugi's.

In addition, it would be doing injustice to the early writers if one regards Ngugi's case as an isolated exception to the rule. Like Ngugi, the early writers used their work to assert the value of traditional culture. In some cases what they wrote was as critical of colonialism as later writing. For example, in the 'proto post-modernist' mixture of fiction and expository writing, *Africa Answers Back* (1936), by the

Ugandan Akiki Nyabongo, an African prince who has been educated by the missionaries returns to his village and marries several wives, which, contrary to what one expects of the literature of the period, enhances rather than harms the protagonist's status as a leader.[17] Most of all, what Nyabongo's text proves is that 'writing back' to the centre is not just a post-colonial phenomenon. Paradoxically, the major difference between Nyabongo and Ngugi, for instance, is not in their critique of the West, but rather their differential access to Western cultural resources and the relative proximity of their texts to oral tradition.[18]

To the extent that the missionaries and colonial publishers did not force writers to imitate Western literary practices, they provided the conditions which sustained what the Sudanese-Ugandan poet, Taban Lo Liyong, refers to approvingly as the 'true sons of Zinjanthropus'.[19] It is inconceivable that the much-acclaimed intervention in the direction of East and Central African writing mounted by the Ugandan writer Okot p'Bitek in the late 1960s would have been possible without his apprenticeship under the East African Publications Bureau. His first novel, written in Luo, *Lak Tar Miyo Kinyero wi Lobo* (*Are Your Teeth White? Then Laugh*) was published by the East African Literature Bureau in 1953. Indeed, the work that catapulted Okot to fame, *Song of Lawino: A Lament* (1966), was a literal translation of *Wer Par Lawino*, originally written in Acholi. Thus, contrary to popular critical opinion, the output of missionary and colonial institutions of literary production was not always a direct expression of colonial and Christian ideology.

The combination of autobiography and the story of the nation gave rise to political autobiography such as J.M. Kariuki's *Mau-Mau Detainee* (1960), Kenneth Kaunda's *Zambia Shall Be Free* (1962), and Mugo Gatheru's *Child of Two Worlds* (1964). There are, in addition, autobiographies which solely focus on the life of an individual rather than using an individual's experiences as a means of representing the ethnic group or nation. One such text is *I Will Try* (1965) by the Malawian novelist Legson Kayira, which is about the journey Kayira made on foot from northern Malawi to the Sudan before finding his way to the United States of America. Like a good mission-educated Malawian, Kayira took with him a copy of the Bible and *Pilgrim's Progress*. The link with missionaries is also evident in the fact that Kayira uses the motto of the Livingstonia Mission for the title of his book. Kayira may have seen himself as a latter-day David Livingstone exploring uncharted territory. However, to the extent that such biographies betray a certain unholy narcissism, it can be argued that they represent the beginning of a secular mode of self-representation.

Apart from monographs, print media in the form of newspapers and magazines played an important role in the emergence of literature in East and Central Africa. During the colonial period, there was a strong tradition of the school magazine in most of the region, which later evolved into literary magazines. Most of these were based at university campuses: *Penpoint* at the University of Makerere, *Darlite* at Dar-es-Salaam, *Nexus* at Nairobi, *Odi* at the University of Malawi, and *The Jewel of Africa* at the University of Zambia. These magazines provided writers with easily accessible local publishing outlets. There were also other magazines with looser connections with the university campus, among them: *Transition*, founded in Uganda in 1961 and co-edited by Rajat Neogy and the Nigerian poet, Christopher Okigbo; *The East African Journal* launched in Uganda in 1964; and *Two-Tone* founded in the late 1960s in Zimbabwe.

Another important factor in the development of literature in the region is the increase, after independence, in the number of indigenous publishing houses committed to promoting local literature: for example, the East African Publishing House, The Tanzanian Publishing House, the Zambian Neczam, Mambo Press, and the Zimbabwe Publishing House. It must be noted that not all publishing houses facilitating the growth of literature in the region appeared on the scene just before or soon after independence. In Zimbabwe, Mambo Press, which was the first publishing house in the country to promote the work of budding black Zimbabwean writers, had been established long before the country became independent. Similarly, Montfort Press, which is owned by the Catholic Church of Malawi, imaginatively switched from being a typical missionary press solely churning out religious material to publishing secular literature when there was need to launch the Malawian Writers Series.[20] Furthermore, the efforts of the indigenous publishing houses have been augmented by the increased interest in the literature of the region by multinational publishers such as Heinemann, Macmillan and Longman, some of which have offices in Nairobi and Harare. It is also significant that both local and multinational publishing companies recruited a number of graduates as editors, an example of which is Jonathan Kariara who joined Oxford University Press in Nairobi upon graduating from the University of Makerere.

However, the influence of universities on the literature of the region goes further. Universities provided the region with a new breed of writers whose command of English was more accomplished than that of the writers of the earlier generation. Besides, these were writers who had been brought up on the Great Tradition rather than *Pilgrim's Progress*. The early creative effort of the new writers betrays a marked degree of cultural plagiarism. Chris Wanjala reports that: 'in the late fifties, a Makerere College Undergraduate wrote on *The Anomaly of Humanity*, dabbling in the metaphysical tradition, where man is seen as a creature of baffling nature, basically an unknowable creature'.[21] Not much came out of these early endeavours at first, with the result that in the early 1960s East and Central Africa were universally regarded as a literary desert. Here, there was no equivalent of a Chinua Achebe, or a Peter Abrahams to speak of. Desperate to do something about the embarrassing literary barrenness of East Africa, Taban Lo Liyong resorted to an unusual source of inspiration. He says that after failing to give a convincing lecture on East African writing to a group of fellow Africans because there was little literature to discuss, he immediately set out to became a writer, which he did as follows:

> I walked to my apartment, threw my bookcase on the bed and sat next to it. I then held my big head between my powerful hands. I squeezed it, and squeezed it hard, till it thought. When thoughts came, they poured like tropical rain: big and fast. I pulled out a pencil and a paper and wrote fast, capturing every drop of thought.[22]

Apart from such individual Herculean fits as Taban's, there were other collective catalytic moments, one of them being the Conference of African Writers of English Expression held at the University of Makerere in 1962, which brought together such eminent names as Wole Soyinka, Chinua Achebe, Christopher Okigbo, Lewis Nkosi, Bloke Modisane, Ezekiel Mphahlele and Langston Hughes. The contribution of writers from outside to the development of writing in the region was further evident at the 1964 Ranche House College National Creative Writer's Conference which brought Zimbabwean writers in contact with those from South Africa such as Wilber Smith.[23] These conferences greatly awakened interest in writing in a region which had lagged behind West and South Africa. The feeling of being part of a community of writers emerging from a common history of colonial oppression, which Ngugi mentions, must have encouraged local writers to tell their own particular history of colonialism and decolonisation.

The major motivating force behind the early literature in English from the region was the desire to represent the African past from an African perspective so as to challenge the often negative constructions of Africa found in colonial narratives.[24] The refutation of the colonial universe of history took diverse forms: reconstructing pre-colonial Africa, representing the advent of colonialism, dramatising life under colonial rule and the struggle for independence.

The past was a dominant theme of the works, such as Solomon Mutswairo's *Feso*, published during the transition from the age of mission presses and government bureaux to contemporary post-colonial writing. Originally written in Shona, and published in 1956 by the Rhodesian Literature Bureau, and translated into English by the author in 1974, the novel uses pre-colonial Africa as a metaphor for the colonial situation. *Feso* is a story about the conflict between two ethnic groups in seventeenth-century Zimbabwe.[25] The warlike Vanyai regularly attack their peace-loving neighbours, the Vahota. Under a brave general by the name Feso, the Vahota not only manage to defend themselves successfully against their adversaries, but also conquer and absorb them into a new political unit founded on the Vahota political philosophy which emphasises peace and good neighbourliness. The novel was banned by the colonial government in Rhodesia as it was easily recognised as an allegory of the conflict between Africans and Europeans over Zimbabwe.[26] The hostility of the colonial government to the novel underlines the extent to which the project of recovering the African historical universe, both during and after the colonial period, served more than just a nostalgic retrieval of the past; it was a site where the construction and privileging of an autochthonous African identity functioned as a device for foregrounding the alienness of the colonial formation.

One of the few instances of poetic representation of the advent of colonialism is the much anthologised poem, 'Stanley Meets Mutesa', by David Rubadiri. Like Samkange's novels, Rubadiri's poem seeks to rewrite a specific event in the history of colonialism. The adventures of 'explorers' such as Henry Morton Stanley and David Livingstone were staple reading for pupils in the region. Evidently these accounts celebrated the 'explorers' contribution to British imperial expansion. What Rubadiri does is to reinscribe the African in the story, thereby activating the silent space of alterity in colonial discourse. He does this by shifting the focus to the African porters who accompanied Stanley:

> The thin weary line of carriers
> With tattered dirty rags to cover backs;
> The battered bulky chests
> That kept on falling off their heads.
> Their tempers high and hot
> The sun fierce and scorching . . .[27]

Here, Stanley is not glorified in the manner of the colonial textbook, but diminished, as he is presented as being no different from a slave master. Furthermore, the poet suggests that undiscriminating traditional hospitality may have been the Baganda's Achilles heel, since it made them misrecognise the moment of colonial penetration:

> The tall black king steps forward,
> He towers over the thin bearded white man
> Then grabbing his lean white hand
> Manages to whisper
> 'Mtu Mweupe karibu'
> White man you are welcome.
> The gate of polished reed closes behind them
> And the west is let in.[28]

Unlike Rubadiri's, Ngugi's representation of the past does not work with a concept of history which lays emphasis on precise documentary evidence. Ngugi's *The River Between* (1965) depicts colonialism as an event that had not been totally outside the collective consciousness of African society: the seer Mugo wa Kibiro foretells the arrival of Europeans. It is, however, the divisive impact of colonialism on the community that is explored in the novel, as the newly converted Christians of Makuyu are pitted against the traditionalists from Kameno. The only two characters, Muthoni and Waiyaki, who attempt to reconcile tradition and Christianity suffer death or alienation. Thus Christianity produces new forms of difference for which there are no readily available solutions.[29]

The early days of European incursion in Africa also feature in *The Tongue of the Dumb* (1971) by the Zambian novelist Dominic Mulaisho. Like Ngugi's *The River Between*, the novel presents the conflict between tradition and Christianity, bringing into it the relationship between a given ideology and the way it is understood and applied by those adhering to it. Both the missionary, Father Oliver or Chiphwanya, and Lubinda, the custodian of African tradition, are shown to be ruthless and narrow-minded agents of their respective belief-systems. Thus the novel is less a simple portrayal of the ideological conflict between Western and African culture than a critical reflection on how the deployment of a simple Manichean dichotomy in the analysis of the history of colonisation inevitably ignores those instances when a particular implementation of an aspect of an ideology is mediated by local power struggles among members affiliated to that ideology. Both Chiphwanya and Lubinda react to each other not solely as representatives of their respective religious and cultural ideologies, but also in order to undermine someone from their own community.

As well as retrieving the pre-colonial past and the history of colonisation, writers from East and Central Africa have examined the history of resistance to colonial rule. Ngugi's first published novel, *Weep Not Child* (1964) was the first novel in the region to examine the moment of resistance to colonialism and the psychological effects of colonial violence. The author recreates the experience of growing up during the Emergency through the young protagonist, Njoroge, whose dream of attaining education is shattered when he is expelled from school because his brothers have joined the struggle against the colonial forces. Njoroge learns that he cannot stand outside history. *Weep Not Child* shows Ngugi already questioning the limitations of personal goals which do not include the needs of the community as a whole. The difference between Njoroge and Kihika in Ngugi's *A Grain of Wheat* (1967) best exemplifies Ngugi's growing conviction that the pursuit of education as a means of social mobility leads to the reproduction of the same forms of hierarchy as those of the colonial social formation. Unlike Njoroge, Kihika inscribes his identity in the needs of the collective rather than in the colonial ideology of self-improvement.

It is in *A Grain of Wheat* that Ngugi gives a more comprehensive and complex study of the war of liberation in Kenya as he attempts to situate the Mau-Mau movement in the history of the Kenyan nationalist struggle and to demonstrate that, far from being an organisation that was merely violent, as has sometimes been claimed, it sprung from a history of incessant colonial brutality.[30] Ione Leigh's view that 'Mau-Mau is no liberation movement. It is an evil, malignant growth, a dark, tribal septic focus, and it has to be destroyed', is typical of the representation of the Kenyan war of liberation in the colonial press and the literature written by apologists of colonial rule in

Kenya.[31] However, the novel also introduces a theme that will become increasingly central to Ngugi's later work – the betrayal of the ideals of the liberation struggle by the leadership.

In Zimbabwe too, the struggle against the colonial political system has inspired a large body of writing. Wilson Katiyo's *A Son of the Soil* (1976) looks at the production of colonial subjectivity through state apparatuses of law and order, and the hero's eventual realisation that his future lies in aligning himself with the nationalist forces of liberation. Like Ngugi, Katiyo argues that it is colonial violence that engenders violent anti-colonial resistance. If Katiyo's novel is a study of the gradual process of counter-identification with colonial ideology, Freedom Nyamubaya's anthology of poetry, *On the Road Again* (1986), is a record of the life of a freedom fighter. In her poem, 'Of Course, it's not the same', she contrasts the colonial or settler soldier with the freedom fighter:

> Soldiers specialise
> in killing people
> per instruction
> with firearms!
> A profession like doctors.
>
> BUT!!!
>
> Freedom fighters
> shelter people
> Under the shadow of death
>   By soldiers
>   by warfare
> Of course, it is not the same.[32]

Furthermore, in her poem 'The Native Intellectual', Nyamubaya bemoans the marginalisation of the freedom fighter when the struggle is over.[33]

The wide diversity of response to the war is evident in Musaemura Zimunya's and M. Kadhani's anthology of Zimbabwean poetry, *And Now the Poets Speak* (1981). For the Zimbabwean poet and novelist Chenjerai Hove, one cannot fully grasp the magnitude of psychological and physical damage engendered by war – even if it is a war of liberation – without widening one's field of investigation to include the seemingly unheroic life of ordinary people. As Emmanuel Ngara observes, Hove's concern in his anthology, *Up in Arms* (1982), 'is with the effect of the war on the common people and on the fighters as victims of war's cruelty'.[34] Hove's attempt to look at the whole community demonstrates an awareness of the danger of only focusing on the great deeds of the heroes of the war of liberation.

It is perhaps the need to problematise the role of heroes of the nationalist struggle that informs Charles Mangua's satirisation of Mau-Mau leaders in *A Tail in the Mouth* (1972).[35] Mangua, like his compatriot Meja Mwangi – in his novels such as *Carcase for Hounds* (1974) and *A Taste of Death* (1975) – has appropriated nationalist history for a popular fiction that relies heavily on American thrillers and detective fiction, thus inadvertently bringing back a form of cultural colonialism that would have shocked the leaders of the Mau-Mau struggle.[36] It is possible to read the sensational and irreverent portrayal of the history of the liberation struggle as a symptom of the growing disillusionment with post-colonial regimes in the region, one of the major themes of recent work.

The critique of post-colonial social formations has concentrated on issues of cultural alienation, corruption and dictatorship. The most celebrated work from the region on the question of cultural alienation is Okot p'Bitek's *Song of Lawino: A Lament* (1966), in which Lawino, a traditionalist, castigates her husband Ocol for losing his manhood through his uncritical devotion to Western culture and lifestyle. She takes it upon herself to remind Ocol, and others like him, of the value of traditional culture:

> Listen Ocol, my old friend,
> The ways of your ancestors
> Are good,
> Their customs are solid
> And not hollow
> They are thin, not easily breakable
> They cannot be blown away
> By the winds
> Because their roots reach deep into the soil.[37]

The song delivers a thematic and stylistic discourse of cultural authenticity. Through the use of a form of English that reads and sounds like an African language, Okot manages to bring the literature written in English in the region closer to its immediate cultural context. As he says, his ambition is to effect a 'total demolition of foreign cultural domination and the restoration and promotion of Africa's proud culture to its rightful place'.[38] However, Okot's critics have accused him of being superficial in his social analysis of cultural alienation. According to Ngugi, Okot is 'in danger of emphasising culture as if it could be divorced from its political and economic basis'.[39] More important, as Ngugi has argued recently, writers such as Okot, who sought to decolonise African aesthetics through the medium of English, still subscribed to the primacy of English as a language of cultural expression, thus inserting their radical authenticity within the very symbolic framework it was intended to undermine.[40] Okot's *Song of Lawino*, in its linguistic and formal syntheses, exemplifies little cultural authenticity and more hybridity. Nevertheless, Okot's songs were to have a profound influence on other East African writers, particularly in Uganda, Kenya and, to some extent, Malawi.

Without exaggerating Okot's influence on the literature of the region, it can be argued that his success contributed to the increased confidence in the use of oral and traditional material in literature which can be observed in the work of writers such as Robert Serumaga. Serumaga used traditional mime and dance for his stage plays like *Renga Moi* (1974) and *Majangwa* (1974). The use of elements of oral tradition in drama is also evident in Steve Chimombo's play *The Rainmaker* (1974) which is based on the Mbona rain-cult of southern Malawi. Chimombo's play, which seems to aspire to Soyinkan verbal density, suggests that, with regard to the use of oral material in drama, Okot may have been one of many available sources of inspiration.

However, Okot's impact on the local scene is perhaps most obvious in the area of popular literature where his poetic form, which gave the songs a populist edge, provided writers such as David Maillu with a model through which they could represent the problems of urban life in an idiom that was closer to their readers than the language of American popular literature which they sometimes relied on. Okot's influence is detectable in Maillu's narrative poems such as *My Dear Bottle* (1973) and *After 4.30* (1974). It would also appear that it was Okot's focus on the decadence of the educated urban-dwellers that struck a chord with the concerns of the popular writers. In a nutshell, Okot p'Bitek can be said to have bridged the gap between popular and high literature, which saved the literature of the region from developing into a purely elite cultural practice. It is ironic, however, that Okot's poetic form, fashioned for purposes of liberating the African from cultural alienation, is employed by the writers of popular literature to celebrate the very condition it was meant to cure. As some critics have pointed out, the song has been used by writers like David Maillu for an urban pornography.[41]

Not all applications of Okot's model have been in the vein of *After 4.30*. In the narrative poem, *The Orphan* (1968), by the Ugandan poet Okello Oculi, the song becomes the means by which the orphan is given a voice through which to chastise a cruel and irresponsible world. Oculi seems to subscribe to that strain of existentialism that emphasises the idea that man is alone in the universe.[42] Oculi's concern with social outcasts resurfaces in *The Prostitute* (1968) where the prostitute is shown as a victim of other prostitutes, the African elite, who employ their opulence and political positions in order to exacerbate rather than diminish the suffering of the underprivileged. It is the vision of an egalitarian society that informs Oculi's interest in the problem of cultural authenticity.

The concern with economic issues in writing is given greater ideological solidity in the socialist interpretation of social relations that we find in the plays of the Ugandan writer Mukotani Rugyendo. His play, *The Barbed Wire* (1977), tells the story of how a group of landlords expropriated land from peasants. However, in the end the peasants get their land back and establish a communal system of land ownership. Rugyendo's socialist realism is similar to Ngugi wa Thiong'o's post-humanist work. Beginning with *Petals of Blood* (published in 1977), Ngugi adopted a Marxist interpretation of neo-colonialism. The novel dramatises the exploitation of peasants by the local comprador class in conjunction with international capital, a theme that Ngugi articulated in his collection of essays *Homecoming* (1969). The theme was elaborated further in his 1980 play *Ngaahika Ndeenda* (*I Will Marry When I Want*, 1982) which drew Ngugi into the domain of popular theatre and brought him in direct conflict with the Kenyan government.

Ngugi's detention in 1977 highlighted the fact that unequal social and economic relations were in fact mediated through the one-party state dictatorship. This theme was taken up by writers in Uganda and Malawi. In his novel *No Bride Price* (1967), Rubadiri looks at the way individuals inhabit and interact with bureaucratic power, thus contributing unknowingly to the creation of despotism. The novel, like Peter Nazareth's *In a Brown Mantle* (1972), is also a study of conditions which lead to military government.[43] Taking the theme further, the Ugandan playwright, John Ruganda, uses his play, *The Floods* (1980), to plumb the nature of brutal dictatorships. Evidently, the play is an attempt to record one of the darkest moments in the history of Uganda, the period of Idi Amin's regime. Serumaga's existentialist novel, *Return to the Shadows* (1969), examines the degree to which individualism enables some members of the intellectual elite to turn even such moments of national crises to personal advantage. The protagonist cynically and regularly profits from defending members of governments overthrown by the military in the full knowledge that his clients, who stand little chance of avoiding the death-sentence, will be desperate to pay any price and are unlikely to return to ask for a discount.[44]

The issue of dictatorship dominates Malawian writing. It features in Legson Kayira's novel *The Detainee* (1974) and Lupenga Mphande's and Innocent Banda's verse, for example.[45] Furthermore, Felix Mnthali's collection of poetry, *When Sunset Comes to Sapitwa* (1980), brings to the critique of dictatorship a philosophical approach within which the abuse of political power is seen in terms of fundamental questions about the relationship between self and society. In Jack Mapanje's *Of Chameleon and Gods* (1981), the poet attempts to fashion a language through which to circumvent the government-imposed censorship and provide an alternative narrative of the story of the nation.[46] Mapanje's poetry speaks from within the discourse of everyday language, even when aspects of oral tradition are brought in. Though more outspoken in its criticism of the Malawian dictatorship, Jack Mapanje's collection of poetry *The Chattering Wagtails of Mikuyu Prison* (1993), written after his release from political detention, employs similar devices of defamiliarisation as his previous work.[47] In contrast to Mapanje, Steve Chimombo's poetry achieves subversive concealment through a dense interweaving of local myth and contemporary politics.[48] As for Frank Chipasula, it is the contrast between home and exile that underpins his poetic output.[49]

In the region, the analysis of power is not just limited to the critique of formal political and social relations, but extends to other sites of difference such as dominant gender and aesthetic ideologies. Here, again, Ngugi features highly, as in most of his work, especially that produced after *A Grain of Wheat* (1967), he has tried to locate unequal relations of gender in the context of capitalist relations of production and distribution. In *Petals of Blood* (1977), for instance, Wanja is exploited in terms of both her class and gender. Similarly, in *Devil on the Cross* (1982), the rich smuggler who contemplates investing his money in a factory manufacturing human parts, and endowing himself with two penises is rudely surprised when his wife asks him: 'Why do you want to have two? tell me: what would you use two for? . . . If you have two then I must have two. We must have equality of the sexes . . .'[50] However, Ngugi represents a handful of men seriously exploring the question of gender ideology in the region. Mostly, it has been women, by no means many, who have brought the issue to the fore of cultural debate in East and Central Africa. The Kenyan writer, Rebeka Njau was one of the first writers in the area to give women more than a general ideological illustrative function in narrative. In Njau's *Ripples in the Pool* (1978), as Jane Bryce-Okunlola has suggested, female subjectivity is more concretely presented than in the work of Ngugi wa Thiong'o.[51] Njau's concern with gendered subjectivity was first expressed in her early work, the play *The Scar* (1965). And recently, in her novel *Nervous Conditions* (1988), Tsitsi Dangarembga has examined the interplay between traditional and Western discourses of gender in contemporary Zimbabwe.[52]

However, some writers do not easily fit in the general thematic categories elaborated in the foregoing discussion. The most obvious example is Dambuzo Marechera, whose *House of Hunger* (1978) and *The Black Insider* (1990) are closer to the Western aesthetic on the indigenisation continuum than any other text from the region. The manuscript reader from Nairobi aptly described *House of Hunger* as an expression of Western existentialism.[53] However, Marechera's aesthetic alienation has nothing to do with the use of Western philosophy or literary values as such, since many African writers have, in varying degrees, appropriated elements of Western culture. It is more to do with the subject position from which Marechera writes: unlike a self-confessed valoriser of Western tradition such as Taban Lo Liyong who nevertheless speaks from an indigenist position, Marechera speaks from outside the culture of his origins and from a place in the centre of the metropole. Thus for Marechera the centre was more than a place of exile – it was home. If Marechera wrote back to the centre, he did so as a diasporic subject who, despite being critical of the centre, still upheld the integrity of the Western symbolic system. Marechera's incorporation is more acute than that of the writers who wrote for the mission presses or the bureaux. However, it is not necessarily the case that writing from within the centre produces the subject position found in Marechera's work. A text which demonstrates the possibility of using modernist and post-modernist Western forms for an enhanced African writing practice is Abdulrazak

Gurnah's novel *Paradise* which was shortlisted for the Booker Prize in 1994. Gurnah employs a combination of Western and African narrative form, exemplifying a way of engaging with the most current Western literary conventions without allowing them to overwhelm the cultural distinctiveness of his practice.

Ngugi wa Thiong'o has successfully employed this method in his work written in Gikuyu such as *Matagari* where certain aspects of Western tradition, in particular the Bible, are used as narrative devices for a critique of neo-colonialism. Nevertheless, with Ngugi's decision to stop writing in English, a position that is by no means widely shared by writers in the region, the pendulum has swung completely to the indigenous pole. Even if Ngugi is in a minority, his decision will obviously enhance the status of writing in indigenous languages. However, Ngugi's new-found authenticity is part of the tradition founded by the much maligned writers of local language school-readers. Thus Ngugi's project is only radical in the context of the failure of post-colonial writers to carry out a meaningful dialogue with their local literary heritage.

In conclusion, when one looks at the history of writing in East and Central Africa closely, it is evident that the distinction between colonial and post-colonial writing is not as clear-cut as is presented in some influential models of post-colonial literary history. The dominant preoccupation throughout the history of the literature of the region has been with the place of African culture in the new cultural dispensation. It is true that the discourse of cultural authenticity during the colonial era was predominantly mediated through colonial and Christian ideology, but even under such conditions of cultural surveillance, a number of writers produced work which, in its own limited way, undermined the self-evident plausibility of the colonial project. It is equally true that cultural production in the post-colonial era is not itself free from the determining influence of the Other. One can only conclude from this that the suggestion that the literature of post-colonial societies evolves from a moment of absolute colonial hegemony in the past to a moment of freedom in the present post-colonial period disregards the co-presence of colonised and autonomous spaces in each phase of the development of the literature. Furthermore, such conceptions of literary history unwittingly collude with nationalists' myths of history in which the post-colonial moment is often uncritically regarded as representing the absence of colonial hegemony. It is proposed here that such linear and teleological models of history need to be replaced with a concept of history which takes each historical period as essentially constituting a dialectic of identification and counter-identification with dominant ideology or the other.

Notes

1. W.D. Ashcroft, Gareth Griffiths and Helen Tiffin, *The Empire Writes Back: The Theory and Practice in Post-Colonial Literatures* (London, 1989).

2. Edward Said, *Orientalism: Western Conceptions of the Orient* (London, 1978). There are exceptions to the rule, such as Doris Lessing's *The Grass is Singing* (1950), which, unlike most colonial novels, attempts to come to terms with the brutality of colonialism.

3. W.D. Ashcroft et al., *The Empire Writes Back*, p. 6.

4. Ibid., p. 4.

5. Ngugi wa Thiong'o, 'The African Writer and his Past', in Christopher Heywood (ed.), *Perspectives on African Literature* (London, 1971), p. 7.

6. Simon Gikandi, 'The Growth of the East African Novel', in G.D. Killam (ed.), *The Writing of East and Central Africa* (London, 1984), p. 234; and Taban Lo Liyong, *The Last Word: Cultural Synthesism* (Nairobi, 1969), p. 12.

7. Ngugi wa Thiong'o, 'The African Writer and his Past', p. 3.

8. See Ismael Mbise, 'Writing in English from Tanzania', in G.D. Killam (ed.), *The Writing of East and Central Africa*, pp. 54–69.

9. Chris Wanjala, 'Imaginative Writing Since Independence: The East African Experience', in Ulla Schild (ed.), *The East African Experience: Essays on English and Swahili Literature* (Berlin, 1980), p. 9.

10. M.W.K. Chiume, *Dunia Ngumu* (Dar-es-Salaam, 1973), and *Charu Ndi Mazgora* (Lusaka, 1963).

11. See Peter Nazareth, 'Waiting for Amin: Two Decades of Ugandan Literature', in G.D. Killam (ed.), *The Writing of East and Central Africa*, pp. 7–35.

12. See Steve Chimombo, 'Evangelisation and Literacy in Malawi', *Religion in Malawi*, vol. 2, no. 1 (1988), p. 25.

13. Ngugi wa Thiong'o, *Decolonising the Mind: The Politics of Language in African Literature* (London, 1986), p. 67.

14. See Dennis Duerden and Cosmo Pieterse (eds), *African Writers Talking* (London, 1972), p. 122.

15. Ngugi wa Thiong'o, 'An Interview with Students at Leeds', *Cultural Events in Africa*, no. 1 (1967), p. 2.

16. For comments on the Christian content in Ngugi's works, see for example Adrain Roscoe, *Uhuru's Fire* (Cambridge, 1977), pp. 171–2; and Peter

Nazareth, 'The Second Homecoming', in Georg Gugelberger (ed.), *Marxism and African Literature* (London, 1985), p. 122.

17. Akiki Nyabongo, *Africa Answers Back* (London, 1936).
18. Ngugi has acknowledged the influence of Conrad and Lawrence on his early work. See 'Ngugi's Interview with Dennis Duerden', in D. Duerden and C. Pieterse (eds), *African Writers Talking*, pp. 122–3.
19. See the Preface to Taban Lo Liyong's *The Last Word* (Nairobi, 1969), p. 157.
20. See Bernth Lindfors, *Kulankula* (Bayreuth, 1989).
21. C. Wanjala, 'Imaginative Writing Since Independence', p. 12.
22. T. Lo Liyong, *The Last Word*, p. 26.
23. See Adrian Roscoe and Mpalive-Hangson Msiska, *The Quiet Chameleon: Modern Poetry Central Africa* (London, 1992), pp. 96–7.
24. S. Gikandi, 'The Growth of the East African Novel', p. 234.
25. See *Feso*, in *Zimbabwe Prose and Poetry* (Washington DC, 1974).
26. See G. Kahari, *The Search for Zimbabwean Identity* (Gwelo, 1980), and T.O. McLoughlin, 'Black Writing in English from Zimbabwe', in G.D. Killam (ed.), *The Writing of East and Central Africa*, pp. 101–4.
27. David Rubadiri, 'Stanley Meets Mutesa', in Jonathan Kariara and Ellen Kitonga (eds), *An Introduction to East African Poetry* (Nairobi, 1976), pp. 28–9.
28. Ibid., p. 30.
29. See David Cook and Michael Okenimkpe, *Ngugi wa Thiong'o: An Exploration of His Work* (London, 1983), pp. 26–47.
30. The Mau-Mau war began in 1952 and continued until 1956.
31. David Maughan-Brown, *Land, Freedom and Fiction* (London, 1985), p. 20.
32. Freedom Nyamubaya, *On the Road Again* (Harare, 1986), p. 31.
33. Ibid., p. 44.
34. Emmanuel Ngara, *Ideology and Form in African Poetry* (London, 1990), p. 116; Chenjerai Hove, *Up In Arms* (Harare, 1982).
35. See Bernth Lindfors, 'Kenyan Literature', in Leonard Klein (ed.), *African Literatures in the Twentieth Century: A Guide* (Harpenden, Herts, 1988), pp. 85–6.
36. For a good discussion of Mwangi and Mangua, see Angela Smith, *East African Writing in English* (London, 1989), and Angus Calder, 'Meja Mawangi's Novels', in G.D. Killam (ed.), *The Writing of East and Central Africa*, pp. 177–91.
37. Okot p'Bitek, *Song of Lawino: A Lament* (Nairobi, 1972), p. 29.
38. Okot p'Bitek (ed.), *Africa's Cultural Revolution* (Nairobi, 1973).
39. See Ngugi wa Thiong'o, 'Introduction', on O. p'Bitek (ed.), *Africa's Cultural Revolution*, p. xii.
40. Ngugi wa Thiong'o, *Decolonising the Mind*, pp. 8–9.

41. See Bernth Lindfors, *Popular Literature in Africa* (Trenton, New Jersey, 1991), pp. 47–60.
42. Okello Oculi, *Orphan* (Nairobi, 1968), p. 15.
43. See Peter Nazareth, 'Waiting for Amin', pp. 12–13.
44. Ibid., p. 14.
45. See Anthony Nazombe (ed.), *The Haunting Wind: New Poetry From Malawi* (Blantyre, 1990), and *Index on Censorship*, vol. 18, no. 9 (1989).
46. Jack Mapanje, 'Introduction', *Of Chameleons and Gods* (London, 1981).
47. Jack Mapanje, *The Chattering Wagtails of Mikuyu Prison* (London, 1993).
48. For an extended discussion of this view, see Mpalive-Hangson Msiska, 'Geopoetics: Subterraneanity and Subversion in Malawian Poetry', in Abdulrazak Gurnah (ed.), *Essays on African Writing*, vol. 2 (London, 1995); Felix Mnthali, *When Sunset Comes to Sapitwa* (Lusaka, 1980). Chimombo has so far published three collections of verse: *Napolo Poems* (Zomba, 1987); *Python! Python!* (Zomba, 1992); *A Referendum of The Forest Creatures* (Zomba, 1993).
49. Frank Chipasula, *O Earth, Wait for Me* (Braamfontein, 1984), *Whispers in the Dark* (London, 1991).
50. Ngugi wa Thiong'o, *Devil on the Cross* (London, 1982).
51. Ngugi wa Thiong'o, *Decolonising the Mind*, p. 8.
52. Tsitsi Dangarembga, *Nervous Condition* (London, 1988); Rebeka Njau, *Ripples in the Pool* (London, 1975).
53. See Flora Veit-Wild's 'Introduction' to Dambuzo Marechera, *The Black Insider* (Harare, 1990), p. 6.

Part II
Issues and Problems

4 *What is African literature?: ethnography and criticism*

Kadiatu Kanneh

> To know how I am and how I have fared, you must understand why I
> resist all kinds of domination including that of being given something.
> (Nuruddin Farah, *Gifts*, 1993)

The reading and criticism of African literatures has given rise to a series
of related issues which can be broadly summarised by the question:
What is African literature? How does the rubric 'African literature' relate
to, construct or reflect national boundaries, cultural definitions or
racial histories? Should reading African literatures insist on a recognition of the cultural or philosophical *difference* of what is African
within these texts, and would that, in turn, be a task for anthropology
or a specifically 'African' critical theory?

Christopher Miller's discussion of the interpretation of African
literatures relies on an examination of cultural or theoretical projection onto a text. How might we approach a 'right' reading of a
literature without being misled by 'Western' theory? The question, in
Miller's essay, manages to escape the conclusion that authentic
communion with an African text is possible only (if at all) from the
pure African him/herself – a matter of inherent or contextual coincidence.
Miller's question is primarily aimed at the difference between the
Western critic and the non-Western text. Or, rather, it is staged as a
confrontation between Western literary theory or criticism and its
subordination of an African text. For Miller, the argument is a cultural
one, which needs assistance from ethnography and its problems: 'It
becomes evident from the start that contact with African literature will
involve contact with, even dependence on, anthropology.'[1]

The apparent excesses of this claim, that the reading of literature is
always, consciously or unconsciously, the exercise of power through

ssumption of knowledge over others, directly faces theory's other
n on the irreducible self-reflexivity of literary interpretation. In
other words, Miller insists on the *conscious* awareness of how literary
criticism is also a cultural battleground where a *resigned* acceptance
of the inevitability of seeing only oneself within the text is also an
appropriative act inseparable from the politics of Western academe.
Between recognising the impossibility of truly knowing or representing
the (African) 'Other', and being aware of the Other's challenging and
inescapable presence, one is left, according to Miller, with all the
difficulties of anthropology.

What an anthropology of literature might mean arises, I would
argue, at the same moment one asks how 'Africa' and literature might
be said to coincide in the first place. Categorising and then making
sense out of what is African implies a speculative distance between
object and interlocutor. One interprets difference into knowledge in a
process of dialogue and *translation*. A definition of what is African
might then read as that which, on some level resists European surveillance and domination, that which needs to be translated or
subdued from its discrete independence into the realm of the same.
Miller's observation that very different readings may emerge of an
African text if interpretative skills are allowed to arise from the culture
in which it is situated is a timely response to critical techniques which
currently dominate the academy as somehow universal. This process
becomes more complicated, however, when considering literature
itself as a form of representation with its own histories, theories and
alliances. The subject, author, philosophy, language or values of a
novel do not possess a necessarily simple or coterminus relationship
with each other. Before we can approach the difference, or not, of
African from European or Western literature, we are compelled to
undertake a detour, or rather, get beneath the surface to examine what
have been called philosophical, racial or cultural oppositions between
Africa and Europe, and what this might mean.

The arguments of Ngugi wa Thiong'o about the politics of cultural
independence and domination introduce a debate which appears to
have clear definitions and answers for our earlier question: 'What is
African literature?' Ngugi's contentions provide a valuable corrective
to the widespread temptation to approach literature and criticism in
isolation from the ongoing battles for economic, linguistic and social
self-determination by African peoples. For Ngugi, literary creativity
as well as literary criticism is irrevocably caught up in issues of

representation and power, which forces any discuss
literature' in several particular directions. Intere.
immediately bypasses the very question we have pos
irrelevant detour from the proper, underlying probl
African literature?' must, for Ngugi, give way to 'How .
dominated?' The problems which emerged from tl   ...u
conference of 1962, 'A Conference of African Writers of English
Expression', which form the basis of Ngugi's impatience, do, however,
throw up some crucial issues. The questions about the African-ness of
African literature which the conference foregrounded are summarised
by Ngugi in this way:

> Was it literature about Africa or about the African experience? Was it
> literature written by Africans? What about a non-African who wrote
> about Africa: did his work qualify as African literature? What if an
> African set his work in Greenland . . . were African languages the
> criteria? . . . What about French and English, which had become African
> languages? What if an European wrote about Europe in an African
> language?[2]

In terms of Miller's argument – that theoretical approaches to
literature may not be simply generalisable but need to be checked by
other traditions echoing in or forming the text – the difficulties of
finding or pinning down these other traditions becomes apparent.
What do we mean by 'Africa' or a literature categorised by nationality,
culture, race or place?

Ngugi's statement: 'If . . . if . . . if . . . this or that, except the issue:
the domination of our languages and cultures by those of imperialist
Europe' (*Decolonising*, p. 6) focuses on what he sees as the crux of the
issue for African literature. African languages and cultures are placed
at the centre of African literary criticism precisely because these have
been and are at the point of attack and displacement in the imperialist
confrontation between Europe and Africa. In both *Decolonising the
Mind* and *Moving the Centre*, Ngugi associates language very closely
with culture so that the two almost work on an axis of inter-
changeability. Both language and culture are the blueprints of identity
and value for a nation or a people, leading Ngugi to assert that
'Language as culture is the collective memory bank of a people's
experience in history' (*Decolonising*, p. 15). Although conceding that
culture is like a constantly moving river: 'It is like studying a river in
its very movement, that is in its very being as a river',[3] it is also an

Nyasha

ganic whole – a slowly mutating but particular identity in itself: 'In this sense society is like a human body which develops as a result of the internal working out of all its cells and other biological processes' (*Centre*, p. xv).

In a sense, then, Ngugi can accept flux and change within, and communication between cultures, on the basis of significant, discrete identities. The 'gift' of European languages to African cultures, because performed as an act of domination, not reciprocity, results in a literature which hovers uneasily in the twilight between Europe and Africa. After thrusting aside any engagement with the long quarrel over the (proper) constitution of African literature, Ngugi unavoidably enters the fray. African literature written in French, English or Portuguese, for example, is *not African* literature, but 'Afro-European literature' (*Decolonising*, p. 27). What is African is located in what has become 'traditional' African culture, carried and understood through indigenous languages. This neat resolution of the problem of definition by reference to the (continuing) history of cultural imperialism does not, of course, end there. If 'Africa' is located in the (largely oral) histories of African languages, then issues of literacy, audience and the plurality of the modern world would seem to place insurmountable obstacles in the path of Ngugi's protest for African literature. Ngugi's struggle, however, is mounted precisely at this point of contention between what is often labelled the 'traditional' and the 'modern'. If the modern world is the technological economy of literate societies, it becomes necessary for Africa to also take its place within the structures of modernity. If there is a critical debate within and about literature, Africa has been denied an equal platform in order to participate on its own cultural, hence linguistic terms. Ngugi disallows the debate to fall into a long lament for an African past *before* Europe and insists instead that Africa take its place *alongside* (rather than behind) Europe in a fair exchange of cultural gifts.

The argument could be taken one stage further, and a closer exploration of what could be termed classic African literary criticism seems, implicitly, to have done that. Miller's evocation of anthropology as the necessary shadow haunting our reading contributes to the notion of African literary criticism as a negotiation of differences. In this light, Africa can exist only as what is (claimed or made to be) *different from*, outside or against, Europe. This moves us, stealthily, to the implications of Jean-Paul Sartre's statement on revolutionary action in the preface to *The Wretched of the Earth*: 'We only become what we are by the radical and deep-seated refusal of that which others have made of us.'[4] Ngugi's struggle to claim a place for African literatures in a longed-for world centred on a multiplicity of different cultures is as much an argument for retaining the tension of those boundaries – without which the refusal cannot take place – as it is an argument for communication.

The three dimensions which are repeatedly run together in discussions of African literature – its definition, the constitution of African culture, and the validity of a specifically African literary criticism – carry with them the serious danger of removing African literature into the realm of *cultural difference* away from literature itself. What needs to be questioned, then, is how far ' literature itself', or literary criticism, is motivated by *implicit* cultural biases. To this end, cultural criticism may offer a way in.

Henry Louis Gates's dismissal of what he calls the 'anthropology fallacy',[5] refers, particularly, to the repeated and long-standing habit of shunting African literatures into a space outside art and literary figuration and into sociological data. Re-applying the use of 'anthropology', certain resonances within African texts, belonging to traditions and metaphors outside the 'canon' of literary theory may, usefully, be incorporated into more sensitive readings of *literary* signification. The danger centres around the problems of anthropology itself, and its tendency towards a holistic vision of Africa as one internally coherent and systematic – or spiritual – difference. Gates's significant contention against Black and African texts being read only as windows directly onto social reality, needing no artistic or imaginative mediation, needs to be approached at a tangent from the acceptance of Black African literatures as needing identical reading strategies as those *already formulated* by the academy. Gates's insistence that theoretical complexity should not be denied Black/African texts,[6] that they demand to be read on a range of levels, needs to be balanced against (and not necessarily at odds with) Anthony Appiah's statement against the grandiose authority of Western theory: '. . . there is surely something appealing in the notion of African theories for African texts . . . contemporary theory has often sponsored techniques of literary interpretation that yield somewhat uniform results. Our modern theories are too powerful, prove too much.'[7] The tension between these points of view acts both as a corrective to a treatment of Black African literatures as mysterious *cultural* but not complex *literary* material, and as a warning against the subordination of the specific, challenging nature of African literatures to an arrogant levelling by culturally blind literary theories.

African literary criticism has founded itself on projects of decolonisation and nationalist independence movements. Conferences, journals and books about African literature and criticism increase from the years of African independence from European colonisation. The arguments within these texts reveal a tortured relationship between and resistance to cultural imperialism in such a way that claims of equality interchange with assertions of radical difference. Chinweizu, Jemie and Madubuike's thesis in *Toward the Decolonisation of African Literature* provides a self-conscious scrutiny of African identity through literary criticism in terms which both reject and mirror European critical standards. Ngugi's rejection of European languages in the name of African literary decolonisation becomes replaced here with a rejection not of the English language, nor of the values of English literary criticism *per se*, but of the hypocritical or ignorant *application* of these values to African literature. Thus, the sense of reversal or counter-attack is limited by and conducted within the institutional terms of English Literature.

In a characteristically direct passage, the *bolekaja* critics make an unflinching claim for the independence of African literature:

> But African literature *is* an autonomous entity separate and apart from all other literatures. It has its own traditions, models and norms . . . separate and radically different from that of the European . . . sometimes altogether antithetical . . . even for those portions of African literature which continue to be written in European languages.[8]

The autonomy and separateness of African literature is here celebrated within an implicit notion of organic unity. Any critical models would, from this passage, be assumed to arise from the internal coherence of the literature itself and its exclusive development. This radical developmental difference is partly explained by a description of its roots in African orature which, when recognised, must place the evaluation of African literatures outside the preoccupations of 'euromodernist criticism' and its 'mutilations' (Chinweizu, p. 2). 'Afrocentric' criticism, which the *bolekaja* critics insist should take the place of the egocentric European assessment of 'the proper, the beautiful, or the well done' (Chinweizu, p. 3), must be founded in a sensitive, well-informed interrogation of the *history* of African artistry:

> Furthermore, African orature is important to this enterprise of decolonizing African literature, for the important reason that it is the incontestable reservoir of the values, sensibilities, aesthetics, and achievements of traditional African thought and imagination outside our plastic arts. Thus, it must serve as the ultimate foundation, guidepost, and point of departure for a modern liberated African literature.
>
> (Chinweizu, p. 2)

The insistence on African orature as the 'historically indisputable core of the canon of African literature' (Chinweizu, p. 13) is made, not simply to distance it from the linear narrative of the English literary canon, from which African literature would merely constitute a deviant 'overseas department' (Chinweizu, p. 3), but also to assert rhetorically, a radically different *value system* and *temporality*. What is located in the Eurocentric criticism with which Chinweizu, Jemie and Madubuike take issue is the imposition of a literary time-scale where African novels are assessed according to the traditions of late nineteenth-century European realism,[9] and African poetry succeeds or fails against the standards of '20th century European modernism' (Chinweizu, p. 3).

In order to counteract and write against this Eurocentric attack on African aesthetic standards, the *bolekaja* critics fight the claim that African writers have *failed* European literary values and at the same moment substitute these norms and expectations with others that are *naturally in time with* African life: 'the vital nourishment of our African traditions and home soil . . . the vibrancy, gusto and absolute energy of our African oral poetry which is so firmly and deeply rooted in the African home soil' (Chinweizu, p. 3). This also, by an imperceptible or *natural* move, constitutes 'cultural values' and 'national ethos' (Chinweizu, p. 12). By insisting that African literature, as an observable and qualitative object, has its distinctive origins in oral traditions, the *bolekaja* critics are able to circumvent the contention that African literature springs directly from its European equivalents. Notions of an essential force, occurring naturally within and belonging to Africa, which informs the particularity of African literature, would seem to push the critics' argument into a cultural or even a (racial) biological determinism. What is also significant in Chinweizu's argument is the problem of *time difference* which, alongside an awareness of *distance* between (distinct) cultures, is a central tenet of anthropology. This anxiety and obsession with temporality as an assessment of African culture(s) and literature in the 'ethno-

losophical' texts *about* African literature as well as *in* African
erature itself, rises out of the history of anthropological writing about
other 'cultures' or 'races'. What is often intrinsic to theories of cultural
difference is a notion of mapping *discrete* human groups at particular
places on a path to modernity. Johannes Fabian's argument in *Time
and the Other*, which explores the creation of anthropology as a
discipline, a project and a profession, insists on a structural 'Politics
of Time'.[10] Any 'knowledge of the other', in Fabian's discussion, is
fundamentally informed by a politics of temporality which positions
the object of anthropological investigation in a relationship *outside*
the interlocutor's *present*, and dislocated from the possibility of
contemporal *dialogue*.

Anthropology's 'other' has often been constructed out of a
conception of 'cultures' as discrete entities, entirely separable from
each other in *space*, and 'racially' as well as geographically distinct.
The relationship between anthropology and imperialism, and its
concomitant relationship with theories of unequal races is well
documented. Talal Asad, for example, associates anthropology
directly with the 'unequal power encounter between the West and the
Third World . . . an encounter in which colonialism is merely one
historical moment'.[11] This 'encounter' has given rise to both a
'sustained physical proximity' (Asad, p. 17), and a structure of exploitation which ensured that observation, the taking of knowledge and
the writing of information, was always of, from, and about the *non-
European* Other. The concept of race which informs and lies behind
the concept of separate human cultures within the history of
anthropology is one which Fabian claims to rest on an idea of
'evolutionary time', where both *past* cultures and *distant* living
societies become 'irrevocably placed on a temporal slope, a stream of
Time – some upstream, others downstream' (Fabian, p. 17). In order
to view the contemporary human world, anthropological discourse
has often resorted to a form of 'typological time' (Fabian, p. 23), which
allows different societies to be classified in terms of a quality of *states*
rather than a measure of change or movement. In this way, the quality
of dynamic *development* is one which is differentially attributed to
particular societies. Thus, 'savage', 'tribal', and 'animist' cultures or
races can be identified by anthropologists as *fixed* in their difference,
outside or before history.

The relationship between ethnography about Africans and colonialism of Africa is evident in travelogues and novels, often written by

members of the British colonial service, and 'ethnophilosophy', which incorporates African literary criticism and presents itself as either resistance to, or resolution of the problems of colonialism. An example of the British 'colonial travelogue' is Frederick Migeod's *A View Of Sierra Leone*, published in 1926. Migeod is introduced as 'Colonial Civil Service, retired', and he presents in his preface an account both of the reasons for his study of the people of the (then) colony and protectorate and some of the methodological problems involved. He classifies his own position repeatedly as 'the Anthropologist', and makes continual allusions to 'official publications', 'anthropological information', and the possibility of 'a general reference book to the colony',[12] making clear that his work is to be placed within and in dialogue with a politically sanctioned store of colonial literature and 'knowledge'.

In order to verify his generalisations about 'the simple savage', Migeod can glibly include an anecdote about 'a political officer in a distant colony' to illustrate a feature of Sierra Leonean 'native' activity. Yet he insists on the significance of the *specific* landscape of a people in order to produce an accurate account of them: 'An anthropological student cannot draw just deductions unless he is perfectly acquainted with the environment of the tribe he is studying' (Migeod, p. ix). This generalising tendency to reduce the totality of empire to a type of savagery *already known*, and to simultaneously provide careful geographical detail concurs with Fabian's notion of how a particular (colonial) concept of time serves as an implicit method for 'studying' cultures dispersed in space. Lord Avebury's *On the Origin of Civilisation and Primitive Condition of Man*, which precedes Migeod's study by over twenty years and narrows the British empire into a sweeping 'study of savage life',[13] spells out more clearly the meaning of Migeod's 'savage': 'The study of the lower races of men, apart from the direct importance which it possesses in an empire like ours, is of great interest . . . the condition and habits of existing savages resemble in many ways . . . those of our own ancestors in a period now long gone by' (Avebury, p. 1). This evolutionary development of 'races' is not always an upwards movement, which illustrates how the civilising mission of colonialism gains part of its validity: 'It has been said by some writers that savages are merely the degenerate descendants of more civilised ancestors, and I am far from denying that there are cases of retrogression' (Avebury, p. 3). As with Migeod, dispersal in space is of less significance in terms of cultural or racial difference than the time schema of empire: 'different races in similar stages of development often present more features of resemblance to one another than the same race does to itself in different stages of history' (Avebury, p. 11).

If 'cultural difference' as a concept emerges from the 'culture gardens' in Fabian's discussion, or the higher and lower 'races' of anthropologists like Avebury, an approach to African literature which sees only otherness risks these totalising and essentialising strategies. Fabian's argument relies on a bid for 'Intersubjective Time' in anthropology, which refuses any absolute distinction between the temporalities of one culture and another, and relies instead on the dynamics of human interaction and communication (Fabian, p. 24). However, in his insistence on 'coevalness', on a recognition that all societies are 'of the same age' (Fabian, p. 159), Fabian cannot dismiss the reality of confrontation between 'cultures'. If coevalness rules out notions of divided evolutions, and disallows the identity of the present to be defined solely within the terms of Western modernity, it cannot rule out the violence of cultural domination and the negotiation of difference and resistance between and within human societies: 'What are opposed, in conflict, in fact, locked in antagonistic struggle, are not the same societies at different stages of development, but different societies facing each other at the same Time' (Fabian, p. 155). James Clifford's question, asking how and if we *can* represent (other) cultures, is forced to move away from a reliance on exclusive totalities decipherable from each other,[14] and to accept a more fluid but still active understanding of cultural identity as 'an ongoing process, politically contested and historically unfinished' (Clifford, p. 9).

In this light, cultural difference cannot be an outdated pre-occupation which needs to be pushed aside in favour of a more 'universal' or 'innocent' field of communication. Having been perceived and mapped by colonialist anthropologies, difference still operates in terms like 'modern' and 'traditional', which have become metaphors of contested space *within* and *between* societies, nations or 'cultures'. Although unequal power over resources of knowledge and dissemination of information has spawned documents like Migeod's 'view' of Sierra Leone, the struggle over representation emerges quite clearly within his text, where the generalised Mende, Temne or Limba 'native' informant constantly challenges the authority of Migeod's observations. For Migeod, the problem is partly the 'mercenary nature' of 'natives' who demand payment for giving information and, in this way, attempt to redress the balance of exploitation. In addition, the

control over knowledge is one which slips between the cer
colonial power to the extent that anthropological study i
reliant on and at the mercy of the native. The informant
engaged in a dialogue of cultural give and take, but is us
resource. Recognising that the 'inquirer' is 'assuredly regard\   as a
very big fool by the simple savage', Migeod never accepts the
possibility of a reciprocal conversation, or of the subversion behind
the activities of the 'naughty' informant. His attitude and desire is
succinctly revealed in a phrase which shows exasperation as well as a
clear wish for human African resources to remain under the
microscope: 'I have mentioned just a few incidentals connected with
collecting information as regards the human species. The botanist,
zoologist or geologist has an easy time in comparison. The objects of
his research, if not passive, at least cannot lie to him' (Migeod, p. x).

That accurate information often escapes the surveillance of Western
eyes through the wit and evasion of human subjects is now a recognised
fact of ethnographical study. However, resistance to the ambitious
gaze of Western colonial anthropology involves a close relationship
with its tenets, and has left African literary and cultural criticism in a
difficult net of choices. Is Africa essentially, or even significantly, Other
to the West, and how can African literature or its criticism negotiate
the struggle between 'modernity' and 'traditional' societies? If cultural
difference does, very clearly, operate in, for example, the nationalist
resistance of some African writing, or the racism of most Western
literature, then both African and Western literary criticism is forced
to contend with issues that the newly self-reflexive politics of
anthropology, as well as the difficulties of African independence, have
had to confront.

The cultural essentialism haunting the arguments of the *bolekaja*
critics, where Africa becomes a totalised vision of Otherness,
summarised in the phrase 'Africa is simply not the West' (Chinweizu,
p. 30), is born of the assumptions which structure the studies of
colonial anthropology. The critics work within the terms of the English
literary values with which they are confronted and this leads them to
claim the equal fulfilment of these values in African literatures while
demanding that they be assessed by wholly other traditions and
aesthetics. Their notion of 'culture' is implicitly a philosophy of racial
determinism, which allows their reading of African culture to include
the pan-African (or Black) world. In this way, African-ness over-
reaches itself to become an expression of *national* identity, *racial*

identity, political consciousness and heritage, achieving its only coherence in opposition to the (White) West. The book is dedicated to 'the black world', but in such a way that African-ness – 'one drop of black blood' – although essential for inclusion, is subordinated to matters of personal choice and cultural commitment.

The relationship of the beliefs of either Ngugi or the *bolekaja* critics to racial determinism is complicated. Both parties take race almost for granted in their discussions of African identity, nationalism, cultural consciousness and revolutionary thought, precisely because the 'decolonising' struggle to which the critics link the writing and criticism of African literatures has, particularly from colonial literatures and cultural anthropology, been constructed as a racial one. What are consistently conflated within these texts are 'culture' and 'race' which work together as essentialist terms while allowing a possible disconnection between culture/race and consciousness/decolonisation; or a lamented fissure between an 'African world' and an 'African world view'.

Following Fabian's arguments on ethnography, the struggle to read the difference of Africa has repeatedly been framed as a battle between the traditional and the modern world/artist/view. It is this opposition which explicitly informs the crisis of aesthetics and values confronting critics of African texts. Emmanuel Obiechina analyses the distinction between the 'traditional artist' and the 'modern artist' in terms of a duality *within* African society,[15] which has, I would argue, become the expression of a radical confrontation between ('the true') Africa and the (encroaching, eroding) West. The deep and justifiable anxiety which emerges out of a dislocation which is starker and more threatening in contemporary Africa than it is in Britain, has led to a radical difference of direction and context for African and European writing. The weight of a visibility and Otherness which has been conferred in terms of race and exoticism upon African peoples and cultures has resulted in a literature which – particularly through the medium of European languages – tends towards a self-conscious representation of African people to themselves. Appiah's summary of the split between traditional collaboration and modern individualism – which acts as a tension within African literatures and for African writing – is useful here. He describes it in terms of 'a profound difference between the projects of contemporary European and African writers: a difference I shall summarise for the sake of a slogan, as the difference between the search for the self and the search for a culture' (Appiah, p. 118). Appiah appraises the stance of the *bolekaja* critics in terms of 'cultural nationalism' (Appiah, p. 96), or 'nativist nostalgia' (Appiah, p. 95), which can never extricate itself from its presumed enemy. Chinweizu, Jemie and Madubuike's attack on Western modernity and its assumptions falls, according to Appiah, into the trap of nativist 'culture', where 'Africa' becomes a common denominator of a spiritual, traditional and philosophical consciousness, essentially separate from the time of the West.

It must be said that African, or 'Afrocentric' writers and critics have many sides to defend, due to the 'schizophrenic asymmetry' (Chinweizu, p. 149), of prejudiced European criticism. The alternative to a call for a specifically *African* literary criticism (with tension still around the term 'Africa'), has often been the call for *universal* literary values, where cultural blindness takes the place of and helps to neutralise cultural fear. Chinweizu's annoyance at calls for 'universal truths' which act merely as euphemisms for *European* truths is justified.[16] Rand Bishop's reading of the history of African criticism under the opening question: 'By what standards is African literature to be judged?'[17] quotes a string of European critics in the 1960s whose approach to African literature swung from a defensive call for the universality of literature and humanity, to a disappointed longing for Otherness and radical cultural and literary *difference*.[18] Robert P. Armstrong, in his paper for the African Studies Association in Chicago (1964), is quoted tautologically claiming that the African-ness of African literature is that it is African (Bishop, p. 1), and that this can be demonstrated, not through national languages, but through 'metaphor, symbol, situation . . . ' (Bishop, p. 1). In the Conference of African Literature and the University Curriculum at Fourah Bay College, Freetown, in 1963, the perennial question: 'What is African Literature?', was again debated with the accepted definition being voiced by the Canadian critic, T.R.M. Creighton, that 'African literature' is 'any work in which an African setting is authentically handled, or to which experiences which originate in Africa are integral' (Bishop, p. 21). Cyprian Ekwensi, a year later, claims that African literature is based on African character and psychology: 'This means that the main theme may be anthropological, traditional or modern, but the traits, temperaments and reactions of the characters will be peculiarly African due to influences of tribe, culture and history.'[19]

The arguments about language have ranged from Obiajunwa Wali's claim that language *defines* literature,[20] to Cheikh Hamidou Kane,

Ezekiel Mphahlele and Chinua Achebe's claim that 'African reality' is already 'African' in complex, hybrid ways where, in fact, writing and indigenous languages do not have an equivalent relationship.[21] Given this still complicated terrain around the questions of what constitutes African culture and its connection with literature, the *bolekaja* critics' summary that a 'judicious exercise of commonsense is what is partly called for' (Chinweizu, p. 15), in determining inclusion in 'the canon of African literature' (Chinweizu, p. 13), has a ring of irony about it.

African cultures and literatures cannot be pushed idealistically or superstitiously into a place of spiritual isolation beyond and outside Western infiltration for evident historical reasons. The arguments surrounding Africa's 'otherness' are already formed and caught in a syncretic and conflicting struggle with the West, and Africa's over-determination as well as its invisibility is part of that struggle. Gates's resolution of the issue in terms of *Black* texts is an acceptance of their 'double heritage',[22] weaving Black and European traditions together. What is significant about this 'resolution' is that it increases, not diminishes, the immense demands of Black texts. By pluralising sources and influences, while not reducing the effects to a polemic of sociological observation, Gates manages to slide the double corner of difference and equality. The relationship between African literatures and cultures is not a perfect mirroring. Reading literature demands a sensitivity to aesthetics and figuration *in addition to* representation. However, modes of signification and reading rely on traditions and values which are also cultural and often in contest.

Two texts which come out of the ethnophilosophical genre of writings about Africa are Jahnheinz Jahn's *Muntu* (1961), and W.E. Abraham's *The Mind of Africa* (1962). Both texts confront, in great detail, these issues of plurality within African literature(s) and culture(s). Jahn explores the clash between European influence and traditional Africa by accepting the link between 'modernization' and Europe, but not the conflation of a traditional and a 'real' Africa. For Jahn, contemporary African culture is reaching a crisis of survival whose resolution lies in the creation of 'neo-African culture', a blend of 'modern' Europe with 'traditional' Africa in order to produce 'a modern, viable *African* culture . . . out of the whole'.[23] Evading the fallacy that there ever was *one* traditional African culture, Jahn nevertheless discusses a spiritual or philosophical 'common denominator' of 'African-ness', which, through a process of *development into* history, moves from 'primitive' to 'modern' expression (*Muntu*, p. 17).

As Wole Soyinka, in *Myth, Literature and the African World*, attempts to express the African world view through Yoruba ritual archetypes and social ideologies,[24] Jahn discusses the neo-African culture through the 'common denominator' of Bantu philosophy. While disclaiming the idea that culture is *innate*, he discusses it as a *spiritual phenomenon* based on rational human understanding, and expressed in the world view of Bantu tradition, which is characteristic of *all* sub-Saharan Africa. In this way, African authors and artists hold the key to neo-African culture as a unified whole. Crucially for Jahn's argument, this view is based in a dialectical relationship with colonial ethnology, and its foundation *outside* the politics of independence is irrelevant: 'The Africa presented by the ethnologist is a legend in which we used to believe. African tradition as it appears in the light of neo-African culture may also be a legend – but it is the legend in which African intelligence believes' (*Muntu*, p. 17). Abraham attacks Jahn for this reliance on spiritual/political *belief* rather than *fact*, and moves the issue of authentic African literature into an engagement with 'traditional' Africa, which must be represented in African literatures in order to produce something different from and equal to English literature. For him, 'real' Africa, as a unified concept, is to be found in the rural peasantry, and its paradigm is the world view of the Akan in Ghana.[25]

It is vital to resist formulations of a holistic African world, culture, or world view which can be discovered, recovered or re-appropriated. Africa, with its plural cultures and influences, has no paradigm and cannot be reduced to a single political aspiration or spiritual unity. This does not mean that African literatures should be denied their specificity, their cultural differences, the complex textures of traditions, genres and influences. African literatures pose particular and significant challenges to literary criticisms which are not sensitive to this plurality of voices. It is a relatively simple matter to attack the theoretical inadequacies of arguments which insist on Africa's independence and (cultural) difference. It is a lot more difficult to incorporate, into reading practices, an awareness of the politics of resistance, the crises of representation and the layers of reference and signification which inform and form African texts. The most difficult point to accept, for Western literary criticism, might still be that Africa is not always thinking of, or speaking to the West, and that, at moments, it escapes.

Notes

1. Christopher Miller, 'Theories of Africans: The Question of Literary Anthropology', in Henry Louis Gates (ed.), *'Race', Writing, and Difference* (Chicago, 1986), pp. 281–300, 282. Further page references are cited in the text.
2. Ngugi wa Thiong'o, *Decolonising the Mind: The Politics of Language in African Literature* (London, 1986), p. 6. Further page references are cited in the text.
3. Ngugi wa Thiong'o, *Moving the Centre: The Struggle for Cultural Freedoms* (London, 1993), p. 27. Further page references are cited in the text.
4. Jean-Paul Sartre, Preface to Frantz Fanon's *The Wretched of the Earth* (1961; Harmondsworth, 1985), p. 15.
5. Henry Louis Gates, 'Criticism in the Jungle', in H.L. Gates (ed.), *Black Literature and Literary Theory* (London, 1984), p. 5.
6. H.L. Gates, writing of 'the multifarious demands of the texts of our tradition', asks, 'Who would seek to deny us our complexity? Who, indeed?': 'Criticism in the Jungle', p. 4. Further page references are cited in the text.
7. Kwame Anthony Appiah, *In My Father's House: Africa in the Philosophy of Culture* (London, 1992), p. 103. Further page references are cited in the text.
8. Chinweizu, Onwuchekwu Jemie and Ihechukwu Madubuike, *Toward the Decolonization of African Literature*, vol. 1: *African Fiction and Poetry and their Critics* (Washington DC, 1983), p. 4. The term 'bolekaja' is translated as 'Come down let's fight!'; a western Nigerian term, which the critics use to claim 'we are *bolekaja* critics, outraged touts for the passenger lorries of African literature' (p. xii).
9. 'Most of the genuinely technical charges would appear to attempt to impose canons of the 19th century European "well-made novel" upon the 20th century African novel, entirely disregarding both the tradition of African orature and the revolution in the techniques of the European novel initiated by Proust, Joyce and Kafka, and extended by Faulkner, Hemingway, Beckett and many others': Chinweizu et al., *Toward the Decolonization of African Literature*, vol. 1, p. 87.
10. Johannes Fabian, *Time and the Other: How Anthropology Makes its Object* (New York, 1983), p. x. Further page references are cited in the text.
11. Talal Asad, *Anthropology and the Colonial Encounter* (London, 1973), p. 16. Further page references are cited in the text.
12. Frederick William Hugh Migeod, *A View of Sierra Leone* (New York, 1926), p. xi. Further page references are cited in the text.

13. Right Hon. Lord Avebury, P.C., *On the Origin of Civilisation and Primitive Condition of Man: Mental and Social Condition of Savages* (sixth edn; London, 1902), p. 5. Further page references are cited in the text.

14. James Clifford, *The Predicament of Culture: Twentieth-Century Ethnography, Literature and Art* (Cambridge, MA, 1988), p. 274. Further page references are cited in the text.

15. Emmanuel Obiechina, *Culture, Tradition and Society in the West African Novel* (Cambridge, 1975), p. 73.

16. Appiah's observation on the work of the *bolekaja* critics is useful here: 'Indeed, it is characteristic of those who pose as anti-universalists to use the term "universalism" as if it meant "pseudo-universalism", and the fact is that their complaint is not with universalism at all. What they truly object to – and who would not? – is Eurocentric hegemony *posing* as universalism': K.A. Appiah, *In My Father's House*, p. 92. These debates about universal truths have a long history in criticism of African literatures. Rand Bishop quotes Dorothy Blair, a South African, speaking at the Conference of African Literature and the University Curriculum, at Dakar in 1963, where she claims that 'understanding of suffering is universal'. In this way, cultural and historical context are rendered unimportant. See R. Bishop, *African Literature, African Critics: The Forming of Critical Standards, 1947–1966* (New York, 1988), p. 3. Chinweizu *et al.*'s fury at this attitude emerges in such phrases as 'imperialist motherhens . . . They cluck: "Be Universal! Be Universal!" ': *Toward the Decolonization of African Literature*, vol. 1, p. 89.

17. R. Bishop, Preface to *African Literature, African Critics*, p. xi.

18. Bishop cites Blair, Stuart and Lilyan Lagneau-Kesteloot at the Berlin Conference of African Poets in 1964, who chided Africans for being too imitative of Europeans: R. Bishop, *African Literature, African Critics*, p. 2.

19. Cyprian Ekwensi, *Nigeria Magazine*, no. 83 (1964), pp. 294–9: quoted in R. Bishop, *African Literature, African Critics*, p. 22.

20. See O. Wali's 'The Dead End of African Literature?' *Transition*, no. 10 (1963). Ngugi quotes from the article what he perceives to be its most significant message, 'that the whole uncritical acceptance of English and French as the inevitable medium for educated African writing is misdirected, and has no chance of advancing African literature and culture': *Decolonising the Mind*, p. 24.

21. R. Bishop, *African Literature, African Critics*, p. 31.

22. H.L. Gates, 'Criticism in the Jungle', p. 4. See also K.A. Appiah's comment, 'But for us to forget Europe is to suppress the conflicts that have shaped our identities; and since it is too late for us to escape each other, we might instead seek to turn to our advantage the mutual

interdependencies history has thrust upon us: *In My Father's House*, p. 115.

23. Janheinz Jahn, *Muntu: An Outline of Neo-African Culture* (1958; London, 1961), p. 16. Further page references are cited in the text.

24. Wole Soyinka, *Myth, Literature and the African World* (1976; Cambridge, 1990).

25. 'I believe that there is a *type* of African culture, and that this type is essentialist in inspiration. The essentialist view of man underlying this type finds expression in the art, the ethics and morality, the literary and the religious traditions, and also the social traditions of the people': W.E. Abraham, *The Mind of Africa* (Chicago, 1962), p. 42.

5 Fiction as an historicising form in modern South Africa

Michael Green

'History is history and it should remain so.'
                    (Dr Hendrik Verwoerd, Durban, 26 August 1963)

'. . . history is impossible, meaningless, in the finite totality, and . . . in the positive and actual infinity . . . history keeps to the difference between totality and infinity.'
                    (Jacques Derrida, *Writing and Difference*, trans. Alan Bass (London, 1978, p. 123)

In her review of the first volume of the *Oxford History of South Africa* (1969), Shula Marks criticises this 'apogee of the liberal tradition of South African historiography'[1] for its failure to use the 'abundance of resources [available] to construct a picture alive with real people and events'.[2] She is speaking particularly of the section on the Eastern frontier, but the implication is for a broader application which can be traced to a general trend in the historiography of the 1970s. Marks's criticism aligns itself with what Raphael Samuel identifies as a new movement towards 'the recovery of subjective experience' in which the aim was 'to personalise the workings of large historical forces'.[3] Thus Marks writes of the '100 years of warfare on the Eastern frontier' as 'in many ways a dramatic story, punctuated by colourful episodes and personalities', and decries the omission of the 'eccentric individuals' with which the 'frontier . . . brimmed'. By way of example she lists van der Kemp, de Buys, Alberti, Ngqika, and Ndlambe, adding: 'one could extend the list indefinitely; their story, however, has still to he written'.[4]

Several of these figures *had* had their stories written at the time Marks was writing – albeit not in a form generally taken into account by historians. De Buys and van der Kemp had featured as protagonists in historical novels written by Sarah Gertrude Millin, *King of the Bastards* (1950) and *The Burning Man* (1952) respectively, and many of the others listed or implied by Marks were strongly featured in Millin's novels. The currency of these figures in their fictionalised form was no limited one either: '*King of the Bastards* was then one of the best-selling novels in the history of South Africa', Millin's biographer, Martin Ruhin, tells us.[5] While the appearance of this cast of characters in novels (and popular novels at that) has isolated the fact of their representation from professional historiographical concerns, it is worth re-examining the distinctions that preserve this isolation.

History and fiction

In most history writing, the general neglect or dismissal of historical fiction suggests a clear demarcation by historians between these two forms of discourse, but the line between them may be seen to be a shifting one.

> 'To make the past present, to bring the distant near.' It seems a modest enough task: it is what we have come to expect of any novelist with a pronounced sense of history: 'to invest', as Macaulay put it, 'with the reality of human flesh and blood beings whom we are too much inclined to consider as personified qualities in an allegory'. In defining the duties of the historical novelist which were once those of the historian, the English essayist uses a language which would surely find immediate emotional responses from those of our writers haunted by the African past and who are trying to develop strategies for 'bringing the distant near'.[6]

In this passage from 'History as the "Hero" of the African Novel', Nkosi indicates just how easily the 'duties' of the historian and the historical novelist may be shared or swapped according to context. Historical fiction makes different demands in relation to history writing in different contexts. What distinguishes the categories is institutionalised practice, not formal essences; which is not to say the distinction does not exist, only that it can at times be significantly reassessed. Such reassessment seems especially necessary in Southern Africa when much historical revisionism is practised outside academic institutions, often taking a 'literary' form.

Southern African writers, all-too-aware of the biased and frag-mented versions of their history[7] produced by institutionalised history writing and historiography, find that a central preoccupation in their work is, as Bessie Head puts it, 'a search as an African for a sense of historical community'.[8] They echo in every genre Matsemela Manaka's definition of the role of theatre, which, he says, 'should reconstruct a people's history and cultural values'.[9] A related impulse must surely be seen to inform all serious deployments of history in fiction. The underlying or overt thrust of such works is historical revisionism, even if the reasons for and methods of resorting to the strategies of fiction may vary widely.

Revisionist historiography in South Africa has shown itself to be increasingly aware of this point. The social history movement, of which Marks was to become a leading figure, has had particularly good reason to develop the connections between history writing and fiction. Both in content and form, as Marks's comments must suggest, the writing of social history comes close to modes that intersect with structures commonly associated with fiction – or, to be more precise, a certain mode of fiction: realism.

Social history and literary realism

Now the dominant approach in South African history writing, social history has renewed interest in narrative, biography ('life history'), and human experience. This is neatly summarised in another well-known social historian's professed aim of writing 'an analytically informed chronicle of the warm, vibrant and intensely human struggle of people'.[10] The implications of this statement by van Onselen underline the ways in which, in both content and form, social history shares literary realism's interests: its selection of subject matter privileges the average, the ordinary, the everyday – 'the history of the person in the street', as Belinda Bozzoli puts it,[11] or the much vaunted 'view from below'. Its mode of representation favours the creation of a sense of actual experience – the 'referential illusion' in which, as Roland Barthes has demonstrated, 'the historian tries to give the impression that the referent is speaking for itself' by 'absenting himself' from his writing and treating language as if it gives transparent access to the real.[12] It comes as no surprise, then, that sessions concerned with culture – in which the literary is often, not unproblematically, given a prominent status – have now become a standard feature of social history forums such as those of the History Workshop at the University of the Witwatersrand.

Nicholas Visser, a literary academic, was asked to give one of the Keynote Addresses at the 1990 History Workshop, at which for the 'first time . . . a full "cultural" component [was] deliberately and fully incorporated into the proceedings'. He expressed the hope that 'the various disciplines might be made mutually enriching',[13] but other academics were more cynical about the interaction between history and literature as they stand. David Attwell, in his account of this History Workshop, stated that literary or cultural scholars who work within the confines of social history 'are always going to play the role of handmaiden to the more powerful, more coherently marshalled, more politically cogent discourses of history'.[14] In this he follows J.M. Coetzee who, in a talk for the 1987 *Weekly Mail* Book Week, said of the 'novel and history in South Africa today', there is 'a tendency, a powerful tendency, perhaps even a dominant tendency, to subsume the novel under history'. 'Speaking as a novelist', Coetzee objected to 'the appropriating appetite of the discourse of history' and 'the colonisation of the novel by the discourse of history'.[15]

If, as we have seen, history for Nkosi was once the hero of a dominant genre within the African novel, then history – at least in certain important forms – would seem to have now become something of a villain for some writers and academics concerned with the South African novel. It is important to note, however, that what is at issue in Coetzee's view are the all-too-often unquestioned foundations of 'history' as conceived within the present dominant mode of Southern African historiography. More specifically, it is social history's claim to a privileged grasp of reality, reflected in the emphasis we have seen that it places on the mode of realistic representation, that is a problem for Coetzee. The nature of his objections in this regard are clear:

> I reiterate the elementary and rather obvious point I am making: that history is not reality; that history is a kind of discourse; that the novel is a kind of discourse, too, but a different kind of discourse; that inevitably, in our culture, history will, with varying degrees of force-fulness, try to claim primacy, claim to be a master-form of discourse, just as, inevitably, people like myself will defend themselves by saying that history is nothing but a certain kind of story that people agree to tell each other – that . . . the authority of history lies simply in the consensus it commands. . . . I see absolutely no reason why, even in the South Africa of the 1980s, we should agree to agree that things are otherwise.[16]

It is only an apparent irony that the point ultimately made here is that history and literature find an ever-deepening intimacy as the horizons of the questions set for them are pushed back. The reference to a particular historical situation in Coetzee's concluding sentence in the above, draws our attention to the historicity of history, to the fact that the concept of 'history' has a history, and that it operates in certain and often conflicting ways in specific places at specific times. Obviously, this has implications for the relationship between literature and history which, as has been pointed out, must be seen as historically variable too.

The willingness of social historians to grant literature an important place within their project has not remained necessarily and automatically the progressive gesture it has been assumed to be in the work of, say, Stephen Clingman, a literary scholar who has close ties with social history. In his essay on 'Literature and History in South Africa', he asks 'what is the legitimate use of fiction for historiographic purposes?', and his answer turns upon a hypothesis that fixes literature in a relationship with history that is highly contestable in Coetzee's terms. 'If literature is to have a real historical value,' Clingman writes, 'we must regard it in the inclusive sense, having to do with its larger significance in embodying the ways of life, patterns of experience, and the structures of thought and feeling of communities and classes at large.'[17] The problem here is not that literature is read back *into* history; it is that the initial hypothesis governs, limits even, the effectiveness of the ways in which this might be done. Clingman's next question illustrates the effect of the logic of granting the initial 'if' of his first question. He asks 'what kind of evidence?' literature offers the discipline of history, and answers that 'fiction writes out, within its hypothetical and potential frame, the normally hidden issues, complexities, and deeper perturbations of society'. Although he emphasises that 'fiction is *never* simply historical "illustration"',[18] this typically social historical view of fiction being, in the final analysis, 'evidence' for history is exactly what Coetzee wishes to resist.[19]

Coetzee rejects the type of novel which 'operates in terms of the procedures of history and eventuates in conclusions that are checkable by history (as a child's schoolwork is checked by a schoolmistress)'. The type of novel which interests Coetzee 'operates in terms of its own procedures and issues in its own conclusions', 'evolves its own paradigms and myths, in the process . . . perhaps going so far as to show up the mythic status of history – in other words, demythologising history'.[20] This is the programme that overtly informs Coetzee's first novel *Dusklands* (1974) and, on a different scale, his later work, *Foe* (1986). *Foe* differs from *Dusklands* in the far more overt intimacy it accords social and literary history, as they are fused in such a way as to render any separation impossible.

The 'historical novel' and continuous history

In the course of his argument in 'The Novel Today', Coetzee does away with a generic distinction once so crucial to the meeting of history and fiction within one form: 'we are not – I should make it clear – talking about what used to be called "the historical novel" ', which he defines as 'the novel that self-consciously and on the basis of explicitly historical research sets out to re-create on its own terms a given time in the past'.[21] While Coetzee would no doubt favour emphasis being placed on 'its own terms', I would like to concentrate on two phrases – both temporal – which are important in his brief setting-aside of 'the historical novel': 'used to be' and 'in the past'. These two references to *the past* are distinct but related. To begin with 'in the past': standard definitions of the historical novel give the historical aspect of their category an exclusively past tense. Ian Glenn, for example, says of Daphne Rooke: 'She is the most serious historical (as opposed to political) novelist of South Africa',[22] where 'historical' takes the weight of the past and 'political' the burden of the present. Jacques Berthoud makes the same point about Nadine Gordimer, defining her work as 'more political than historical'. 'If she is a historical writer, as she claims to be,' he continues, 'then the term requires qualification. If the past, as it is usually understood, enters into [her stories], it does so by virtue of the attention she gives to the present.'[23]

In their distinction between 'political' and 'historical', Glenn and Berthoud follow a particular sense of the word 'history', one which Raymond Williams calls the 'established general sense' which has 'lasted into contemporary English as the predominant meaning'; that is, history is 'an account of real *past* events' and 'the organised knowledge of the *past*'. Yet this generally acknowledged sense of 'history' co-exists somewhat uneasily with 'history' in another, more modern and controversial sense:

> It is necessary to distinguish an important sense of history which is more than, although it includes, organized knowledge of the past. . . . One

way of expressing this new sense is to say that past events are seen not as specific histories but as continuous and connected process. Various systematizations and interpretations of this continuous and connected process then become history in a new general and eventually abstract sense. Moreover . . . history in many of these uses loses its exclusive association with the past and becomes connected not only to the present but also to the future.[24]

This distinction has proved crucial to the invalidation of the historical novel as a discrete genre, and it lies behind the other reference to the past in Coetzee's comments upon the form: 'what *used to be* called "the historical novel" '. Here he is following a pervasive contemporary practice which, having severed 'history' from its exclusive association with *the past*, concludes that the novel form's general fidelity to the continuous process of history makes the isolation of those novels engaged with the past in a specific genre or sub-genre quite superfluous.

Such a manoeuvre regarding literary form depends upon a particular sense of 'history' , one we may trace back to Georg Lukács. He initiated the use of Hegelian Marxism in which history (rather than economics, the class struggle, the state or social relations) became the primary element in the methodology of Marxism, and it is this perspective which leads to his rejection of the validity of the genre:

> One could go through all the problems of content and form in the novel without lighting upon a single question of importance which applied to the historical novel alone. The classical historical novel arose out of the social novel and, having enriched and raised it to a higher level, passed back into it. The higher the level of both historical and social novel in the classical period, the less there are really decisive differences of style between them . . . the ultimate principles are in either case the same. And they flow from a similar aim: the portrayal of a total context of social life, be it present or past, in narrative form.[25]

The 'total context' referred to here includes, pre-eminently, as the connectedness of present and past suggests, a unified sense of 'history'. The very attribution of a specific genre to the 'historical novel', claims Lukács, rests on a failure to grasp this connectedness: 'the social reason for creating the historical novel a genre or sub-genre in its own right is . . . the separation of the present from the past, the abstract opposition of the one to the other'.[26]

A study of a Southern African novelist's use of history which depends upon just such a refusal to separate past and present is Stephen Clingman's *The Novels of Nadine Gordimer: History from the Inside*. This work is saturated with a Lukácsian historical perspective: 'Gordimer's novels prove what Lukács pointed out some time ago: that there is no separable "historical novel" as a genre. Gordimer' s novels, mostly written in the present, establish deep links with broader and more continuous processes because it is here that they find the meaning of the present.'[27] In doing without the generic category of the historical novel, Clingman develops, as the subtitle to his book makes plain, an even stronger sense in which Gordimer is an historical writer. He sees Gordimer's fiction as 'historical' precisely because in it 'history' is no longer tied exclusively to the past. The various ways in which Clingman defines Gordimer as a historical writer have, in fact, very little to do with the past. Gordimer's 'historical consciousness' lies in her 'close observation', and 'in this observation [her] eye is fixed resolutely on the present'. She is also an historical writer for Clingman because, for her, 'social and private life are seen as integrally related'. Here, history enters as externality, with no hint of association with the past: 'the exploration of history and character, of external and internal worlds, becomes entirely indivisible'.[28] Gordimer is historical for Clingman at another level, because 'her aim is to deliver the kind of fictional judgement whose vindication might be the verdict of history'. In order to achieve this, the future must be added to her historical perspective: each of Gordimer's novels 'ends with a vision, and it might properly be called an historical vision. It is a vision of the future, from the present.' In this, Clingman goes beyond Lukács's merging of past and present and identifies the future – which Lukács explicitly excluded from his historical concerns – as an important aspect in the 'totality' which embodies Gordimer's 'specific historical consciousness'.[29] Here we have, then, a full sense of history as a 'continuous and connected process'.

This is a strong case for maintaining the distinguishing category of the historical even in the absence of a specific association with the past. Crucially, however, it collapses the distinction we saw Glenn and Berthoud making between the 'historical' and the 'political', which turned upon maintaining the distinction between past and present. There is a danger, however, that in holding the historical *present* continually before us, we risk effacing the historical *past* almost entirely.

At the level of setting, this is the effect of Gordimer's view of history on her fiction; her fictional locations are determinedly present-tensed, as we have noted, even when they include the future. The past only appears in passing. Against this we may set the first five novels of Coetzee; their temporal settings almost militantly avoid the present, chiefly finding their fictional locations in the past and future. Such a strategy may be seen as arising from a desire to approach the present from a point of difference, cutting it lose from a connected temporal process within which it is guaranteed a position of dominance. We recognise here an engagement with postmodern assaults upon 'continuous history', especially as far as the status of the historian is concerned.

History and difference

Continuous history is, as Mark Poster puts it in *Foucault, Marxism and History*, 'a means of controlling and domesticating the past in the form of knowing it', and the problem with this is that the historian (and, we may add, the historical novelist) achieves control over the past 'without placing himself or herself in question'.[30] The chief advantage of Foucault's method of stressing *discontinuity* in the historical process is the challenge it presents to the position of the historian. For Poster, Foucault 'attempts to show how the past was different, strange, threatening. He labors to distance the past from the present, to disrupt the easy, cozy intimacy that historians have traditionally enjoyed in the relationship of the past to the present.'[31] I do not mean to pin Gordimer or Coetzee to one side or the other of this debate. Gordimer, it seems to me, escapes the damaging effects of continuous history to the degree that she treats the present *as history* – that is, as I will argue, as a point of resistance to her own position within that present. Coetzee, on the other hand, perhaps allows more than he intends of a continuous history to enter his polemical position when he lets go of the 'historical novel' a little too easily. If the 'historical' as a generic category is abandoned on the grounds that the past as a point of reference is simply subsumed by a narrative constructed in the present, how then can the past serve as a point of difference from which to challenge the present?

To link the present and past within the discipline of history at all is illegitimate from a materialist perspective, Paul Hirst claims, because it depends upon a 'philosophy of history', which is an idealist category:

'If philosophical . . . grounds . . . are rejected then historical investigations need to base their pertinence on some other claim, for example, current political or ideological relevance . . . whether historical investigations are pertinent or not becomes a matter of politics.'[32]

The past, then, becomes essentially an issue in the politics of the present. Stressing the historicity of the present moves quickly into the politics of reconstructing the past. Making this move too quickly, however, risks effacing the historical almost entirely. It seems to me strategically – politically – necessary that we reclaim the historical in the face of such a foregrounding of the present, and the way in which this is best done is by reminding ourselves that, while we may acknowledge that the categories of the historical and the political are radically implicated, the acts of *politicisation* and *historicisation* are not identical. Again, this can be demonstrated by returning to the question of the contemporary status of the 'historical novel'. The legacy of the now apparently defunct issue of the nature and status of this genre leads us to is this central question: How can a work of fiction make of history something both resistant to being appropriated by the present and yet relevant enough to relate meaningfully to the present?

From historical novel to historicising form

Fredric Jameson goes along with Lukács in allowing that 'in our own time it is generally agreed that all novels are historical, in that in keeping faith with the present their object is just as profoundly historical as any moment from the distant past'.[33] While he is prepared to let go of '*history*' as a passive generic or disciplinary distinction, he preserves in his cultural enquiry the vital activity of *historicisation*. He shifts, then, from distinguishing between past and present as a basis for idealist distinctions of genre or discipline, to connecting past and present (and future, it is worth adding) as the basis for the radical activity of historicisation. In this shift lies a way for rethinking the place of the historical within fiction.

The entire structure of Jameson's *The Political Unconscious* finds its origin in tackling what he calls 'the old dilemmas of historicism'. Chief among these is the 'unacceptable option, or ideological double bind, between antiquarianism' and 'modernizing "relevance" or projection'.[34] How can we methodologically accommodate within one practice a reading which aims at, as Catherine Belsey puts it, 'a knowledge of history, albeit the unconscious of history', and a reading which is 'of the present and for the present'?[35] Jameson's answer is, as is well known, that these different emphases must be linked within a single historical narrative, and the narrative he puts forward as the most fundamental is that of 'the Marxian notion of the mode of production'.[36] So grand a narrative is positively scandalous in an age characterised by, as Lyotard would have it, an 'incredulity towards metanarratives',[37] but the historicist approach which Jameson's deployment of narrative allows, is not meant, finally, to appropriate and contain all that is potentially *other* to it; its real thrust is to cross distance without flattening difference. In historical terms, what Jameson is looking for is a way in which the past may be read *from* the present without appropriating it *for* the present: only a genuine philosophy of history is capable of respecting the specificity and radical difference of the social and cultural past while disclosing the solidarity of its polemics and passions, its forms, structures, experiences, and struggles, with those of the present day.[38] In its own way, this has been the aim of what Stephen Greenblatt calls the 'textual practice' (as opposed to theory or doctrine) of New Historicism, but I would claim that it is an identifiable *literary* practice as much as it is a *critical/ historical* one. A work of fiction may be considered as effectively engaging with history if it calls up the past as a point of *resistance* to the present, if the past is allowed to exist in the work in all its *difference* from the present, if the very act of creating the past in the work is powerful enough to hold at bay the appropriation of that past by the present moment of creation. Jerome McGann's description of an historical method of criticism may be read, then, as a model for a particular form of fictional activity.[39]

As a description of a valid historical method, McGann's approach is acutely relevant to contemporary South Africa. His insistence on the way in which the position of the critic – and the point of this chapter is to extend this to the historian and writer of fiction – must be open to the interrogation of his or her subject is an attitude that is important to encourage in people wishing to know a divided community. The resulting sense of a community created out of difference may also be read directly into current attempts to transform the signifier 'South Africa' from a term of deeply contested geographical significance to a national one that is able to encompass fractures of region, ethnicity, gender, and class. History is constantly and urgently mobilised by the different factions created in such a project, and if it is not to be merely subsumed into the prevailing and all too often bloody and vicious present-mindedness, we must find terms upon which it can challenge the present and force the different positions within the present to examine the specificities of their positionality. To do this, history must be accorded a force of its own and treated as valid in itself, as it were, and not simply something entirely open to the manipulation of the present.

This is the essence of historicising form, and I would wish to preserve it as a model for a particular and vital fictional activity. This activity has been developed out of debates regarding critical approach, but my aim has been to identify the ways in which fiction itself may be seen to carry out this function. This does not mean we have neglected the matter of critical approach: a corollary of identifying fiction which operates as an historicising form is that we can approach uses of history in fiction without making the fictional simply evidence for the historical, or the historical merely something subsumed in the fictional. This is because the 'historical novel' as a category defined by its subject matter (the past) gives way in this account to the process carried out by fiction as an historicising form. Furthermore, fiction becomes an historicising form when it so operates upon its material – no longer bound to a particular temporal location, but open to the past, present, and future – as to turn it into history; that is, to make of its historical material a moment of resistance that leads to an intervention within its own moment of production or consumption. In this way, the history a work depicts is no mere reflex of that work's own history, but acts upon its construction within that history in the very act of its construction.

Millin, Rooke, and historicising form

I began by citing Millin's historical novels as examples of historical material that has been overlooked because it is in fictional form. I must end by observing that Millin's careful attention to historical detail – she carried out extensive research for the writing of *King of the Bastards* and *The Burning Man*, both in archives and interviews – does not make either of these 'historical novels' historicising in form. Millin's novels are ostensibly historical in that they are investigations into the origins of racial segregation in South Africa. What they do, in fact, is run together current capitalist racial attitudes with attitudes to race prevalent in the colonial period, and make a case for a monolithic racism informing all South African history. Millin reads apartheid attitudes into the Eastern Cape frontier world of de Buys and van der Kemp, then, with the most surprisingly convincing sleight-of-hand (if the standard myths of South African history are anything to go by), finds in the Eastern Cape frontier of that period an historical justification for apartheid attitudes. Race – and racism – are transhistorical for Millin, and so they can have no history; any attempt to explain them historically must remain, at best, tautological.

Martin Legassick uses exactly the same 'evidence' – de Buys's miscegenation – in support of his thesis that contemporary South African racism *cannot* be directly attributed to early frontier attitudes.[40] The historical material he marshals in support of his case is, not surprisingly, more impressive in terms of accuracy and range than Millin's – although it is, for the most, quite impressionistically presented. This, however, is not what is at stake. If our choice between the positions of the novelist, Millin, and the historian, Legassick, must be made purely in terms of the significance of their explanatory narratives, we must either stand by some sort of moral or political essentialism as a basis for our choice – thus transcending history – or fall back into some sort of relativism which would allow us to explain Millin's and Legassick's uses of history as relevant to their own contexts, and our decision as relevant to ours. This would be an acknowledgement of history that parodoxically refuses to acknowledge the significance of the historical material appropriated by Millin and Legassick and, through them, by us. In all the options of this account, novelist, historian, and critic fail to make their case on *historical* terms.

Many writers – novelists, historians, and even critics – *do* present history in such a way as to challenge their own account of it, and the uses to which their audiences may put it. An example of a South African novelist who, in her use of historicising form, gives the history she works with a real force in the present is Daphne Rooke. Her work is not well known, and I would claim that this is to a significant degree because she worked seriously within the romance mode at a time in which the reception, if not always the production, of South African fiction tended to privilege realist modes. Yet, it is Rooke's use of romance to evoke a disturbing and challenging sense of historical difference in her novels that makes her work extremely important as far as the uses of history in Southern African fiction are concerned.

To illustrate with reference to one of her novels: *Wizards' Country* (1957) was meant to be the first in a trilogy concerned with the clash between traditional, settler, and imperial forces in Natal around the time of the Anglo-Zulu War. Rooke's very success in presenting the past in *Wizards' Country* was ultimately personally disenabling, but for telling reasons; in an interview she said: 'I didn't do the other two because I felt you had to twist your view point, your mind to take the Zulu point on it . . . you eventually come to look at the same thing from such a different angle that it becomes much too difficult.'[41]

What Rooke achieved before giving in to the difficulty of her task is illuminating in terms of the theme of this chapter. The effect of reading *Wizards' Country* is that of entering a radically different realm, yet one entirely convincing in terms of its own informing logic. Its formal perspective – and here I would include idiom, internalisation, and action – is challenging in the difficulty it presented to the moment of its production, and remains so today.

Written as the full force of grand apartheid was getting underway, the exploration of historical difference on ethno-national terms ran dangerously close to providing the kind of cultural support for state policies which Millin's work did. In resisting this, *Wizards' Country* did not sit easily with oppositional efforts that attempted to override the significance of ethnicity. (In this lies its potential current relevance in a climate of resurgent ethnic and regional tension.) The novel's strength lies in preserving the value of historical difference in the face of the appropriation of that difference into structures which exploited it. Imperial forces, as Marks and Atmore remind us, did not so much destroy as take over the centralised powers of the Zulu state, and the extraction of rent from the peasantry depended on maintaining rather than restructuring their productive relations.[42] Out of such determined attempts to maintain historical continuity in order to manipulate it, grew the model for the apartheid state; what needed to be defended was the radical difference of traditional social relations, in order for them to serve at an indigenous challenge to the way in which modern South Africa was being constructed. Rooke's novel, in its presentation of such difference, stands as a statement to the validity of historicisation as a form of resistance to the present's domination of the past.

Notes

1. Shula Marks and Anthony Atmore (eds), *Economy and Society in Pre-Industrial South Africa* (London, 1980), p. 1.

2. Shula Marks, 'African and Afrikaner History', *Journal of African History,* vol. XI, no. 3 (1970), p. 447.
3. Raphael Samuel, 'Editorial Prefaces' in *People's History and Socialist Theory* (London, 1981), pp. xvii–xviii.
4. S. Marks, 'African and Afrikaner History', p. 447.
5. M. Rubin, *Sarah Gertrude Millin: A South African Life* (Johannesburg, 1977), p. 228.
6. L. Nkosi, *Tasks and Masks: Themes and Styles of African Literature* (London, 1981), p. 30.
7. See E. Dean, P. Hartman and M. Katzan (eds), *History in Black and White: An Analysis of South African School History Textbooks* (Paris, 1983), and Marianne Cornevin, *Apartheid: Power and Historical Falsification* (Paris, 1980).
8. B. Head, 'The Search for Historical Continuity and Roots', in M.J. Daymond, J.U. Jacobs and M. Lenta (eds), *Momentum: On Recent South African Writing* (Pietermaritzburg, 1984), p. 278.
9. 'Matsix' (pseud.), 'The Babalaz People', *Staffrider*, vol. 4, no. 3, p. 33. In further support of this point, see Mothobi Mutloatse, *Reconstruction: 90 Years Of Black Historical Literature* (Johannesburg, 1981).
10. Charles van Onselen, *Studies in the Social and Economic History of the Witwatersrand, 1886–1914: New Babylon* (London, 1982), p. xvi.
11. B. Bozzoli, *Class, Community and Conflict: South African Perspectives* (Johannesburg, 1987), p. xiv.
12. Roland Barthes, 'Historical Discourse', in Michael Lane (ed.), *Structuralism: A Reader* (London, 1970), p. 149.
13. N. Visser, 'Towards a Political Culture', *Pretexts*, vol. 2, no. 1 (1990), pp. 69, 77.
14. D. Attwell, 'Political Supervision: The Case of the 1990 Wits History Workshop', *Pretexts*, vol. 2, no. 1 (1990), p. 84.
15. J.M. Coetzee, 'The Novel Today', *Upstream*, vol. 6, no. 1 (1988), p. 2.
16. Ibid., p. 4.
17. S. Clingman, quoted in Belinda Bozzoli and Peter Delius (eds), *Radical History Review: History from South Africa*, vols 46/47 (1990), p. 147.
18. Ibid., p. 149.
19. J.M. Coetzee, 'The Novel Today', p. 3.
20. Ibid., p. 3.
21. Ibid., p. 2.
22. I. Glenn, 'Introduction', *Mittee* (Diep River, 1987), p. 2.
23. J. Berthoud, 'Writing Under Apartheid', *Current Writing*, vol. 1, no. 1 (1989), pp. 82–3.
24. Raymond Williams, *Keywords: A Vocabulary of Culture and Society* (1976; London, 1983), p. 146.

25. Georg Lukács, *The Historical Novel* (1937; Harmondsworth, 1981), p. 290.
26. Ibid., p. 289.
27. S. Clingman, *The Novels of Nadine Gordimer: History from the Inside* (London, 1986), p. 224.
28. Ibid., pp. 8–9.
29. Ibid., p. 13.
30. M. Poster, *Foucault, Marxism and History: Mode of Production Versus Mode of Information* (Cambridge, 1984), p. 75.
31. Ibid., p. 74.
32. P.Q. Hirst, 'The Necessity of Theory', in *Marxism and Historical Writing* (London, 1985), p. 89.
33. Fredric Jameson, *Marxism and Form: Twentieth-Century Dialectical Theories of Literature* (Princeton, NJ, 1971), p. 350.
34. Fredric Jameson, *The Political Unconscious: Narrative as a Socially Symbolic Act* (London, 1981), pp. 17, 18.
35. Catherine Belsey, *Critical Practice* (London, 1980), p. 140.
36. Fredric Jameson, 'Marxism and Historicism', in *The Ideologies of Theory: Essays 1971–1986*, vol. 2: *The Syntax of History* (London, 1988), p. 172.
37. Jean François Lyotard, *The Postmodern Condition: A Report on Knowledge*, trans. by Geoff Bennington and Brian Masumi (1979; Minneapolis, 1984), p. xxiv.
38. F. Jameson, *The Political Unconscious*, p. 18.
39. Jerome McGann, 'The Text, the Poem, and the Problem of Historical Method', in J. McGann (ed.), *The Beauty of Inflections: Literary Investigations in Historical Method & Theory* (Oxford, 1985), p. 132.
40. M. Legassick, 'The Frontier Tradition in South African Historiography', in S. Marks and A. Atmore (eds), *Economy and Society in Pre-Industrial South Africa*, pp. 44–79; see especially pp. 65–7.
41. I am much in debt to Ian Glenn for allowing me free access to this important and unpublished interview, conducted at Daphne Rooke's previous residence in Australia, in 1989.
42. See S. Marks and A. Atmore's Introduction to *Economy and Society in Pre-Industrial South Africa*, p. 19.

6 Empires of the imagination: Rider Haggard, popular fiction and Africa

Terence Rodgers

> *How thinkest thou that I rule this people?*
> *I have but a regiment of guards to do my bidding, therefore it is*
> *not by force . . .*
> *My empire is of the imagination.*
>
> (H. Rider Haggard, *She*, 1887)

Rider Haggard's empire

In the Victorian literature of empire, Africa loomed large as a subject for political, geographical and scientific debate and for moral and religious controversy. However, it was also an object of intense cultural curiosity and fantasy for the expanding literate and reading public. Among the many writers who became identified with Africa, both as a territory within the imperial gaze and as an imaginative literary subject, Henry Rider Haggard stands out as one of the pivotal and most influential figures of his age.[1] Long either ignored or dismissed by modern critics as merely a late-Victorian storyteller who specialised in rumbustious tales of adventure, with Africa as a convenient and exotic backdrop, Haggard's literary and cultural significance is now undergoing a process of substantial reassessment. One of the general reasons for this rethinking is the burgeoning interest in the relationship between imperialism and culture, which has become a rich and diverse field of academic debate and publication.[2] But another and more specific reason is the gathering appreciation, particularly among literary historians, that Haggard's extensive writings on Africa, and in particular his core fiction of the 1880s, not only reflected Victorian attitudes towards the 'dark continent' in an age of imperial expansion and colonialism, but served to direct and define these attitudes through the construction of an imagined Africa.[3]

Haggard's narrative and textual Africa, both Saharan and sub-Saharan in focus, fitted comfortably into a more extensive Victorian dream of empire and possessed both fictive and cultural power. On one level, it undoubtedly helped to condition Britain's own developing imperial identity and the colonial discourses with which it was associated. But at another level and no less importantly, his writings helped to produce durable models of African identity and Otherness which were compatible with current ideas about geography, race and human evolution, and to project them into the deeper reaches of educated and common understanding. In this sense, Haggard's African terrain, his specifically African 'empire of the imagination', may be seen not just as complementary to, but as an integral component of the cultural apparatus of British imperialism and its mechanisms of propaganda, subordination and control at the *fin-de-siècle* and for some time beyond. Indeed, as Wendy Katz has underlined recently in her outstanding critical study of the writer, Rider Haggard's fiction, 'only superficially innocuous, contributed generously to the process of shaping of the imperial mentality' and 'towards fostering [the] limited moral consciousness', which characterised the British colonial system in its heyday.[4]

As a distinguished member of a large group of writers who dominated the market for popular fiction in Britain during the period *c.*1880–1920, Haggard was not, of course, alone in subscribing to this imperial project and in exerting some influence. Alongside Haggard, such contemporaries as John Buchan, Flora Annie Steel and Rudyard Kipling, to name but three, self-consciously constructed a fictional world of empire which served to entertain and 'inform' the reading public, but also to legitimise British colonial expansion and control in Africa, Asia and elsewhere.[5] Complementing this, the widely disseminated works of explorers such as H.M. Stanley and Mary Kingsley, together with those of academics and Darwinistic social theorists like Benjamin Kidd, were read as providing an empirical and 'scientific' basis to the imaginary imperial landscapes which dominated such a large segment of late Victorian popular fiction.[6] However, what marked out Haggard's contribution as a whole from the canon of Victorian narratives about empire and Africa was its volume, its distinctive form, and the diversity and power of its images. The purpose of this chapter is to examine some of the general features of this contribution to writing on Africa and to provide some pointers for further reading and debate. In the process, it will also attempt to explain Haggard's central and enduring importance by indicating how, through his discourses, black Africa was positioned and imbued with multiple meanings for the imperial elites, the domestic masses, and for colonial consumption.

Romancing Africa

To some extent, Haggard's impact on the literary scene, both during his lifetime and after, was the product of sheer hard work and industry. Haggard wrote quickly and often. During the course of his career he produced nearly sixty major works of fiction and many short stories, together with ten works of non-fiction, which included an auto-biography (published after his death in 1925) and numerous articles and pamphlets.[7] This tremendous output reflected Haggard's fertile mind and the span of his public activities and private interests. The former ranged from colonial service under the Lieutenant Governor of Natal (1875–79) to work on various Royal Commissions (1905–14) on imperial and socio-economic issues. His private interests were equally broad. These included agricultural improvement, Egyptology and Orientalism, occultism and the social work of the Salvation Army. Between the pursuit of these activities and interests, which have been well documented by his biographers, Haggard managed a substantial country estate in Norfolk, stood for Parliament as a Conservative candidate and traversed the British empire. In short, Haggard was no ordinary late-Victorian man of literature and *belles lettres,* comfort-ably ensconced in the salons of the imperial metropolis. On the contrary, in the context of the Victorian literary intelligentsia, Haggard has to be seen both as an exception and as exceptional.

Haggard produced his first novel in 1884 when he was twenty-eight, but within the space of two hectic years he had written the important works of fiction that were to make his career and reputation: *King Solomon's Mines* (1885), *She: A History of Adventure* (January 1887) and *Allan Quatermain* (July 1887). The critical and public reception of these books catapulted Haggard from obscurity to literary stardom, with considerable financial rewards for the young writer.[8] But they also made him a subject of controversy. Among many of his contemporaries, he was seen as a literary upstart and sensationalist whose sole purpose was to exploit a public appetite for violence and sex. Following the publication of *Allan Quatermain* for example, one magazine accused Haggard of championing the 'culture of the horrible' and violating public decency. In the same year, other reviewers accused him of sponsoring 'the literature of gross excitements and vulgar display' and of pandering to working class 'craving[s] for coarse and violent intoxicants'.[9] Haggard denied these accusations vehemently but, as even his admirers admitted, they carried a grain of truth. For all his considerable imaginative talents, he was neither a controlled nor particularly subtle stylist and his narratives could be repetitive, self-indulgent and, in places, crude. Partly for these reasons, despite his celebrity Haggard always remained on the fringes of the English literary establishment.

In 1912 Haggard was knighted; however, this was more in recognition of his political and official activities rather than any renewed literary achievement. In fact, after 1887, Haggard was treading water as a writer. No less than fifty-six other novels followed, many of them popular with the critics and public alike, including *The People of the Mist* (1894), *Benita: An African Romance* (1906), *The Ghost Kings* (1908), *The Yellow God: An Idol of Africa* (1909), and *The Holy Flower* (1915), together with a number of pioneering but now hardly discussed stories which were directly centred on black African native life and culture, notably *Nada The Lily* (1892) and the Zulu trilogy, *Marie* (1911), *Child of Storm* (1913) and *Finished* (1917).[10] But Haggard was never to regain fully the powers of originality and the public acclaim which were his in the 1880s. By the First World War his reputation, together with the sales of his books, were in decline and, by the time of his death, Haggard had come to be seen as one of the relics of the Victorian age, entitled to respect perhaps, but hardly worthy of modern critical attention.

As is well known, much of Haggard's life, as well as his fiction, was bound up with Africa, particularly Egypt and the central and southern regions. Haggard first went to the continent as a young imperial adventurer in 1875, and thereafter it was to exercise a special fascination over him and to provide a rich subject for literary exploitation. His three most famous novels were promoted by his publishers and received by his reading public as weird and astounding tales of adventure. However, they also constituted a loose imperial trilogy which transparently contained an allegorical sequence of a confident and expansionist Britain encountering, exploring and overcoming black Africa. The nature of this engagement, as depicted by Haggard, was multifaceted. First, it was physical: force and violence featured heavily in the stories. The meeting was also presented as psychological and cultural: the scheme of Western knowledge and Christian values were pitted against a mystical and superstitious African Other. Haggard's Anglo-African encounters were also emotional: attraction and sympathy for Africa and Africans were depicted alongside repulsion and fear. Finally, the encounters were sexual, with human attraction and the desire for physical possession being expressed with an explicitness which was unusual for the literature of the time.

Haggard's fictional encounters with Africa and the powerful motifs which were generated in the texts took place, of course, alongside the real thing; that is, the European encroachment into Africa during the nineteenth century, culminating in the so-called 'scramble for Africa' in the 1880s and 1890s and the British entanglement in Southern Africa. The timing of his personal literary encounter with Africa and appropriation of it as a subject therefore cannot be reckoned as mere chance. For, although Haggard's imperial trilogy clearly drew on his own experiences and reflected the nature of his African preoccupations, it was also clearly designed to promote and exploit a deep and growing public interest in the continent. Not surprisingly perhaps, largely on the basis of his writings and travels, Haggard also acquired a reputation as an African expert and, in particular, as an authority on black African tribal life and culture.[11] Even though Haggard assumed this mantle, he clearly had no great ambition to compete with the great empirical Africanists of the day. Rather, along with others, like his mentor Andrew Lang and rival Robert Louis Stevenson, he saw himself first and foremost as an exponent of a reconstructed genre of masculine romance which he was forthright in championing as superior to the literary realism and naturalism which was then in vogue.[12]

At the height of his fame in the 1880s, Haggard was publicly acclaimed as 'King Romance' by a friendly critic.[13] The title bestowed was both welcomed and appropriate as throughout his career he carefully segregated his literary output into two categories: 'Novels' and 'Romances'. The former, of which on his own estimate he wrote twelve, were usually conventional stories of 'society' set in rural England and concerned with love and marriage, personal fortune and misfortune, with topical angles such as political corruption, divorce and social reform. However, Haggardian romance as exemplified in his African imperial trilogy of the 1880s, had a different focus, agenda and significance. The literary theorist Northrop Frye defined romance as 'the literature of wish-fulfilment', and argued that it represents an intrusion of the 'it might have been' into the 'it was'. While the real world keeps these two, like dreaming and waking, in continual opposition, the popular appeal of romance, he suggests, rests in its ability to dissemble the boundaries between the actual and the potential.[14] Romance, in other words, allows for the construction of alternative visions of reality. This description of the genre, at least in part, fits much of Haggard's narrative practice. Here, and at its most commonsense level, romance takes the form of an adventure story where the attraction for the reader lies in an abundance of action in an unknown environment which contrasts sharply with the ordinariness and familiarity of the domestic scene. In this limited sense, it has been suggested, Haggardian romance can be read as a journey and escape from the banalities of late-Victorian domesticity into fantasy land- scapes at the frontiers of empire.[15]

Yet, Haggard's fiction was more than simply a supplement to a well-established canon of escapist literature. When he began to reinvent himself as a romance writer in the mid-1880s he was also helping to reshape and diversify the genre in two related ways: first, in his 'orientalist romances' which, beginning with *Cleopatra* (1889) and *The World's Desire* (1890) were concerned with ancient Egypt and the Middle East and the rise and fall of their great peoples;[16] and secondly and more importantly for this discussion, through his 'colonial romances' which centred on black Africa. In *King Solomon's Mines* and many of his colonial romances down to 1914, this proved to be a literature wherein the discourse of adventure was blended with recognisable gothic elements; a literature of obscure maps and parchments, new continents, lost empires and eldorados, suspense and terror and, finally, strange and wonderful happenings in which science and technology, on the one hand, and the occult and the supernatural on the other, featured prominently and were given the same status.[17] It was, in short, a richly laden narrative which elevated modern imperialism to the level of mythology, but which at the same time also provided a referenced and decodable allegory of imperial conquest, control and challenge which had an obvious relevance to contemporary events in central and southern Africa.

The structure of Haggard's imperial allegories about Africa altered very little over the expanding corpus of work that he classified as romance. The essential element usually consisted of a quest motif, a formal dramatic device which enabled a layered narrative of meaning to unfold through the encounter with the unknown and successive revelations of the incredible. Around this device, which he introduced for the first time and with great effect in *King Solomon's Mines*, and repeated immediately in the next instalments of his trilogy, Haggard was able to identify, discuss and reflect upon a range of issues that were crucial to Victorian imperialism and, specifically, to the imperial engagement with Africa. These included the idea of Africa as the 'dark continent' or (in Haggard's imagery, predating Conrad) 'the heart of the darkness',[18] the dichotomy between 'civilisation' and 'savagery', the meaning of progress, the defining characteristics of 'Englishness', the primacy of race and class, and notions of sexuality, particularly female sexuality. In this sense, and like most romance novels, in Haggard's fiction characterisation was less important than narrative and dialogue. Nevertheless, he did create some memorable characters, most notably his male imperial hero, Allan Quatermain, who appears in eighteen of Haggard's stories, and his female African anti-hero, Ayesha, who featured in four novels. Quatermain, like Conrad's equally phlegmatic Marlow, functioned as the narrator and reflective voice, 'thinking my thoughts and looking at life through my eyes', and was instrumental in defining the complex relationship between the 'imaginary' and the 'real' in Haggard's imperial landscapes.[19] Thus, beneath the paradigm of imperial heroism, Quatermain's deep role was as a vital mediator between the reader and the narrative, and text and context.

Mapping Africa

Two of the most distinctive and recurring motifs in Haggard's colonial romances are the 'mapping' and cataloguing of the African continent. In this regard, *King Solomon's Mines* is the pivotal text. Here, three intrepid Englishmen, Allan Quatermain, Sir Henry Curtis and Captain John Good, set off on a journey to central Africa in search of a hidden kingdom ('Kukuanaland') and its great diamond treasures, armed with an ancient map which has come into their possession through mysterious circumstances. The device of the map, which was reproduced in the text as an artifact, immediately helped to create an illusion of geography, territory and place for the reader. Put another way, it asserted a geographical authenticity in the context of a fiction.

...agem of authentication was strengthened by markers which
...e subject. In Haggard's colonial romances as a whole, many
...ich claimed the existence of imaginary tribal kingdoms and
...les, there are references to the white colonisation of Southern and
Central Africa, contemporary colonial administrators, to the history
of black tribal empires, such as the Zulus, Mashona and Matabele and
to known academic works on colonial matters.[20] In so locating 'Africa'
for the reader in terms of territory and subject, Haggard's romances
also engaged in what appeared to be a systematic classification and
cataloguing of black African life, peoples and customs. Thus, for
instance, alongside the lengthy and detailed descriptions of the African
landscape which appear in his imperial trilogy, Haggard bombarded
the reader with details about the flora and fauna of his imagined/real
Africa, and no less interestingly for his audience, the physical
appearance and the social, moral and sexual practices of his imagined
and real African peoples.

Haggard's positivism, his concern with the delineation of colonial
time and space and with the accumulation and ordering of 'knowledge'
about Africa was a characteristic feature of the imperial enterprise.[21]
In the Victorian imperial archive of knowledge, serviced by many disciplines and sources, 'fact' slid easily into myth in the pursuit of a vast
imagined community of colonial peoples united by the *pax Britannica*,
albeit divided by race, custom and economic development. In
Haggard's case, however, the process of the acquisition, referencing
and cataloguing of data about black Africa also provided a convincing
framework within his fiction for a series of critical discourses. Of these,
one of the most evident but also problematical, and permeating most
of his fiction, was the old Enlightenment dichotomy between
'civilisation' and 'savagery'.

Like many Africanists of his day, influenced among other things by
current archaeological hypotheses as well as ethnological debates,
Haggard made a clear distinction between north and sub-Saharan
Africa in his mental mapping of the continent, locating the former and
its peoples within the oriental rim of the ancient Mediterranean world
and, therefore, within the pale of 'civilisation'. In many of his African
romances, the grounds for this differentiation of Otherness between an
'Oriental Africa' and black Africa was spelt out clearly for the reader:

> [T]hey were interesting in their way; tall spare men, light coloured with
> refined, mobile faces. Here was no negro blood, but that of some ancient

people such as Egyptians or Phoenicians; men whose forefathers had been wise and civilised thousands of years ago, and perchance had stood in the courts of Pharaoh or of Solomon.[22]

Conversely, and in line with this logic of differentiation, Haggard appeared to subscribe to the Victorian construct of sub-Saharan Africa as the 'Dark Continent' peopled by savages, gripped by 'superstitious madness' and ravaged by slavery; or, put another way, Africa as a psychological and physical realm of corruption, destruction and death.

This dualistic conception of Africa was a central feature of Haggard's colonial narratives from their earliest practice. Nowhere was it more evident than in *She* where the protagonists, Horace Holly and Leo Vincey, search out Ayesha, the ageless, all-knowing but wicked Egyptian princess who presides over the black and primitive 'Amahagger', literally, in the 'dark interior' of central Africa. Yet at the same time (and a feature which has attracted the notice of several sympathetic critics), Haggard's writing seemed at moments to hint at a form of cultural relativism in which African tribal society and 'Africanness' might be compared on at least neutral terms with white Anglo-Saxon society. 'Ah! this civilisation, what does it all come to?' Haggard's English hero, Quatermain, muses:

> Full forty years and more I spent among savages, and studied them and their ways; and now for several years I have lived here in England, and in my own stupid manner have done my best to learn the ways of the children of light; and what do I find? A great gulf fixed? No, only a very little one, that a plain man's thought may spring across. I say that as the savage is, so is the white man, only the latter is more inventive, and possesses a faculty of combination; save and except also that the savage, as I have known him, is to a large extent free from the greed of money, which eats like a cancer into the heart of the white man.[23]

Haggard's dislike of western materialism and his empathy towards African native life were frequently struck chords in both his fictional and non-fictional writings. This empathy was further underlined by his willingness to create heroic African characters in the well-established tradition of the 'noble savage'. In *Nada the Lily*, a major contribution to that tradition, Haggard was certainly one of the few nineteenth-century English novelists (if not the first), to pen a serious novel about pre-colonial black Africa and to confront the reader with an autonomous African voice. Equally, his earlier representation of the figures of Umbopa and Umslopagaas in the imperial trilogy was notable at certain points in allowing their human and specifically male virtues to transcend their twin signifiers of inferiority; black and servant status. Moreover, scenes such as the disrobing of Umbopa in *King Solomon's Mines* also involved an apparent and provocative celebration of the sexual power of male black figures, an approach which was visually echoed in the revised and illustrated edition of the novel:

> Sir Henry told me to ask him to stand up. Umbopa did so, at the same time slipping off the long military great coat which he wore, and revealing himself naked except for the moocha round his centre and a necklace of lions' claws. Certainly he was a magnificent-looking man; I never saw a finer native. Standing about six foot three high he was broad in proportion, and very shapely. In that light too, his skin looked scarcely more than dark, except here and there where deep black scars marked old assegai wounds. Sir Henry walked up to him and looked into his proud, handsome face.[24]

Such positive images in Haggard's writing, implying at least a common humanity and rough equality between the imperial incomer and the native host in Africa were rare and in fact misleading. As Katz asserts: 'Any idea of unity between black and white in Haggard's fiction is a unity of unequals.'[25] Rather, the dominant approach to colour and race in the imperial narratives was conventional for its time in its strategy and objectives. Thus Haggard's heroes, notably the ubiquitous Quatermain, but also other less-remembered ones, such as Alan Vernon in *The Yellow God* and Captain Oliver Orme in *Queen Sheba's Ring* (1910), are presented as paragons of English and imperial virtue: rational, intelligent, moral and brave; though this was a stereotype which always left some room for the eccentric behaviour popularly associated with 'Englishness' and the marauding English gentleman abroad. Haggard's imperial villains, where they appear, are generally Boers, people of mixed race or Portuguese Jews, a fact which reflected a persistent anti-Semitism in his work and, of course, the social milieu of which he was part. These characters might be further stigmatised, having embraced 'the wilderness as a last resource . . . and sank to the level of the savages among whom they lived', a deterioration which could be finalised through intimate relationships with black African women.[26]

Like Haggard's representation of Africa as a whole, his construct of black Africa admitted some differentiation in Otherness. In most of his colonial romances and short stories, he voiced a fulsome admiration for the Zulu nation and its famous chiefs, Chaka, Dingaan and Ceteweyo. In the second book of his Zulu trilogy, Haggard prefaced his novel with a lengthy discussion of the Zulus, commending their military prowess and their 'primitive virtues'.[27]

The rich cultural and folk heritage of the Zulu nation also gave Haggard an acknowledged source for his stories and provided the inspiration for his best known African 'noble savages', Umbopa and Umslopagaas. In several of his later novels he bemoaned the decline of traditional African tribal life, and in particular the disintegration of the Zulu nation within the emerging South African colonial state:

> Now everything is changed, or so I hear, and doubtless in the balance, this is best. Still we may wonder what are the thoughts that pass through the mind of some ancient warrior of Chaka's or Dingaan's time, as he suns himself crouched on the ground . . . and watches men and women of the Zulu blood passing homeward from the cities or the mines, bemused, some of them, with the white man's smuggled liquor, grotesque with the white man's cast-off garments, hiding, perhaps, in their blankets examples of the white man's doubtful photographs – and then shuts his sunken eyes and remembers the plumed and kilted regiments making that same ground shake as, with a thunder of salute, line upon line, company upon company, they rushed out to battle.[28]

Even so, across the full span of Haggard's work, although a privileged position was always reserved for the Zulu people in his ethnological map of black Africa, the representation of Africans, more than anything else followed and reinforced existing negative and inferior stereotypes: the African as savage, the African as child, faithful manservant, buffoon and sex object – all framed in the discourse of the colonial romances. Interestingly, his African villains, of which there were by necessity many, were frequently ascribed with diabolic and supernatural powers, such as the witch 'Gagool' in *King Solomon's Mines* and the wizard 'Zikali' in the Zulu trilogy. This contributed to a construct of black Africa and 'Otherness' which was notable in several respects, not least for its polarities. In Haggard's colonial romances, Africa itself was presented as containing both utopian promise and dystopian danger. The prospect of the continent as the cradle of an 'earthly paradise' was contrasted with 'those dark parts of Africa . . . that . . . were dark indeed'.[29] Black nobility, as suggested, was juxtaposed against indigenous evil; black Africans such as Umbopa might in some cases be admirable and admired, but more often they were presented as fearful and to be feared. But between these polarities the Africans were rarely permitted to rise above servant status, and where they did, it was usually as exceptional objects of physical curiosity or sexual voyeurism.

For different reasons, for Haggard's Victorian audience and contemporary readers alike, it is the persistent downgrading of black Africa as a whole, and of the African, that stands out in his colonial romances: in the first case because it was expected; in the second because it exemplifies some of the conceptual and linguistic archaeology of racism. Thus, for example, most signs of 'civilisation' in Haggard's black Africa, both imaginary and real, were attributed to the Near Orient, and specifically to ancient Egyptian, Phoenician or Semitic penetration and colonisation rather than to the skills of indigenous cultures. As Haggard confidently told his readers in introducing a short story on the subject: 'Zimbabwe is only one of a group of ruins . . . built by civilised men in the heart of Africa.'[30] Likewise, the completeness of African humanity itself was interrogated. 'What a man he was, if indeed, he could be called quite human', Haggard wrote in describing one African.[31] Time and time again Haggard depicted his Africans, even his heroic ones, as possessing animal and beast-like characteristics, as possessing 'filthy paws', 'thin voices as rats speak', 'nostrils agape like the horse's', as moving 'as a monkey springs', 'angry as a wounded buffalo', 'screaming like little monkeys'. The reader also frequently encounters Africans who are explicitly identified with animals, such as Gagool (monkey) and the 'baboon woman' in *Allan's Wife* (1889), 'Otter', the black manservant in *The People of the Mist*, and 'Magepa the Buck', in a short story of the same title published in 1912.[32] The net and witting result was a crude sort of anthropological reductionism, as in this description of Hans, a Cape bushman and Quatermain's faithful retainer:

> 'A dog, I expect, or perhaps it is Hans. He curls up in all sorts of places near to where I may be. Hans, are you there?'
> A figure rose from the gardenia bushes.
> '*Ja* I am here, Baas.'
> 'What are you doing, Hans?'
> 'I am doing what the dog does, Baas – watching my master'.
> 'Good', I answered.[33]

Like animals too, Haggard seems to suggest, Africans are expendable. In almost every one of his major colonial romances, beginning with *King Solomon's Mines*, African wildlife and natives alike are slaughtered on a massive scale with an apparent indifference by imperial adventurers, usually inferior in number, but possessing superior military knowledge and technology. Black Africans, for their part, exhibit the blood-lust of the beast, as well as seeking to kill whites, enslave, mutilate and butcher each other in the most brutal and goriest of fashions using traditional weapons, particularly the axe. Thus Africa itself seems to be reduced to the simple categories of the non-rational and the primitive. As Haggard himself expressed it in one of his early essays, and subsequently reiterated many times through the voice and reflections of Quatermain: Africa 'was like coming face to face with great primeval Nature, not nature as we civilised people know her, smiling in cornfields, waving in well-ordered woods, but Nature as she was on the morrow of the Creation.'[34]

Haggard's mapping and cataloguing of Africa, with its accompanying ethnological and cultural narratives, was thus essentially a reductionist project, although one which possessed internal tensions. The colonial space of the African present was shown as providing, first, a glimpse into the roots of human evolution and civilisation and, second, a reminder and warning of the fragility of progress and the regressive pull of the 'beast within'. As Norman Etherington has pointed out, 'Again and again Haggard marches virtuous men into the wilderness where they reveal hidden savage impulses and confront the awesome mysteries of their deepest inner selves.'[35] For Haggard's readers and certainly for some of his critics, this was undoubtedly a disconcerting, if not subversive spectre. What made it palatable, apart from its obvious distancing in the difference of Africa, was the important accompanying messages of self-discovery and imperial regeneration.

Running parallel to the ethnographic, cultural and degeneration/regeneration narratives are the discourses of gender. This is the lens through which the interiors of Haggard's African romances have been most frequently examined in recent scholarship, and understandably so. Much of the literature and language of empire, including Haggard's romances, was constructed in terms of masculine narratives. These were romances for men and boys and, as Haggard was to boast in one instance, without 'a *petticoat* in the whole history'.[36] But in fact, and in more ways than one, the opposite was the case. English women figured prominently in some of Haggard's colonial romances, just as they did in the real territory of empire. More substantively, his colonial narratives involved the explicit gendering of Africa as female and the sexual mapping of its internal 'virgin space'. In *King Solomon's Mines*, the map that leads Quatermain and the reader to Kukuanaland, and ultimately to a vast treasure of diamonds, is patently the outline of a female torso. The explorers must pass through 'two enormous mountains . . . like the pillars of a gigantic gateway . . . [and] shaped exactly like a woman's breasts'.[37] After negotiating 'Sheba's Breasts', they proceed down Solomon's Road to a triangle of mountains called the Three Witches, where they must descend into the 'mouth' of the treasure cave. Through this feminised landscape, the 'female body' of Africa thus becomes an object of the imperial gaze and male desire, and an obvious metaphor for colonial penetration and domination, but also, for the sexual exploration and classification of the continent. As Rebecca Stott has pointed out: 'The fantasy is that of a passive body, naked . . . and half asleep. Africa invites . . .'[38]

Haggard's 'empire of the imagination', like Kipling's imperial India, was indeed an empire of sexual fantasy and opportunity, but also carnal danger. In *She* and its sequel, *Ayesha: The Return of She* (1905), together with the surprisingly neglected, *Wisdom's Daughter* (1923), Haggard created his most controversial and discussed 'African' character, Ayesha or She-Who-Must-Be-Obeyed. As Sandra Gilbert and Susan Gubar and many others have argued, Haggard's invention of this ultimate *femme fatale* betrayed both contemporary fears about female emancipation at the imperial centre (and the need to restate patriarchial law), and the lure of uncontrolled female sexuality at the colonial margins.[39] However, and a point which is often overlooked, although Ayesha is part of the 'body' of Africa, she is not at one with it. Ayesha is better understood as a product of Haggard's Orientalist interests and imagination rather than of his encounter with black Africa; a white immortal Egyptian princess, like Leo Vincey and Holly, an intruding force in the African 'heart of the darkness'; but a would-be coloniser of white men as well as black territory. Significantly, Haggard was to resubmit the basic idea of white femininity occupying the core of black Africa, albeit in a less aggressive human form, in conjuring up the idea of the 'Zu Vendis' Queens in *Allan Quatermain*, and reworked variations on this theme in several of his later colonial romances.[40] Partly because of this fixation, there was always very limited scope in his romances for any acknowledgement of a competing black African female beauty, except and only where it could be redefined in terms of a dominant caucasian or semi-caucasian racial paradigm. Likewise, black sexuality could only be made intelligible and erotically convincing for Haggard's assumed readership by validating it against the aboriginal – a definition that was unacceptable, as we see in this description of 'Mameena' in *Child of Storm*:

> There, standing in a beam of golden light . . . stood the most beautiful creature that I had ever seen – that is, if it be admitted that a person who is black, or rather copper-coloured, can be beautiful.
>
> She was a little above the medium height, not more, with a figure that, so far as I am a judge of such matters, was absolutely perfect – that of a Greek statue indeed. . . . Her features showed no trace of the negro type; on the contrary, they were singularly well cut, the nose being straight and fine and the pouting mouth that just showed the ivory teeth between, very small. Then the eyes . . . set beneath a smooth broad forehead on which the curling, but not woolly, hair grew low. . . . The hair, by the way, was not dressed up in any of the eccentric native fashions, but simply parted in the middle. . . .[41]

But Haggard's depiction of the beauty of Mameena, like the better known Ayesha, is invested with an aura of sexual danger and an implied sexual knowingness which exposes the depth of Victorian patriarchial anxieties.

> A lovely woman, truly; and yet there was something not quite pleasing about that beautiful face; something, notwithstanding its childlike outline, which reminded me of a flower breaking into bloom, that one does not associate with youth and innocence.[42]

Even so, where black female sexuality and power was explicitly recognised in Haggard's African romances, it was like the figure of Africa itself, an object of male imperial scrutiny and generally trapped in a colonial discourse which controlled the terms of its visual inspection and classification. This ensures that black female sexuality in the texts, while possibly challenging the male and imperialist integrity of Haggard's explorers, cannot compromise that integrity. Thus, in *King Solomon's Mines* Quatermain could speak approvingly of the sexually provocative native dancing-girls 'now whirling round and round, now meeting in mimic warfare, swaying, eddying here and there, coming forward, falling back in ordered confusion, delightful to witness'.[43] But where the overt threat of inter-racial sexual union loomed, as ultimately it does between the eccentric Captain Good and the simple native girl, Foulata, the narrative interceded. As a dying Foulata tells Quatermain of her love for Captain Good, in almost a confessional situation: 'Say to my Lord, Bougwan, that – I love him, and that I am glad to die because I know that he cannot cumber his life with such as I am, for the sun may not mate with the darkness, nor the white with the black.'[44] In this sense, it might be said, Haggard's colonial romances constructed a model of supposedly intrinsic African female sexuality and sexual power – pale, beautiful and erotic – which was as exhilarating as it was a pure fantasy and deception, and closed off the reality of the black female Other.

Haggard's significance for writing and Africa is both historical and actively contemporary. As one of the now acknowledged architects of colonial discourse, he undoubtedly helped to create and consolidate the components of an English-language narrative about Africa which, with some modifications, and despite serious challenges, persisted throughout the twentieth century in various forms – journalism, popular literature and film. Seen in its own *fin-de-siècle* context, Haggard's fiction demonstrated and continues to underline the essentially homologous nature of the British imperial project in which politics, literature and 'knowledge' were intertwined to create an 'empire of the imagination' and which drew deeply on the Victorian popular fascination with global exploration and colonial incorporation. A large part of post-colonial literary practice both inside and outside Africa has since been devoted to the decolonisation of that imperial fantasy along with its adjuncts of linguistic and textual ethnocentrism. In this respect, it might be argued, it is Rider Haggard and his popular fiction, rather than Joseph Conrad's modernist narratives, which stand out as occupying the dominant and most telling ground in the recent history of literary constructions of Africa. But what also makes Haggard particularly interesting and relevant today, apart from the unrivalled scope and scale of his writing on Africa, are the numerous tensions and latent contradictions within his colonial romances, some of which have been identified in this chapter. These not only offer valuable insights into the Victorian assembly of the imperial Self and Western notions of African place and identity, but also into the irrepressible imperial urge to explain, catalogue and commodify Africa.

Notes

1. His biographers include Lilias Rider Haggard, *The Cloak that I Left: A Biography of the Author Henry Rider Haggard K.B.E.* (London, 1951); Morton Cohen, *Rider Haggard: His Life and Works* (London, 1960); Peter Berresford Ellis, *H. Rider Haggard: A Voice From the Infinite* (London, 1978); D.S. Higgins, *Rider Haggard: The Great Storyteller* (London, 1981); and Tom Pocock, *Rider Haggard and the Lost Empire: A Biography* (London, 1993).

2. Notable theoretical insights into this relationship have been provided by Edward Said in *Orientalism: Western Conceptions of the Orient* (London, 1978) and *Culture and Imperialism* (London, 1994), and in more conventional terms through the work of many historians. See, for example, John M. Mackenzie (ed.), *Imperialism and Popular Culture* (Manchester, 1986). A useful addition to the literature is Nicholas Thomas's *Colonialism's Culture: Anthropology, Travel and Government* (Cambridge, 1994).

3. The critical canon on Haggard is an expanding one. The major books are Norman Etherington, *Rider Haggard* (Boston, 1984), and Wendy R. Katz, *Rider Haggard and the Fiction of Empire* (Cambridge, 1987). Detailed discussion of Haggard's fiction can also be found in Alan Sandison, *The Wheel of Empire: A Study of the Imperial Idea in Some Late Nineteenth and Early Twentieth-Century Fiction* (London, 1967); Brian Street, *The Savage in Literature* (London, 1975); Martin Green, *Dreams of Adventure, Deeds of Empire* (London, 1980); David Dabydeen (ed.), *The Black Presence in English Literature* (Manchester, 1985); Patrick Brantlinger, *Rule of Darkness: British Literature and Imperialism 1830–1914* (Ithaca, NY, 1988); Sandra M. Gilbert and Susan Gubar, *No Man's Land*, vol. 2: *Sexchanges* (New Haven, CT, 1989); Elaine Showalter, *Sexual Anarchy: Gender and Culture at the Fin de Siècle* (London, 1992) and Rebecca Stott, *The Fabrication of the Late Victorian Femme Fatale* (London, 1992). Other significant works include: Norman Etherington, 'Rider Haggard, Imperialism and the Layered Personality', *Victorian Studies*, vol. 22, no. 1 (1978), pp. 71–87; David Bunn, 'Embodying Africa: Woman and Romance in Colonial Fiction', *English in Africa*, vol. 15, no. 1 (1988), pp. 1–27; and Rebecca Stott, 'The Dark Continent: Africa as Female Body in Haggard's Adventure Fiction', *Feminist Review* vol. 32 (1989), pp. 69–89. The standard bibliographical guide is D.E. Whatmore, *Rider Haggard: A Bibliography* (London, 1987).

4. W.R. Katz, *Rider Haggard and the Fiction of Empire* p. 153.

5. For the wider view on Africa in the literature of empire, see P. Brantlinger, *Rule of Darkness* ch. 6. Haggard's close relationship with Kipling is noted by his biographers and is chronicled by Morton Cohen in *Rudyard Kipling to Rider Haggard: The Record of a Friendship* (London, 1965).

6. See, for example, Frank McLynn, *Hearts of Darkness: The European Exploration of Africa* (London, 1993).

7. A useful checklist of Haggard's publications is provided by P. Berresford Ellis, *H. Rider Haggard*, pp. 269–77.

8. For example, 8,000 copies of *King Solomon's Mines* were produced and sold by Haggard's publisher, Cassell, between September and November 1885, rising to 31,000 in the following year. The total production of each of Haggard's first two novels, *Dawn* (February 1884) and *The Witch's Head* (December 1884), had been less than 500.

9. 'The Culture of the Horrible: Mr Haggard's Stories', *Church Quarterly Review* (January 1888), and 'The Fall of Fiction', *Fortnightly Review* (September 1888): cited in D.S. Higgins, *Rider Haggard*, pp. 121, 126–7.

10. 'So-called' because the trilogy charts the downfall (via the African exploits of Allan Quatermain) of the Zulu empire in its confrontations with Boers and the British.

11. Haggard's authority as a commentator on African affairs dated from early articles on the subject and from his first book, *Cetywayo and his White Neighbours* (1882). In the wake of his literary success he was appointed Honorary Chairman of the Anglo-African Writers Club and became a director of the *African Review*, a prestigious weekly magazine which published his articles and short stories. This celebrity status also brought him into contact with other notable Africanists of the day, including Olive Schreiner and Cecil Rhodes.

12. Andrew Lang (1844–1912), influential Scottish anthropologist, poet, novelist and co-author of Haggard's thirteenth novel, *The World's Desire* (1890). On the literary and sexual politics of Victorian romance, see W.R. Katz, *Rider Haggard and the Fiction of Empire*, ch. 2; E. Showalter, *Sexual Anarchy*, ch. 5; and Jean Radford (ed.), *The Progress of Romance: The Politics of Popular Fiction* (London, 1986).

13. See P. Berresford Ellis, *H. Rider Haggard*, p. 119.

14. J. Radford (ed.), *The Progress of Romance*, pp. 8–9.

15. M. Green, *Dreams of Adventure, Deeds of Empire*, pp. 229–34, and David Trotter, *The English Novel in History 1895–1920* (London, 1993), p. 142.

16. Haggard's Orientalist interests came to dominate his later life and work and were reflected in a string of novels, including *Pearl Maiden* (1903), *The Way of the Spirit* (1906), *Morning Star* (1910), *Moon of Israel* (1918), *Wisdom's Daughter* (1923) and *Queen of the Dawn* (1925).

17. For a fuller discussion of 'imperial gothic', see P. Brantlinger, *Rule of Darkness*, ch. 8.

18. Haggard, *She*, ed. Daniel Karlin (Oxford, 1991), p. 273. An alternative modern edition is *The Annotated She: A Critical Edition of H. Rider Haggard's Victorian Romance*, ed. Norman Etherington (Bloomington, IN, 1991).

19. Haggard, *The Days of My Life: An Autobiography*, 2 vols, ed. C.J. Longman (London, 1926), pp. 85–6.
20. Haggard also validated many colonial romances by dedicating them to his personal imperial heroes, such as Sir Theophilus Shepstone, Lord Curzon and Theodore Roosevelt.
21. See Thomas Richards, *The Imperial Archive: Knowledge and the Fantasy of Empire* (London, 1993).
22. Haggard, *Benita: An African Romance* (London, 1906), p. 92.
23. Haggard, *Allan Quatermain* (1887; London, 1894), p. 4.
24. Haggard, *King Solomon's Mines*, ed. Dennis Butts (Oxford, 1989), pp. 48–9. The revised illustrated edition was published by Cassell in 1905 with illustrations by W. Russell Flint (1880–1965).
25. W.R. Katz, *Rider Haggard and the Fiction of Empire*, p. 135.
26. Haggard, *The Ghost Kings* (1908; London, 1935), pp. 43–4.
27. Haggard, *Child of Storm* (1913; London, 1914), p. iv.
28. Ibid., pp. vi–vii.
29. Haggard, *The Holy Flower* (London, 1915), p. 108.
30. Haggard, 'Author's Note', *Elissa: Or, The Doom of Zimbabwe* (London, 1917). This story first appeared in 1898 in a serialised form. See also Haggard's revealing essay, 'The Real King Solomon's Mines', published in *Cassell's Magazine* in July 1907.
31. Haggard, *Child of Storm*, p. 29.
32. See Peter Haining (ed.), *The Best Short Stories of Rider Haggard* (London, 1981).
33. Haggard, *The Holy Flower*, p. 57.
34. W.R. Katz, *Rider Haggard and the Fiction of Empire*, p. 8.
35. N. Etherington, 'Rider Haggard, Imperialism and the Layered Personality', p. 86.
36. Haggard, *King Solomon's Mines*, p. 9.
37. Ibid., p. 85.
38. R. Stott, 'The Dark Continent', p. 79.
39. For the further development of this idea, see Anne McClintock, 'Maidens, Maps and Mines: *King Solomon's Mines* and the Reinvention of Patriarchy in Colonial South Africa', in Cherryl Walker (ed.), *Women and Gender in Southern Africa since 1945* (London, 1990), pp. 97–124.
40. Notably *Benita* and *The Ghost Kings*.
41. Haggard, *Child of Storm*, pp. 67–8.
42. Ibid., p. 68.
43. Haggard, *King Solomon's Mines*, p. 179.
44. Ibid., p. 281.

7 Stars in the moral universe: writing and resistance to colonialism

Ed Marum

Resistance to colonialism has long been a regular feature of African writing. The anti-colonial spirit has perhaps been most powerfully expressed through fiction and poetry, but has also taken other forms. The purpose of this chapter is to provide a general introduction to the issues, themes and perspectives reflected in the literature and to comment on some major figures in the colonial and post-colonial debate, outlining the perspectives they offer on the subject of the writer in Africa and on the relationship between the writer and the society in which he or she lives and works.

Even now, when the subject of African literature has been well researched and documented on an international scale, there is little agreement as to a definition of 'Africa' in the theory and criticism the subject has produced. Similarly, 'colonialism' continues to mean different things to different people (among them, African writers). Writers and critics emerging from different historical positions across the nineteenth and twentieth centuries have demonstrated their own bias and prejudice, for the term is primarily a socio-political one, concerned with a view of social reality seen from a range of philosophical, political and economic perspectives. These perspectives have naturally shaped and informed the work of generations of African 'wordsmiths' in poetry and prose.

Similarly, movements within individual countries in the direction of (or away from) nationalism, or intellectual shifts towards or away from state-imposed systems and structures, have also informed and conditioned the writer's task. Because of the complexity of the history of Africa itself and the multiracial, pluralistic character of the continent, it is impossible to make easy assertions about perceptions of colonialism on a broad scale or to document the innumerable versions of colonialism the literature has generated. However, I hope here to register the sense of fascination many writers have had and continue to have with the subject, and to provide some examples from which more detailed analysis may be possible. In doing this, I shall refer to a range of writers and critics who form part of the colonial discussion and from whom much more can be learned as to the salient characteristics of African literatures in English.

The nineteenth-century background

From a wide range of perspectives it has been the relationship between Africa and the West that has determined the issues addressed in the writing of resistance. An indication of the complexity of the issues is provided in the following extract by Gérard:

> Africa is the last continent to have been subdued by European power. Its literary evolution followed a pattern that combines in a specific way features already perceptible in the Dominions and in Southern Asia. By the time European expansion started in earnest in the last few years of the eighteenth century, Africa was divided into two cultural zones. The peripheral areas of the North and East had literate elites responsible for a written tradition dating back to several centuries: Ethiopia had its own script, mainly used for hymnal poetry and homiletic prose in the church language, Ge'ez, a situation which was comparable to that of Latin in the Western Middle Ages or Church Slavonic in Eastern Europe; in Islamic Africa the Arabic script and language had produced a significant amount of religious and historical works in the North while the Arabic script had been used for transliterating the vernacular tongue, Swahili, along the Eastern coast. South of the Sahara, lay the vast *terra incognita* of the Blacks, whose verbal art was still confined to oracy.[1]

Despite having what could be described as a rather patronising tone, this piece begins to state the position regarding the multifaceted nature of languages in African societies and the many contexts which shape the nature and character of literacies across the continent. Lynch's summary of the historical development of the African slave trade at the beginning of his important book provides an informative context from which to view writers who subsequently articulated resistance to colonialism:

> The nineteenth century was probably the most humiliating century in the history of the Negro [sic] race. The African slave trade which had

reached new high proportions in the eighteenth century continued to flourish, despite the well-intentioned efforts of the British to stop it and the legal prohibitions imposed upon it by European and American nations. A vast contraband trade supplied the enormous demands for slaves on the plantations of the Americas. On the western coast of Africa this was not effectively brought under control until the 1860s; and in these same years in East Africa, the Arab trade in ivory and slaves caused widespread and unprecedented devastation. Not until the last decade of the century was the traffic successfully combated. Africa had 'bled her life's blood at every pore', and needed resuscitation.

In the New World, the beginning of the century saw the vast majority of Negroes in slavery. Although the system had been abolished in the British West Indies in 1834, and in the French and Danish West Indies in 1848, it continued a vigorous life in the United States, Cuba and Brazil. So entrenched was slavery in the southern United States that it took the Civil War (1861–65) to bring about its downfall. In Cuba and Brazil, final emancipation did not come until 1886 and 1888, respectively. And even after their emancipation, Negroes of the New World were, for the most part, regarded and treated as inferior members of society.[2]

The continuing encroachment of Europe into Africa in the nine-teenth century further complicated the nature of debate on colonial issues. E.W. Blyden, for example, the subject of Lynch's book, proved to be largely responsible for the development of such concepts as pan-Africanism, intellectualised arguments regarding the African personality and the development of theories of Negritude. (The latter term is defined and placed in an historical context in a later section of this chapter.) Blyden was probably the most important influence in the nineteenth century in shaping contemporary and later historical expressions of the 'negro question', in terms of changing perceptions of African identity. His suggested solutions regarding the redefinition of the 'negro's' role in national and social developments have made a major impact upon subsequent African thought and writing. He makes the following comments regarding explorations of Africa:

> These discoveries have turned the attention of Europe to Africa with renewed curiosity and interest. And, very recently, this interest has so much increased that the competition among the leading European Powers for the possession of territory on the coast has been described by the London *Times*, with no touch of exaggeration, as 'The Scramble for Africa'.

A European writer, delighting in epigrammatic rhetoric, has recently said, 'The eighteenth century stole the black man from his country; the nineteenth century steals his country from the black man.'[3]

Although Blyden had the ability to turn lacerating phrases to good effect and was instrumental in influencing black attitudes to colonial expansion, his position on the development of the African race can be questioned. A keen supporter of Islam, he has been accused of 'an alternative racist preoccupation with purity of blood', for example.[4] Nonetheless, his influence upon subsequent literature and thought is major in that he saw 'the peoples of Africa not just as Africans, but as members of a dispersed Negro race inhabiting both sides of the Atlantic'.[5] In the development of the Pan-African movement he has been an influence upon writers and thinkers approaching the issue of black identity from a wide range of perspectives and is one of a group of West African politicians who contributed to the creation of a nationalistic sentiment in opposition to colonial expansionism. During his lifetime, (1832–1912), he published two seminal collections, *Liberia's Offering* (1862) and *Christianity, Islam and the Negro Race* (1867). Although these works, as Fyfe has shown, reflect some inconsistencies in argument and outlook, they also transmit Blyden's support for Islam as well as his specific racism. They additionally provide good illustrative material which demonstrates the power, seriousness and romantic appeal behind Blyden's position as an influential rhetorician.[6]

His particular blend of romanticism was tempered by a caustic and sometimes savage wit which strongly impressed those who heard and read him. Blyden's views on Christianity, for example, had major implications for the Black sense of identity. He believed that Christianity had come to debase the Negro: 'All tendencies to independent individuality are repressed and destroyed. Their [the negroes'] ideas and aspirations could be expressed only in conformity with the views and tastes of those who held rule over them. All avenues to intellectual improvement were closed against them, and they were doomed to perpetual ignorance.'[7]

Blyden's view that black and white could not live together, particularly in the United States, was coupled with his belief that 'Nature's Laws' would help keep the Europeans out of a renationalised Africa whose future history, in his view, needed to be rewritten and be redirected to revivify and extol self-respect among Africans. Above all, however, it was his achievement to provide for the Black peoples what Fyfe has called that 'new vision of themselves in relation to their ancestral home'.[8]

Many of the writers who came after him (including those who have articulated black consciousness in the twentieth century around versions of Negritude, as well as its intellectual opponents) owe much to Blyden. He helped to give African writers a framework with which they could begin to address the issues of being African. Recent work has documented his and others' contribution to the intellectual and literary inheritance of the twentieth-century writer.[10] In helping to articulate problems, and by suggesting possible and, for some, contentious solutions to them, Blyden handed down an important legacy.

Views of colonialism in the twentieth century

Many of the writers, philosophers and critics who followed the lead Blyden gave in the fight against colonialism have gone on to document in specific ways their own versions of evolving African identity in both poetry and prose. I shall draw attention to some of the important literary figures in the resistance movement and to the themes and issues they address.

One of the foremost modern writers, and now widely recognised as a major world novelist, is Chinua Achebe. It is perhaps unsurprising that one of the clearest tributes to Achebe has come from a fellow major African novelist, Ngugi. In an important essay on African history, Ngugi places Achebe at the forefront of innovation in the African novel:

> What the African novelist has attempted to do is restore the African character to its history. The African novelist has turned his back on the Christian god and resumed the broken dialogue with gods of his own people. He has given back to the African character the will to act and change the scheme of things. Writers like Chinua Achebe have paved the way.[11]

This passage is interesting because it links Ngugi with the nineteenth-century view Blyden articulated; Blyden demanded that a new African consciousness should replace the fractured colonised African character; and Ngugi sees Achebe as having helped to do the job Blyden wanted done. The passage also implies Ngugi's radical Marxist stance, clearly evident in his own fictional treatment of the African issue in such major works as *Weep Not Child* (1964), *Between* (1965) and *A Grain of Wheat* (1967). In this respe course, at a far remove from Blyden, but the two expres different ways the same wish to see a rebirth of African ide consciousness. Yet, while there have been major critical differences regarding Ngugi's own contribution to the African novel, the work of Achebe has been generally welcomed and celebrated.[12] Like the other writers, Achebe recognises the historical inheritance of the African; rather than allot blame, however, he is concerned to find out where mistakes were made in order to better understand the divisions and strife to which colonialism gave birth.

In his first great novel, *Things Fall Apart* (1958), Achebe documents the transitional period in African history when the indigenous leader Okonkwo comes face to face with the colonial pressures for change brought to bear on an ordered tribal social-system. Okonkwo is both hero and villain, noble protagonist and vanquished victim in Achebe's eyes. Part of the pathos of the social documentation lies in Okonkwo being caught between the two worlds of Africa and the West, of testifying to, but also in part ironically bringing about, his own downfall and with it the erosion of the traditional tribal culture so important to him. One must agree that Achebe's sources include the 'traditional lore, indigenous customs, and the oral tradition of Africa'.[13] It also needs to be stressed, however, that he has pushed the frontiers of the African novel forwards by confronting the predicament of the modern man caught in a culture clash. The insight into and sensitivity towards the question of individual and social identity that Achebe demonstrates in this work is exceptional, and the novel has rightly come to be seen as a major landmark in African writing in English, despite the paternalistic views of some critics.[14]

Achebe's later work, in part, develops the central theme of his first novel, continuing to present fiction as documenting important facets of social history and emphasising the continual interplay of, and conflicts between, past and present. His second novel, *No Longer at Ease* (1960), centres around Okonkwo's grandson, Obi, who returns to Nigeria after a university education in England, to find himself caught, as was his grandfather before him, between African and European cultures. Like his grandfather, he becomes a victim of his own weakness as well as of the pressures placed on him by a tribal culture whose values and attitudes he can no longer exemplify, nor believe in. The difference between the two men lies in their chronological situation, in that Okonkwo is never a part of the Western culture; he marks its meeting with the African tribal traditions. His grandson, however, has inherited the colonial legacy of previous generations, has lived through a period of colonial expansion and the dilution of traditional tribal culture. His plight therefore reflects a more developed, sophisticated colonial influence upon Nigeria than did his grandfather's.

Achebe's third novel, *Arrow of God* (1964), again centres around a cultural victim. In this case, however, the character is Ezeulu, a priest of the god Umuaru, who comes into conflict with both his tribe and the Western government's representative, Winterbottom. His fate, like those of Achebe's other heroes, is to demonstrate that no individual is greater than his people; he becomes another victim unable to relate past to present. In *A Man of the People* (1966) Achebe returns to the theme of political corruption he first introduced through Obi in his second novel. The treatment here focuses upon the party political struggle between Odili, the central characer, and Chief Nanga, a corrupt politician. The novel has been criticised, as has Achebe's previous work, for the unconvincing nature of the storyline and for defects in character presentation. In part, I believe this stems from a failure to recognise the developing objectivity of the author towards the issues presented; there is a movement from the first to the third and fourth novels that signifies an awareness of increasing complexity in moral issues and a distancing from easy political answers. This is all the more evident in his most recent work, *Anthills of the Savannah* (1987), produced twenty-one years after his previous novel. Like his other works, this novel attempts to present a balanced and considered view of moral conflict between different value systems, represented in *Man of the People* by the two central characters. Although it clearly retains strong links with his earlier novels, there is about *Anthills* an aura of optimism; the last sections of the book reflect a view that, despite political upheaval, there are signs of a possible future for Africa's peoples – indications that the struggle for self-definition continues into the present, and may be successfully passed down the generations into tomorrow.

The move to radicalism

Achebe can be said to be very much the father figure of modern African literature in English. One of his 'followers', and a writer who is curiously linked to the issues Blyden identified in a previous century, Ngugi wa Thiong'o, has also made an important contribution to literary development, although, as I have indicated, his work is of a very different character. Much of his fiction has been conditioned by his experience in Kenya and East Africa, where history has determined a different colonial inheritance from that of Achebe's Nigeria. As Bardolph explains:

> Paradoxically, the British presence in colonial times also worked against the establishment of a European type of fiction: Kenya, unlike Nigeria, was meant to be a settlers' colony, a white man's paradise. Later, in high density areas like the Highlands of Kenya, the modernisation brought by the railway and the Christian missions was felt by many to be alienating. As early as the 1920s, the Kikuyus in those areas fought for their culture, and before the independence of Kenya, in 1963, the Mau-Mau rebellion and the ten years of Emergency connected the British presence with a language that could never be accepted easily.[15]

Ngugi's career demonstrates this last point well. *The River Between* (1965) chronologically predates his first novel, *Weep Not Child* (1964), and shows how the arrival of Christianity divides two neighbouring peoples – the people of Makuyu and Kameno. While the latter remain pagan, religion proves to be a source of conflict. The young woman Muthoni attempts to reconcile personally her wish to be a 'woman in the tribe', in proper Kenyan tradition, with being a Christian, but dies as a result of illness. In a sense she becomes one of the 'martyrs' that figure in Ngugi's fiction. For him this is a central theme: 'The people who apparently lose and die as persons, in fact have an effect. Their work is carried on by other people who come after them. . . . An individual's importance is not only the life he leads in this world, but the effect of his work on other people after he has gone.'[16]

Another characteristic of Ngugi's work is the incorporation of historical events and movements into the fictional process. He has thus been described as a documentary historian of a particular kind, while others see him as a social realist and part of a larger movement in African literature.[17] Onoge, for example, quoting Fischer, sees a common standpoint between Ngugi and another important African novelist, Ousmane:

> The socialist realist artist – or intellectual for that matter – shows the world as changeable. And because of his historical materialist outlook,

his prospective vision is a positive statement on behalf of the revolutionary aspirations of the exploited classes. Thus it is not enough for the artist to disassociate himself from the decadent environment by the adoption of a self-distancing, contemptuous, satirical or reformist attitude.[18]

Ngugi himself has consistently argued for the exercise of moral responsibility on the part of the African writer, as he states here:

I believe that the African masses will build a place to feel at home. For they are not alone. In Asia, in Latin America, in Black America, the people are fighting the same battle. I believe the African novelist, the African writer, can help in this struggle. But he cannot do this if he insists on a liberal posture. He must be committed on the side of the majority. . . .[19]

In his celebrated novel, *A Grain of Wheat* (1967), Ngugi incorporates a wide range of issues while looking back at Kenyan history, including the period of colonialism, the Mau-Mau movement, the fight for freedom, and the independence ceremony. Schipper has commented perceptively that, 'The author first presents his "file-cards" of the real objective facts, how it went in reality, how it had been told in the newspapers. In the next section the narrator, changing from third-person to first-person narrative technique, recalls his own experiences, the independence festivities in the village.'[20] This fusion of the personal and the general characterises Ngugi's work, and helps explain the sharp immediacy of his treatment of both pre- and post-colonial eras. Bardolph's comments on his early work are also helpful in understanding his particular vision of Africa:

how distant from the vision of Achebe, the 'elder brother' he admired and wanted to emulate. Not for him the 'culture clash' symmetries of so much West African writing. It is too late to describe, even through imaginative recreation, the first encounter between a white man and a 'pure', 'authentic' African culture. What is at stake is the division in each family, not between East and West, but between conflicting projects, all of them African.[21]

Ngugi's novelistic technique of 'exploded chronology' marked out a very distinctive place for his later fiction.[22] This was further developed by his abandonment of English as a medium and the shift to writing in Gikuyu, his mother tongue, in order that he might speak directly to the people. His subsequent arrest, in December 1977, is a reflection of the political power of his work and testifies to the fact that, from his perspective, post-colonial Kenya also suppresses in its own fashion and is seen to act in league with foreign colonial powers. In so doing, the state exerts a new kind of slavery.[23]

There can be no doubt that Ngugi's radical stance stems from real-life experience of the colonial legacy and from his view of the writer as one of the people. His achievement as a writer has been to carry forward the sense of Africa as a nation in its own right, with its own identity founded on the indigenous cultures of the people. Interestingly, the literary critic Schipper links Ngugi's *Detained* (1981) with another published diary, Amadi's *Sunset in Biafra* (1973), as a developing form in African literature. Ngugi is not alone in this respect, for Sembene Ousmane has also contributed in a major way to our understanding of the African writer's concern with class relations.

Ousmane and the social novel

Ousmane's early novel, *God's Bits of Wood* (1960), registers class consciousness through his support for the peasants and proletariat. In an interview, he gives a clear account of his position:

> The African writer must stand in the midst of society and at the same time observe this reality from the outside. . . . I participate in the developments of society and note these. I am a fighter, I know what I want to change in society and this facilitates my work as a writer. You are right in stating that my works develop along with the society in which I live, with its ups and downs, its defeats and its victories. . . . We started from a colonial system. This system is now partially hidden behind the façade of the black bourgeoisie. My work as a writer is narrowly associated with the struggle for real independence. In Africa, we first thought that in 1960 with Independence paradise would come. Now we know better. The whites have left indeed, but those in power now behave in exactly the same way. . . .[24]

Ousmane wishes to identify with the people at large; he has been 'educated' through discussion with peasants, and sees himself as speaking on behalf of social groups in conflict with the more powerful sectors of society; whether these are black dockers in a racist France in *The Black Docker* (1956), or the poor fighting against the powerful and rich in *Xala* (1973). His trade-union training and allegiance to unionism have been powerful forces behind his work. Early critics of his work focus on features of his style, but often betray a weak sense of the issues with which he sees himself involved. Carter's review of *God's Bits of Wood* is characteristic in this respect. Referring to Fanon, Carter says that Ousmane is concerned with

> 'the wretched of the earth' – the striking railway workers on the Dakar–Niger line, the date being 1947–48 and the villains being the French. The format is that of prose epic – an epic of holding out, of incidental suffering and deprivation, of long endurance insecurely sustained by hope, of an ordeal of French hypocrisy, the rather desperate failure of scruple and moral toe-hold of the late colonists. Amongst the press of events otherwise not too coherent, there is an epic march of women, of which the full catalogue of cruel incident is ferociously detailed for us – but of all of it the shape in the end is that of History, always at best a stand-in Muse. A certain dullness, the weariness of recorded cruel fact infects the narrative.[25]

Carter goes on to say that the book is 'not a true art of fiction', but fails to say what he believes the true art of fiction is. His response perhaps reflects the difficulty for a Western reader in 'placing' such work against the very different forms of the Western novel's tradition and history. It is significant that criteria of judgement are often not articulated in such responses. If, for comparative purposes, we place these remarks alongside those of such an eminent African writer and critic as Soyinka, we meet a very different level of understanding of Ousmane's work:

> We are made conscious of a new society in the process of coming to birth. Sembene's ideology is implicit, he does not allow its rhetorical intrusion, but makes it organic to the process of birth. The strategy of struggle determines the one ideological resolution, translate it how one will. An egalitarian discipline has been enforced upon the community by the goals and the ordeals of the strike, by the knowledge of colonial indignity with its imposition of an inferior status on the indigene, its wage-discrimination and inadequate social facilities.[26]

The clarity of Soyinka's analysis is based on a communal African response to the colonial threat, and this threat is 'reduced in scale' by Ousmane in order to stress the positive features of African resistance and self-definition. Soyinka points out that the fate of the colonists is here 'of no interest to the author except in so far as it may by contrast illuminate the virtues of the new vision of society'.[27] Ousmane's contribution, even on the basis of this work alone, to what Soyinka terms the process of 'artistic retrieval' in Africa, lies in his reformulation of social issues in the novel in such a way as to shift the balance of interest towards new definitions of the African, at the expense of outmoded colonialists.[28] The characters in his books are engaged in the struggle for political and economic freedom, while also pursuing a quest for cultural and linguistic independence.

Ousmane's work has also carefully documented social shifts in Senegal in the thirteen years between *God's Bits of Wood* and *Xala*, tracing the movement from group values to the individualism of the late 1960s and early 1970s, and the accompanying pursuit of Western style materialism and 'independent enterprise'. Chreachain-Adelugba has commented on the latter work as showing Africa how it should not live, and sees it as a warning for the 'businessmen' of 'independent' Africa as to 'the impotence which will inevitably befall them if they persist in their two inter-related follies: in being "businessmen without funds" and in ignoring the existence of the beggars they themselves have created'.[29]

It needs to be emphasised that Ousmane's general position, has been to move beyond the 'rehabilitation of the past' and a concern with 'retrospective fixation', towards a more proactive assertion of an African stance which is socially committed.[30] Onoge deals with this issue and raises a number of interesting perspectives, placing Ousmane in a general movement towards a 'pan-African and, indeed, a proletarian–internationalist outlook'.[31] This larger, social concern is demonstrated in the corpus of his work and forms part of the general post-Negritude stance taken by a range of African writers in recent years.

Negritude and post-colonialism

The development of Negritude among French-speaking writers and intellectuals marked another twentieth-century literary phenomenon centred around versions of Africa. It was in many respects quite distinct from the resistance to colonialism reflected in the English-speaking African world, but had, in common with it, a central desire to assert the issues relating to black consciousness.

Césaire's important *Return to My Native Land* (1939) articulated a particular view of Negritude founded on the assertion of a pre-colonial African inheritance. Much of his poetry is based around his Martinique childhood. The colonial-inheritance theme, as I have attempted to show, has been central to African writing through the twentieth century and takes on particular significance in the largely

...an poetry the movement produced. Césaire himself is one
...t poets. Numerous definitions of negritude, however,
...the literature. For the present, I shall use Irele's broad but
...xpressed definition:

> ...ıde can be taken to correspond to a certain form of Pan-Negro
> feeling and awareness, and as a movement, to represent the equivalent
> on the French-speaking side of what has come to be known as Pan-
> Africanism. It thus forms a distinctive current of a larger movement of
> black nationalism, inasmuch as the French-speaking black intellectuals
> involved in the movement faced special problems in their relationship
> to French colonial rule, which gave a particular dimension and quality
> to their reaction. . . . It is with respect to this formal expression of the
> black nationalist consciousness – or to be more precise, of black cultural
> nationalism – that a second and closer sense of the term negritude can
> be defined. . . . In this sense, Negritude has come to mean the ideology
> which was either implicit in the production of the literary school
> associated with the French-speaking black intellectuals or came
> expressly to be formulated for it.[32]

Thus we are able to see, through the creation and development of
Negritude, the transmission of resuscitated cultural values clearly
embedded in Blyden's earlier message to the black people. Césaire's
poetry is a central twentieth-century expression of such concerns:

> Listen to the white world
> appallingly weary from its immense effort
> the crack of its joints rebelling under the
>   hardness of the stars
> listen to the proclaimed victories which trumpet
>   their defeats
> listen to their grandiose alibis (stumbling so
>   lamely)
> Pity for our conquerors, all-knowing and naive![33]

Césaire's ' hardness of the stars' reflects Blyden's earlier metaphor; the
African writer throws light on the colonial issue by exposing the moral
impossibilities inherent in the coloniser's stance. The celebration of
being black which is Negritude is socially and culturally affirmative.
Perhaps the most important voice in the movement, however, partly
because of his ability to articulate issues, is Leopold Senghor, who
defines Negritude as 'l'ensemble des valeurs culturelles du monde
noir'.[34] Unlike Sartre, who saw Negritude as a stage through which

the black experience had to pass in order to move towards a society without racism, Senghor saw Negritude as reflecting the spirituality of the black man, his inner feelings and very identity. His poetry, in consequence, celebrates a romantic attitude towards black experience through what have been called 'rhapsodic assertions' about the black man.[35] His views are characteristically expressed in an essay on religion: 'The African's contribution to the religious sense lies in his faculty of perceiving the supernatural in the natural, his sense of the transcendental and the active self-abandonment that accompanies it, the self-abandonment of love.[36] Senghor's transcendental romanticism, allied to his Roman Catholicism, created a celebratory poetry which has become famous:

> New York! I say to New York, let black blood
> flow into your veins
> Cleaning the rust from your steel articulation
> like an oil of life
> Giving your bridges the curve of the hills, the
> liana's suppleness.[37]

Irele has crystallised Senghor's views on Negritude to good effect:

> The underlying assumption . . . is that each race is endowed with a distinctive nature and embodies, in its civilization, a particular spirit. Each race has its genius, and is apt for a particular kind of expression conforming with its genius. And Senghor postulates just such a nature, such a genius, for the Negro race. The whole edifice of Senghor's Negritude rests on this foundation: the idea of a collective soul of the black race constituting the unifying concept of 'the collective personality of black peoples' which Senghor makes synonymous with Negritude.[38]

The tendency towards traditionalism, which is necessarily linked to many facets of Negritude, has been criticised by many English-speaking writers in Africa, including Mphahlele. Writers like Ngugi and Ousmane have moved beyond its limitations towards a more radical social view. Negritude, however, was at its time a legitimate rejection of colonialism and a positive assertion of blackness. Historically, it occupies a paradoxical position, as did Senghor himself, who, as President of Senegal, oversaw a country still largely influenced by French history, culture and materialism and in part clung to a romantic view of France which allowed him to forgive the colonial master. Awoonor sums up the character of the movement:

In these contradictions are revealed the basic emotional nature of Negritude – the eternal exile's designation of himself. Non-rationalist philosophy has to admit as its basic antithesis a rationalist outlook which was responsible for pragmatic solutions to simple questions of survival, shelter, food, and politics in the African world long before the European presence. Neo-symbolism and surrealism are elegant literary concepts that may have nothing to do with the black man's *real* estate in our times.[39]

Both English- and French-speaking Africans have strongly registered their sense of identity through indigenous poetry and prose fashioned to define anew the African personality and the richness of those cultures which together constitute Africa's post-colonial nature. If it is only relatively recently that we have come to appreciate the power and quality of black writing in Africa, it is in part because of a narrow Eurocentric view of culture which has dominated our curricula and thinking, in schools and universities, since before the nineteenth century. It is more than ironic that the very struggle to resist colonialism was for many African writers the spur to self-expression. Their struggles parallel the continuing political struggles of the African peoples, for, as Nkosi points out, 'modern African literature as such can be said to have achieved its present status concomitantly with the maturation of the long struggle for political independence and the achievement of the modern state in Africa'.[40]

There can be no doubt that the expression of resistance to colonialism which characterised African writing in the period up to the 'seventies has strong and historical roots. We now celebrate African writers who for too long have been unread or unacknowledged. Sartre is characteristically brilliant in describing the reasons for this, implying, as he does so, the whole history of colonialism which sought to define the world in white terms, and opposition to which has produced instead a pluralist world view which we cannot but welcome as being long overdue:

> For the white man has enjoyed for three thousand years the privilege of seeing without being seen. . . . The white man, white because he was man . . . lighted like a torch all creation; he unfolded the essence, secret and white, of existence. Today these black men have fixed their gaze upon us and our gaze is thrown back in our eyes; black torches, in their turn, light the world.[41]

Notes

1. Albert Gérard, *Contexts of African Literature* (Amsterdam, 1990), p. 19.
2. H.R. Lynch, *Edward Wilmot Blyden – Pan-Negro Patriot* (Oxford, 1970), p. 1.
3. Edward W. Blyden, cited in C. Fyfe (ed.), *Christianity, Islam and the Negro Race* (Edinburgh, 1967), p. 337.
4. Paul Edwards and D. Dabydeen, *Black Writers in Britain 1760–1890* (Edinburgh, 1991), p. 208.
5. Christopher Fyfe (ed.), *Christianity, Islam and the Negro Race*, p. xii.
6. Edward W. Blyden, cited in C. Fyfe (ed.), *Christianity, Islam and the Negro Race*, pp. 150–1.
7. Ibid., p. 13.
8. Ibid., p. xii.
9. Judith Gleason, *This Africa* (Evanston, IL, 1965), p. xv.
10. A good example can be found in P. Edwards and David Dabydeen, *Black Writers in Britain 1760–1890*. This work draws attention to 'forgotten' but important and influential black writers, and has a very useful bibliography.
11. Ngugi wa Thiong'o, 'The African Writer and His Past', in Christopher Heywood (ed.), *Perspectives on African Literature* (London, 1971), p. 7.
12. See, for example, Clive Wake, 'The Political and Cultural Revolution', in Cosmo Pieterse and Donald Munro (eds), *Protest and Conflict in African Literature* (London, 1969). Wake says the 'poetry of pre-independence speaking Africa was not very good, nor was it very inspiring', and describes Ngugi as 'a young writer who has it in him to produce valuable work' (p. 49). Similarly, Eustace Palmer talks of Ngugi's 'apparent stylistic ineptitude' and thinks him 'modestly successful': *An Introduction to the African Novel* (New York, 1972), pp. 9–10.
13. Eustace Palmer, *An Introduction to the African Novel*, p. ix.
14. Ibid., p. 5.
15. J. Bardolph, 'East Africa', in Bruce King (ed.), *The Commonwealth Novel since 1960* (London, 1991), p. 50.
16. Ngugi, quoted in Robert Serumaga, 'A Mirror of Integration', in Cosmo Pieterse and Donald Munro (eds), *Protest and Conflict in African Literature*, p. 75.
17. Meneake Schipper, *Beyond the Boundaries: African Literature and Literary Theory* (London, 1989), p. 137.
18. O.F. Onoge, 'The Crisis of Consciousness in African Literature', in George M. Gugelberger (ed.), *Marxism and African Literature* (London, 1985), p. 36.
19. Ngugi wa Thiong'o, 'The Writer and His Past', in *Homecoming* (London, 1972), p. 46.

Meneake Schipper, *Beyond the Boundaries*, p. 137.

21. J. Bardolph, 'East Africa', pp. 52–3.
22. Eustace Palmer, *An Introduction to the African Novel*, p. 27.
23. Ngugi wa Thiong'o, *Detained: A Writer's Prison Diary* (London, 1981), p. xi.
24. Meneake Schipper, *Beyond the Boundaries*, p. 40.
25. D. Carter, book review, in E.D. Jones (ed.), *African Literature Today*, no. 5, 'The Novel in Africa' (London, 1971), p. 139.
26. Wole Soyinka, *Myth, Literature and the African World* (Cambridge, 1990), p. 118.
27. Ibid., p. 120.
28. Ibid., p. 121.
29. F.N. Chreachain-Adelugba, 'Self and Other in Sembene Ousmane's *Xala*', in K. Ogunbesan (ed.), *New West African Literature* (London, 1979), p. 102.
30. O.F. Onoge, 'The Crisis of Consciousness in African Literature', pp. 36–7.
31. Ibid., p. 39.
32. Abiola Irele, *The African Experience in Literature and Ideology* (London, 1981), p. 68.
33. Aerne Cesaire, *Return to My Native Land* (London, 1969), p. 76.
34. Leopold Sedan Senghor, 'L'Esthetique Negro-Africain', quoted in K. Awoonor, *The Breast of the Earth* (New York, 1976).
35. Kofi Awoonor, *The Breast of the Earth*, p. 154.
36. L.S. Senghor, in J. Reed and C. Wake (eds), *Prose and Poetry* (Oxford, 1965), p. 39.
37. Ibid., p. 157.
38. A. Irele, *The African Experience*, pp. 70–1.
39. K. Awoonor, *The Breast of the Earth*, p. 158.
40. Lewis Nkosi, *Tasks and Masks: Themes and Styles of African Literature* (London, 1981), p. 1.
41. Jean-Paul Sartre, *Black Orpheus*, trans. S.W. Allen (Paris, n.d.), pp. 7–8.

8 Writing, literacy and history in Africa

Gareth Griffiths

During 1993 the Program of African Studies Seminar at Northwestern University in the United States announced that its theme would be Material Inscription in African Cultures. The choice of theme for this internationally renowned seminar was clearly designed to address the fact that in 1993 we needed to be reminded that for the majority of people in Africa writing has never been the principal means of expression or communication, and that many other forms of material inscription, such as in ritual, dance, communal performance, sculpture, carving, dying, weaving, and ceramics, would take precedence over writing in any comprehensive historical description of African culture. This truth makes it even more significant that in the contemporary representation of Africa a concern with written inscription has been so dominant.

Although almost all accounts of African cultures insist on the importance of oral culture, and insist on its equal status in an abstract sense, there is little doubt that for all practical purposes the oral has been displaced by the written in the majority of texts concerned with African culture written in the last twenty years. This, despite the fact that for the vast majority of the people of Africa literacy is still an unachieved ideal, and that for most African people the oral world of speech and of non-written cultural exchange is the world they inhabit on a daily basis. In fact, even within the sphere of writing itself, the principal contemporary concern with writing can be seen to be mainly with writing in ex-colonial languages, not the writing which has developed since the seventh century in African languages.[1] The earlier attempts of Jahnheinz Jahn and Albert Gérard to promote the study of African literatures as the integrated study of writing in both African indigenous languages and in ex-colonial languages seem to be less and less in evidence. Even where they exist, they form only a small part of the contemporary criticism and scholarship lavished on anglophone, francophone, and, to a far lesser extent, reflecting its relative decline in status as a world language in the twentieth century, lusophone writing in Africa.[2]

The politics implicit in this situation is evident. The displacement indicates the degree to which the new cultural elite of Africa has been hybridised by several centuries of Euro-American contact. It indicates, too, perhaps, that the impact of concepts of the modern are bound up in contemporary Africa with the privileging of modes of written inscription over alternative inscriptive modes, or over a recognition of the continuing importance of oral communication in the lives of most Africans. The emphasis on writing as an essential feature of modernisation is also bound up with the access written forms give to the 'world languages' of the ex-colonial powers. Thus even the work of the consciously nationalistic and decolonising African critics such as Chinweizu in Nigeria or Ngugi in Kenya are concerned not with the recovery of the oral but with its transmission into the contemporary forms of African writing. On the other end of the same continuum the popular contemporary oral forms are turning to the modern high-tech inscriptive modes of television and film for their new lease of life. It is to television, for example, that the popular folk-opera troupes (themselves, it is worth noting, relatively recent hybridised forms) of Western Nigeria have turned for a financially viable contemporary outlet. It is in popular television series and programmes that you will find the most extensive use of traditional story or of fable, and the most widespread use of indigenous languages in contemporary representations of Africa in countries such as Nigeria. It seems unlikely that even the most strenuous and politically correct revaluation of the hierarchy of contemporary communicative modes such as that implicitly sought by the Northwestern programme is likely in the near future to alter this as a contemporary sociological condition governing the representation of African culture and African peoples. For obvious reasons the drive to literacy and to modern mass-communication systems both in African languages and, even more, in the languages of the ex-colonising powers is a leading part of the programme of most contemporary African nations who seek modernisation as a necessary precondition to international economic and political recognition and to the fiscal development support which this entails. Language in the form of writing, literacy and modern mass-media communication is, in this respect as in many others, bound up with contemporary social conditions and with the power relations they represent. For this reason it is worth looking briefly at the history of literacy, and of writing, and the ways in which it has developed in an intimate way with the power relations of African cultures and the various cultural forces acting upon these cultures from the seventh century to the present day.

African cultures had not, prior to the first sustained incursions of Arab cultures into the Maghreb from the seventh to the eleventh centuries, and into the regions of sub-Saharan West Africa and Eastern Africa from the eleventh to the fourteenth centuries, developed extensive written systems, with the notable exceptions of those of Ancient Egypt, and of the Nilotic and Ethiopian regions (which had received earlier Arab influences from the Yemen region leading to the development of the Ge'ez and old Amharic scripts and literatures).[3] Most linguists and anthropologists agree that the few proto-alphabets which existed prior to the introduction of the Arabic script in these areas were employed mainly as a form of mnemonic in sacred inscriptions. The absence of writing, the form of material cultural inscription dominant in the invasive cultures of both the Arab/Islamic and Euro/Christian incursions, is of great significance in shaping the perceptions of Africa and its people from the earliest times, and in beginning the long process of constructing them under signs of primitiveness, culturelessness, historylessness and so forth, as well as under such potent binarisms as black/white, 'pagan'/civilised etc. This process has recently been related solely to the processes of nineteenth- and twentieth-century colonialism and the discursive regimes it set in place, but it must surely be seen to precede these in many significant ways. Vitally important though the history of colonisation since the European expansion of the fifteenth to twentieth centuries has been, the stress on this has tended to deny Africa its much longer pre-European and pre-colonial history.

The association of Africa with Arabic culture and with the cultural forms which accompanied the introduction of the Muslim religion into many areas of East and West Africa from the eleventh to the fourteenth century, an influence which has continued to the present day, is of at least as much significance in the privileging of certain cultural forms over others, and in the beginnings of processes of self-construction and self-representation for the peoples of these regions. Arabic and Muslim culture, it should be recalled, laid as much stress on the importance of writing as did the Judeo-Christian strand of European culture when this became part of the construction of European cultural patterns in the post-classical period. The Arabs see themselves, together with the Jews and Christians, as part of a unique group, the people of the book (*ahl al Kitāb*), to whom the revelation of God has been entrusted through the prophets, and so the idea of the stability of the sacred material inscription of writing is central to their conception of cultural worth. The encounter with peoples who did not have even the limited access to the word of God that the earlier prophets Moses and Jesus had provided in their incomplete and unsuccessful earlier revelations leading up to the final revelation of the Quran was a central feature of the encounter of the Arab invaders, especially after the domination by the end of the tenth century of the orthodox Malikite school of Sunnite Islam across most of the Maghreb. This orthodox form was that which was dominant in the influence on the Western Sudan from then onwards too. In East Africa the intercourse of peoples seems to have been much more restricted, with the Muslim presence being confined for longer to the settlement of the coasts, though in the north of the region a long development of the Afro-Arabic coastal cultures and the hybrid languages they developed (*ki-swahi*) led to a substantial cultural colonisation of the interior, as it did in areas such as Mozambique and Zimbabwe in the south where there was also a strong cultural influence on the peoples and cultures of the interior.[4] Even in the southernmost regions of East Africa where the society of the coastal cities was doubtless Islamic but not Arabic, the classic feature of Islamicisation that lasted historically was the veneration of the written word, which persisted even where there are traces neither of any Islamic institutions nor of mosques.[5]

Thus it can be seen how, to the Arab invasive influence as much as to the modern Christian invasive influence, the idea of the written text represented a fundamental sign of superior cultural value and identity. The Arab cultures of the East African littoral, and of the sub-Saharan Sudanese kingdoms stressed the importance of the text in identifying the Muslim from the indigenous peoples in ways significantly like later European practice, but since the bulk of the contact in the Western Sudan was through trade rather than through conquest in the traditional sense, and through the conversion of the merchant classes and eventually the rulers of important empires, such as medieval Mali, Bornu-Kanem etc., rather than through a military consolidation of trade,[6] the nature of the Arab relationship with the African peoples is distinctive from that of the nineteenth-century European colonisers in a number of important respects. Nevertheless, the idea of writing and of literacy as a sign of social distinction and worth as well as a means to political power clearly did have a strong role in effecting the assimilation of the peoples of Africa to a different religion and culture in the period of Arab influence, as in the later period of European influence and colonial domination. Despite differences between the processes in East and West Africa, in both those regions the test of social standing and power was not strictly one of blood or race, but rather of culture, and the test of this was having entered the world of writing through which alone the word could be perceived and understood.[7] Commenting on this process in the Western Sudan, I. Hrbek notes that within the Sudanic kingdoms of medieval Africa,

> one of the great problems of the imperial rulers was how to secure the allegiance of other subjected pagan clans and peoples which possessed totally different ancestor and land cults from those of the ruling dynasty. A universal religion such as Islam seemed to offer a suitable solution; an effort was made to implant it at least among the heads of other lineages and clans and to establish a new common religious bond. The increasing extent of the empires made the effective administration of the realm more complicated; in this respect the help of Muslim scribes, and other literate persons was indispensable for correspondence and the control of state affairs. The influence of Muslim clerics at the courts must have been great, thus preparing the ground for the conversion of the ruler and his family.[8]

Of course, for the majority of people the acts of writing and reading would be performed for them by a special class, by the mullah or priest, and in this respect the situation is not so different today. What is crucial is not the possession of writing by the bulk of the individuals in a society but its privileging over other forms of communicative means as a distinguishing feature of the cultural and political elite. An examination of the process by which this group effected an Islamicisation of these societies (and the degree to which, despite Islam's formal claims to be a brotherhood of believers beyond cultural difference, this involved an Arabisation of these cultures) shows a fascinating parallel with the later processes by which European cultures and religons effected purchase on the societies of Africa, and tends to give the lie to the simplistic assertions that Islam is 'African' in some more authentic sense than the later hybrid acculturalisations associated with African Christianity. Thus one scholar remarks:

it was normal, at the outset, for educated Malinke, Fulani, Soninke, Berbers or Negro-Berbers . . . to think in Arabic, write in Arabic and produce commentaries on books belonging to the Islamic tradition. This Islamo-centrism no doubt made the universities of Timbuktu seem less brilliant than black Africans today would wish, as they can discern in these universities, as far as present knowledge goes, hardly a trace of their cultural past. This being so, there is only one comment to be made: the Muslim scholars belonged to a fairly closed world and were still a minority group facing a mass of adherents of African traditional religion, whom they thought themselves duty bound to convert and perhaps to guide towards other styles of life: thus they were not predisposed to become enlightened historians of the African past or even sympathetic observers of the life of the autochthonous societies which they considered to be 'pagan'.[9]

Significantly, too, as both Dramani-Issifou and Hrbek have noted, the successful spread of Islam depended on the development both of a sense of the higher qualities of civilisation implicit in the Arab world, that is to say an Arabisation of African cultures among the ruling and administrative classes,[10] and the emergence of a

class of learned Muslim scholars and clerics of Sudanese origin . . . as an important event in the history of Islam in Africa south of the Sahara. It meant that from then on Islam was propagated and spread by authochthons armed with the knowledge of local languages, customs and beliefs; this knowledge facilitated their missionary work and assured them a greater success than that obtained by their North African co-religionists in earlier times. In the eyes of the Africans Islam ceased to be the religion of white expatriates and, because it was now carried by Africans themselves, it became an African religion.[11]

Although this is, as Dramani-Issifou admits, a contentious and problematic area, open to wide and biased levels of interpretation in the absence of really effective sources, one cannot help but be struck by the degree of similarity between these scholarly accounts of the spread of Islam and Arabic culture and those of the later European colonisers. Both have writing at their centre, and the script is the ultimate tool of conquest – as mastery of it is of acceptance by the conqueror. For this reason the control of the patronage of writing has been a powerful and recurring weapon in African history from the earliest times, and it has involved the development of special classes of people who have acted as translators/cultural transmitters and who have facilitated the hybridisation of the indigenous cultures.

The positive benefit of the Islamic invasions in offering not only the language of Arabic as a communicative mode but also the script as a tool for the consolidation of a widespread and effective lingua franca in East Africa (Ki-Swahili) created from a fusion of Arabic and the various Afro-Arabic coastal languages and for the writing down in West Africa of such indigenous languages as Fulani and Wolof, needs to be noted. The *ajami* writings which resulted (writing which used Arabic orthography to write down African languages) were an important feature of the literary output of both East and West Africa. In East Africa, they took the form both of Ki-Swahili texts and the use of Arabic script to create a body of indigenous texts in the local languages in places such as Madagascar. In West Africa, after the first exclusive use of Arabic script for Arabic writing there developed numerous examples of the use of Arabic script to develop a writing system for local languages such as Wolof and Fulani.[12] Again, one detects similarities in this process to the impact in the nineteenth century of the missionaries of Christianity (especially in its Bible-centred Protestant forms) who not only introduced the Bible in direct translation but also undertook the task of transcribing the indigenous languages into European orthographies and of compiling dictionaries and grammars, to facilitate the teaching of their converts, a process which led to the rapid development of writing in those languages, mainly sacred and devotional in form. As in the case of the Islamic process detailed above, the personnel of this venture rapidly expanded to include indigenous converts such as the famous Samuel (Ajayi) Crowther, the first black African bishop.[13]

At a later date, when Europeans first encountered Africans in large numbers with the development of the West African slave trade in the eighteenth century (just as when the Arabs first encountered the Berbers of North Africa, the people of the East African littoral and, later, the peoples of the Western Sudan), it is significant that the implicit test of the absence of civilisation was the lack of an effective writing system. Without this sign of inscriptive permanence the complex and subtle oral cultures of the region were rapidly discounted and overlooked in favour of the cultural values carried along as baggage by the inscriptive forms of the invasive cultures.[14] It was the absence of writing which, for both major invasive influences on indigenous African cultures (Arab/Islamic and Euro/Christian), served to justify the development of theories of racial and cultural superiority. Likewise, when the slaves who were taken to Europe and America became the privileged playthings of their liberal masters, and were taught the European arts, it was their unexpected ability to master the art of writing which was seen as the principal sign of their educability and of their possession of a soul. The literary texts produced by the slaves who were taught to read and write English, such as Olaudah Equiano or Phyllis Wheatley, served to confirm both the possibility of salvation for African peoples and, ironically, to confirm the distance that the bulk of Africans needed to travel in order to be available for salvation. Writing and its acquisition became the marker both of the possibility of her/his assimilation to the civilised world and of the Africans' difference, which made such a process of salvation both necessary and justifiable.

In the late eighteenth and nineteenth centuries the patronage of writing and of literacy as a device for conversion and salvation lay not in the hands of enlightened individual slave-owners, but was institutionalised under the great Protestant missionary societies which developed along with the anti-slavery movement, and which laid central emphasis on the provision of the scriptures to the pagan peoples they sought to convert. The early pre-colonial Catholic missionary attempts, which had signal success elsewhere, did not have much success in sub-Saharan Africa. Thus, for example, the Portuguese, to whom West and South Africa was the first leg of their explorations and eastern expansion, did not have the same success in these regions that they did in South and South-East Asia, and in East Asia. There is no African equivalent to Alexander de Rhodes or to Francis Xavier. Yet arguments of proximity would make one wonder why. So would the seemingly commonsense notion that where no organised and stable large-scale religious movements existed prior to the missionaries' arrival, the task would prove easier. In fact this was not so. Apart from the fact that Africa did not represent such a rich field for commercial exploitation in this period and so was a less glittering prize (the Portuguese desire was, in the first instance, for the spices of the East rather than the slaves or even the gold of West Africa), it is worth speculating that it may well have been more difficult for missions to function in a region which had no directly comparable if different cultural infrastructure and inscriptive hierarchy. Thus, in Thailand or Macao for de Rhodes or in South-West India, China, or Japan for Xavier and his fellow Jesuits, the difficulties lay in penetrating and subverting a system which despite its differences was, at least, recognisable to them. These were civilisations erected, before all else, on writing and on bodies of decipherable scriptures and texts. In Africa the absence of a cultural text recognisable as such to the European invaders meant that there was no group which could be easily 'converted' by a process of cultural transposition, that is by the supplanting of one such 'text' by another. If this precluded the granting to the religions of Africa the status of alternative (if inadequate) religious revelations, accorded by even nineteenth-century Christians to Islam, Hinduism, Buddhism, Taoism etc. (analogous with the Arab construction of earlier cultures such as Judaism and Christianity as inadequate forms awaiting completion by the seal of the prophet, Muhammed), it also made it difficult to identify how these almost unrecognisable, unwritten cultural forms could be effectively opposed or overcome.[15] As with the Arabs so with the new invasive cultures, the process required the development of an autochthonous class who could form an effective invasive bridge between the pre-written cultures and those of the proselytising culture. In China or in India such a class could be brought into being by the subversion of existing literate classes. In Africa such a class first had to be created via the processes of literacy education. As an example, the penetration of West Africa by the missionary societies was effected finally by the classic agent of change, the dispossessed intellectual, creolised by education. The role conditions requisite for this figure were not those of a convert alone. What was required first was the creation of the pre-conditions for the emergence of a literate cultural 'elite'. Only such a created group could be successfully allied to the inscriptive and communicative forms of the dominant culture by education. Education into literacy was the pre-condition of conversion for this crucial first generation of autochthonous Christians, as it was for the first generation of African Muslim converts. The figure of Samuel (Ajayi) Crowther, first student to be admitted to the College at Fourah Bay in Sierra Leone, founded by the Church Missionary Society in 1827, was the earliest of these local figures in West Africa. In order for a subversion to occur, the Christian missionaries, like their Islamic precursors, had first to create the conditions for the dominance of their text over alternative modes of inscription; they had to create an African class who *could* be converted in a meaningful sense by being taught to acknowledge the intrinsic superiority of the new inscriptive modes over those of the indigenous cultures. For this reason, literacy education became the primary means by which the Christian missions sought to effect change and set up the conditions for conversion, unconsciously echoing the processes of their Islamic precursors some eight centuries earlier. From the nineteenth century until well into the 1940s the missionary societies were not only the dominant educative force in establishing literacy in Africa, but also the major patrons of writing and the written text.

From the beginning of what, rather ironically, perhaps, we have to recognise is a concept of history limited by our dominant contemporary notion of culture as coterminous with written records, the written text is implicated in the process of effecting cultural and political change: the act of writing is indissoluble from the act of social control that it brings about. At the same time, the establishment of writing as the dominant mode and the literate class as its transmitters creates the possibility for a re-appropriation of the techniques of writing and reading to an oppositional mode. As in so many of the features of colonialism, the processes of change and influence can run both ways. While the bulk of the new writing produced in the scripts and forms provided by the missionaries of both Islam and Christianity is sacred, and devotional, fixed and conservative in character, as has been noted, there are a number of ways in which these texts, by the complex process of ambivalence and mimicry[16] implicit in all dominating invasive discourse, begin to construct the possibility for the dismantling of that dependent position which defines them as objects of the discourse.

It is easier to indicate, however inadequately and sketchily, how this might be so in obviously dominating and hierarchised modes of cultural exchange such as slavery (or even of religious conversion), where the precondition within which the relationship defines itself is the unquestioned superiority of the dominator over the dominated. It is harder, but perhaps even more crucial, to see how this process continues even in more liberal enterprises such as in the development of secular educational systems and in contemporary publishing ventures.

I have said that the mission presses were the dominant publishers of texts in Africa until the 1940s. I have also noted that if the ideal goal was general literacy, in practice, the pre-condition for successful conversion was the creation of a specialist class of literate Africans. This group could both serve as the conduit for the transmission of sacral texts and dogma and, equally important, though less obviously, embody a living proof of the power and prestige acquirable by the mastery of the communicative mode of writing in the place of other earlier forms of inscription. These figures, from African bishops such as Crowther, to local priests and lay catechists, litter the landscape of African culture in the nineteenth and twentieth centuries. They are frequently the fathers of the current generation of secular writers (for example, Achebe), or are figures who articulate crucial tropes in the negotiation of relations between the past and present modes of culture vying for the contemporary African space in literary texts (for example, the Professor in Soyinka's *The Road* (1965)). They represent the pre-conditions for the emergence of the present elite of secular African intellectuals whose dominant inscriptive mode is writing. The emergence of this group is illustrated by the alliance which can be traced between the missionary presses of the 1930s and 1940s and the emergent intellectuals of modern Africa. For example, the publications of the United Society for Christian Literature include both texts by figures who continued to ally themselves with the missions and missionaries and those by intellectuals from whom the new generation of independence leaders and fighters were to emerge; for example, the Ghanaian leader J.B. Danquah,[17] who later died in a colonial prison during the struggle for independence, or Jomo Kenyatta,[18] the political leader of the Mau-Mau Liberation Movement and the first President of independent Kenya. These figures were not only educated by the missions but were also dependent upon their presses to achieve the status of print at all. That this resulted in tensions can be seen from the disclaimer which the missionary publishers inserted as a preamble to the Africa's Own Library series which was published in the 1940s and which includes the Kenyatta text mentioned above:

> This series is designed primarily to introduce books written by African authors who, as far as possible, are left to express their own views in their own words. The society cannot always guarantee the accuracy of what is written nor necessarily associate itself with all the views expressed. The desire is to afford a medium whereby Africans may give, to us and to their fellows, the benefit of African knowledge and opinion. The society is always ready to consider appropriate material.

The liberal desire to be seen to be the people who were bringing to Africans the ability to speak was constrained by the desire to guide and shape what would be spoken, and by the slow realisation that this was not possible or even, the liberal conscience insisted, desirable in terms of the stated aims of equality before Christ and respect for cultural difference. In the case of the text by Kenyatta referred to here, the ethnographic descriptive text favoured by early missionaries as part of the process of enculturing the primitive people by enabling them to study their own cultures and valorise them within a suitable denigratory hierarchy of implicit alternatives is now available for subtle subversion as when, as in this case, it becomes the means to insist on the re-inscription of the history of the colonised written out of the record by colonial historical mythography. As the disclaimer's ambivalent tone suggests, this new liberty provoked equally complex reactions in the missionary bodies themselves by the late 1940s. Similar complex relations can be seen in the early literary texts published under missionary control, or by educational institutions and publishers with strong missionary connections; for example, in the Danquah text referred to here, in earlier texts such as Thomas Mofolo's *Chaka*[19] or in what is almost certainly the earliest African novel in English, published by an African born on the continent and not transported as a slave, Joseph J. Walters' *Guanya Pau*.[20]

Albert Gérard has recorded how, through the 1920s and 1930s, in line with the educational policy which flowed from the Lugardian theory of indirect rule, the colonial administrations in anglophone Africa sought to establish organisations which would encourage the spread of literacy in the indigenous African languages. Thus he describes how in Northern Nigeria Rupert East was deputed in the 1920s to set up a Translation Bureau which, as well as supervising the translation of school-texts into Hausa, broadened its scope to publish two books dealing with the history and customs of the Hausa and their neighbours. This ampler scope became formalised when the institution was turned into a Literature Bureau, which was situated in Zaria, and which deliberately tried to foster Hausa creative writing in the Roman script (Gérard, 1981, p. 62). The task, as seen by people like East, was not just to get the younger educated Hausa intellectual to write in a script accessible to and compatible with the systems of the European colonial power, but to persuade her/him to move away from the traditional conservative forms and to write prose fiction on the Western model. As East saw it, in a piece replete with the racial and cultural assumptions of the period, the difficulty was that

> The influence of Islam, superimposed on the Hamitic strain in the blood of the Northern Nigerian, produces an extremely serious-minded type of person. The art of writing, moreover, being intimately connected in his mind with his religion, is not to be treated lightly. . . . To these

people, therefore, the idea of writing a book which was frankly intended neither for edification of the mind, nor the good of the soul, a story book which, however, followed none of the prescribed forms of story-telling, seemed very strange. . . . In short, it was necessary to explain to a very conservative audience a conception which was entirely new, and of doubtful value if not morality.[21]

There can be no clearer example of how the use of writing and the forms associated with its cultural origins have the profoundest effects on the values, social function and aesthetic structures of the texts they produce, and how these in their turn can never hope to be innocent of a further consequence in shaping and re-shaping the society they claim, with equal innocence, to represent.

So far, the examples of influence and patronage discussed can be seen to belong to periods when African cultures were under overt forms of control through directly invasive influence, and so may seem to be of a totally different character from the control exercised by the dominant patronage systems for writing in the post-Independence period. However, it is important to show how the patronage exercised by those who controlled access to publication through the post-war period and after the political independence of many of the African nations in the late-1950s and 1960s continued to influence the nature and content of writing in Africa. Thus, if we consider the relationship between overseas publishers and the varying markets for texts in Africa created by the educational policies inherited from the colonial period we may be able to begin to construct a historiography of writing in post-Independence Africa which gives a proper place to these processes of control in the construction of the form and content of many contemporary African texts. To concentrate, as an example, on the anglophone literary texts of West and East Africa it can be noted how in anglophone cultures (where the educational system of the colonial period had stressed education in both the indigenous and colonial languages, and in which the secondary schools were designed to feed tertiary institutions which continued the education of the African elite *inside* the country, at least to the end of the undergraduate level of study), a growing market was created after Independence in countries such as Ghana, Nigeria, Kenya etc., for locally produced texts which reflected the new interests and concerns of the post-colonial cultures.

Such models emerged, of course, as African writers responded to the need to redress and reassert the past in their own terms. The classic Nigerian text in this case is Chinua Achebe's *Things Fall Apart* (1958).

Achebe has described in various places how he was led to write this text, at least in part, in response to the inadequacies of the colonial white texts describing his culture and its past; notably, the bathetic representation of Africans and African culture in Joyce Cary's *Mister Johnson* (1939).[22] But there is, of course, a sense in which the Achebe text, liberating though its form and content are in formal and thematic terms *vis-à-vis* the earlier white textual representations of African culture, might also function repressively, in so far as it became the definitive template for the establishment of a generation of contact novels whose market was the new educational system, hungry for local texts, and whose controlling agent of supply was the foreign publishing giant, Heinemann.[23] The role of Heinemann and, to a lesser extent, Longman at a later date with its Drumbeat series, in this process, echoing the earlier functions of the great imperial publishing cartels earlier in the century, was in many ways a consciously liberal one. The long-term consequences of these ventures were in no sense intended. Yet, in a sense, the process parallels the problems and difficulties that the missionary ventures of the 1920s, 1930s and 1940s faced. The Heinemann African Writers' series, for example, both established African writing in English (and in French for an English audience) in a useful and significant way while simultaneously creating the genres and forms which then became established as characteristic and representative of contemporary African writing. Like the efforts of the early Literature Bureaux of the colonial period, it could be said that the series created the thing it claimed to have been designed to serve.

The process of commissioning works led to a standardisation of theme and form, a standardisation which can be seen at its worst in the derivative texts of someone like T.M. Aluko, and at its best in the rather more original reworkings of the themes and periodisations of the role-model writer (and first editor of the series) Chinua Achebe, in the work of a writer like Amadi or, in East Africa, of Ngugi. The fact that the themes and forms were so readily translatable across the huge gulf of geography and culture from West to East Africa in a way which allowed and, in a sense, encouraged the direct influence of the Achebe model on the early work of Ngugi is fascinating evidence of the power of the cultural template as it reflected the perceptions of the publisher and general editor as to what was or was not appropriate African content and form. What is so significant is how this perception was able to override and overdetermine the huge historical and cultural differences within the regions and locales the texts sought to represent in a way acceptable to both the local educational market and to the world audience.[24] That this process was, to a large extent, unconscious, both driven by the market demands of the education system, and impelled by the liberal desire to proselytise the exciting new developments in contemporary African writing in the most praiseworthy way (within the normal motivation of a fair profit to justify the venture) does not wipe out the degree of influence such a series had in shaping the very nature of writing in English in Africa from 1958 until the 1980s. Indeed the influence is still present, though fading as the growth of the market for educational and popular literature strengthens the possibilities for locally owned publishing ventures to find a viable audience for their products.[25] The relative lack of success of the equivalent Heinemann Caribbean series may reflect the fact that most of the Caribbean writers were resident in London (as Kenneth Ramchand's foundation study notes[26]) and so had a direct uncontrolled access to the competing range of publishers available there. Significantly, most of the texts in this series were reprints, whereas the texts in the Heinemann African Writers series were usually original texts, and often, in the early days, commissioned works. In a number of significant ways, a series such as Heinemann African Writers' created much of the contemporary anglophone literature in Africa, and it did so to service a secular market, that of education, which had as its motivating ideology the modernisation of African culture, just as the missionary venture had had Christianisation as its motivation. In this respect, despite the differences of goal and intention, the role of the liberal educational publishers of the 1960s, 1970s and 1980s is uncomfortably close in a number of respects to that of the missionary presses and to the government Literature Bureaux of the colonial period. In fact, it is arguable that their almost exclusive concentration on writing in the ex-colonial languages and seeming lack of interest in commissioning translations of works originally written in the indigenous languages, at least until the recent publication by Heinemann of the self-translations of Ngugi's later texts written in Gikuyu,[27] makes the output of such publishers, in certain respects, as directive and invasive as that of the missionary presses and the colonial publishing institutions.

The point of making such a comparison is not to be provocative nor destructive of the important gains that resulted from these ventures for the development of writing in English in many parts of Africa. It is not to score some point in a fruitless contest of political correctness and moral superiority. The forces that construct and determine cultural activities are the product of the conditions prevailing at the time, and they are to be judged by the values and motives of that time, if they are to be judged at all. The point of suggesting the importance of analysing such forces is to suggest that the contemporary control of writing and literacy through the institutions of the education system and through the infrastructure of the international publishing cartels needs to be made part of any account of the shaping historiography of writing in contemporary Africa. It is also to indicate the need to see these contemporary ventures much more clearly as a modern instance of a much older, characteristic feature of African cultural relations with the outside world since the earliest foreign incursions on the continent. It is, if you like, the last chapter of the long story of the means by which Africa has been persuaded to represent itself, at least in its elite modes, in 'written' rather than 'oral' forms, and in the scripts and genres of the invasive cultures rather than in those of the indigenous cultures which preceded them. These processes of inter-cultural contact and conflict have been both positive and negative in their overall effect, but they cannot be neglected or overlooked in seeking to understand how writing, literacy and history have been interwoven in constructing the conditions which have determined the development of the representation of African cultures.

Notes

1. References are given in the European form of tenth century AD, although for the Arab world which dates its history from the Hegira, or emigration of Mohammed and his followers from Mecca to Medina (622 AD), the tenth century AD is the fourth century, and so on.

2. This is not to say, of course, that this is how things should be, nor to deny the fact that African scholars continue to make immense efforts to provide expert and effective accounts of indigenous language writing. But, despite these elements and the fact that publishing has been on the increase in African languages in recent years, Albert Gérard's 1981 plea in the lecture 'Linguistics and the Emergence of Vernacular Writing' for an extension of the work needed in both translating and commenting on the large body of work in African indigenous languages has not been met, and is still outpaced by the many commentaries on the literature in the ex-colonial languages published each year. On the other hand, the redress of this situation cannot be in terms of a refusal to engage in debates about African writing in English, or in French etc. Arguably, the rivalry centring

on fruitless issues of political correctness needs to yield to a more generous extension of funds for scholarship in the areas less likely to be sustainable by publishers relying on the existing market for texts, commentaries, and histories of the literatures and texts in the ex-colonial languages.

3. See, for example, Albert Gérard's *African Language Literatures: An Introduction to the Literary History of Sub-Saharan Africa* (London, 1981), pp. 7–21, and the essay 'Fifteen Centuries of Creative Writing in Black Africa' in his *Contexts of African Literature* (Amsterdam, 1990), pp. 47–60.

4. For a fuller account of the complex nature of the spread of Islam into Africa, see M. Elfasi and I. Hrbek (eds), *Africa from the Seventh to the Eleventh Century*, vol. III, Unesco General History of Africa.

5. For an account of this process, see I. Hrbek, 'Stages in the Development of Islam and its Dissemination', in M. Elfasi and I. Hrbek (eds), *Africa from the Seventh to the Eleventh Century*, vol. III, pp. 88–90.

6. The Islamic invasion is, in some respects, a mirror-image of the European in that it begins in the Maghreb from the seventh century as a military venture which is then consolidated by trade. Likewise, in its expansion into the Western Sudan where, after the conquest of medieval Ghana by Abu Bakr in the second half of the twelfth century and the subsequent failure of this military incursion, it is by trade and missionary (*marabout*) proselytisers that Islam continues to spread and consolidate itself.

7. The practice of laying claim to 'Arab' or 'Yemeni' descent is, as various commentators have noted, a recurring feature of Sudanic praise poetry and the dynastic legitimacy claims of its rulers as late as the nineteenth century. For an extreme example, see A. Gérard, *African Language Literatures* (p. 51), where in a praise poem by Bauba Jariida the Fulani lord Ahidjo is described as the handsome European from Garwa and as the white Arab, while in a poem by Moody Yaawa the Fulani claim to superiority, based on Arab racial purity, over Southern black pagans and their culture is a marked feature of the text. Elsewhere Gérard notes (p. 77) that even in Islamic cultures such as Madagascar, where the racial origin of the earliest of the Malagasy peoples is probably Indonesian, the tendency to legitimise Islamic cultural rulers by claiming Arabian origin persists: [a Malagasy manuscript] 'recounts the arrival of one Ramakararube, coming from Mecca in search of a suitable settlement and thus introducing Islam, allegedly in 1164 (AH 542) – as is usual in non-Arab Muslim countries, the leading clans are in the habit of claiming Meccan descent'.

8. I. Hrbek, 'Stages in the development of Islam and its dissemination', p. 76.

9. Z. Dramani-Issifou, 'Islam as a Social System in Africa since the Seventh Century', in M. Elfasi and I. Hrbek (eds), *Africa from the Seventh to the Eleventh Century*, vol. III, p. 112.

10. Ibid., pp. 112–15.
11. I. Hrbek, 'Stages in the Development of Islam and its Dissemination', p. 78.
12. Significantly, in these areas where *ajami* script was in use the first Christian missionaries prioritised the attempt to convert the people to the use of a romanised rather than an arabic script to write the indigenous languages with varying degrees of success. What is significant about this is how it stresses both the practical political importance of controlling writing in a form more easily accessible to the owners of political power, and the symbolic weight given to the idea of the sign for language in its written form being one identified with the invasive culture concerned. It is a significant modification within the anglophonic colonial culture's policy of indirect rule and the maintenance of indigenous cultures.
13. See, for example, A. Gérard, 'Linguistics and the Emergence of Vernacular Writing', p. 62 *et passim*.
14. The term 'invasive culture' is used rather than invasion culture, since the process was never simply one of direct military conquest in either case. Some recent historians have argued that it was hardly so at all in the case of the Arab/Islamic intervention in many regions of sub-Saharan Africa, and that in the case of the European/Christian intervention at least, it was not predominantly so in the early period of the encounter. In both cases it was rather an incursion of small groups of private merchants who, in conjunction with local rulers, consolidated trading and slaving networks and then through exploration, infiltration and missionary activity (amateur and professional) sought to consolidate this influence and establish settlements and permanent spheres of influence. That in the period from about the 1870s onwards in the case of the European powers the character of the process changed radically to one of direct military conquest and the imposition of colonial governments of expatriates is, of course, a crucial difference, and one which underpins contemporary recuperations of Islam as a more African religion and culture than Christianity. But both ventures share at different stages this more complex and arguably more important and influential mercantile and cultural invasive process in which the power of writing played a crucial role in defining the power relations which prevailed and the discursive regimes within which people were constituted and represented. Of course, the history of Southern Africa differs in a number of crucial respects in the substantive forms and in the implemental timetable of these processes, and it needs to be treated separately in ways beyond the scope of this chapter.
15. As A. Gérard has noted, the two early Catholic attempts at a catechism in the Kongo language (produced in 1556 and 1624) failed to generate any further creative activity: *Contexts of African Literature*, p. 62.

16. The implication of the subversive possibility of colonialist discourse in its mimicry of the discourse to which it is constructed as enabling 'other' is, of course, central to many recent critical texts; notably those of the critic Homi Bhabha.

17. Joseph B. Danquah, *The Third Woman: A Play in Five Acts* (London, 1943).

18. Jomo Kenyatta, *My People of Kikuyu and the Life of Chief Wangome*, Africa's Own Library, no. 1 (London, 1944).

19. Thomas Mofolo, *Chaka: An Historical Romance* (London, 1931). The text was, of course, developed when Mofolo had a close association with the missionary system of patronage.

20. Joseph Walters, *Guanya Pau: A Story of an African Princess* (Cleveland, OH, 1891). For an account of this remarkable early African English text, see John Victor Singler, 'The Day Will Come: J.J. Walters and Guanya Pau', *Liberian Studies Journal* vol. XV, no. 2 (1990).

21. Rupert E. East, 'A First Essay in Imaginative African Literature', *Africa*, vol. IX (1936), iii, pp. 350–7: quoted in A. Gérard, *African Language Literatures*, p. 63.

22. Abdul R. JanMahomed has likewise illustrated how this intertextual relationship works and the nature of its complex reflexivities: *Manichaean Aesthetics: The Politics of Writing in Colonial Africa* (Amherst, MA, 1983).

23. For an interesting and rather self-flattering account of this process and the Heinemann involvement in it, see 'Playing Midwife to Genius', *New Africa* (August 1992), pp. 38–9.

24. Significantly, in the *New Africa* article above, Sir Alan Hill notes that 'I remember Fred Warburg [of Secker and Warburg] telling me that Tutuola's *The Palm Wine Drinkard* (1952) was the only sort of African book that he would want on his list as "it represented the real Africa". For this very reason Tutuola's work was anathema to many educated Nigerians – to whom his linguistic virtuosity seemed plain illiteracy.' The article continues: 'In contrast here was a polished work from a completely unknown author. "In *Things Fall Apart* we now had something entirely new from Africa", Hill remembers, "a novel which affirmed permanent human values; and which expressed those values in terms which the Western-educated reader could understand".' The irony of this observation which implicitly enshrines an alternative view of what 'ought' to represent Africa is self-evident. It is also interesting to wonder if, measured by the criteria implicit here, not only Tutuola but all the more recent texts which seek actively to reflect and employ oral cultural forms, such as Syl Cheney-Coker's *The Last Harmattan of Alusine Dunbar* (1990) or Ben Okri's *The Famished Road* (1991), would have been unacceptable to the autochthonous intellectuals and overseas publishers

dominating the scene in the 1960s and 1970s. Indeed, what would have been the fate of Ngugi had he offered Heinemann *Matagari* in 1964, rather than *Weep Not Child* with its acceptable theme and its title from Walt Whitman echoing the acknowledgement of a link to European forms and concerns in Achebe's own Yeatsian title?

25. Though, sadly, this window of opportunity for local publishing is in contention with a general crisis of documentation confronting Africa, and many other areas of the less developed world, in the 1990s.

26. K. Ramchand, *The West Indian Novel and its Background* (London, 1970).

27. An obvious early exception to this is Wole Soyinka's translation of the Yoruba writer D.O. Fagunwa's *The Forest of a Thousand Daemons*, published by Nelson in 1968. Of course, Nelson had published the book first in 1938 and so, presumably, still had the rights. However, such exceptions prove the rule that, in general, the publishers who initiated the upsurge in the publication of African writing in the late 1950s and 1960s did not have the translation of indigenous writing as a significant part of their programme for introducing African writing to a world audience.

9 Oral tradition as history

Robin Law

Before the relationship between 'oral tradition' and 'history' can be discussed, some preliminary issues of definition have to be addressed. The term 'oral tradition' itself presents some difficulty. Not all 'oral history', in the sense of historical information recorded in an oral form, is strictly oral tradition, since much of it consists of information obtained from eyewitnesses of, or participants in, the events concerned, and comprising recollections of their own observations or experiences. Such oral testimony is, therefore, first-hand evidence, albeit normally recorded retrospectively.[1] The term 'tradition', however, strictly implies a chain of transmission, and 'oral tradition' denotes information transmitted as well as recorded orally, comprising the informant's recollections not of his or her own experiences but of what he or she was told by others (whose statements, in turn, may have represented recollections of statements by others earlier in the chain of transmission). 'Oral tradition' is therefore, by definition, a form of second-hand or hearsay testimony. It differs from other types of hearsay evidence (such as contemporary rumours) in that the information in it has been transmitted vertically, through time, rather than horizontally, across space.

Some confusion can also be caused by insistence on the 'oral' character of oral tradition, which is implicitly or explicitly commonly contrasted to written historical sources. While the term 'oral tradition' is normally understood to consist of testimony recorded orally by modern researchers in the field, the 'orality' of oral tradition resides more critically in its mode of transmission than in the form in which it is eventually recorded. Indeed, until the recent invention of sound recording, oral traditions could only be recorded in writing (and even nowadays, sound recordings are regularly transcribed in writing), so that, once recorded, 'oral traditions' necessarily themselves become written texts. And since traditional material has been recorded in writing for many centuries, a great deal of 'oral tradition' comes to the modern historian already in written form. From a historian's point of view, the critical distinction is not between written and oral sources, but between contemporary and traditional ones. 'Oral tradition' does not cease to be 'oral tradition' merely by being recorded in writing.

It should also be stressed that the category 'oral tradition' covers a wide range of different sorts of material. A basic distinction can be drawn between traditions which have, in principle, a fixed text (such as poetry and songs, but also including some forms of prose recitation) and those which comprise merely a body of information which may be verbalised in a variety of ways; in general it may be assumed that, other things being equal, traditions that have fixed texts will tend to be transmitted with less alteration than those with free texts. A related (but overlapping rather than identical) distinction may be made between those traditions whose preservation and transmission is entrusted to specialists, and those transmitted more informally, by anyone interested in doing so. Here again, the preliminary working assumption would normally be that the existence of specialist custodians of a tradition constitutes in some measure a guarantee of its accurate transmission. If, however, as is often the case, the specialist tradition-bearers are closely associated with the ruling authorities of the society concerned, the presumption of more accurate transmission is counterbalanced by the evident fact that the operations of such official state historians are likely to be more susceptible to politically motivated censorship and manipulation.

Although oral tradition has been utilised in the study of many fields of history, in recent years it has been associated especially with the history of sub-Saharan Africa, and more especially of sub-Saharan Africa during the pre-colonial period (that is, the nineteenth century and earlier). The most useful and influential recent analyses of the historical use of oral tradition have been written by historians of Africa, and have drawn most of their illustrative material from African history.[2] When the serious study of African history at universities in Africa, Europe and America began in the early 1950s, from the outset great emphasis was placed on the use of oral tradition. This reflected the conviction that there was for Africa south of the Sahara a relative dearth of contemporary written sources, and that emphasis needed therefore to be placed on less conventional sorts of historical sources, including, above all, oral tradition. There was an element of exaggeration in this view, since sub-Saharan Africa was not by any means wholly non-literate (a circumstance which has also had a significant influence on the character of local oral tradition). Written sources survive for many African societies – most obviously, Islamic societies with written sources in Arabic (and occasionally, in African languages written in Arabic script), but also some coastal societies under European/Christian influence which produced written documents in European languages.[3] More widely, there were many societies which, although themselves non-literate, were in touch with literate societies through trade, and for whose history there are therefore written sources produced by outsiders. It remains true, however, that this sort of written documentation is limited and (more critically) uneven in its incidence and coverage. Oral tradition remains the only source for the history of some African societies, and the only form of internal source for many.

It may nevertheless be that rather too much was made of the supposed novelty of the use of oral tradition. The use of oral tradition as a significant source had, in fact, been a normal feature of historical research, back to the 'Father of History' himself, the Greek historian Herodotus in the fifth century BC; and it was characteristic of both Christian and Islamic historical scholarship in medieval times. One consequence of this is that 'oral tradition' is the basis for many classical written sources, as well as being the only source available for the history of non-literate societies.

Quite apart from such remoter antecedents, in the study of the history of sub-Saharan Africa itself, the academic historiography which developed from the 1950s had been preceded by a tradition of historical writing by local amateur scholars, often making extensive use of oral tradition, which stretched back well into the nineteenth century. This interest in the study and writing of the history of indigenous African societies had arisen initially in West Africa in the late nineteenth century, as part of a wider movement of 'cultural nationalism', which involved the study of indigenous African culture and religion as well as history, and attempts to develop a vernacular literature (including the recording of indigenous oral literature).[4] This movement arose essentially out of a crisis of identity among European-educated (and Christian) West Africans, faced with growing racial prejudice and discrimination from Europeans, and responding to this rejection by European culture by seeking to re-establish an identity with indigenous African culture. The most vigorous early tradition of such local historical studies emerged among the Yoruba of south-western Nigeria, where writing on Yoruba history (mainly in English, but with some works in the Yoruba language) began on a significant scale from the 1880s onwards.[5] An especially distinguished example was the *History of the Yorubas* of the Revd Samuel Johnson, a Yoruba clergyman, written in 1897 (although not published until 1921).[6] Elsewhere in West Africa, similar early historical work was produced on the Gold Coast (modern Ghana) to the west, where the Revd C.C. Reindorf, another African Christian clergyman, published his *History of the Gold Coast and Asante* in 1895.[7] A tradition of historical writing of comparable antiquity existed among the Buganda (of modern Uganda) in East Africa, where Apolo Kaggwa published *Basekabaka be Buganda*, a history of the kings of Buganda in the Luganda language, in 1901.[8] Much of the 'oral tradition' used by modern historians, in fact, is taken at second-hand from the writings of such literate local scholars, rather than recorded in oral form.

In Europe, however, a more sceptical attitude towards oral tradition had begun to develop from the eighteenth century onwards. The Scottish social philosopher Adam Ferguson, for example, in his essay on the history of 'civil society', written in 1767, dismissed the traditional accounts of Classical Antiquity on the grounds that traditions were necessarily distorted in the process of their oral transmission:

> They are, for the most part, the mere conjectures or the fictions of subsequent ages; and even where at first they contained some degree of truth, they still vary with the imagination of those by whom they are transmitted, and in every generation receive a different form. They are made to bear the stamp of the times through which they have passed in the form of tradition, not of the ages to which their pretended descriptions relate.[9]

A similarly sceptical attitude towards oral tradition was taken by the author of one of the earliest European attempts to study the history of African societies, Archibald Dalzel (another Scotsman), in his history of the kingdom of Dahomey (in the modern Republic of Bénin) published in 1793: 'the blacks have no records, but those traditional ones, the legends of their bards; which are so politically affected, that they are but little to be depended upon'. In consequence, Dalzel argued that the history of a state such as Dahomey would have to be based mainly on the evidence of outsiders, the European traders who visited or resided in it. For the period prior to European contact, therefore, nothing could be known with any confidence. 'All before this time stands on the ground of tradition, which is ever more or less precarious, in proportion to the number of relators, and the frequency of repetition.'[10] By the twentieth century, it was conventional wisdom among professional historians that history could be based only upon written documents, and that the history of non-literate societies, including most of Africa, was therefore effectively irrecoverable: 'History only begins when men take to writing.'[11]

The pioneers of academic African historiography in the 1950s, therefore, in seeking to emphasise their use of oral traditions, were obliged to address the methodological issues which this involved, in order to vindicate the professional legitimacy of their project. This was done most systematically and influentially by Jan Vansina, a Belgian historian (though later settled in the United States of America) who had worked in Central Africa, in his classic study *Oral Tradition*, originally published in French in 1961 (and in English translation in 1965). Vansina insisted that oral traditions could be subjected to the same sort of criticism as any other sources. Such criticism was partly internal to the tradition concerned – to assess not only the likely reliability of the original information from which a tradition is ultimately derived, but also the likelihood of its having been accurately transmitted down to the present; but partly also external – by comparison with other available sources referring to the same events. Vansina acknowledged the many difficulties presented by the interpretation and evaluation of oral traditions, but argued that they were, in principle, no different from those arising with regard to any sources, including written ones. He did concede that additional possibilities of distortion arose out of the process of oral transmission itself. All documents are likely to be distorted by the particular circumstances which generate them, but written documents, once created, may survive by inertia, and thus be preserved unchanged from their original form. Oral traditions, by contrast, can only survive by being constantly repeated, and each repetition (as Adam Ferguson had pointed out) provides both an opportunity and potentially (since the precise purpose for which the tradition is used may change over time) a motive for further distortion. Even Vansina, therefore, regarded oral traditions as affording 'a lower degree of probability' than other sorts of historical sources.[12] He maintained, however, that oral traditions, like any other sources, could be utilised to the extent that they were subject to corroboration through comparison with other evidence, and that the material with which a tradition might be compared included not only written documents (where these were available), archaeological and linguistic evidence, and inferences from comparative ethnography, but also (critically) other oral traditions: if two or more independent traditions agreed, this was good ground for supposing that they were accurate.

Vansina's *Oral Tradition* became a sort of moral charter for a whole generation of historians seeking to use oral tradition for the reconstruction of the pre-colonial history of African societies. It is now clear, however, that early considerations of the use of oral traditions in African history, including that of Vansina, very substantially underestimated the problems involved, and over-simplified the relationship between oral traditions and history. The last twenty or so years have seen a significant refinement of our understanding of oral traditions, which has changed our perceptions of their nature in ways which radically problematise their use as historical sources. The measure of this transformation of our understanding can, indeed, be seen by comparing the original 1961 version of Vansina's *Oral Tradition* with the subsequent (1985) version, which is greatly revised and indeed so totally rewritten that it was felt appropriate to give it a new title, *Oral Tradition as History*. There are two main areas where earlier perceptions have had to be rethought: evaluation of the accuracy of transmission of traditional material, and interpretation of the meaning of its content.

First, with regard to the problem of how far traditions were preserved and transmitted accurately before being recorded, Vansina's original approach rested explicitly upon an analogy with written documents: his concept of reconstructing a 'chain of transmission' from a supposed original testimony through various oral informants down to the version(s) eventually recorded by the modern historian, depended upon an analogy with the copying of manuscript documents, and thus on the transfer to the field of oral tradition of techniques of textual criticism well established in the analysis of classical and medieval written sources. Vansina's assumption was that through comparison of variant versions of a tradition, and knowledge of the general conditions under which traditions were preserved, transmitted and performed, an 'archetype' could be reconstructed, which would approximate the original testimony from which the tradition derived, and which would, by implication, be effectively equivalent to a first-hand, or at least contemporary, source. (Although, of course, the concept of reconstructing an original text can, strictly, be applied only to those traditions which had a fixed verbal form, it was presumed that this approach could also be applied, albeit more loosely, to traditions with free texts, for which the original content or 'plot' could, in principle, be reconstructed.)

Against this approach, it may be argued, first, that the analogy between oral traditions and written manuscripts breaks down, because in the case of oral traditions it is highly misleading to think in terms of an original text which is more or less accurately reproduced at each link in the chain of transmission. In oral performance, there is not in fact a 'text' to be copied – indeed, the very concept of an oral 'text' comes close to being self-contradictory, since the 'text' exists only in the act of performance. Moreover, Vansina' s concept of a 'chain of transmission' assumed that different traditions were preserved and transmitted essentially independently of each other; although he acknowledged the existence of diffusion of traditional material from one society to another, he gave little attention to the problems arising from it. In fact, however, it is increasingly clear that tradition-bearers very commonly combined material from different sources, and that in consequence one is obliged to assume as a working hypothesis a great degree of interdependence among traditions within and even across societal boundaries: this, again, undermines the documentary analogy, since it implies a textual ancestry so complex as to make the reconstruction of an archetypal text quite inconceivable.[13]

As an illustration of this problem, may be cited the particular case of the incorporation into oral traditions of material derived from written sources. This has received a relatively great amount of detailed attention, in part of course because it is easier to document than the influence of wholly oral traditions upon each other. This phenomenon of borrowing into traditions from written sources has generally been termed 'feedback' by historians of Africa.[14] Many African societies, as was noted earlier, had some contact with literacy, even in the pre-colonial period, and all have become literate during the present century. Alongside the oral transmission of traditions, written accounts of local history, including written recensions of oral traditions, have been published and circulated, in some cases (as in Yorubaland) for over a hundred years before the present day. There is increasing evidence that traditions still current orally have been heavily influenced by written accounts. As the author of a general analysis of oral tradition published in the early 1980s, David Henige has insisted, in most areas of the world (and certainly in all of Africa), 'uncontaminated oral tradition simply does not exist any more'.[15] Especially clear, given the long history of Islamic influence in much of Africa, is the borrowing into local oral traditions of material and themes from the Quran and other Islamic written sources. Yoruba tradition, for example, as already recorded by Samuel Johnson in the 1890s, traces ethnic origins to a migration from Mecca, presenting the ancestral Yorubas as expelled followers of a king of Mecca called Lamurudu, who was overthrown by the supporters of a man called Braima for relapsing from Islam. Although formerly often interpreted more or less at face value, as evidence for origins from the Near East, it is now generally agreed that this story represents a straightforward case of 'feedback' or borrowing ultimately from written sources – 'Lamurudu' and 'Braima' being the Nimrud and Ibrahim (Abraham) of Arabic accounts (and ultimately of the Old Testament), and the whole story merely reproducing well-known Muslim sagas of the confrontation of Nimrud and Ibrahim at Mecca.[16]

More generally, it may be suggested, much of the earlier discussion of the problem of accurate transmission of oral material in practice proceeded from an unacknowledged but pervasive analogy with the memorisation of a written text, where the *memorandum* is objectified and serves as an invariant source for and check upon the *memoratum*, with a consequent failure to confront systematically the practical implications of true orality. If one looks at some of the detailed work which has been done on the differences between the ways in which information is handled and preserved in oral and literate societies,[17] the overwhelming impression obtained is of how practically difficult it was for a purely oral society to remember anything, or (even more critically) to know whether what it remembered was remembered accurately. To be remembered with any chance of accuracy, oral information had to be recast in a readily memorable form, characteristically in a stereotyped formula (such as proverbs), a process which itself ineluctably compromised the accurate preservation of that information.

In addition to these problems of contamination or distortion of traditions through the mechanics of their transmission, even if the content of traditions is, for purposes of argument, assumed to have been accurately transmitted and recorded, serious problems arise over the interpretation of this content. For all the methodological sophistication of Vansina's and other early work on African oral tradition, there was underlying it an essentially literalistic approach, which implicitly assumed that the narratives in oral traditions were not in principle dissimilar to those in written documents. It should be stressed that by 'literalistic' here is not meant 'uncritical', since it was of course recognised (and indeed emphasised) that traditions (like contemporary written documents) might be selective and distorted in various ways, being based upon incomplete information, affected by bias, moulded by general cultural values, and often consciously falsified or even fabricated. But traditional narratives were nevertheless assumed generally to deal with real people and real events, to be in essence historical documents, even if they were very defective or distorted ones.

Here again, there has in recent times been much important work, principally by anthropologists rather than historians, which has argued persuasively that, at least in very many instances, it is misleading to treat oral traditions as being, even in intention or profession, historical records of real events. Very often, it is suggested, traditions must be understood rather as making normative or cosmological statements – expressing general ideas of the nature of values and institutions. The narrative form in which they are cast is only superficially historical, and their content is, in essence, not historical at all. Traditions may, of course, incorporate material which is historical – in the sense of reflecting real historical events – as well as purely invented material; but any such inclusion of genuinely historical material is merely incidental to their essential nature. Especially influential in this connection, even though itself the subject of much critical and sceptical commentary, has been the 'structuralist' analysis of Central African traditions of origin by the Belgian anthropologist Luc de Heusch, *The Drunken King*, originally published in French in 1972.[18]

The point will be illustrated here by a single (but, it is here argued, representative) example – from the West African kingdom of Dahomey.[19] The traditions of Dahomey attribute many of its central political and social institutions to a specific ruler, Wegbaja, who is said to have ruled during the second half of the seventeenth century and to have won recognition as 'king' by the local village chiefs, principally by the lavishness of his gift-giving to them, and in particular to have established judicial order, suppressing the right of private vengeance and monopolising the right of capital punishment. Although modern scholars have recognised that Wegbaja in Dahomian tradition is a sort of 'culture hero', on whom all national institutions tend to be fathered, so that his personal achievements have doubtless been exaggerated, this tradition has generally been treated as essentially historical, partly perhaps because it fits into a well-established tradition in anthropological theory, which sees the power of the state growing at the expense of the component lineage groups of society – 'the revolutionary change by which local groups surrendered their right of independent action in the settlement of criminal cases'.[20]

It may be argued, however, that this is to misunderstand the real meaning of the traditions of the creation of kingship by Wegbaja. The picture of judicial anarchy and general lawlessness prior to Wegbaja's advent, which is implied by the traditions, is inherently suspect, if treated as a straightforwardly historical account, but this is not in fact the only interpretation of it which is conceivable. It is clear that in Dahomian thought a central function of monarchical authority was the maintenance of judicial order, this conception being given dramatic expression during the interregnum between the death of one king and the formal installation of his successor, during which criminal and even murderous acts might be committed with impunity – the idea being that justice was guaranteed only by the king, and ceased to exist when there was no king. The traditions of Wegbaja, it can be suggested, express the same idea in historical (or rather, pseudo-historical) form, with the Hobbesian 'state of nature' in this instance imagined as actually existing prior to the institution of monarchical authority rather than as a hypothetical alternative to it. The essential content of the traditions, on this view, is the normative judgement that the alternative to monarchy was anarchy, rather than the historical assertion that such a monarchless state of anarchy had once actually existed. They tell us nothing whatever, therefore, about the historical process whereby the kingdom of Dahomey emerged.

Likewise, claims of genealogical links between the ruling dynasties of African kingdoms are often misunderstood, if they are treated as historical statements. For example, Dahomey was preceded as the major power in the area by a kingdom called Allada (which Dahomey conquered in 1724), and its authority was challenged after 1724 by the kingdom of Porto-Novo. According to Dahomian traditions, Dahomey and Porto-Novo were founded by two brothers, who had contested the succession to the Allada throne and then left to found their own kingdoms. In fact, it is clear from other evidence that

Dahomey and Porto-Novo were not contemporaneous foundations, as the traditions imply in making their founders brothers, something like a century in fact separating the establishment of the two kingdoms. And while it is clear that the kings of Porto-Novo were indeed descended from the earlier kings of Allada, it is extremely improbable that the kings of Dahomey were so descended. At any rate, despite considerable European interest in the historical traditions of Dahomey during the eighteenth century (of which Dalzel's *History*, cited earlier, was the most elaborated instance), no contemporary record of such a claim was recorded before the 1790s. An obvious interpretation of these problems is to suppose that the traditions have been distorted for political purposes, to legitimise the authority of the kings of Dahomey, seeking to clothe the authority which Dahomey had acquired by force in a cloak of traditional legitimacy. This charge of falsification, however, may be inapposite, or at least inadequate, since it implicitly assumes that the ostensible purpose of traditions in Dahomey was to preserve an accurate record of past events. It might be more accurate to consider the traditions as expressing in an historical (or pseudo-historical) form Dahomey's self-image. The real historical basis of the tradition is that Dahomey in the eighteenth century aspired to the position of regional paramountcy earlier enjoyed by Allada, and that Porto-Novo was the principal rival to Dahomey for this pre-eminence. The supposed filiation of the Dahomian royal dynasty to that of Allada, with the presentation of the founders of Dahomey and Porto-Novo as brothers, is best interpreted as an expression of these perceptions in a genealogical idiom, rather than as a claim to literal kinship. Rather than making historical assertions which can be shown to be false, the traditional genealogy expresses perceptions of Dahomey's contemporary (late eighteenth- and nineteenth-century) situation; the question of its historical accuracy, as commonly conceived, does not really arise.

While these sorts of problems are now very widely appreciated, it is commonly assumed that traditions are nevertheless usable as historical sources; indeed, it has been claimed that, by assimilating much of the criticisms of the traditions offered by anthropologists, historians have refined their methodology of interpretation, thereby achieving greater rather than less certainty. This position is adopted, for example, in most of the essays in an important anthology on oral tradition in Africa published in 1980, entitled *The African Past Speaks*.[21] The editor of this anthology, Joseph Miller, formulates the claim explicitly: 'if [historians] now believe less of what they hear in oral sources, they can justify more rigorously their acceptance of that bit of each narrative that they accept as historical'.[22]

It is questionable, however, how far this optimistic assessment can really be sustained. Reading through the illustrative case studies offered in *The African Past Speaks*, it is difficult to find anywhere a wholly convincing demonstration of the usability of oral traditions as historical sources. What several of the contributions do show, is that if we know the history of a society independently of its traditions – that is, if we can compare the traditions with other sorts of evidence (principally contemporary sources, though archaeology, linguistics and comparative ethnography may also be useful) – then we can make sense of its traditions, and sort out how they are related to history, and which elements in them are historical. In the absence of this sort of external control, however, the use of traditions remains problematical. Scholars can offer different 'readings' of the historical significance of traditions, and we may find this or that reading subjectively plausible, but the procedure remains inescapably arbitrary in that it does not usually seem possible to demonstrate rigorously that one 'reading' of the traditions is correct, or even preferable to the others. It may well be that in time the scholarly community will evolve a truly scientific approach to the analysis of oral traditions (as it did for written documents during the eighteenth and nineteenth centuries), but for the moment it must be said that the historical use of oral traditions, without corroboration from other categories of source material, remains, in the final analysis, unvalidated by any systematic rules of historical inference.

It should not be concluded from the foregoing, however, that no effective progress has been made in the historical analysis of oral traditions. In the first place, our refined understanding of the ways in which oral traditions are distorted and biased has a positive as well as a negative side for the historian seeking to make use of them. Even if the value of traditions as historical records is undermined, their potential as historical sources is not thereby necessarily totally compromised. Even traditions which are demonstrably tendentious, or symbolic, may be of great historical value, if they are regarded as potential evidence not for the actual events which they purport to describe, but rather as evidence for pre-colonial propaganda and ideology. To turn Adam Ferguson's criticism of oral tradition on its head, traditional stories may be better evidence for 'the times through which they have passed in the form of tradition' than for 'the ages to which their pretended descriptions relate'. The traditions of King Wegbaja, for example, may tell us nothing about Dahomian history in the seventeenth century, but they do tell us a great deal about Dahomian concepts of kingship as they existed in the nineteenth century. The way ahead for the study of oral traditions may lie more in their contribution to pre-colonial African intellectual history, than in the reconstruction of particular historical events.

Secondly, we should recognise the potential value in the understanding and assessment of oral traditions of the contemporary European (and sometimes also Arabic) sources – a potential as yet little exploited by historians of Africa.[23] European written sources offer some degree of control in the evaluation of traditions, not merely in the sense that we can sometimes compare traditional and contemporary accounts of the same events, but also, and more critically, because we can often find recensions of early versions of traditions preserved in European written sources, which can be compared with the versions of the same traditions recorded more recently. For example, the traditional saga of the foundation of Dahomey exists in at least five versions recorded independently by European visitors during the pre-colonial period, including two from as early as the second half of the eighteenth century. Comparison of such early recordings of traditional history with each other and with versions recorded in the twentieth century affords useful insight into the ways in which traditions have changed over time. It may be suggested, in fact, that it is only by the exploitation of this sort of written evidence for the history of development of traditional stories, that we will be able, in the long run, to develop any sort of rigorous methodology of interpretation and evaluation of oral traditions as historical sources.

Notes

1. For a treatment of 'oral history' which concentrates on such first-hand reminiscences of recent history, see Paul Thompson, *The Voice of the Past: Oral History* (Oxford, 1978).
2. See especially Jan Vansina, *Oral Tradition: A Study in Historical Methodology* (London, 1965), and *Oral Tradition as History* (London, 1985); also David Henige, *The Chronology of Oral Tradition: Quest for a Chimera* (Oxford, 1974) – a study whose value extends far beyond

narrowly chronological issues – and *Oral Historiography* (London, 1982).

3. See, for example, the diary of Antera Duke, an African merchant of Old Calabar (in south-eastern Nigeria), written in English, and covering the years 1785–88, which is reproduced in Daryll Forde (ed.), *Efik Traders of Old Calabar* (London, 1956), pp. 27–115.

4. See P.F. de Moraes Farias and Karin Barber (eds), *Self-Assertion and Brokerage: Early Cultural Nationalism in West Africa* (Centre of West African Studies, University of Birmingham, 1990).

5. See Robin Law, 'Early Yoruba Historiography', in *History in Africa*, vol. III (1976), pp. 69–89.

6. Revd Samuel Johnson, *The History of the Yorubas*, ed. O. Johnson (London, 1921).

7. Revd C.C. Reindorf, *The History of the Gold Coast and Asante* (Accra, 1951).

8. Translated into English by M.S.M. Kiwanuka as *The Kings of Buganda* (Nairobi, 1971).

9. Adam Ferguson, *An Essay on the History of Civil Society*, ed. Duncan Forbes (Edinburgh, 1966), p. 76.

10. Archibald Dalzel, *The History of Dahomy* (1793; London, 1967), pp. 1–2. This pioneering work, it should be stressed, was not undertaken as a disinterested work of scholarship, but as a polemic in defence of the slave trade: see I.A. Akinjogbin, 'Archibald Dalzel: Slave Trader and Historian of Dahomey', *Journal of African History*, vol. VII, no. 1(1966), pp. 67–78.

11. Professor A.P. Newton, dismissing the possibility of studying the pre-colonial history of Africa in 1922: quoted in J.D. Fage, *On the Nature of African History* (Inaugural Lecture, University of Birmingham, 10 March 1965), p. 3.

12. J. Vansina, *Oral Tradition*, p. 186.

13. This problem of composite ancestry can also arise, of course, with regard to written texts, but it seems to be more pervasive and insoluble in the case of oral traditions.

14. See, for example, David Henige, 'The Problem of Feedback in Oral Tradition: Four Examples from the Fante Coastlands', *Journal of African History*, vol. XIV, no. 2 (1973), pp. 181–94.

15. D. Henige, *Oral Historiography*, p. 85.

16. See further, Robin Law, 'How Truly Traditional is Our Traditional History? The Case of Samuel Johnson and the Recording of Yoruba Oral Tradition', *History in Africa*, vol. XI (1984), pp. 195–221.

17. For example, Walter J. Ong, *Orality and Literacy: The Technologizing of the Word* (London, 1982).

18. Luc de Heusch, *Le roi ivre où l'origine de l'Etat* (1972), trans. Roy Willis

as *The Drunken King, or, The Origin of the State* (Bloomington, IN, 1982).

19. For further discussion, see Robin Law, 'History and Legitimacy: Aspects of the Use of the Past in Precolonial Dahomey', *History in Africa*, vol. XV (1988), pp. 431–56. For a reconstruction of the early history of Dahomey, based on a combination of contemporary European and local traditional sources, see R. Law, *The Slave Coast of West Africa 1550–1750: The Impact of the Atlantic Slave Trade on an African Society* (Oxford, 1991).

20. W.J. Argyle, *The Fon of Dahomey: The History and Ethnography of the Old Kingdom* (Oxford, 1966), p. 90.

21. Joseph C. Miller (ed.), *The African Past Speaks: Essays on Oral Tradition and History* (Folkestone, 1980). An essentially similar stance is adopted by Paul Irwin, *Liptako Speaks: History from Oral Tradition in Africa* (Princeton, NJ, 1981).

22. J.C. Miller, 'Preface' to *The African Past Speaks*, p. x.

23. But for an exceptional example of what can be done in this direction, see David Henige, ' "The Disease of Writing": Ganda and Nyoro Kinglists in a Newly Literate World', in J.C. Miller (ed.), *The African Past Speaks*, pp. 240–61.

10 *Popular writing in Africa*

Jane Bryce-Okunlola

80 kph	God will take care of you
100 kph	Guide me O thou great Jehovah
120 kph	Nearer my God to thee
140 kph	This world is not my home
160 kph	Lord I am coming home
Over 180	Precious memories.

(Text in the windscreen of a Nairobi taxi, 1990)

Do not urinate here – again
(Notice on the outside wall of a popular bar in Lagos, 1991)

If we are to attempt a definition of 'popular writing' in Africa, these two texts demonstrate several of its essential features. The first, the taxi driver's prayer, incorporates a tongue-in-cheek intertextuality with 'official' culture in the form of Christianity or establishment religion, and a whole-hearted embrace of fast living, the hectic pace of an urban lifestyle with its attendant dangers. The second, the admonition to inconsiderate drinkers, adds to these a pragmatic acceptance of imperfect material conditions and human weakness, and an unsqueamish straight-forwardness about bodily functions. Furthermore, the do-it-yourself production of these texts, handwritten and displayed on available surfaces for public consumption, and their contexts – the taxi, the bar – speak of the sociological parameters within which most popular culture functions: the urban lower to lower-middle class, living as much by its wits as by petty trading, small retailing, manual skills or on the lower echelons of bureaucracy.

'A sideways glance': theorising popular writing

Can we, however, really call these 'texts'? Was there any consciousness on the part of their producers of participating in a creative process? Certainly, in the case of at least the second example, is it not purely functional and devoid of all artistic aspirations? Such a distinction, relying as it does on the producer's intention, is largely irrelevant. In the light of deconstructive theory, 'writing' has expanded beyond its narrower, literal meaning of marks-on-a-page, or what has been described as 'merely graphic conventions'[1] to signify instead a whole network of systems of meaning, in which 'texts', seen as methodological fields, are constantly in a state of process. Critics of African orature (Barber, Irele) have demonstrated how the Derridean deconstruction of the Western Metaphysic of Presence – the idea that 'writing' is a more or less faithful transcription of elements of speech – was already quite obvious to African writers and readers, for whom orature can never be 'reduced' to writing-as-marks-on-a-page. In the Derridean sense, orature *is* 'writing', and so are road signs, bread labels, or an admonition scrawled in paint on a wall.[2]

Writing on Yoruba *oriki*, Karin Barber claims for deconstructive criticism that it 'seems to fit oral texts like a glove . . . oral texts are what deconstructive critics say all literature is – only more so'.[3] (The qualification, 'seems', is important here, as she ultimately concludes that what deconstruction leaves *out* is 'questions about power and ideology – raised so insistently by *oriki*' (p. 514), precisely as a result of its being trapped in an epistemology which alienates texts from their human agents: producers and consumers.) Abiola Irele, too, insists on the paramountcy of orature and an aesthetic of fluidity and participation:

> Despite the undoubted impact of print culture on African experience and its role in the determination of new cultural modes, the tradition of orality remains predominant, serving as a central paradigm for various kinds of expression on the continent . . . [it] functions as the matrix of an African mode of discourse . . . [and] thus represents the basic intertext of the African imagination.[4]

I take the intertextuality of orature and so-called 'popular' literature as fundamental. This is partly a matter of aesthetics; for example, the relationship identified by Emmanuel Obiechina between Onitsha Market pamphlets and folktale, or the episodic narrative structure and sequential pattern noted by Griswold and Bastian in some Nigerian romance fiction. It is partly also a matter of 'popular writing' being a discursive space inhabited by many different kinds of text – drama, songs, spoken poetry, proverbs, archetypes, gossip, political slogans and speeches, newspapers and magazines, to name a few – which works of fiction draw on not simply as reference points but as a way of invoking, in immediate, accessible and condensed form, a range of shared meanings.[5]

It is here that the Bakhtinian distinction between 'official' and 'unofficial' cultures comes into play. This, I find, bearing in mind Barber's caveat about the significant differences between Bakhtin's 'central type of the unofficial . . . the medieval carnival' and African popular culture, is quite simply the most appropriate and least problematic way of classifying 'popular writing'.[6] It places it as the 'other' of both official or canonical writing and traditional orature. It is, in Barber's words, the 'fluctuating, undefined and shapeless space between . . . two positive terms' – 'traditional' and 'elite'. It allows us to accept the essentially experimental, innovative nature of popular writing – in the sense that its producers feel free to use, abuse or ignore established conventions, and to combine disparate elements without regard to critical norms. Such a practice requires an equally adaptive critical response, and where this is absent, the uneasiness that results is all too evident. There is, for example, a purist strain in African literary criticism which strongly objects to the materialism, sexism and con-servatism of much popular fiction. As Raoul Granqvist states: 'Among traditionalists of the right and left within the academy popular culture is frequently defined as unitary or stultifying mass culture in opposition to free and authentic literary cultures.'[7] It is my contention that the notion of 'authenticity' – the real, original, truly repre-sentative, essential Africa – is one that should be laid to rest for all time. What popular writing shows above all is that 'Africa' is a site of competing and contested meanings, of manifold voices and strategies of expression, and cannot be reduced to a single, univocal, homo-geneous text. Popular writing, in the same way as Bakhtin's 'unofficial' culture, is perpetually in process, incorporative, heterogenous and – a Bakhtinian term – dialogic.[8]

Granqvist establishes that, in relation to African popular culture, 'What has been at the core of the debate is, as a matter of fact, what we are concerned with here, the discriminatory and selective rules governing the popular narratives and their risk of always being encapsulated or integrated into a dominant meta-narrative' (Granqvist, p. 3). Let us apply this analysis to the position adopted by Holger Ehling in the same collection. In an essay on recent popular writing in Nigeria, he inclines to the view that 'popular' is an economic index only, designating 'a commodity which fulfils certain needs in response to a demand from the "market"', and has no other purpose than to entertain.[9] Such writing, 'written for the purpose of mere entertainment and . . . of inferior aesthetic quality [is] generally called "trivial" literature . . . ' (Ehling, p. 155). It is obvious that what this leaves out of account is the whole question of power relations; who produces the literature known as 'trivial', for whom, its relationship to the canon, its (often concealed) subversive tendencies, and who is in the position of 'policing' language by the deployment of such a value-loaded term as 'trivial'? The drawback with this perspective is that, preoccupied as it is with surface, it does not enable us to read its 'surplus meaning' (Barber, 1987, p. 64), that latent sub-textual oppositional voice frequently suppressed beneath the constraints of genre or the sense of what may or may not be said.[10]

An African sociology of popular literature

Emmanuel Obiechina, whose work, *An African Popular Literature: A Study of Onitsha Market Pamphlets,* was published in 1971, cites various forerunners, but his is probably the most widely read and detailed seminal study of this much written-about phenomenon.[11] Reading Obiechina against Bakhtin, however, the surprising number of correspondences which emerge (considering the differences in time and place: Africa in the first half of the twentieth century and medieval Europe) suggests a theoretical approach to African popular writing which addresses 'questions about power and ideology'.

Obiechina informs us that Onitsha Market literature arose as a result of a confluence of influences and circumstances: increased literacy in southern Nigeria, population explosion, rural-urban migration, increased technology (including printing) and an incursion of new ideas, aspirations and desires with the return of soldiers from the Second World War. More poetic is Chinua Achebe's foreword, in which he describes Onitsha, a town on the east bank of the Niger, and site of a market which was 'one of the most splendid of its kind in West Africa, if not in the whole of Africa' (Obiechina, 1972, p. 8). What Achebe evokes is Onitsha's peculiar situation as a site of transition, of margins and crossings, both physical and temporal, cultural and religious. It is, in effect, a limbo zone between the spirit world (of dead ancestors, gods, the unborn) and familiar, everyday 'reality'.[12] The encounter between colonialism and tradition is here represented as an encounter of equals, or rather as one encounter among many in a fluid and changing situation. History tells us that this was far from being the case, that it was in fact something closer to how Bakhtin describes the hegemonic relationship of Greek culture to Roman: 'From start to finish, the creative literary consciousness of the Romans functioned against the background of the Greek language and Greek forms' (Lodge, p. 140). This is an apt description of how African written literature, too, was born: in the context of a colonial language, a new religion, Western education and inherited literary forms and values. The outcome was, in Bakhtin's term, 'polyglossia': a process of transformation whereby speakers of a particular language come to see that language (and its whole cultural superstructure) through the eyes of an alien language (and culture) and are thus enabled to construct 'a working hypothesis for comprehending and expressing reality' (p. 140). To summarise, Bakhtin builds a case for the birth of the (European) novel out of 'the struggle between two tendencies . . . one a centralising (unifying) tendency, the other a decentralising tendency', so that it 'senses itself on the border between the completed dominant literary language and the extra-literary languages that know heteroglossia' (p. 140). The form that most typifies this situation is parody, which undermines the seriousness of the dominant culture by using its characteristics playfully.

Onitsha Market literature conforms to a remarkable degree to this description. Published as short pamphlets between the 1940s and 1970s, it was aimed at helping the newly literate, urban population make sense of its situation – one where the old rules were being severely questioned, whether in questions of courtship, marriage, business or general deportment. Obiechina says that Onitsha Market pamphlets *and* the novel were 'forms whose very novelty presented them to young educated Igbo writers as an aspect of the challenge of modernity that must be met' (Obiechina, 1971, p. 8). In the process of meeting this challenge, both the traditional and the new, much sought-after Western way of life are parodied. This again evokes Bakhtin's description of the novel as a carnival travesty of 'serious' classical forms. The provenance of the pamphlets – Onitsha Market – is, like carnival, a public space where forms of expression as well as material goods for sale are typified by their variety – their heteroglossia. 'Serious' forms travestied include both the Bible and Shakespeare (icons of the foreign system introduced through colonialism), and a range of other English authors who are freely quoted and misquoted in a joyful intertextuality which has little regard for 'authenticity', or the ownership of text. Just as in medieval Europe, Latin and church liturgy were the object of parody by the vernacular languages, so the English canon and Christianity provide the ground for the Onitsha writers to try out their newly acquired or invented skills of expression. Obiechina tells us that biblical and Shakespearean references provided ratification, the stamp of authority, evidence of the education and enlightenment of the author, but also sonorous language and marvellously wrought phrases for which writers and readers had been prepared by the rhetoric of orature. Orature is indeed shown to be, as Irele says, the 'central paradigm' and 'basic intertext of the African imagination'.

This is true not only in the love of elaborate language, but of what another commentator, Donatus Nwoga, calls the 'graph of justice', based on the traditional belief that 'at the end of punishment and disgrace comes salvation and forgiveness', as opposed to the Christian notion of 'eternal hell for the evil doer.'[13] This is not true of all popular literature, for example, both the prostitute mother, Maria, and her promiscuous daughter, Nancy, die at the end of W.E. Mkufya's *The Wicked Walk*. Cyprian Ekwensi's celebrated novel *Jagua Nana*, however, does exemplify this tendency, with its Lagos prostitute heroine first undergoing a retreat in her eastern village, before re-emerging to become a successful Onitsha business woman.[14] Another feature of both Onitsha pamphlets and popular literature in general which may easily be misread is their apparent adherence to 'Western individualism', as opposed to a more communal 'traditional' ethos.[15] This, however, is an overly simplistic opposition, as Obiechina demonstrates (Obiechina, 1971, p. 8). He detects the same 'democratic and adventurous spirit' at work in Achebe as in eastern Nigerian popular fiction, but interprets this less as a buying into Western materialism than a concern for 'otherwise anonymous little people' arising from Igbo tradition itself. As in the literature, which exhibits ambivalence towards rather than rejection of tradition, there is no straightforward binary opposition of modern/traditional. Rather, the two are equally significant aspects of a single phenomenon, informing and modifying each other.

Getting words on to paper: the publishing industry

Onitsha is not the only place to have given rise to a popular literature, only one of the first and best documented. We have dwelt on it at length in the belief that it provides a paradigm for the discussion of more contemporary popular fiction, not only in itself and its material conditions of production, but as an object of theorisation. The correspondences noted between Bakhtin and Obiechina are cited to suggest a strategy for the reading of popular writing which will be as elastic as possible, in recognition of its 'unofficial', transgressive, syncretic and innovative nature.

A salient point to emerge from the Onitsha paradigm is the central role played by the publishing industry in the production of popular literature. To an extent, all writing whether elite or popular, is conditional on forces determined by the marketplace – what sells, what is acceptable to editors and publishers' readers, what conforms to a particular imprint's view of itself. The major canonical vehicle for anglophone African writing, the Heinemann African Writers' Series (HAWS), for example, founded on the bedrock of *Things Fall Apart* (1958), characterises itself as including 'almost all the leading names of African literature', as 'authoritative', and publishing 'only the best that is available in whatever genre', as though such terms as 'excellence' (beloved of New Criticism) were transparent and needed no mediation.[16] Those popular texts which have been admitted to HAWS have seen a corresponding alteration in their status, which interestingly demonstrates the instability of the demarcation popular/ elite.[17] Ekwensi's *Jagua Nana*, for example, is now regarded as a 'classic', though Jagua's frank celebration of her sexuality was viewed with disapprobation by critics on its appearance in 1961. (The increase in feminist readers and critics may also have something to do with it.)

Nigeria has not only produced elite presses in competition with Heinemann (such as Onibonoje Press, which launched its own African Literature Series, Fourth Dimension, Spectrum, and others), but popular presses and imprints. Olayia Fagbamigbe, according to James Gibbs, 'was an innovative publisher who . . . understood the enthusiasm of the Nigerian reading public for books by James Hadley-Chase and Bertha M. Clay . . . and encouraged local writers to cater for the Chase–Clay readership'.[18] As a result, under the imprint Eagle Romance, titles such as *Broken Love*, *Love in the Clouds*, *Half a Love* and *The Love Thief* began to appear, while other Ibadan firms,

Paperback Publishers Limited and Spectrum, jumped on the bandwagon with Egret and Sunshine Romance. The best-known and most interesting series, however, is Macmillan's Pacesetters, partly because its writers write with greater awareness of the thriller and romance formulae and how these may be coopted to serve a local readership. This series, which has been the focus of a certain amount of critical attention, includes some of the best-known popular writers.[19] It is heavily dominated by Nigerians such as Helen Ovbiagele, Kalu Okpi, Buchi Emecheta and Agbo Areo, though writers from Kenya (David Maillu), Ghana (Christine Botchway and Atu Yalley), Zimbabwe (Hope Dube and Senzenyani Lukhele), Sierra Leone (Yema Lucilda Hunter) and elsewhere, have also contributed.

Apart from these, there are also small presses which exist to publish a single author's books, such as Flora Nwapa's Onitsha-based Tana (which also publishes children's fiction) and Fakunle Major Press, producer of Funmilayo Fukunle's romantic novels. Heinemann belatedly started its own romance imprint in 1992, Heinemann Heartbeats, to which Pacesetter writer Kalu Okpi has contributed with *Love Changes Everything* (1993). The innovative writer Ken Saro-Wiwa, author of *Sozaboy: A novel in Rotten English* (1985), published himself and other writers through Saros International. Even so, the declining economic situation in Nigeria over the last decade or so has inevitably affected the publishing industry. The cost of ink and paper, the problems of distribution, the exorbitant cover price, all mean that fewer books get made and sold. Yet Nigeria, with its vast population (80 million at the last count) is incomparably better off in this respect than smaller countries with fewer resources and a more restricted reading public. A case in point is Nigeria's West African neighbour, Ghana.

It is necessary at this juncture to acknowledge that the popular writing of each region is an outgrowth of its own specific circumstances, so as to avoid treating it as one homogeneous entity. Barber has suggested that 'some cultures have a long history of seeking and assimilating novelty while others do not', and that 'the innovatory disposition was characteristic of trading cultures', such as the West and East African coasts. Indeed, she posits: 'Innovation within the cultures of these trading societies was not merely the result of culture clash, population movement or slow cultural diffusion: it was actively sought and creatively incorporated into an assimilative tradition' (Barber, 1987, p. 42).

In spite of a common trading disposition, there are differences even between two West African countries, like Nigeria and Ghana. Though Ghana has a history of published fiction going back to J.E. Casely-Heyford's novel, *Ethiopia Unbound* published in 1911 (the first West African novel; later followed by R.E. Obeng's *Eighteenpence* in 1943), and a great flowering of talent in the immediate post-Independence (1957) years and the decade following the downfall of Nkrumah (1966–76), virtual economic collapse has since reduced Ghanaian writing to a trickle. While this is less true of 'elite' writing, which finds publishers overseas or through a local publisher such as Woelie, established specifically to provide an outlet for 'the cream of Ghanaian creative writing' (personal interview with Atsu Dekutsey, publisher), it is markedly so of popular fiction. Richard Priebe identifies three strands of 'popular literature' in Ghana: comic opera, or what is more commonly known as concert party, 'a multi-generic dramatic event' which still thrives; the lyrics of highlife music, the predominant musical form of West Africa from the 1930s to the 1960s, but whose influence spread much further afield; and popular writing.[20] Another critic, Ime Ikiddeh, attributes 'the late rise of popular fiction in Ghana' (though he cites J. Benibengor Blay's *Emelia's Promise*, published in 1944, as probably the earliest example) to the lack – so unlike Onitsha – of an indigenous printing industry.[21] Publishing in Ghana has, since Nkrumah, been dominated by the Ghana Publishing Corporation, while private enterprise was curbed in Nkrumah's era. Though there are independent publishers in Ghana today, they are severely constrained by costs and forced to concentrate their resources on the lucrative area of text-book publishing, apart from the already-mentioned Woelie.[22] In an essay on popular writing in Ghana, Priebe gives a detailed analysis of the publishing background and current situation (1978) of various popular writers.[23]

What the example of Ghana shows is the symbiotic relationship of popular literature and the publishing industry, and its dependence therefore on economic forces. It also reinforces the necessity, in Africa, of taking the wider view of 'popular writing', since book production is so vulnerable to economic contingencies. Other non-'written' forms, however – television, drama, popular songs, radio poetry broadcasts, concert party, popular syncretic prayer-forms and a contemporary secular entertainment-form based on the Asante tradition of *nwonkoro*, women's praise-singing and other songs, all survive and thrive, though they remain invisible to the print-bound researcher.[24]

'When money speaks it is women who hear' (Ghanaian [Chokosi] popular song)

To move across the continent to East Africa, in particular Kenya, is to be plunged into what has variously been called 'erotic realism' (Peter Nazareth), the ' "he ha" school of soft-pornography' (Bernth Lindfors), 'a cacology fed on neo-colonist pulp' (Christopher Mulei) and 'porno-aesthetics' (Chris Wanjala). As long ago as 1968 (until 1972) Longman Kenya sponsored a 'crime and passion' series in Kiswahili, *Hadithi za Kusimama* (literally: 'stories to make you stand' or 'titillating stories'). Strongly resembling Onitsha Market in their penchant for modern, urban settings and loose women, the titles too (as Bernth Lindfors points out) recall Onitsha: *Yote Hukosa Yote* (*He Who Wants All Loses All*, 1968); *Mwerevu Hajinyoi* (*A Clever Man Does Not Shave Himself*, 1971); *Uhalifu Haulipi* (*Crime Does Not Pay*, 1971); *Mwisho wa Mapenzi* (*End of Love*, 1971) and *Kwa Sababu ya Pesa* (*Because of Money*, 1972).[25]

The same combination of sensationalism and moralism/didacticism is evident in Onitsha pamphlet titles like *Money Hard To Get But Easy To Spend*, *Why Boys Never Trust Money – Monger Girls*, *Beware of Harlots and Many Friends – The World is Hard* and *Beauty is a Trouble*, suggesting some correspondences in both the social conditions which generated the texts and their aesthetic parameters. A crucial difference that has been observed between Nigerian and Kenyan popular literature, however, is the relative pessimism and negative view of the city in the latter. Barber sees this in the light of different forms of colonialism – 'indirect rule' versus settler colonialism, as pertained in Kenya, as a result of which there was a large-scale land 'alienation' and uprooting of peasant populations.[26] Nigerian cities have their slums, with similar problems (inadequate supplies of piped water and electricity, overcrowding, insanitary conditions and makeshift housing) but they lack an essential feature of 'squatter settlements' like Nairobi's notorious Mathare Valley – a deracinated population.

The fantasy of 'everlasting love' triumphing over all obstacles is a recurring feature of romantic fiction by women, not only in Kenya. Funmilayo Fukunle's novels invariably end with the woman vindicated through love, in spite of realistic portrayals of the vicissitudes of Nigerian married life – being supplanted by a younger wife, hostility from other wives in a polygamous setting, the tragedy of infertility, the influence of the extended family.[27] This is markedly different from many male-authored novels, where the emphasis tends to be on retribution, though many do also feature the male protagonist's regeneration through a woman. In the former category, *The City Kid* (1973) by the Ugandan Edwin Luwaso, shows how a young man's search for material success in Kamobi (a composite of Kampala and Nairobi) and his downfall through debt and corruption are directly linked to his involvement with an expensive city woman, Rosemary Kimaga.[28] Like Owino's Aggy, John Ouma is all too eager to leave his village backwater for the fast pace and opportunity of the city. Peering through a shop window, he meditates on how little has changed in the decade since Independence:

> There was last year's calendar with a picture of the President on one wall – and that was new compared with the Aspro advertisement over the door, now permanently browned by dust. Progress, it seemed to John, was being concentrated in the towns; and the villages . . . were being ignored. Well, that meant one thing for John: he had to leave the village and find a new life in the city.   (p. 8)

In the city, John quickly falls prey to Rosemary's consumerism, her demands for nights in hotels and weekends at the coast, till he is forced to involve himself in forging receipts for his boss to make extra money. Rewarded for this by Rose's desertion of him in favour of a junior government minister, John drives in a frenzy to 'the sprawling shanty known as sikenyi', provenance of the lethal home-brewed beer and prostitutes. This potent combination reduces John to a state of waking up next day in a sewer, covered in vomit, wet with urine, and without his watch, his wallet and his car. As he staggers away, 'John had the feeling that he was walking away from the jaws of hell' (p. 66).

The City Kid, published by Africa Christian Press, sees John spiritually transformed through the intervention of a Christian friend, accepting Jesus, repenting of his past, and returning to the village to visit his parents. He now sees his ambitions as illusory: 'Instead of being free, he had become the slave of personal habits and social pressures which he could not control' (p. 94). It is perhaps not surprising that a text with an overtly Christian intention should see prostitutes as inhabitants of 'hell', but the prostitute, in various manifestations, is an abiding figure in popular writing. Kwabena Nketia, describing a concert-party performance in 1961 by the Atlanta Trio, says the Ghanaian play 'was based on the story of two girls who had different attitudes to life. One . . . was a prostitute who did not see any point in marriage, and the other a girl of good character who chose to marry, even though this meant a lower standard of living, fewer dresses, fewer jewelry and less money to spend. The prostitute ends in disgrace, while the other girl is blessed with children and a happy home.'[29]

As Obiechina points out with reference to Onitsha, traditional morality was frequently reinforced by Christianity, rather than overtaken by it. One of the functions of popular writing, apart from entertainment, is to warn the reader/consumer of the dangers inherent in city life, largely constituted by 'harlots, independent women, mostly lip-painted ladies [who] love bachelors . . . because they know that bachelors have a long way to go with them . . .' (Obiechina, 1973, p. 59). There is an obvious gender bias in this representation, which points to the exclusively male authorship (and probably predominantly male readership) of Onitsha pamphlets, as of the earlier examples of popular writing elsewhere on the continent. Ikeddeh tells us that: 'In Ghanaian fiction, the woman is almost invariably the cause of friction and disruption.' (Ikiddeh, 1988, p. 76). Though there is no doubt that this is indeed a powerful stereotype, it is not always so clear cut. K.A. Bediako's *Don't Leave Me Mercy!!* (1966) vacillates between a representation of Mercy as a money-grabbing witch and a sincere woman caught between respect for her father and love for her husband.[30] It is similarly undecided as to whether Owusu, her husband, is a besotted fool or a hard-hearted and unforgiving man. The long drawn-out narrative of marital problems leads to a very conservative lesson in wifely deportment, which reinforces traditional morality at the same time as appearing to criticise it. This ambivalence destabilises the apparent certainty of the text's ideological position, allowing a space for the operation of desire, the seductiveness of transgression, the barely repressed power of feminine sexuality.

The same elements of ambivalence and attraction are evident in F. Senkoro's essay *The Prostitute in African Literature*, in which he evokes a 'literature flooding with dayless cities, "notorious" red-light streets, "shebeens" and cheap cafés filled with girls of the street, ladies of the night, and painted women beckoning from numerous windows and balconies, using all their professional tactics to attract the eyes of critics.'[31] Here, critics (depicted as fastidiously avoiding contamination by contact with 'the numerous stinking slum areas in the world of African literature' (p. xi) are *ipso facto* implicated in the issue of prostitution, just as David Maillu is accused, in *Unfit for Human Consumption* (1973), of 'laying all the blame on the prostitutes and

at the same time using their bodies to make his books sell . . . a pimp
who prostitutes his characters for money' (p. 10). Fastidious avoidance
will make neither the 'stinking slums' nor their representation in
popular writing go away. The figure of the prostitute is metonymic of
the post-colonial malaise: cultural imperialism, economic dependency
and political corruption. As Senkoro says, 'Everyone is guilty of
prostitution, the prostitute herself is only a symptom' (p. 37).

The Kenyan writer, Ngugi wa Thiong'o's prostitute heroines are an
obvious symbol of redemption, but not all works of popular fiction
can be dismissed as merely exploitative. Though Kenyan critic Chris
Wanjala excoriates Charles Mangua's *Son of Woman*[32] as proposing
passivity, acceptance of weakness, apathy and 'blind conformism',[33]
it can also be read as a utopian projection of the possibility of change
and transformation for people trapped in a cycle of poverty-induced
crime. The Tanzanian writer, W.E. Mkufya's *The Wicked Walk*, cited
by Senkoro as depicting the city as 'a microcosm of a neocolonial
society, with most of its predicaments' (p. 37), treats Maria and Nancy
with exemplary realism in its analysis of the material conditions which
lead first the mother, then her daughter, to use their bodies for
economic survival. It is, however, in the writing of women that
women's situation as objects (rather than instigators) of exploitation
is most fully explored.

Popular writing – loud, insistent, brash, crude, but also dynamic,
exciting, pleasurable – challenges the critical project which would seek
to construct 'African Literature' in a particular way, for particular
purposes. The dichotomy perceived by Wanjala between 'Ngugism'
and 'Mailluism' in Kenya, goes hand in hand with a narrowly
prescriptive tendency which decrees for the artist that s/he 'must depict
the social and historical view of the environment he lives in, so that
what is socially healthy becomes a component of men's historical
self-awareness'; and for the critic that s/he 'must strive to reform
popular taste, to stress that Ngugi . . . is a better and truer writer than
Maillu' (Wanjala, 1980, p. 217). I would contend that this dichotomy
is a projection of the class perspective of the onlooker. As Barber
observes: 'The people's arts represent what people do in fact think,
believe and aspire to. . . . It is surely crucial that we respect and pay
attention to that very conservatism and misogyny if we are to
understand why and how people collaborate in their own oppression'
(Barber, 1987, p. 8). Maillu, indeed, sees himself less as a commercial
exploiter than an educator, and many of his readers concur. When he

canvassed his audience through questionnaires included in the novel, *The Kommon Man*, published by his firm Comb Books (later reborn as Maillu Publishing House), a flood of correspondence resulted.[34] Apart from the indubitable element of sexual titillation, the reader response was characterised by its seriousness. As Wanjala summarises, 'They argue that Maillu will be remembered as a God-appointed social reformer and an enemy of moral corruption' (Wanjala, 1980, p. 240). Certainly, his subjects – prostitution in *After 4:30*, the situation of domestic servants in *The Ayah*, drunkenness in *My Dear Bottle* – are supremely those of concern to his readership.[35] It is debatable, too, whether Ngugi's saintly Guthera (*Matigari*, Heinemann, 1989) is a 'better and truer' prostitute's portrait than Emili Katango in *After 4:30*.

That he also sees his low-life ('stinking slum') subjects in a serious and reflective light is evidenced by his authorship of a non-fictional work, *Our Kind of Polygamy* (Heinemann, 1988), in which he considers African marriage and sexual customs from every point of view: historical, social, economic, moral, reproductive, psychological, religious, in relation to 'love' and 'faithfulness', and the contemporary version of polygamy – 'concubinage', or the keeping of girlfriends or 'outside women'. His conclusion is characteristically pragmatic: 'If concubinage is a less evil than prostitution, it is better to go for it. We begin to learn and develop for the better by accepting the necessary evil as the starting point. . . . How can we say that blessed are the merciful when we limit that mercy? How can we love one another when we limit the dimensions of that love?'[36] In Kenya, Maillu proposes, social and cultural factors have created a situation where women who find it hard to get husbands are condemned and scapegoated. Is this special pleading for the right of men to indulge themselves sexually, or is it an attempt to confront the contradictions of Christian morality in a traditionally polygamous setting?

Conclusion

Even a woman writer of romance fiction, like the Nigerian Helen Ovbiagele, displays an extraordinary pragmatism in the matter of sexuality. The heroine of *Evbu, My Love*, though she attains the ideal of romantic love and monogamy, does so by way of being a call-girl and the girl-friend of a rich expatriate.[37] Aggy, in *Sugar Daddy's Lover*, similarly starts out with stereotypical, Western formula notions of romantic love, exaggerated to the point of burlesque. The first time

Abed gives her a lift in his car, she is so primed with romantic expectations that it only takes one look from him to trigger them:

> I felt him gazing at me and I looked up. Our eyes met . . . from then on, whenever he changed gear, he made sure that he touched my knee and smiled. His touch conveyed a message to me which ran through my body like fire. Then he suddenly seemed younger. He *was* younger! . . . Now I knew I already loved him dearly, whatever his age was.
>
> (pp. 5–6)

Exaggerated as this is, it does address one very prevalent aspect of gender relations in Africa, the 'sugar daddy' phenomenon, described by the character, Frank, in *The Wicked Walk*, in the following terms:

> Sugar daddies . . . make money through big salaries and underground businesses or through naked corruption. They make more money than they need and use the extra to seduce women and destroy young girls, school girls. They forget their high ranking positions in the government and become moral dirt betraying the society which put them into leadership. These are sugar daddies.
>
> (p. 83)

In this novel, Nancy is indeed destroyed, dying in the course of a harrowing abortion which exploits to the full her powerlessness in the face of Magege, her lover, and the doctor, his friend. Aggy's story, perhaps in accordance with women writers' insistence on the power of love to transform reality, ends more positively. While Mkufya's is a didactic realist work, Ovbiagele and Owino wrench the romance formula, with its element of fantasy, to fit the shape of contemporary urban African social imperatives. The female protagonists of their works are not passive dreamers, but active agents in their self-transformation, who struggle and suffer to achieve their aspirations. But all three of these texts, and most of those under discussion, are preoccupied with the question of power relations. The overriding obsession with sex, love, marriage, money and material possessions may very well signify a deeper concern with the social inequality and ruthless political cynicism which pervade the continent, a concern displaced onto personal relationships and the seductive lure of wealth. Both of these speak of a desire for change in the *status quo*, tempered by the reality of poverty and political disenfranchisement. African popular writing provides a space for the rewriting of power relations, for transformation, above all, for *pleasure* in a harsh world where pleasure is not just an escape but a challenge.

Notes

1. Christopher Norris, *Deconstruction: Theory and Practice* (London, 1982), p. 39.
2. My own use of the word 'writing' in this chapter slides between the Derridean and the 'older' conventional meaning. I have found this, to an extent, inevitable, given that I am both attempting to focus on those texts available as marks-on-a-page (popular novels/fiction) and to contextualise them in the wider field of popular culture of which they are one manifestation.
3. Karin Barber, 'Yoruba *oriki* and Deconstructive Criticism', *Research in African Literatures*, vol. 15, no. 4 (1984), p. 498.
4. Abiola Irele, 'The African Imagination', *Research in African Literatures*, vol. 21, no. 1 (1990), p. 56.
5. This operates too in 'official' or 'canonical' literature; for example, in Ayi Kwei Armah's invocation of proverbial wisdom in his title *The Beautiful Ones are Not Yet Born* (London, 1968), which, with its orthographical peculiarity, signals a consciousness of the strength and resilience of 'popular' as opposed to 'elite' culture, which pulls strongly against the perceived pessimism of the novel's explicit content. When, too, Ngugi wa Thiong'o, in his novel *Matigari* (London, 1987), wishes to evoke a particular atmosphere in a bar in Nairobi, he only has to mention that the popular Kiswahili song 'Shauri Yako', with its swinging Zairian guitar accompaniment, is playing.
6. Karin Barber, 'Popular Arts in Africa', *African Studies Review*, vol. 30, no. 3 (1987), p. 64 (further page references are cited in the text).
7. Raoul Granqvist, 'African Popular Discourse and Aspects of Regulation: Two Perspectives', in R. Granqvist (ed.), *Signs and Signals: Popular Culture in Africa* (Stockholm, 1990), p. 3 (further page references are cited in the text).
8. See Mikhail Bakhtin, 'From the Pre-history of Novelistic Discourse', in David Lodge (ed.), *Modern Criticism and Theory* (London, 1988) (further page references are cited in the text), and *Rabelais and His World*, trans. Hélèn Iswolsky (Bloomington, IN, 1984).
9. Holger Ehling, 'The Biafran War and Recent English Language "Popular" Writing in Nigeria', in R. Granqvist (ed.), *Signs and Signals*, p. 154.
10. Jurgen Martini, 'Sex, Class and Power: The Emergence of a Capitalist Youth Culture in Nigeria', *Journal of African Children's Literature*, vol. 1 (1989), p. 54.
11. Ulli Beier (1962), Donatus Nwoga (1965), Nancy Schmidt (1965), H.R. Collins (1968), Bernth Lindfors (1970), among others.
12. This construction of Achebe's calls to mind Wole Soyinka's 'Fourth Stage', the zone of transition between the living, the dead and the unborn

in Yoruba cosmology, as described in an appendix, 'The Fourth Stage' in *Myth, Literature and the African World* (Cambridge, 1976). Soyinka's Fourth Stage, however, is entirely metaphysical, and tragic – the abyss into which all creatures must enter before they can cross from one world to another, 'vortex of archetypes and home of the tragic spirit' (p. 149).

13. Donatus Nwoga, 'Onitsha Market Literature', *Transition*, vol. 4, no. 19 (1965), p. 31.

14. W.E. Mkufya, *The Wicked Walk* (Dar-es-Salaam, 1977); Cyprian Ekwensi, *Jagua Nana* (London, 1987).

15. For an exposition of this point of view, see Gerald Porter, 'Market Forces: Onitsha Pamphlets and the Post-colonial Experience', in R. Grandqvist (ed.), *Signs and Signals*, pp. 173–81. He argues that 'the pamphlets are overtly seeking to promote a specific model, the self-sufficient individual . . . in every sense an imported concept, a construct based on colonial stereotypes promoted by the mission schools' (p. 173). He concludes: 'Onitsha market literature has subverted the traditional structures of Igbo society and substituted a tension-filled, Euro-centred concept of the Individual . . . a hybrid filled with neurotic anxieties and guilt' (p. 181).

16. Adewale Maja-Pearce, 'In Pursuit of Excellence: Thirty Years of the Heinemann African Writers' Series', *Research in African Literatures*, vol. 23, no. 4 (1992), pp. 126–7.

17. Titles by the popular writer Cyprian Ekwensi which have been published by HAWS (with their series number): *Burning Grass* (2), *People of the City* (5), *Lokotown* (19), *Beautiful Feathers* (84), *Jagua Nana* (146), *Restless City* (172), and *Survive the Peace* (185). By Kenyan popular writer, Meja Mwangi: *Kill me Quick* (143), *Carcase for Hounds* (145), and *Going Down River Road* (176). By Nigerians, Nkem Nwankwo: *Danda* (67), and *My Mercedes is Bigger than Yours* (173); and Eddie Iroh: *Forty-eight Guns for the General* (189), and *Toads of War* (213). There are also two of Asare Konadu's: *A Woman in her Prime* (40) and *Ordained by the Oracle* (55), first published as *Come Back Dora!* by Anowuo, Accra, in 1966, and Bediako Asare's *Rebel* (59). Publication by Heinemann has the great advantage to students of accessibility outside the continent.

18. James Gibbs (ed.), *A Handbook for African Writers* (London, 1986), pp. 128–9.

19. For critical essays, see Virginia Coulon, 'Onitsha Goes National: Nigerian Writing in Macmillan's Pacesetter's Series', vol. 18, no. 3 (1987) *Research in African Literatures*; Jurgen Martini, 'Sex, Class and Power: The Emergence of a Capitalist Youth Culture in Nigeria', *Journal of African Children's Literature*, vol. 1 (1989), pp. 43–59; Jane Bryce, 'Popular Writing by Women in Nigeria: The Pacesetter Series', *Kunapipi*, vol. 16, no. 3 (1993). It is a sad reflection on the state of Nigeria's economy that,

while Macmillan Nigeria used to lease publishing rights for Pacesetters, which enabled it to choose and publish its own titles and gave local writers and readers much more immediate access, it is no longer able to afford to do so.

20. Richard Priebe (ed.), *Introduction to Ghanaian Literatures* (New York, 1988), p. 6.

21. Ime Ikiddeh, 'The Characters of Popular Fiction in Ghana', in R. Priebe (ed.), *Introduction to Ghanaian Literatures*, p. 73.

22. Eric Ofei, then President of the Ghana Book Publishers Association, in a paper to the National Book Congress, Accra, 1991, gives the following information: 'There are about 15 well-known private publishing houses currently in existence . . . and they publish between three and 12 titles including reprints in a year. . . . However, there are many one-man publishers around . . . mostly author-turned-publisher who issue teaching notes . . . and sell to students' (p. 4).

23. Richard Priebe, 'Popular Writing in Ghana: A Sociology and Rhetoric', *Research in African Literatures*, vol. 9, no. 3 (1978), pp. 401–8. In 1991, I spent six weeks in Accra courtesy of the Leverhulme Trust, researching (among other things) popular fiction. Interestingly, the two popular novels I did pick up were both by Asare Konadu, one published under his pseudonym, K.A. Bediako: *Don't Leave Me Mercy!!* (Anowuo, 1966); and *Devils in Waiting* (which says 'this edition 1989' but has no date of first publication and is not listed in either of the bibliographies provided by Ikiddeh and Priebe, so it may well be one of the few popular novels to have been published in Ghana since the 1970s).

24. I am grateful to Esi Sutherland-Addy, in 1991 Deputy Secretary for Education and a lecturer at the University of Ghana, Legon's Institute of African Studies, for information on these popular cultural forms.

25. Bernth Lindfors, 'A Basic Anatomy of E. A. Literature'. Paper to the African Literature Association, March 1979.

26. K. Barber, 'Popular Arts in Africa', p. 52.

27. Funmilayo Fakunle, *The Sacrificial Child* (1978); *Chasing the Shadow* (1980); *Chance or Destiny?* (1983), all published in Oshogbo by Fakunle Major Press.

28. Edwin Luwaso, *The City Kid* (Nairobi, 1973). It is worth noting that, in a sense, religious publishers have been implicated in the growth of popular literature from the start. Mpalive Msiska, in an unpublished manuscript 'The Politics of Love and Marriage in African Popular Literature', contends that it is an outgrowth of the English language mission-school readers and the vernacular writing promoted first by mission presses such as the International Committee for Christian Literature (founded 1926) and the International Institute of African Languages and Culture (founded in the late 1920s). Literature Bureaux were also established in

countries under British colonial rule for the same purpose. Msiska, like Obiechina, attributes the new concept of 'romantic love' between individuals, and the ideal of life-long monogamy, to Christian influence. That Christian publishers have continued to involve themselves in the production of popular literature is evidenced by the fact that the 1947 edition of Benibengor Blay's *Emilia's Promise* and Asare Konadu's 1964 novel *The Wizard of Asamang* were both published by Waterville, a Presbyterian press. The publishing arm of the Christian Council of Churches, Asempa, is active today in Ghana, promoting fiction with a Christian message.

29. J.H. Kwabena Nketia, *Music, Dance and Drama: A Review of the Performing Arts of Ghana* (Legon, 1965), p. 43.

30. K.A. Bediako, *Don't Leave me Mercy!!* (Accra, 1966).

31. F.E.M.K. Senkoro, *The Prostitute in African Literature* (Dar-es-Salaam, 1982), p. xi.

32. Charles Mangua, *Son of Woman* (Nairobi, 1988).

33. Chris Wanjala, 'The Culture of the Uniformed Man: His Problems of Alienation', *For Home and Freedom* (Nairobi, 1980), pp. 218–21.

34. David Maillu, *The Kommon Man* (Nairobi, 1975).

35. David Maillu, *After 4:30* (Nairobi, 1974); *The Ayah* (Nairobi, 1986); *My Dear Bottle* (Nairobi, 1973).

36. David Maillu, *Our Kind of Polygamy* (Nairobi, 1988), p. 182. The relationship between Maillu and the 'elite' publisher Heinemann is indicative of the Kenyan situation. Like Nigeria, Kenya has a multiplicity of publishing houses (thirty-six in Nairobi alone, according to Heinemann senior editor, Leteipa ole Sunkuli). The local branch of Heinemann is now (since 1991) 85 per cent Kenyan owned. In 1975, Heinemann started its own 'popular' imprint, which only really moved into gear with the indigenisation of the company, and its increasing autonomy. Again according to ole Sunkuli, after ten years it 'finally found its level among school children and salespersons' (personal interview, 1990). One needs to know that 40 per cent of Kenya's population is under eighteen for this statement to be seen in proper perspective. Popular literature, with its large school-based readership, actually subsidises 'elite' literature which sells less. The example given by ole Sunkuli was Marjorie Oludhe-Macgoye's novel, *Coming to Birth*, which he called a 'one-off', and which won the Sinclair Prize for Fiction in 1986, the year it was published by Virago in the United Kingdom.

37. Helen Ovbiagele, *Evbu, My Love* (London, 1980).

11 *African writing and gender*

Lyn Innes and Caroline Rooney

This chapter can but serve as an introduction, or dated postscript, to the many 'in-prints' of the interfolds of African writing and gender. The attempt, nevertheless, is to fashion or re-fashion a narrative of the inscriptions of gender in African writing, a story of ellipses that has its own ellipses and yet remains . . . opportune.

The title of this chapter may be spelt out or printed out as follows: 'African Writing . . . and Gender'. 'Gender' would thus appear to be an afterthought or, perhaps, the admission of an omission. This is not only a speculative consideration, for it may be claimed that in historical terms, African women's writing finds its moment of appointment in the omissions of African men's writing. However, while it may be claimed that the question of (female) gender is what a would-be male universe leaves out, or gives secondary place or inadequate space to, it is not only this post-universalist category. For, 'gender' in the West is also the privileged categorical imperative, the differential which eclipses other possible differentials, such as race, class, region, generation, and so on. In so far as other possible differentials can be subsumed by the gender differential, it may be and has been used to universalise what are really class-specific and regionally specific norms. The tyranny of a gender differential is thus potentially and historically imperialistic.[1] In the writings of African women, there is a notable disengagement with the isolated elevation of gender as an all-absorbing determinant. This is not simply a matter of giving consideration to other differentials and determinants, but of giving consideration to their cooperation or non-cooperation on a number of fronts. Nonetheless, while *African* women are not only 'women' (if we mean by this a centrally defined world-wide class), it would seem that the burdens and issues of gender are to be borne by the female sex. Or, whoever 'fathers' or conceives of gender as an imperative, it is usually the presumed or assumed responsibility of women to 'bring it up'.

'Beginning again'

Canonically speaking, modern African writing may be said to begin with Achebe, Ngugi, Soyinka. In particular, for a number of African women writers, it is Achebe who is the father of this renaissance. The Nigerian writer, Flora Nwapa, in an anthology of interviews with African women writers, speaks of him as the one who 'has inspired all of us'.[2] Achebe's inspirational importance lies in his revision of Western productions of African inferiority through the informed depiction of Igbo society in his early novels. What African women writers first took up from Achebe was the project to extend and supplement or revise his depiction of traditional society. In Achebe's early novels of rural Igbo life, the roles and experiences of women may be said to be marginalised. Writers such as Nwapa, Ama Ata Aidoo, and Buchi Emecheta recapitulate Achebe's point of departure, addressing colonial blindspots, while they also address the blindspots in this very point of departure, with regard to both gender and writing. This venture, then, assumes a recapitulation of the counter-discursive representationalist project, while also interrogating its pretensions, at least implicitly. That is, while the impetus may be to complete and, paradoxically, re-orientate the account to date by addressing what it ignores, what is at the same time called into question is the authoritative representation of a pre-given reality (whether it be 'African society' or 'African womanhood'). In Achebe's writing an interplay between mimeticism and ironic mimicry may already be discerned with particular reference to competing depictions of Africa. The first question to be pursued here is how gender is implied or marked within this scenario.

For anglophone African writers the departure from colonialist representations of African societies often also departs from models established by francophone African writers such as Leopold Senghor. Thus, in *A Man of the People* (1966), his fourth novel, Chinua Achebe parodies earlier African writing in the nationalist mode, when he cites a poem by his fictional young and idealistic leader of the Common People's Convention, Cool Max. The poem is titled 'Dance Offering to the Earth Mother'.[3] The parody here is fairly clearly directed towards the Negritude school, and especially the poetry of Senghor, with its long line, its concern with cultural assertion of the kind which Frantz Fanon contemptuously dismissed as the culture of the museum, and, above all, its imaging of Africa as the lovely, but despoiled mother. Despite his ironic view of Senghor's romanticism, Achebe is to some extent caught up in that kind of nationalism which images the contest for Africa or the nation in gendered terms. It is a trope rather scathingly rejected by the Senegalese woman writer Mariama Ba, who commented:

> The nostalgic songs dedicated to African mothers which express the anxieties of men concerning Mother Africa are no longer enough for us. The Black woman in African literature must be given the dimension that her role in the liberation struggles next to men has proven to be hers, the dimension which coincides with her proven contribution to the economic development of our country.[4]

Critics writing about Achebe have focused on what Abdul JanMahomed has called the Manichean Aesthetic, that is, the dialectic in which anti-colonialist writers confront and seek to reverse colonialist writing.[5] In so doing, such critics have averted their attention from the marginalisation of woman characters in Achebe's novels, and his failure to give women a voice or a place in the creation of an African vision of the reconstruction of the nation and its culture. There is, however, a link between Achebe's anti-colonial dialectic and his representation or non-representation of the feminine, the female, and African women.

Achebe's novels also focus on a context between a son and his father, or a father figure, and characteristically feature a determination by the father to impose his will and way of life upon his son, a determination and a contest which mirrors the contest between coloniser and colonised. Like much nationalist fiction and drama, Achebe's first two novels narrate a kind of complex Oedipal struggle in which the contestants are always males of different generations, and the contested land, or a character who symbolises the land, is female. This plot is almost obsessive in the writing of the Negritude school, where warrior sons are called upon to redeem an Africa who is mistress and mother, but one also finds it in a great deal of other African nationalist writing: one might cite Mumbi in Ngugi's *A Grain of Wheat* (1967), Dede in Awoonor's *This Earth, My Brother* . . . (1971), Araba Jessiwa in Armah's *The Healers* (1975), Ireyise in Soyinka's *Season of Anomy*

his nationalist contest both complicates and intensifies the
ontest that the American critic Harold Bloom used as his
for *The Anxiety of Influence* (1975), in which he argued
that each generation of writers misreads and rewrites the most
influential writers who precede them, their literary fathers. Yet another
complication comes from the anxiety of the artist son to declare his
relevance to the nationalist struggle at a time when political and
military activity may be seen as the way forward and as a means of
asserting manhood and manliness in contrast to the coloniser's representations of the colonised as childlike or effeminate. Ashis Nandy
argues that the psychology of colonialism and anti-colonialism
produces extreme dichotomies between definitions of the masculine
and the feminine; the two terms cannot be perceived as overlapping.[6]
As a result, issues of masculinity and femininity are often foregrounded
in nationalist writing, and are intertwined with the issues of conflict
between generations, and conflict between coloniser and colonised. In
Achebe's *Things Fall Apart* (1958), Ani, the earth goddess, is the
arbiter of morality and good conduct. Her priestess, Chielo, possesses
supernatural power and authority, and she alone can silence the
aggressive Okonkwo. At the same time, Okonkwo's fear of being
thought weak and effeminate distorts his whole psychology and his
relationship with his son and wives. He and the rest of his clan dismiss
Unoka, his musician father, for being too much like a woman, and
Okonkwo forbids his son Nwoye to listen to folk tales and songs,
which he sees as the province of women. And it is his fear of being
thought weak and effeminate that drives him to participate actively in
the sacrifice of his adopted son Ikemefuna.

Achebe's second novel, *No Longer At Ease* (1960), continues as
one of its underlying thematic structures, the opposition between
masculine and feminine and their relation to forms of culture and art.
This is seen most strikingly in the contrast between the rooms of Obi's
parents and their attitudes towards Christianity and tradition. Isaac
Okonkwo worships and preserves the written word. Although he is
the same Nwoye who deserts his father and insists on a harsh
masculinity, he is equally conservative and inflexible in his attitudes
towards those who are outcasts (he cannot contemplate his son
marrying an *osu*, a descendant of slaves) and towards creative song
and fiction – he too rejects folk tradition and wishes to preserve
mathematical and educational texts only. In contrast, his mother seeks
to combine folk tradition in story and song, and her room is filled with

the produce of the land – palm oil, yams, kola nuts. Her reaction to Obi's intended marriage is emotional and instinctive rather than intellectual and patriarchal. The death of Obi's mother and the disappearance of Clara from his life coincide with Obi's decision to become a 'hard-headed realist', to forget his old idealism, and to throw away his poem celebrating 'Nigeria'.

Both of these early novels were written before Nigeria had achieved Independence, and both involve the male/female conflict, and the failure of a harmonious relationship between fathers and sons, male and female linked to a concern with leading and taking responsibility for the nation or the community. In both cases the failure to acknowledge fully the feminine, and incorporate it, leads to an inability to become an acknowledged and acceptable leader. Achebe's next novel, *Arrow of God* (1964), was written after Independence, and interestingly is a novel in which masculine/feminine principles as well as male/female relationships almost disappear. The gods in this novel are all male, whether Ulu or Idemili, and all manmade. And Ulu speaks with and through the voice of a man. This is all the more striking in that Idemili, in particular, is normally in Igbo tradition conceived of as female, and is so acknowledged in Achebe's most recent novel, *Anthills of the Savannah* (1987). Moreover, *Arrow of God* is set at a time when colonial interference in the appointment of local chiefs was strongly, vociferously and often successfully opposed by Igbo women.[7]

Why then does *Arrow of God* fail to notice such involvement of women? Why are they pushed even further into the background than in *Things Fall Apart*? And why are all the gods and their human representatives masculinised? One reason may be that the novel is written after Independence is legally achieved, in 1960, and the novelist's concern is no longer with claiming the right to the land itself; *who* shall possess Mother Africa or the Earth Mother is no longer at issue. What does concern Achebe is the nature of leadership, moral authority and integrity in post-Independence Nigeria, and the values which should inform it. Thus the concern with harmonising masculine and feminine principles is replaced by a concern with finding and defining the right kind of male leader in a contest between three members of the older generation – three fathers, the priests of Ulu, Idemili, and the District Commissioner where all three are replaced by the sons, so that 'henceforth the yam will be harvested in the name of the son'. In *Things Fall Apart*, however, the novel ends with one father, the colonial one, replacing another. In *No Longer At Ease*, the son,

Obi, abandons the women and the feminine principles they represent, leaving Obi, 'a beast of no nation', as a fellow countryman describes him at the doctor's waiting-room, when he and Clara are waiting to arrange the abortion of their child, an abortion which can be read symbolically as the premature killing of the embryonic nation.

That concern with finding the right kind of male leader is also at the forefront of *A Man of the People* (1966), but in this novel the focus is not only on the values which are appropriate, but also on the actual activity of electioneering and courting the voters. Here the contest is not for the land, but for the people, and the political rivalry between Chief Nanga and Odili and Max is mirrored and also intensified by their rivalry over two women, Elsie and Edna. Indeed, the responses of the electorate are largely displaced in the novel by the responses of the women, who come to stand for two kinds of young new voter: the urban voter, who is seen as fickle, materialistic, and easily seduced, represented by Elsie, and the rural voter, represented through Edna as semi-literate, relatively naïve, still tied to traditional family values and loyalties. There is, of course, a third woman whom Odili seeks to get on his side, Mrs Nanga, who remains firmly loyal to her husband and to traditional values and commitments. There is a similar trio of women in Sembene Ousmane's *Xala* (1974), again representing an older wife tied to traditional values, a second who is out for what she can get, and a third who is a victim of family greed and male desire for sexual status. Both novels end with a riot and the suggestion that there is a fourth kind of woman to admire and win over; Eunice and Ramatoulaye are portrayed as idealistic young women who can unite an allegiance to tradition with an idealistic socialism, while remaining loyal to their partners and fathers.

What happens in the post-Independence novel, we would suggest, is that the feminine principle embodied in the land, in Mother Earth, is replaced by female types – whose symbolic function is to represent the people, the voters who make up the nation. They are there to be wooed and seduced, and claimed by the hero and prospective leader, and their role is to enhance both the masculinity and the political authority of the leader, not to participate in or actively pursue the leadership or themselves become involved in politics. Here too the struggle is between father and son figures, and Odili seeks to usurp Chief Nanga, his erstwhile teacher, scoutleader and father figure, in the affections of Mrs Nanga and also of Elsie and Edna. As Elleke Boehmer puts it, in the nationalist scenario the male characters are typically metonymic.[8] It may be added, with a difference of emphasis, that while the male characters are naturalised, the female characters retain their metaphoric and symbolic status so that they serve as the trope of masculist truths, while the realist text may serve to obscure this representationalist imbalance.

It can be argued, as Florence Stratton has done, that African women writers such as Grace Ogot, Flora Nwapa, Buchi Emecheta, and Mariama Ba have been caught up in a dialogue with African male writers which is equivalent to the anti-colonialist dialectic which has been foregrounded in the work of those male writers.[9] This 'equivalence', however, is unsettled somewhat by both an acknowledged indebtedness and certain mutuality of concerns, already touched on, and by different forms of 're-writing' to be addressed later in this chapter. Nwapa belongs to the same generation as Achebe, and comes from the same area of Eastern Nigeria. She has the distinction of being the first Nigerian woman novelist, although critics have often dismissed her first novels as containing 'mere gossip',[10] lacking structure, or as being too slight. Recently, women critics such as Stratton have sought to reassess Nwapa's work, and have argued that both the form of her novels and the plots and characters are to be seen in the light of her attempt to write women into the nation as active characters and subjects rather than as metaphoric objects of the national struggle. Nwapa's early novels do not explicitly take up the colonial and anti-colonial narrative. Instead, titles proclaim the focus on specific women, the eponymous heroines, and recreate a context which ignores what is usually regarded as the substance of history.

Both this focus on individual heroines and the form of the novels, consisting largely of dialogues between women, and of stories told through dialogue, anecdote and a kind of choric commentary, suggest that Nwapa has been influenced by Achebe's use of oral forms, but at the same time is seeking to challenge him. Her concern is to write in women, to give them a voice, to create the world of women, and to insist that women did not hear of culture for the first time from men. Here, women, who have been given only a marginal space in Achebe's novels, are placed right at the centre, and the world of men is relegated to the margins, as Achebe relegated the world of the English colonisers to the margins. And just as Achebe sought to show that the world of Igbo men was self-sustaining, had its own validity, and could exist independently of the worlds and values of the Europeans, if only it were allowed to do so, so too Nwapa recreates a world of independent and self-sustaining Igbo women, whose life is disrupted only when men and their values interfere.

Through their speech and conversation, Nwapa also manages to reveal the variety and productivity of women's activities. Achebe's women are almost always seen as wives and mothers; Nwapa's male characters exist only as husbands, sons or lovers. Women do discuss husbands and children, but they are also engaged in planting, harvesting, healing and trading. Indeed, it is not domestic pursuits, but marketing which provides the chief focus for the women, and is the means by which they gain status. It is not the appearance of the new moon, but the market days which regulate time and give structure to their lives. But as Ifi Amadiume demonstrates in her sociological study, female goddesses allow women to challenge male authority and establish their own spheres of power most effectively. Nwapa's two early novels endorse Amadiume's assertions, and the Woman of the Lake deity, Uhamiri, like the Idemili identified by Amadiume, becomes for both her heroines a source of status, identity and resistance.

Ama Ata Aidoo rewrote Achebe in a different way, taking on the historical issues and themes that he had made the subject of his novels, although some of her tactics are comparable to Nwapa's. Aidoo has spoken of Achebe's importance to her: it was reading his early novels, she tells us, which inspired her to write, and she has always remained a great admirer of his work.[11] Nevertheless, her writing brings to the fore certain lacunae in Achebe's work.

Aidoo's first major work was not a novel but a play, *The Dilemma of a Ghost* (1965), written when she was only twenty-two. First performed in 1964, this play echoes and re-examines a number of the concerns explored in Achebe's second novel, *No Longer at Ease*. Both works focus on the return of a been-to, his inability to conform to the expectations of his family, and his inability to choose between individual self-fulfilment and his desire to please his family and community. Both works also feature an outsider as the object of the young man's desire, a young woman who is the descendant of slaves, and therefore an outcast. And both works also take up the issue of motherhood and childbearing as a focus for ambivalence about individualistic and communal values, played out as a conflict between romance and tradition. But, whereas Achebe's novel has Obi and his point of view at its centre, Aidoo gives greater space to the heroine, Eulalie, and to the community of women in the home village of Ato, the been-to son. Aidoo's choice of the medium of drama, rather than fiction, allows her to give even stronger voice to women, although within that medium she draws on techniques analogous to those used by Nwapa – specifically, a series of choric dialogues involving two village women, and carrying much of the off-stage action, but also dialogues between and about different generations of women. This allows her, as it does Nwapa, to make women's roles metonymic rather than metaphorical – they are sisters, daughters, mothers, traders – and to voice the differences and ambivalences in their attitudes. As in Achebe's novel, the been-to hero is finally left isolated, unable to find a place in either society; but unlike Achebe's novel, the outcast heroine, the descendant of slaves, is finally reconciled with the hero's mother, and the bonds between women prove stronger than the bonds between mother and son.

Aidoo's second play, *Anowa* (1970), was written three or four years later and is set at a time in Ghana equivalent to the beginning of *Things Fall Apart*. It spans a longer period and ends at a time equivalent to that of *Arrow of God*. Thus it begins just before the first impact of colonial intrusion and ends at a period when collaboration with the coloniser has already changed Ghanaian society. Like the two Achebe novels, it seeks to recreate a traditional oral culture which draws on proverb, anecdote and folktale for its language. And like Achebe's novels, Aidoo's play is concerned with the flaws, including the existence of slavery, which make the indigenous society vulnerable. In *Things Fall Apart*, a son is alienated from his conservative father, deserts the home of his ancestors, and joins the Christians. In *Anowa*, a daughter is alienated from her conservative mother, deserts her ancestral home, and seeks fulfilment in romance. Nwoye is alienated and leaves his community because he cannot accept the norms of masculinity set by his father; Anowa leaves her home and bitterly argues with her mother because she cannot accept the norms of femininity set by her mother. Both *Things Fall Apart* and *Anowa* end with the suicide of the hero, and in both cases that suicide is related to a fear of emasculation.

Anowa is condemned by her elders for 'behaving as though she were the heroine in a story' (p. 64). Thus the issue is whether women have the right to step from the margins to become central to the story. And here Aidoo makes the two groups of people – women and slaves – marginalised in *Things Fall Apart*, central in their very marginality.

Aidoo's play is also centrally concerned with gender roles. Anowa insists on doing everything her husband does – trading, carrying the heavy animal skins, she sees herself as a partner. For Kofi, her husband, the employment of slaves allows him to treat Anowa not as a partner but as a wife – that is, one who has no function other than to dress beautifully, to be a mark of his status, and to bear children. Anowa refuses to become a mere adornment through the adornment of herself; she does not have children, and so she has no function at all for Kofi.

The issue of gender roles, before and after colonialism, is also taken up in Aidoo's short stories. 'For Whom Things Do Not Change' asks about the definition of manhood, and treats ironically but also compassionately the psychology of the African man who can retain his self-respect when cooking English food for his master – even his black master – but cannot conceive of cooking for his family.

What emerges here, albeit in a generalisation, is that men are inferiorised by colonisation with respect not only to their African identities, but also with respect to their masculine identities. Women, alternatively, would appear to be, in this colonial or neo-colonial situation, less affected in both fortunate and troubling ways. That is, while the self-worth of women is not undermined in the manner that it is for men, outlined above, these women remain at a certain remove from the sites, grand or meagre, of historical negotiations. What is it to the wife in Aidoo's story whether her husband is the servant of a white man or a black man? The husband's problem is, by proxy, her problem. But, then again, it is not *her* problem.

'Between mothers, daughters, sisters . . . '

While Aidoo's *Dilemma of a Ghost* focuses on the dilemma of a man caught between two histories and two cultures, Aidoo is also concerned with the predicament of women who are not so much caught between cultures and histories as no longer having a place in either world. This double non-belonging, as opposed to split allegiance, might be spoken of as the dilemma of the daughter figure, as opposed to son and mother figures. The predicament, somewhat prefigured in *Anowa* in spite of its pre-colonial setting, allows for a certain swerve away from the narrative necessity of addressing male-authored agendas. It is the daughter figure's 'line of flight and fight' that is followed in Aidoo's *Our Sister Killjoy* (1977), a novel that more definitively marks a break with male addressees and male cultural go-betweens while sustaining a Pan-Africanist critique of imperialism.

Our Sister Killjoy concerns the travels of a young African woman in Europe and, as such, presents us with the interruption of an imperialist postmodernist culture by the return of the colonised subject. In order to foreground the importance of the 'African and gendered' identity of the protagonist, it is initially useful to place *Our Sister Killjoy* alongside prominent Western postmodernist texts of roughly its time, such as Thomas Pynchon's *The Crying of Lot 49* (1965) and Margaret Atwood's *Surfacing* (1972). In all three texts a critique of a de-humanised, amnesiac late-capitalist society is performed through the use of female protagonists who, by virtue of their gender, are allowed a certain critical detachment from the male corporatist 'plot'.

In order to produce a telling political difference between Atwood's text, with its eco-feminist concerns, and that of Aidoo, the following unfairly manipulative but useful juxtaposition can be made. In *Surfacing*, a bird that has been trapped and killed provokes the following response from the protagonist: 'Why had they strung it up like a lynch victim . . .' (p. 110). In *Our Sister Killjoy*, the protagonist, Sissie, counters the assertion that 'This earth belongs to us all. We can perch anywhere' (a phrase which also echoes a proverbial formulation in *Things Fall Apart*) with the objection: 'But we are not birds. . . . Our needs are more complicated than those of birds, aren't they?' (p. 129). A bird described as a 'lynch victim'? 'But we are not birds.' For Sissie, the critique of Western patriarchy and imperialism involves challenging its epistemic and actual violence with an epistemic violation.[12] The concerns of African peoples cannot be conflated or confused with those of other constituencies, such as eco-feminism or animal rights, and the female-centred, or even female-decentred, postmodernist text is to be interrupted by the dis-identifications of an African woman. In *Our Sister Killjoy*, Sissie comes to refuse the friendly, over-friendly, overtures of Marija, a housewife, like Pynchon's Oedipa Maas, 'a captive maiden having plenty of time to think' (*The Crying of Lot 49*, p. 13). Sissie, at first flattered by the attention she receives in Europe, particularly from Marija, ultimately cannot allow herself to be seduced: she will not respond to the demand for love that the working husband, that wage slave, fails to supply. In refusing to take the German husband's place, she re-duplicates it in not meeting Marija's, the wife's demand, as Sissie realises. She realises that she comes to occupy the place of ungiving white male, empowered by the vulnerability of another person. In the household of Europe, her choice is between standing in for the white man, through compensating for his failings, or standing in for the white man, through repeating his heartlessness.

This double bind is emblematic of how a gender differential cannot be ideologically universalised without de-stabilising its essentialist premises, namely that women are women always and equally so. An ensuing topic of the novel concerns an ironic treatment of a heart-transplant, that of an African's heart into an ailing white man. In his preface to Frantz Fanon's *The Wretched of the Earth*, Sartre notes that Fanon has given up on addressing a 'dying white culture,[13] a move that Aidoo's protagonist, Sissie, makes. Sissie, having refused the demands and desires of European others, goes on to interrogate her African brothers' inability to break with Europe in order to re-orientate these men towards the problems and crises besetting African countries. Sissie's most telling confrontation is with an ambitious doctor in the following exchange:

> 'But you can see how by remaining here someone like me serves a very useful purpose in educating them to recognise our worth . . . ?'
> 'Educating whom to recognise our worth, my Brother?' I asked.
> 'The people here,' he said.   (p. 129)

What Sissie's questioning serves to indicate here is that this Brother has made a symbolic identification with the European, or has set up the white person as an ego ideal, in the sense that Slavoj Žižek defines this positioning: 'identification with the very place *from where* we are being observed, *from where* we look at ourselves so that we appear to ourselves likeable, worthy of love'.[14] In Aidoo's novel, this question of a symbolic identification with Europe is reserved for the male characters. One reason for this would seem to be that it is the African sons who are generally educated and sent abroad in the role of providers for their families, and that it is these men, in particular, who seek to redeem a racial inferiorisation within the arena of European culture (as explored by Fanon in *Black Skins, White Masks*). The question remains, then, how it is that the character of Sissie, an educated African woman, with access to Europe, manages to preserve a persistent critical distance from European demands and complicities. Answers may be conjectured from the text.

First, her filial relation to Africa is different as a daughter figure. It would seem that the daughter manages to retain a certain narcissistic identification with a Mother Africa, while the African son's relation to a Mother Africa is of a more obviously Oedipal character, as already argued. The daughter's narcissistic identification with Africa would appear to be, as presented in *Our Sister Killjoy*, explicable, at least some extent, in terms of Žižek's definition of an ideal ego, as opposed to ego ideal. According to Žižek, identification with an ideal ego entails 'identification with the image in which we appear likeable to ourselves'.[15] The narcissistic taking up of a position in which one is likeable to oneself is signalled at two places. The first is when Sissie, identifying with the lustrous plums she is given, posits herself as likeable to herself as a young African woman:

> What she was also not aware of, though, was that those Bavarian plums owed their glory in her eyes . . . to other qualities that she possessed at that material time. . . . So she sat, Our Sister, her tongue caressing the plump berries with skin-colour almost like her own . . .   (p. 40)

The second moment is when Sissie, returning to Africa, abandons the love letter she has been writing to the man she has left behind, to address instead her expression of love to Africa, and as the phrasing of the text invites us to consider, also to herself: 'she was back in Africa. And that felt like fresh honey on the tongue. . . . "Oh, Africa. Crazy old continent . . ." Sissie wondered whether she had spoken aloud to herself' (p. 133). It could be argued that Sissie preserves both her own sense of self-worth and her sense of Africa's worth through this incorporating and nourishing 'healthy narcissism', one which is, perhaps paradoxically, both self-affirming and altruistic. There is an argument to be made here for a narcissism that is creative and ethical, as opposed to a narcissism conceived of in solipsistic terms.

Secondly, what is important with respect to this question is the black woman's identification or non-identification with the white woman. Fanon may be said to over-emphasise a symmetry between black men and black women with respect to the assumptions of white masks. If one looks at the literature and statements produced by African women writers, it often emerges that the white woman is not seen to enjoy or occupy a position of superiority as she is marked by her gendered inferiority within her own culture. The idle and isolated housewife or the trivial 'dolly-bird' are not regarded as enviable or viable, particularly among a first generation of post-colonial writers. In *Our Sister Killjoy*, Sissie remarks: 'it seems as if so much of the softness and meekness you and all the brothers expect of me and all the sisters is that which is really western. Some kind of hashed up Victorian notions, hm?' (p. 117). Interviewed by Adeola James, 'Zulu Sofola states: "With European exposure the African educated person has been led to believe that the female is an after-thought, a wall-flower." '[16] She goes on to say: 'There was no area of human endeavour in the traditional system where the woman did not have a role to play. She was very strong and active. . . . In the European system there is absolutely no place for the woman.'[17]

Sofola and Aidoo, while indicating that gender roles may have been clearly demarcated in traditional societies, suggest that hierarchised gender attributes in terms of which women are posited as merely decorative, weak and useless, are a colonial (and capitalist) imposition and legacy, one which African women by no means necessarily interiorise.[18] Speaking from a South African context, Ellen Kuzwayo claims that South African women have been subjected to a double stereotype, as 'black' and as 'women',[19] and in the autobiographical *Call Me Woman* (1985), she celebrates the heroic and insufficiently recognised contribution of African women in the struggle against apartheid. The strength and leadership of African women has been celebrated, justifiably and necessarily, in numerous contexts by both male and female writers,[20] however, there is a danger that this in turn may be posed as a stereotype that distracts from the insurmountable crises and hardships faced by African women.

Bessie Head, a South African writer who suffered ostracism, oppression and statelessness, explores the devastating effects of being radically deprived of a sense of self-worth in her major novel, *A Question of Power* (1974). As far as questions of gender are concerned, the novel may be read for its analyses of sexism and of 'the double displacement of woman',[21] among other possible readings. The central character, Elizabeth, enters into, or is overtaken by, a relationship between two male personae, or in the language of the text 'soul personalities'. For the sake of simplicity, a deliberately vague terminology, in keeping with the literary ambiguity of the text, could be used, whereby the persona of Dan may be referred to as: the personified spirit of racism and sexism. Dan, as the spirit of sexism, torments Elizabeth with her sexual inferiority with respect to the model of women desired by men, by parading before her his harem of pornographic cartoon-strip women: 'Miss Pelican-Beak, Miss Chopper, Miss Pink Sugar-Icing . . . Madame Make-Love-On-The-Floor . . . The Sugar-Plum Fairy . . . Body Beautiful . . . The Womb . . . the list of them was endless' (p. 148). Although Dan has here been suggested to be, in but one formulation, the 'personified spirit of sexism', it is in keeping with Head's anti-essentialism, or refusal to fix and pigeon-hole, that women are shown to be equally capable of sexism. Sexual power is only one of the questions of power explored in the novel, but it may be fair to say that in this text all forms of power are regarded as obscene in so far as they entail a lack of respect for a person's boundaries: a question of subjecthood. 'How had she fallen so low? It was a state below animal, below living . . .' (p. 14).

While Head explores being deprived of a sense of one's own humanity, the gendered dimension of this can be brought out. In these terms, what is at stake is the deconstruction of phallocentric power that does not entail the loss of a subject position for woman. It is the persona of Sello that is used to undo Dan's power, but in the process of this, Sello is accorded the position of the feminine whereby Elizabeth is further displaced: 'She seemed to have only been a side attachment to Sello. . . . Maybe she had made too close an identification with Sello for her own safety and comfort' (p. 25). The feminised Sello (and he is presented in feminine and Oriental, arguably 'Orientalist', terms[22]) comes to occupy any place *she* might have had. The antidote to this predicament would then seem to amount to claiming a speaking position or writing position of one's own; a matter of speaking/writing (for) oneself as opposed to always being spoken for. This is not a case of representing any 'true selfhood' but rather a political question of being granted or gaining access to positions of enunciation. Although it is impossible to detail here, writers such as Head and Aidoo are remarkable for the finding of their own creative idioms, and for their uses of literary forms to suit their purposes.

If African women writers engage with the difficulty of combatting the predicament of 'being spoken for', it is a predicament that they in turn engage with as they take up the responsibility of speaking for the non-literate woman, the 'gendered subaltern', in Gayatri Spivak's term, and terms, one who has even less, if any, access to a position of enunciation. As Robert Young usefully summarises Spivak's position: 'The problem is not that the woman cannot speak as such . . . but that she is assigned no position of enunciation . . . everyone else speaks for her, so that she is continually re-written as the object of patriarchy or imperialism.'[23] What is noteworthy about the position of African women writers with respect to this constituency is that it is one that, in many cases, they have emerged from, and can be said to retain links with. In anthropological terminology, it may be proposed that the native informant writes up her own account, whereby we may suppose (and arguably confirm in close readings) the risks of (mis-)translations are minimised or reduced. While it would be wrong to grant the African woman writer as writer the status of the 'gendered subaltern', it is important to recognise that she may retain a knowledge of, and, sometimes, sustained intimacy with the non-literate or semi-literate worlds of her mothers and sisters. The responsibility of this is registered in the writings and statements of educated African women. As the Kenyan writer and academic, Micere Mugo states: 'One woman's education is for all.'[24] Equally, indebtedness to specifically maternal orature has frequently been registered by African writers as a source of inspiration. Both the stories (orature) and the life stories of village women or non-literate/semi-literate women are transmitted by writers, often in the form of the short story, as in collections by Head and Aidoo among others.[25] One of the advantages conferred by the short-story format is that we are introduced to a number of diverse female characters in different situations, whereby these characters cannot simply be singled out as representative of African womanhood, while a female community yet receives a representation it would not otherwise get.

Bessie Head, who did not come from but became part of a village culture, presents us with the special story of a young woman who, in poverty, repaid an act of kindness with the gift of a bucket of water.[26] The story ends with the words: 'Tell them, those who judge my country, Africa, by gain and greed, that the gods walk about her barefoot with no ermine and pearls.' Head thus confronts foreign audiences with their notion of history with this unhistoric, or seemingly insignificant, act that would remain otherwise unrecorded. Head, in according the woman's act with its own 'glamour' and godliness, speaks of this woman in terms she would be unlikely to speak of herself. What Head does then is to dramatise how this woman in expressing herself has no access to a wider audience, hence the need for the writer's intervention. Indeed, Head's rhetoric draws attention to her role as ambassador of sorts, while the silence of the woman is given particular emphasis in the story.

In a different social and historical arena, the transmission of the otherwise overlooked, local, lived-out knowledges of women is forwarded in the work of the South African writer, Sindiwe Magona. In particular, her collection of short stories, *Living, Loving and Lying Awake at Night* (1992), focuses on the relationship between 'madam' and 'maid' in suburban South Africa, whereas in canonical South African literature the emphasis has arguably tended to fall on the figure of the male servant or urban male worker. Magona uses a collective or inter-changeable 'I' whereby several 'maids' get to tell their stories to each other, and what emerges is a telling collaborative critique of apartheid ideology and practices. For instance, the supposed childlike dependency of the maids is shown to be only an economic necessity, whereas the pathetic childlike dependency of the madams has deeper socio-economic and psychological investments. It is the white woman who is revealed as a captive slave to her idle existence, one to be filled paradoxically through ever-supervising the maid who is employed to enable her idleness (unless she is employed by white men to establish or regulate a whole family lifestyle). The benevolent or occasionally feminist madams are seen as relieving their consciences, still exercising forms of control over their maids, imposing an unwelcome indebtedness on them. Furthermore, the hierarchical racial differential serves to refute gender sameness:[27] 'How can I be a sister to my father, the white woman?' (p. 42). A tricksterish humour arises through the discrepancy between the 'know-all' madams, who think they know who they and their 'ignorant' maids are, and the incisive, witty discourse of the maids that the madams know nothing of. As in Nwapa's writing, gossip and dialogue are prevalent forms. At such a point, it is worth analysing further the question of 'women's voices'.

Following Derrida, in the history of Western metaphysics, speech has been accorded privilege over writing in that it is equated with origins and presence while writing is regarded as derivative, as 'copy'.[28] It may be added that Western culture looks for its origins in what it sees as 'primitive', oral, unrecorded, cultures. Within a colonial/ post-colonial history, it may be said that it is writing that is accorded privilege over orality (as dramatised in *No Longer at Ease*, discussed earlier in this chapter). It is the written word that is taken to be the sign of authority, learning, power, legitimacy, and is associated with progress and technology. Furthermore, it may be pointed out that the gaze and its functions (looking/reading) are gendered as masculine, while the voice is often conversely gendered as feminine. African cultural nationalists (or pan-nationalists) have sought to reassert the value of orature and oral traditions, sometimes in accordance with mother tongues and a return to a 'Mother Africa'.

Is there a difference between the ways in which male and female writers perform this agenda? It is too big a question to answer in so short a space, but a few tentative suggestions can be made with reference to writers under discussion here. It has been noted that Achebe transcribes orature into written form, for instance, strikingly, in the transcription of the use and forms of proverbs. Aidoo, beyond this act of transcription, produces what may be termed a 'spoken writing', whereby we are invited not only to read but almost to hear or to listen. Consider the following examples:

> When we old people speak . . . it is because we see something which you do not see. Our fathers made a proverb about it. They said that when we see an old woman stop in her dance to point again and again in the same direction we can be sure that somewhere there something happened which touched the roots of her life.
>
> (*Arrow of God*, 1964, p. 100)

> 'I say . . .'
> 'They do not say, my sister.'
> 'Have you heard it?'
> 'What?'
> 'This and this and that . . .'
> 'A-a-ah! that is it . . .'
> '*Meewuo!*'
>
> ('The Message', in *No Sweetness Here*, 1988, p. 38)

'Spoken writing', which pays attention to forms of vocalisation, while not the prerogative of the woman writer, is striking in the work of Aidoo and also notable in the work of Nwapa, Magona and Grace Ogot, among others. This inscribed vocalisation is more obviously noticeable in poetry and plays, but it is there too in prose writing. With respect to the latter, writers such as Head and Aidoo might be described, also, as strongly oratorical writers. That is, speech-making is not only included within the narrative (as a framed citation), but can become its mode of address. As far as gossip as a form either within or of writing by African women is concerned, we cannot evaluate it as 'mere' or 'idle'. In Magona's stories, for instance, its status as 'mere' or 'idle' serves as a screen for the production and circulation of a 'knowing otherwise', the use of which ranges from politicisation to survival strategies. The fact that oral forms play an important part in African women's writing, does not mean that their writing is automatically closer to 'original' sources. Rather, what is original is what is being done with *writing*.[29]

Novels by African women writers, particularly recently, also engage with the new demands of the privileged African woman, one who has moved into the professional middle classes. In novels with such a focus, imperialism and neo-colonialism, as topics of critique, are treated more glancingly and indirectly as the object of concern becomes the

articulation of women's desires and ambitions within mo
contemporary African patriarchal societies. Ironically, at a tim
Western feminists are increasingly trying to 'unlearn their privil
novels such as Aidoo's *Changes: A Love Story* (1991) and ~~Tsitsi~~
Dangarembga's *Nervous Conditions* (1988) address possible cross-
border concerns: a case not of unlearning privileges but of learning
what new privileges might entail. In this respect, there is implicitly a
refusal to be confined to an ethnic role and a refusal to comply with,
say, a gender puritanism, that is, a gender insistence purified of
questions of sexual desire.

The significantly titled *Changes: A Love Story* self-consciously
marks itself out as a 'love story', a self-reflexive or even self-parodying
process that is on-going in the narrative. The narrative serves to place
the love story in citation marks, and it underscores its own
socio-literary turns or swerves and tropes as being such. For instance,
this is how we are taken into the central character's world:

> Driving towards the Hotel Twentieth Century, Esi was completely
> overwhelmed by the vision of so much gold, golden red and red filtering
> through the branches of the coconut palms . . . even she wondered, as
> she later looked for parking outside the hotel, how people who had such
> scenes at their backyards felt on a daily basis . . . the fishermen who
> were packing up their boats down there might have been amused if they
> had heard her thoughts. For at that time, what they were wondering
> was whether the government would fulfil its promise . . .
>
> (p. 310)

The narrative takes us into a conversation between Esi and her friend,
Opokuya, beginning with references to 'house- help' and tea-drinking,
before broaching the topic of Esi's failed marriage due to the
insecurities of her husband who cannot cope with her commitment to
her own successful career. Esi's subsequent quest is for a new form of
partnership between the sexes in which independence may be
combined with sexual and romantic fulfilment. Her attempt to find
this with Ali, as his second wife, fails, as he treats her as a part-time
mistress. The truly loving relationship, a different love story behind
the love story, might be seen to be the warm, mutually supportive
friendship between the two women, Esi and Opokuya. The implication
is that a new relationship between the sexes stands in need of the
simultaneous 'roominess' and close support that friendship can
provide. Such a form of love is envisioned in Head's romantic and

idealistic novel *Maru* (1971) when she writes: 'Maybe it was not even love as people usually think of it. Maybe it was everything else; necessity, recognition, courage, friendship and strength' (p. 99). While both Head and Aidoo take up the theme of romantic love, it is in the attempt to move it away from 'true romance' towards the possibilities of a 'new romance'.

Tsitsi Dangarembga's *Nervous Conditions* concerns the cross-over from traditional rural life into the world of the aspiring black middle-class in late-colonial Rhodesia. Tambu, the female narrator, at an early age rejects her mother's destiny, that of a hard-working rural labourer and wife, orientating herself instead towards her uncle's achievements, as a highly educated man and provider for the extended family. The story of the educational and career achievements of the uncle, Babamukuru, is first narrated to Tambu by her grandmother in glowing terms, and Tambu then regards her uncle's position as the admired place to be aimed for. However, when, through her own conscientiousness, she gains a place at the mission school and becomes part of Babamukuru's household, her perspectives change. While from afar the position and status of both Babamukuru and his wife have seemed admirable, Tambu comes to realise that she has moved from one patriarchal sphere to another. Her aunt emerges as a simpering reinforcer and pacifier of the patriarchal ego, demeaning herself as a woman, or demeaning women, and regarding her career potentials as subservient to those of her husband. Babamukuru, while supportive of equal educational opportunities for both sexes, fosters unyielding conventional and puritanical rules and opinions concerning female behaviour and deportment, a question of a Victorian and Christian colonial legacy. Having moved from a more traditional Shona African society into a more thoroughly colonised and semi-elitist one, Tambu realises that Babamukuru's status and position is really no more available to her than before, simply because of the construction of womanhood in which she is trapped. While Tambu falls into a critical silence, one that fears to incur hostility through the expression of hostility, her sophisticated cousin, Nyasha, more used to the freedoms or lure of freedom of a Western lifestyle, rebels. Nyasha could be read as representing Tambu's split-off anger or as representing an alternative daughterly response to imprisonment within the white-like patriarchal household. Tambu's loss of voice and hysterical paralysis (literally, at one significant moment in the text, when her rural mother is forced into a respectable marriage ceremony), and Nyasha's

rebellion, which turns into an anorexic hunger-strike, are
indicative of the daughter's, or daughters', impasse. The question
hysteria and female adolescence that arise are certainly cross-bor
concerns within the arenas of feminism, psychoanalysis and
psychology.[31] Dangarembga, however, takes her title from Sartre's
paraphrase of Fanon.[32] Fanon writes: 'It is because the Negress feels
inferior that she aspires to win admittance into the white world. . . .
The Negro enslaved by his inferiority, the white man enslaved by his
superiority alike behave in accordance with a neurotic orientation.'[33]
As Homi Bhabha suggests, the colonist's message to the colonised is:
'Be like me, but not too like me.'[34] Given a gendered inflection in
Nervous Conditions, the impossible demand is perhaps: 'Be like
Babamukuru (take up a position in white society), but do not be like
him (do not take up his status and privileges as a man).'

In some respects Dangarembga's novel might be regarded as a
response to a first generation of women novelists in its radical
rejection, shown within the text, of matrilineal lines. However,
Nervous Conditions and *Changes* may be said to share the following
bottom lines with respect to the position of African women:

> The victimisation I saw was universal. It didn't depend on poverty, on
> lack of education or on tradition. . . . Even heroes like Babamukuru did
> it . . . what I did not like was the way all the conflicts came back to this
> question of femaleness.

> *(Nervous Conditions*, pp. 115–16)

> The older women felt bad. So an understanding that had never existed
> before them was now born. It was a man's world. . . . What shocked
> the older women though, was obviously how little had changed for their
> daughters – school and all!

> *(Changes*, p. 107)

This universality of the 'victimisation' or marginalisation of women is
not to be simply equated with the universality of women's oppression
in the West, or East, or globally. Each universality has its stories and
its histories, its own pauses for self-recognition and for re-negotiation:
'Do I think it always must be so? Certainly not. It can be changed. It
can be better.' (*Changes*, p. 111).

Notes

1. See Anita Levy, *Other Women: The Writing of Class, Race and Gender* (Princeton, NJ, 1991).
2. Adeola James (ed.), *In Their Own Voices: African Women Writers Talk* (London, 1990), p. 116.
3. Chinua Achebe, *A Man of the People* (London, 1966), p. 91.
4. Cited in Hans Zell, Carol Bundy and Virginia Coulon (eds), *A New Reader's Guide to African Literature* (New York, 1983), p. 358.
5. Abdul JanMohamed, *The Manichean Aesthetic* (Amherst, MA, 1983).
6. Ashis Nandy, *The Intimate Enemy* (Delhi, 1983).
7. See Ifi Amadiume, *Male Daughters, Female Husbands* (London, 1987) for discussion of the political activity of women during this period, and the importance of a goddess-focused religion for endorsing their economic and political power.
8. Elleke Boehmer, 'Stories of Women and Mothers', in Susheila Nasta (ed.), *Motherlands* (London, 1991), p. 6.
9. Florence Stratton, *African Literature and the Politics of Gender* (London, 1994).
10. *African Writers Talking*, ed. Dennis Duerden and Cosmo Pieterse (London, 1972), p. 26.
11. See, for example, Eldred Jones, 'Locale and Universe', *Journal of Commonwealth Literature*, vol. 3 (1967), pp. 127–31.
12. The terminology employed here is that of Gayatri Spivak. See, for example, 'The Rani of Sirmur', in Francis Barker (ed.), *Europe and Its Others*, 2 vols (Colchester, 1985).
13. Jean-Paul Sartre, 'Preface' to F. Fanon's *The Wretched of the Earth* (London, 1990), p. 9.
14. Slavoj Žižek, *The Sublime Object of Ideology* (London, 1989), p. 105.
15. A. James (ed.), *In Their Own Voices*, p. 105.
16. Ibid., p. 145.
17. Ibid., p. 105.
18. Special consideration may be given here to the fiction of Buchi Emecheta. It may be proposed that over her writing career her heroines are portrayed in increasingly 'internationalised' terms (in their feminism too). In *Destination Biafra* (1982), the heroine is destined for a romance with a white man (with respect to which a Fanonesque analysis may be appropriate). In addition, Emecheta has increasingly aimed for a Westernised/internationalised form of address and audience, as stated by her in *In Their Own Voices* (p. 39).
19. A. James (ed.), *In Their Own Voices*, p. 55.
20. Apart from the fictional works of African women see, for example, Ngugi's *Devil on the Cross* (1982), Achebe's *Anthills of the Savannah*

(1987), Chenjerai Hove's *Bones* (1988), and *Mothers of the Revolution* (1990), ed. Irene Staunton. The former three novels by male writers pointedly pay tribute to spirited women characters, while the latter text is a collection of interviews with Zimbabwean women which registers their crucial contribution to the war of independence.

21. See Gayatri Spivak, 'The Double Displacement of Women', in Mark Krupnick (ed.), *Displacement* (Bloomington, IN, 1983). Spivak addresses how the figure of woman has been used in Western philosophical discourses, but just as her critique may be applied within other contexts, Head's novel engages with a will-to-power that is cross-cultural and trans-historical.

22. Head may be regarded as deploying a stereotype of the Eastern man: see A. Nandy, *The Intimate Enemy*, and Edward Said, *Orientalism: Western Conceptions of the Orient* (London, 1978). Also, Dan may be said to conform to the stereotype of the exceptionally virile black man.

23. Robert Young, *White Mythologies: Writing, History and the West* (London, 1990), p. 164.

24. A. James (ed.), *In Their Own Voices*, p. 100. Mugo attributes this point to a speech made by a non-literate woman.

25. See, for example, Head's *The Collector of Treasures* (1977), Aidoo's *No Sweetness Here* (1988), and Grace Ogot's *Land Without Thunder* (1968).

26. Bessie Head, 'The Old Woman', in *Tales of Tenderness and Power* (Johannesburg, 1989).

27. As in *Our Sister Killjoy*, it is unequal power-relations that serve to gender positions – the place of the masculine is apportioned according to whom (which woman) has power.

28. Jacques Derrida, *Of Grammatology* (London, 1976).

29. The discourses of anthropology and psychoanalysis (as informed by respective practices) might, in addition to literary theory, be of use in theorising, formulating or analysing such a 'listening technique'.

30. See Gayatri Spivak, 'French Feminism in an International Frame', in *In Other Worlds* (New York, 1988).

31. See, for example, Carol Gilligan, Janie Victoria Wood and Jill McLean Taylor, *Mapping the Moral Domain* (Cambridge, MA, 1985).

32. Sartre's paraphrase of Fanon in his 'Preface' to *The Wretched of the Earth* is cited as an anonymous epigraph by Dangarembga who does not cite Fanon himself.

33. Frantz Fanon, *Black Skin, White Masks* (London, 1986), p. 60.

34. See, in particular, H. Bhabha, 'Of Mimicry and Man', *October*, vol. 28 (1984), for the analysis of such a message.

12 *The changing fortunes of the writer in Africa?*[1]

Jack Mapanje

Writers as custodians of African culture?

A little over nine years ago, at the Second African Writers' Conference held in Stockholm, I suggested that the custodians of African culture might have to be African writers, artists and scholars.[2] This was proposed because the guardians of our culture, the politicians and their censors, had failed us; they had turned their duty to be ultimately that of battling to protect their lives against the truths delicately depicted in our multifarious works of art. In order to counteract triumphantly the restrictive censorship laws passed by African politicians and their bureaucrats, I suggested therefore that writers might need to be more creatively aggressive in their approach; for example, they might need to exploit with more vigour and more alertness than hitherto, the oral traditions which the politicians so flagrantly debauched. I argued that in certain cases writers might have to adopt the combatant and complacent tone adopted by their oppressors in order to establish the culture of freedom, justice and truth which they sought, to replace our dictators' alternative culture of silence, lies and fear. I further suggested that writers even peep into the drawers of the censors, in order to circumvent properly, through their art, every move the censors made against them.

I suggested, above all, that in this thankless war against the injustices of the world, the language in which we couched the analyses of one another's artistic efforts, or we used in order to refer to one another, might have to be modified. Such dismissive terms as 'collaborators' versus 'exiles', which we sometimes tended to hurl at one another, needed to be restrained in favour of metaphors of solidarity and tolerance, because for us to succeed in the fight against oppression we must fight together, whether we lived within the country of our birth or outside it. I was not denying the reality of collaborators. The danger of working with those who cooperated with our despots was frankly admitted, but I believed that such people ought to be utilised to our advantage. I believed that how we eventually won our political and artistic liberation would depend upon factors that might be difficult to pin down. Writers should not be dismissed as mere collaborators in virtue of their writing within the walls of dictators, nor need we consider the creative contribution to liberation of exiles necessarily valid merely by virtue of their writing from exile.

I exemplified my claim by pointing to the role that the children of Soweto in South Africa would have been known to have played in the history of the liberation of South Africa from apartheid. The gravity of the writer's situation and our resolve to beat the censors at all costs was typified by the impromptu nature of my paper which was largely oral and anecdotal, the original written paper which had been cleared by the censors having been discarded on flight to Stockholm.[3] My remarks were made in the general context of African dictators, civilian and military, who blatantly abused the North–South divide, the East–West conflict and African oral traditions in their campaigns against those who opposed the imposition of their autocratic rule. I also offered these proposals against the background of Western prevailing attitudes. The West openly colluded with African dictators, like Hastings Banda of Malawi, by apologising on their behalf, in the hope that in exchange the dictators would offer to the West their vote at the United Nations. The West probably saw nothing wrong in dealing with dictators like Banda, whom they had educated anyway. As long as such tyrants appeared to be sufficiently strong to create a buffer of sorts against the other side, they were all right. And arcane contracts were entered into between dictators and the West; some coated in such patronising pronouncements as: 'He's all right! After all, things appear to be peaceful and calm in his country and he, at least, feeds his people.'

In the case of Malawi, of course, the truth as to who fed whom was well known. Even the least politically oriented tourist who watched Banda's mammoth political rallies curiously noted that it was the poor people from the villages and the townships who seemed to feed the dictator. These were forcefully made to offer their money, chickens, eggs, goats and cattle as presents to him. They were coerced into giving up their land so that Banda and his MPs could turn it into farms which would be for the people's benefit, although the produce or the profits never reached the people. Banda even claimed that these farms would help show the people, those he had taken the land from, how modern agriculture operates! Everything was done in the name of, and in gratitude to, Banda, who had liberated the people from the pangs of colonialism and the Central African Federation of Rhodesia and Nyasaland. Nothing was done in the name of the people. And in parliament, communist and socialist ideologies were resoundingly deplored by all.

When writers, journalists and others exposed these contradictions, noting, however obliquely, that it was Banda, his mistress's relatives and his parliamentarians who seemed to be the richer and not the villagers and their township counterparts, their voices were muzzled by the variegated strictures of the repressive regime. It was not only the dictators and their censors whose activities were oppressive. The dictators' Western and other allies too, helped in subtler ways to stifle writers and to suppress freedom and new ideas. Some of the people whom Malawian writers and researchers feared most in the university as well as in government, for instance, were not just the students in our lecture rooms or the local colleagues in the Senior Common Room or in the office, all of whom were obviously used to inform the authorities on what we taught or what we thought. We feared most those Western and other experts, whom the system relied upon to interpret the radical character of our various artistic works and researches. Even innocent reviews that demonstrated the tacit artistic revolution of our verse, stories, plays or novels would have been used by the dictator and his censors against us!

While it cannot be denied that some of the expatriates, perhaps only accidentally, brought the supposed radicalism of our works to the attention of the dictator through their ephemeral discussion with his array of informers, for instance, it was clear that there were others who unambiguously worked for the dictator's intelligence. And it was not difficult to detect them. Often they became remarkable interpreters of our dictator's policy, sometimes after only months of stay in the country. These expatriates supposed themselves to be more proficient on most matters of state than locals; they considered themselves more competent on how the dictator was going to respond to the introduction of this or that new idea which we intended to try out. They shamelessly and alarmingly advised us on the course of action to be taken if we wanted the authorities to approve our projects, effectively killing the idea at source if it was too original for their liking or if it threatened their continued cosy expatriate existence. It was these who discovered our poems or the 'revolutionary' results of the research which we published in some esoteric journal or magazine abroad (that is, in academic or professional journals and magazines that were unknown to the authorities or the censors) and they passed these on to the appropriate authorities for their immediate action. And apart from the intractable 'official clearance' which was always invoked in order to make our creative thinking almost impossible, constant appeal to the 'highest authorities' was made. And when you strayed into the office that was said to give 'the clearance' so that you could see for yourself who 'the authority' really was, the office was manned by an ordinary mortal who told you everything you did not want to know about the sexual goings-on at recent political rallies, the latest higher authorities' money transfers to their banks abroad, and the most current expatriate wife-swapping sagas.

Furthermore, there was atrocious concert of the activities of dictators and their acolytes throughout Europe and Africa, so that writers, artists, scholars and human-rights activists from one dictatorship found it impossible to find refuge in another country. Stories of writers or human-rights activists living in exile in Europe, America, Africa and elsewhere being blown up or killed or having been threatened by agents of African dictators abound. It was this kind of fraternity of dictators that frustrated the progress of genuine freedom and continues to thwart noble attempts at democratisation in Africa today.[4]

The changing context of resistance writing?

Today, as dictators, their censors and their local and expatriate informers undergo astonishing transformation, the context of discussion of the writer's role is somewhat shifting, both ideologically and psychologically. The world has so miraculously revolved on its axis in the last few years that the writer's fortunes appear to have been permanently recast so that perhaps resistance writing will no longer be an important option for the writer. More poignantly, when I was released from prison in May 1991, after my peeping into the dictator's drawer had cost me three and a half years, I found solace in the generosity and warmth of a transformed world community that had been fighting for my release. These included Malawian compatriots at home and throughout the diaspora, distinguished writers, artists and scholars throughout the African continent and abroad as well as revered European, American, Commonwealth and other writers, linguists, journalists, academics, church men and women as well as ordinary mortals. Some activists worked from professional organisations such as International PEN, Africa Watch, Human Rights Watch, Fund for Free Expression, Rotterdam Poetry International, The London Poetry Society, Amnesty International, Index On Censorship, Article 19 and others. Individuals and groups from UNESCO, the European Parliament and the African, Caribbean and Pacific Assembly, and such bodies as the United Kingdom's Association of University Teachers, the Linguistics Association of Great Britain, The Language Society of America, Southern Africa's Linguistics Association for SADCC Universities (LASU), the Association of Nigerian Authors and many other associations whose noble efforts I may not sufficiently acknowledge, adopted me as their prisoner of conscience.

Closer friends and colleagues even travelled from one meeting to another giving lectures about my writing and my situation, and getting participants to sign petitions and appeals for my release in the process. Their messages were exploited by various world media; the numerous international newspapers, magazines, journals, radio and television stations throughout Africa and the West, including the BBC, Radio Netherlands International, Radio Deutsche Velle, Voice of America and others in Africa, Europe and beyond. We can begin to imagine the staggering impact that letters of appeal, petitions, telephones, faxes and telegrammes from such a multitude of people must have had on Malawi's frail but stubborn dictator and his bureaucrats. We can begin to imagine how this kind of universal solidarity would help reinvigorate the hope in humanity of the most impenitent writer or the humbling effect it might have on any writer. But upon release, I also found that the context had shifted in another more politically productive direction. The Berlin Wall had crumbled; with it those brutal practices of communism and socialism that we had got accustomed to accepting. The Cold War was over. The West was playing a different political and economic game. Aid to developing countries, for instance, was being considered only for those rulers who showed some respect for human rights. The notion of 'good governance' was being vigorously pursued, being linked to the call for multi-party politics where single-party politics were entrenched.

Furthermore, closer home the political arena had changed just as dramatically. In South Africa, for example, Nelson Mandela was released. Mikuyu Prison in Malawi had greeted the news with huge grins on the faces of political prisoners. Even those criminal prisoners who were awaiting hanging shared our nervous feeling of optimism in a curious manner. The possible fulfilment of the hope for release which we had abandoned and whose search had become tantamount to one's search for madness began to be imagined. We had two reasons for feeling optimistic. First, we had heard through the usual grape-vine about the world-wide campaign for our release just mentioned, although its extent and effect on the inflexible government of Malawi were not so easy to determine. But more importantly, political prisoners throughout Malawi had appropriated Nelson Mandela as their hero long before I was imprisoned myself. Discussion of his release in Mikuyu Prison therefore was always a source of succour and a boost to our impaired spirit. Besides, we knew that Mandela's release in the context of the brave new world just cited would mean the end of apartheid. And this would not augur well for Banda's political career which had, by and large, relied on the continuation of apartheid for its survival. Hence, in Mandela's release we imagined the permanent shattering of the centre that had sustained our own tyranny for more than thirty years.

Suppose then that the West was serious in its quest for good governance for developing countries. Suppose genuine multi-party politics actually happened on the African continent. Imagine that the bulwark of the dictator's pride and nourishment disappeared. Imagine further, that the United Nations and the World Bank changed their language in support of the oppressed or the new human-rights situation. Imagine particularly that the International Monetary Fund or the European banking system were persuaded to join the race against the buoyant bank statements of our dictators. Well, my first serious reaction would be, 'Praise the Lord!' Secondly, despite the apparent paradox that this situation entailed, that is, despite the nagging feeling one might have had, for example, that here was Africa being patronised to again from Europe (reminiscent of the colonial period), nonetheless this was good news, supposing, of course, that the West was serious and that it did not go back on its word!

Intrinsically, the situation was rather disturbing, for yet again the shame was on Africa. We had allowed our dictators, civilian or military, to run the political arena on their own terms (supported naturally by the West) rather than run it on the terms of the people. So, if in the course of time the West had decided to ditch dictators, the writers' response was probably going to be prudent beaming faces, cautiously remembering the number of African writers who had predicted that the African dictator would eventually have to confront the consequences of his own oppressive rule anyway. Perhaps gentle smiles on those exile writers who had been so fearlessly engaged in human-rights activities from other African and European capitals, could now be imagined. Perhaps writers could be allowed to muse about the possibility of eventually returning home or perhaps positively refashioning that pitiful image of exiles who consistently floated from one Northern summer to another, like restless swallows. Perhaps the honour of traditional artists like *izibongi* or the *griots* (poets), lost at the hands of colonialism, dictatorship or apartheid and at the insolent birth of the printed word, would at long last be somewhat restored. Perhaps then there would be no compulsion for resistance writing?

The birth of the beast of the African dictator?

It is true that colonialism and neo-colonialism have destroyed both physically and mentally the men and women whom it was invented to serve: both masters and servants. It is true that it destroyed the stable balance that might have existed between African rulers and their ruled. It is further true to suppose that where there might have been order and mutual understanding among different African peoples, mistrust, division and chaos were brought about instead. It is unrealistic, however, to conclude that the envious role of *griots* or *izibongi* as the nation's entertainers, historians, poets, teachers and critics at once, or that the respect for African cultural traditions (without assuming that the old political, social and cultural order was necessarily glorious and perfect) will ever be satisfactorily re-established. Only romantics presume that these and many other features of the old African world, which have been permanently destroyed by colonialism with its attendant erroneous philosophy of the truth of the printed word over the verbal, can ever be restored again. It is also ludicrous to continue to blame the West or colonialism for all of Africa's burdens, especially when the continent is largely independent. Africa itself must be held accountable for its own ills. One of these ills concerns our impetuous acceptance of the integrity of the printed word; the supposition, for example, that we cannot learn from our African past because it was mainly verbal. D.T. Niane, translator of Africa's best-known epic, *Sundiata*, blames the exacerbation of this state of affairs after colonialism squarely on the attitude of Western-educated African intellectuals:

> Unfortunately the West has taught us to scorn oral sources in matters of history, all that is not written in black and white being considered without foundation. Thus, even among the African intellectuals, there are those who are sufficiently narrow-minded to regard 'speaking documents' which the griots are, with disdain, and to believe that we know nothing of our past for want of written documents. These men simply prove that they do not know their country except through the eyes of the Whites.[5]

The point has been almost spent throughout the literature on the subject but perhaps it needs repeating: the kind of government that Africa has lived through since the attainment of independence has had just as debilitating an effect on our minds as colonialism. We mentioned above the stifling censorship we lived through in Banda's Malawi and which inherently guaranteed that we did not live any meaningful intellectual and social lives. Malawian citizens generally, not just the writers, artists or scholars that we noted, could not be said to have been in control of their own destinies in the manner that nationals of other independent African countries may be said to have been. We were all reduced to the role of sheer observers in the unfolding of the drama of our own history. And although we ought to be held responsible for this state of affairs to obtain, in the sense that we allowed Banda and his hangers-on to impose their rule on us, it must be conceded that with the various tentacles of repression in place in Malawi, it was almost impossible to initiate anything new or substantive. It is dishonest not to confess (however unpleasant it might seem) that for more than thirty years the beast of dictatorship did perform atrociously superbly in Malawi. The system allowed nobody to be genuinely and positively creative, not even the dictator himself.

We were all supposed to think alike and act alike. Anyone who attempted to do otherwise met walls of censorship or imprisonment, both psychological and physical in every direction. And often the censorship was done subtly, with the intention of making you feel guilty for having effectively done nothing. The naïve philosophy of 'biting the hand that feeds you' was habitually invoked to embarrass us into submission. And for fear of what was to befall us and our families (imprisonment or worse), we chose silence or even self-censorship, which probably made it worse for our creative thinking.

It was impossible even to theorise about the situation in which we were. You were considered 'another intellectual' living in an ivory tower, if you resisted. Again, the idea was to make you feel guilty for being the so-called intellectual or to persuade you into exile if you did not want to conform. Thus we all shamelessly cowered to the status of intellectual or creative morons.

I remember directing an interdisciplinary research project on Malawian orature carried out by university students and staff in the mid-1970s. We decided to publish what we had gathered and analysed (the folk stories, the riddles, the fishermen's chants, the songs that men and women sang at beer parties, the wedding songs, the dance songs, the songs that women sang when they pounded grain) in a bulletin which we called *Kalulu*. But when the first issue of *Kalulu* was selling in the Senior Common Room, it was the then Vice-Principal of the College himself who led the campaign against us, roundly mocking our efforts with the words, 'Another English Department magazine; and we wonder how long this one will last this time?' It was he and his informers who finally warned the censors about the 'dangerous research activities going on in the English Department'. Apparently we had blundered by undertaking the research judiciously (without seeking official clearance). But we failed to see why anybody needed official clearance in order to interview their grandmother about the origin of initiation songs or beer-drinking chants she might have sung in her early womanhood!

And the Vice-Principal's protestations had nothing to do with the academic jealousies over publishing that we often come across on university campuses everywhere. If the commentators had intended to challenge the academic quality of the bulletin, we would have taken the remark as a healthy academic gesture. It was rather that this type of imaginative thinking was to be discouraged because it threatened the despotic ethic under which we all lived. What the authorities patently feared was that we would discover what the people actually thought about the government as we collected the songs, the tales and the chants. But everybody already knew what the people thought. Only the dictator and his bureaucrats refused to see what was going on throughout the country. The students and the local staff engaged in the research always returned to their villages every holiday or at every national independence celebration. They could influence the people against the government then if they really wanted to.

The one phenomenal feature common to dictators and those who pledge loyalty to them is that they persistently refuse to see what even children can see. It was incomprehensible to us, for example, that it should have been the Vice-Principal who refused to see that we merely attempted to define and re-affirm the origins of our culture or our identity through the orature research project. We could not have threatened anybody's authority in the process. Yet in the nature of dictatorships, trying to define anything on one's own terms constitutes an obvious act of punishable rebellion. We were being different when we had no right to be so. The point, of course, was that even culture was supposed to be defined on the dictator's terms. Only the dictator and his legislators knew what was best for the development of the country. Only they knew best who to engage in which projects. That the bulletin was allowed to continue at all was, in part, because the English Department had encouraged some of the safer local academics to do their research degrees in orature when they went to universities abroad: *Kalulu* would be indispensable for their research.

What is mind boggling about this weird scenario is the apparent lack of explanation of the origins of the dictators' brutality. Where and how did they get their absolute power and their intolerance? Where did Africa go wrong? Although we voted our rulers into power, we clearly did not decree the cruelty which followed their rule. If anything, at independence the masses of the African peoples expected their leaders to save them from the bondage of colonialism, poverty, disease and hunger. The power of our dictators could not have originated in their physical constitution because their physique tended towards the frail. It could not have emanated from the West where they had trained for so long, because the West preached with impunity the tolerance embedded in their so-called democratic institutions, the most liberal among them anticipating our leaders to exploit such principles on behalf of the peoples of Africa. It could not have had its birth wholly in the African oral traditions for, even under the most frightful patronage of African kings, queens and chiefs, the *griots*' or *izimbongi*'s reproach of the king's or chief's abuse of power was sanctioned at courts, indeed in certain cases the praise-singers were expected to criticise authority at performances. Whatever the case, *griots* and other artists in ancient Africa would not have endured the persecution of writers and artists still prevalent in Africa today.

The *griot*, the *imbongi* and the writer?

As for the role of the African writer or artist in general, let us begin with the boast of the age-old *griot*, from whom, perhaps implicitly, we have all abstracted the writer's present role.[6] The following boast from the *griot* of the African epic *Sundiata* would have been rather venturesome in Banda's Malawi:

> I am a griot . . . master in the art of eloquence . . . we are the vessels of speech, we are the repositories which harbour secrets many centuries old . . . without us the names of kings would vanish into oblivion, we are the memory of mankind; by the spoken word we bring to life the deeds and exploits of kings for younger generations. . . . My word is pure and free of all untruth; it is the word of my father; it is the word of my father's father . . . ; royal griots do not know what lying is. . . . When a quarrel breaks out . . . it is we who settle the difference, for we are the depositories of oaths which the ancestors swore. . . . Listen to my word, you who want to know . . .
>
> (p. 1)

If this *griot* had toured the villages of Malawi in Banda's time, opening his epic with this boast, he would have been arrested on first performance and detained without trial 'for confusing His Excellency the Life President's people'. His epic would have been banned by Banda's Censorship Board. The *griot* claims too much power for himself. Only Banda was allowed to make such boasts and assume such powers. Only he was the nation's historian, entertainer, innovator and arbiter, as witnessed by the long ornate speeches he often subjected us to, rattling on for hours on every aspect of life, from the relevance to Malawi of traditional English Grammar to the futility of modern mathematics. He was the highest authority on matters of health (although there were more prisons than hospitals in Banda's Malawi!). He knew everything about religion (at mass rallies often bamboozling his village mortals with his being the Elder of the Church of Scotland!). There was probably no government post which Banda never occupied in the thirty-three years of his autocratic rule. When a minister was made to resign or was sacked by him, the ministry reverted to him before he appointed someone else. Banda would not stand *griots* like Sundiata's declaring their agenda thus without 'clearance'!

And after banning *griots* of this sort, the censors and bureaucrats would have searched for alternative words to explain to Banda what modern *griots* (poets) were really like and why they deserved being banished from Malawi society as they had done with Sundiata's *griot*. If they had stumbled upon Auberon Waugh's editorial from the January 1994 issue of *Literary Review*,[7] they would have been satisfied first with the title of the editorial 'On the Baseness and Ingratitude of Poets'. 'Brilliant!' they would have shouted. And they would most likely have settled on the following words to argue their case with their dictator against whichever *griot* or poet they chose to ban or imprison:

> It was – and remains – my experience of life that anyone who describes his vocation as poet, purveying the modern style of formless verse, is invariably among the meanest and most despicable in the land: vain, empty, conceited, dishonest, dirty, often flea-ridden and infected by venereal disease, greedy, parasitical, drunken, untruthful, arrogant . . . all these repulsive qualities, and also irresistibly attractive to the women. We certainly did not want them in the Academy.
>
> (p. 1)

Not only would these words be contorted to exonerate the censors' stereotypical view of *griots* or writers, but they would further skew the role of artists generally and claim, for instance, that such people could not be relied upon as the custodians of our culture.

More importantly, having ignored any comic, ironic or sarcastic import that the editorial might entail, and perhaps invoking Plato's view on the place of poets in society in the process, the censors would probably have proceeded to put the case to Banda that having found the *griot* guilty of 'confusing' His Excellency the Life President's people in the villages, through the *griot*'s boastful song, for security reasons, therefore, they recommended that the *griot* be detained. In the circumstances, might His Excellency the Life President like to sign the detention order for the *griot*'s detention until it should delight His Excellency to have him released at His Excellency's own pleasure? The indisposed dictator would probably have nodded or grunted, pointing in the direction of the notorious prison camps. This is no embellishment of fiction. It is the extent to which our dictators would have gone in distorting the *griot*'s boast or the editor's humour, seeking thereby to silence with a ban, exile or imprisonment those who resisted their power. It is evidently insane for writers to contest for space in such a suffocating climate.

Whither freedom in the new dispensation?

As Africa's controversial novelist and essayist, Ngugi wa Thiong'o has consistently argued, and as is implied in Niane's words above, what Africa needs to rectify, at least in part, the status of its annihilated culture, or to assert its distinction and maintain its identity, is some form of decolonising of the writers' and the people's mind. Writers and their audiences must dislodge from their minds those symbols and images of fear, silence and lies which colonialism and our dictatorships have constructed as an abiding feature of our new culture. But the notion of 'decolonising the mind' must be taken more resolutely than hitherto. It must be recognised in its broadest possible sense in order to appreciate how the *griot*'s and Africa's dignity might be restored. Part of the struggle, perhaps the larger part for those writing from within Africa, given the new dispensation, will obviously include the writers' use of their own African languages. Besides, we hope that those who decide to write in African languages will not stop at writing poems, plays, short stories and novels only. Where this has not already started, writers will begin more earnestly to write their ideas and philosophies on how they see the movement of African societies and African thought in African languages. Those essays by African thinkers that sometimes run the risk of being appropriated as part of the modern European world view of African society and thought because they have been written in European languages should be translated in African languages for the masses of the literate African public to read and enjoy (their Africanness or foreignness). Let there be more journals and magazines in African languages where reviews of recent ideas, movements or books from Africa and the world at large can be published, even in translation.

The vexatious politics of publishing cannot be ignored; but in a world where the computer is performing unimaginable wonders (including that of eluding the dictator), we hope that writers can engage more positively in cheap private electronic publishing. We hope that African writers will not continue to depend on multinational publishing houses which have tended to obstruct certain types of African inventiveness. If the fax revolution and E-mail are about to subdue thoroughly the dictator's absolute stranglehold on our societies, private computer publishing might accomplish even greater feats.

Only by experimenting their resilience across languages, and publishing the results in whatever manner suitable, can those so-called untranslatable concepts in philosophy or science be said to possess or not to possess any form of wholeness. We are certain that at least the vibrancy of the Kiswahili culture of long ago, to take one example, could be resuscitated. We are sure that the audience that is literate in Gikuyu or Kiswahili today will enjoy the Gikuyu or Kiswahili version of Ngugi's *Decolonising the Mind* or his *Moving the Centre*.[8] If the 'book' or the printed word is rejected in favour of the 'oral', this would not surprise us. For example, if modern audio-visual gadgetry (cassette tapes, videos and camcorders or CDs and other modern modes of communication) are preferred, this is fine, as long as the message is disseminated in languages (African, creole or other) which the general reading, listening or other public understands. This type of comprehensive approach to communication with the masses of our audiences may prove to be the most effective and most lasting form of moving the centre (before the IMF and CNN permanently conquer our villages).

What about the African writer then? What role should writers play when dictators disappear from the scene (if indeed they do disappear) and in some cases those African languages they stopped us from using are now at our disposal? What is the role of the African writer or journalist when there is some appearance of free press after the fax revolution's destruction of the dictator's censorship and power, leading to the extraordinary proliferation of the euphoric weekly papers that we read today? Above all, what role will writers play when the masses of our African populations (still suffering from the same diseases and still largely untouched by the fruits of our new liberties) continue seething, mostly in disbelief, with the euphoria of a world without the ubiquitous 'His Excellency the Life President'? How will these newly won freedoms and free press fare with the prospect of other dictators lurking around the corner? To these queries there is one and the same answer: writers and artists must be more vigilant. They must continue to play the role they have always played, to ensure that our societies do not lose sight of whatever liberation we might have gained. We will assume, however questionable it might seem, that this time round the audience or readership is going to heed the writer's search for beauty, truth and justice.

In the new dispensation, writers, like other artists, will continue to sing about the struggle for life because that struggle is endless and ponderously cyclic. The world will forever need more and perhaps better light that the writer has come to symbolise. In the case of Malawi, the immediate role of the writer must be to continue to become the memory of the nation. The writer, the musician and the painter must sing the song of reparation of the names of those heroes and heroines that our despotic regime has obliterated from our history. And these have not all been demigods or demigodesses. Only by doing this can the artist begin to reclaim that enviable role as the memory of humanity. The writer's sensibilities will doubtless be exhausted in other areas. Being rigidly prescriptive about them might make matters unbearable in a world which is striving to become democratic. Some writers will experiment with the beauty of their mother tongue, a situation which we consistently cried out for under our dictator's oppressive regime, and where the nine or so languages of Malawi could not be used in education or creative writing. But those who want to write in European languages will not be stopped. The pluralistic society which Africa is energetically pursuing can best advance from a multiplicity of idiom. Besides, there is a growing population of African children who are born in the diaspora and whose native tongue is English, French, Portugese, Kiswahili, etc.

Therefore, let there be a *veritable* freedom of choice of language, subject matter and mode of expression. Let the writers, the painters, the musicians and other artists genuinely organise those drama, poetry, music and art festivals and exhibitions throughout the land. Let them invite their neighbours in trade across the land and across the seas. As of old, let there be global celebration of human charm, folly and horror without hindrance. Where the liberation war has been sufficiently won, let some writers celebrate their reconciliation with their torturers or with themselves or with both. As some pursue this worthy cause, let others commemorate those images of horror and oppression which have become an indelible part of our precious history. These writers too will hopefully want to move on to other experimental rites of passage thereafter? Whatever the case, we hope the new world will let the song endlessly flow, uncensored.

Before the official end of apartheid, Njabulo Ndebele, one of South Africa's most provocative literary critics and probably the best short-story writer in South Africa, said this about the role of the writer in South Africa:

the task of the new generation of South African writers is to help to extend the material range of intellectual and imaginative interest as far as the subject of life under oppression is concerned. It is to look for that area of cultural autonomy and the laws of its dynamism that no oppressor can ever get at; to define that area, and, with purposeful insidiousness, to assert its irrepressible hegemony during that actual process of struggle. That hegemony will necessarily be an organic one: involving the entire range of human activity. Only on this condition can a new creative, and universally meaningful democratic civilisation be built in South Africa.[9]

I find no cause yet to replace Ndebele's phrase 'life under oppression'. The role of the *griot* or the *imbongi* or the writer has not changed, colonialism or none, dictatorships or none, apartheid or none. It will probably not change. The writer will continue to be an activist on behalf of freedom and justice, beauty and truth, whatever time and whatever place. But perhaps more pertinently, should the masses of our African peoples be in danger of another form of assault, perhaps caused by another set of dictators in this timeless cycle of dictators, it is our sincere hope that writers and artists generally will continue to shout, with their pencil, paper, drum, feet or whatever. Otherwise, all our priceless sweat for the redemption of African cultural identity hitherto would have become another vacuous enterprise.

To conclude, Dennis Brutus, South Africa's robust poet and indefatigable fighter against apartheid, in one of his most moving poems on the strategies for survival that humans often adopt in time of despair against oppression, concludes his short poem appropriately titled 'Somehow we survive' with this delicate line: *somehow tenderness survives*. It is our hope that the cultural and other guises of chaos brought about by colonialism in its numerous manifestations, African dictatorships and apartheid in their abundant semblances, can be repaired, in part, by the writers' tender mode of expression because, in the new dispensation, we cannot afford anything less: somehow the writers' tenderness or sensibility must be allowed to blossom unencumbered. So, if some writers in Africa or elsewhere today have advanced from pen to personal computer, in the same way that entrenched totalitarian governments have given over to multi-party governments, this is clearly remarkable and welcome news for our aesthetic world. But this should not blind us of the real issue: the sphere of the majority of writers and would-be writers in Africa continues to twirl dimly on its axis as if nothing has happened. Whatever the guises of Africa's ostensible advance, discernible in our presumed winds of change (in the case of Malawi as reflected in the new free press), most writers in Africa have no robes of fortune to change into, still less boast about (other than a *luta continua*!).

Notes

1. This is a shortened version of a talk which was first presented to the Africa Society, University of Oxford, 12 February 1994, and was interspersed by a reading of relevant poems.
2. The paper I refer to was eventually published as 'Censoring the African Poem: Personal Reflections', in Kirsten Holst Petersen and Per Wastberg (eds), *Criticism and Ideology* (Uppsala, 1988). The résumé which I provide here expands aspects of the original presentation.
3. The tradition of swapping papers in order to conquer the censors was extensively used in the 1960s and 1970s by such well-known Malawian academics as the radical sociologist Professor Alifeyo Chilibvumbo and others, when they attended conferences whose themes might have sounded too abstruse for the censors to give easy clearance. It was part of the ongoing battle against the censors.
4. Typical of the kind of brotherhood of despots that I have in mind are the recent monstrous disclosures on the portentous correspondence between Kenya's ruling party KANU (Kenya African National Union) and Malawi's ruling party MCP (Malawi Congress Party), where KANU, apparently on request, promised to send undercover personnel and equipment in order to 'help' MCP effectively win Malawi's 17 May 1994 general elections (in the manner that Daniel arap Moi and KANU fragmented Kenya's opposition at its general elections). One paper (edited by Malawi's best short-story writer, Ken Lipenga) which has come into being with the recent vibrant free press in Malawi, *The Nation*, carries a photocopy of the letter from KANU to the MCP with instructions to MCP's Vice-President elect, Hon. Gwanda Chakuamba: 'It is our considered view that our Kenyan personnel will need to be provided with Non De Plumes [sic] to cover their professional background, i.e. to mascarade [sic] as International monitors. On our part we would issue them with appropriate Diplomatic Passports' (28 February 1994). The KANU letter which is dated 9 February 1994 arrived at the Chichiri sub-office of the MCP on the 17 February 1994. It is signed by the Secretary General of KANU, Hon. J.J. Kamotho, EGH, MP, and carries seven bold insersions of the word 'CONFIDENTIAL'.
5. For a fuller appreciation of this matter, see D.T. Niane's introduction to *Sundiata: An Epic of Old Mali*, translated into English by G.D. Picket (London, 1965), esp. p. viii.
6. The role of the writer generally as teacher has been exhaustively discussed in the literature. The central concerns of oral poets and singers such as

Southern Africa's *izibongo* and West Afrca's *griots* are well documented. Reference to the modern African writer as teacher was first made by Chinua Achebe early in his career (in the 1960s): 'The Novelist as Teacher', in *Morning Yet on Creation Day* (London, 1975).

7. The point at issue is that Auberon Waugh's editorial could have been culled in part or in whole by the censors in order to support their censorship or imprisonment of a poet whose work might have displeased the so-called authorities. This passage could easily have been deliberately distorted without apology in order to justify the censors' action. See *The Literary Review*, January 1994, p. 1.

8. At a recent Conference (Testaments: Writers at the Crossroads, 29–30 January 1994) of South African and British-based African and Caribbean writers held in London's Brixton Recreation Centre, where I first made this point, I was reminded by Ngugi's best-known translator and well-known writer herself, Wangui wa Goro, that Ngugi's *Decolonising the Mind: The Politics of Language in African Literature* (London, 1986) and *Moving the Centre: The Struggle for Cultural Freedoms* (London, 1993), are already being translated into Gikuyu for the Kenyan public. 'Praise the Lord,' I said.

9. See Ndebele's crisp chapter, 'The Noma Award Acceptance Speech', in *Rediscovery of the Ordinary* (Congress of South Afrcan Writers, 1991), p. 159.

13 The press in Africa: expression and repression

Adewale Maja-Pearce

> In trying to reduce or eliminate the monopoly of African governments, care should be taken not to go to the other extreme of believing that only an exclusively privately-owned system can fulfil the aspirations of the people.
>
> (Paul A. V. Ansah, 'The Political and Legal Framework for a Free and Pluralistic Press in Africa', 1991)

The Standard newspaper in Kenya, one of the country's three English-language dailies, underwent a dramatic metamorphosis towards the end of 1991. Previously a supporter of President Daniel arap Moi's ruling Kenya African National Union (KANU), it suddenly became one of KANU's most virulent opponents, vying with the more popular *Daily Nation* to unearth malpractices in the higher reaches of government. The reason for the about-turn was provided by a spokesperson for 'Tiny' Rowland's Lonrho Group, the owners of the paper, who claimed that 'corruption in Kenya had reached sickening levels', and that, as a result, 'Tiny Rowland felt he had to make a stand'.[1] This was laudable enough, but deeply unconvincing, for at least two reasons. In the first place, Rowland's sudden conversion coincided with the Kenyan government's decision to back out of a lucrative contract with Lonrho; in the second place, corruption in Kenya was always at 'sickening levels', but it had never bothered Rowland before. On the contrary, as late as 1990 (i.e. when business was good) Donald Trelford, editor of the Lonrho-owned London *Observer*, accompanied his employer to Nairobi in order to deliver a lecture in which he called Kenya 'the jewel in the crown of independent Africa', and advised the government not to be too upset by media 'sniffer dogs'.[2] By 'sniffer dogs' he presumably meant the staff of the outspoken *Nairobi Law*

Monthly, which was then at the height of its campaign against government corruption; worse yet, even as Trelford spoke, his counterpart on the *Law Monthly* was being treated at the Kenyatta National Hospital for injuries sustained following his arrest and detention on unspecified charges of sedition.

To understand the scale of the hypocrisy in all of this we need only compare *The Observer*'s 'stand' over Kenya with its treatment of a report by one of its own correspondents following a visit to Malawi at about the same time that Rowland was apparently undergoing his much-trumpeted sea-change. As everybody knows, Life President Ngwazi Dr H. Kamuzu Banda runs one of the nastiest dictatorships anywhere, comparable only to Romania under Ceausescu or Haiti under 'Papa Doc' Duvalier. 'I will keep them there and they will rot', he once declared in reference to a newly constructed prison for suspected or potential or imagined dissidents. 'And I am going to make sure that in addition to the regular prison warders we have additional warders who . . . will know what to do with these fools'.[3] A clear enough statement, and put into deadly practice by a multiplicity of security forces dedicated to maintaining the 'peace and calm, law and order' which Banda considers the greatest achievement of his twenty-eight-year rule, but which only serves to hide the scale of the corruption that would have been impossible even in Kenya. The bulk of Banda's vast personal fortune has been accumulated over the years through his control of Press Group (formerly Press Holdings), which is involved in every branch of the country's economic activity, including retailing, manufacture, food processing, tourism and, most importantly, agriculture. Banda holds all but one of the company's 5,000 shares; as a recent report on the country made clear, 'human rights abuses have occurred as a means of maintaining Banda in power in order to amass further wealth'.[4] The previous managing director of Press Holdings, for instance, was only recently released after ten years in detention for criticising Banda's business practices.

As with all dictators, Banda has never under-estimated the role of the media in ensuring his grip on power, which is why there is no independent press in Malawi. Both the country's newspapers, the *Daily Times*, which appears Monday through Friday, and the *Malawi News*, a weekly published on Saturday, are mouthpieces of the ruling Malawi Congress Party. Every issue of either paper is required to lead with a front-page story on Banda himself, preferably with an accompanying photograph: 'Ngwazi arrives in Zimbabwe'; 'Ngwazi attends reception at meet'; 'Ngwazi holds talks with the Queen'; 'Ngwazi plants a tree at Victoria Falls'; 'Grand welcome awaits Ngwazi', were the successive headlines in the *Daily Times* during the Commonwealth Heads of Government Meeting in October 1991. No mention of human rights or multi-party politics, the twin themes of the meeting, but then both these undesirable imports – 'The Malawi system, the Malawi style is that Kamuzu says it's that, and then it's finished. Whether anyone likes it or not, that is how it's going to be here'[5] – had already been decisively pre-empted as an option for Malawi at the annual Party Convention held a few days earlier. In the words of the *Daily Times*:

> When opening the Convention, the Life President told the delegates to discuss whether or not they wanted multi-party democracy. At the Convention, the delegates, a representation of political, traditional, religious and civic leaders from the grassroots level categorically rejected the multi-party system.[6]

The stranglehold on alternative voices is extended to the foreign media. Journalists are banned from entering the country, period. An exception was made in May 1991, when representatives of the British media were included in a Foreign Office delegation to examine conditions in the Mozambican refugee camps. One of the journalists was Julie Flint of *The Observer*, who looked beyond 'Malawi's admirable treatment of the refugees' and wrote a scathing account of 'the totalitarian, highly personalised regime that is living proof that repression can work'. Her article, 'Land of the Funny Peculiar', pointed out, among other things, that the recent release of some high-profile political prisoners, including Jack Mapanje, the internationally respected poet, and George Mtafu, the country's only neuro-surgeon, was merely an attempt 'to curry favour inside and outside Malawi – especially with aid donors whose goodwill is absolutely crucial'.[7] She also poked fun at the more absurd manifestations of this 'government-by-whim', where women can be imprisoned for six months for wearing trousers (the Decency Dress Act of 1973), and where a popular record was banned in order to save the sensibilities of the 'Official Hostess':

> How is it possible, for example, to remain straight-faced about censorship when Simon and Garfunkel's 'Cecilia' – 'Cecilia/ I'm down on my knees/ I'm begging you please/ To come home' – is banned, just

as Ms Kadzamira is going through a rocky phase in her relationship with the Life President and lets it be known that she prefers to be called by her middle name, Tamanda?[8]

On a more sinister note, she also revealed the extent to which Banda will go to silence his critics. She alluded, for instance, to one political prisoner 'whose only offence was being the brother of a journalist critical of the regime . . . '. She also added that the brother in question was himself murdered in a firebomb attack on his house in Lusaka, the capital of neighbouring Zambia.

It is enough, for our present purposes, that there was not an untrue word in the entire article. The following week, however, *The Observer* published a response by John Tembo, Kadzamira's uncle and Banda's heir-apparent, in which he sought to refute what he was pleased to call 'this ill-informed and opinionated article',[9] but which was little more than a self-serving propaganda exercise by a man who, in the words of the original article, 'is cordially loathed by most Malawians', a sentiment I have heard repeated on a number of occasions. Nowhere did Tembo address any of the issues raised. To rub the salt in further, *The Observer* appended an abject apology: '*The Observer* regrets any errors contained in our report last week and is glad to give Mr Tembo this opportunity to reply.' But not even this, it seemed, was enough to satisfy the Malawian authorities. The following week, yet another apology was offered 'to His Excellency the Life President of Malawi, Ngwazi Dr. H. Kamuzu Banda, Mama C. Tamanda Kadzamira and the Honourable J.Z.U. Tembo for any embarrassment or grief suffered as a result of our "Dateline" of 16 June . . . ', together with a letter from the Malawian High Commissioner in London reiterating Tembo's manufactured outrage.

Predictably, *The Observer*'s main rival, *The Sunday Times*, went to town on this 'humiliating climbdown', and pointed out what everyone already knew: that Lonrho has extensive business interests in Malawi, 'including textile manufacturers, tea and sugar estates, a brewery and a motor distributor'; and that, in applying the required pressure, the Malawian government had 'achieved a notable coup: the muzzling of one of Britain's national newspapers'.[10] So much, at any rate, for Rowland's revulsion at the 'sickening levels' of corruption that, in Kenya, placed him alongside the otherwise contemptible 'sniffer dogs' who were prepared to risk torture and imprisonment for believing that governments should be held accountable, and that citizens (not subjects) should be free to monitor what those same governments do in their name. But this was politics, or rather business, the pursuit of which sometimes entails unexpected alliances.

It is possible, of course, that the editor of *The Observer* will argue that he knew very well what he was doing when he published Julie Flint's article, and that the humiliation which both he and his reporter were subsequently forced to endure in order to balance the Lonrho books was worth the price of exposing the devil's own work. That's as maybe, and as irrelevant, in its own way, as the fact that Banda (not for the first time) finds himself out of step with everybody else. Whatever the Ngwazi's own personal predilections, the argument for democracy has largely been won, hence the spectacle of one African dictator after another standing up on the public platform in Harare in 1991 to affirm their commitment to the democratic values they had been busy suppressing for three decades. Internal pressure from restless populations and external pressure from 'Western' aid donors has ensured that even President Moi has been forced to give way to the demands for political pluralism, and with it the fundamental freedoms; but the behaviour of the Lonrho-owned press might serve as a useful warning to those who imagine that it is enough to exchange government ownership of the media for the dubious virtues of the marketplace for all else to follow. Africa is not Europe. In terms of the media especially, the conditions that apply in the one do not apply in the other, a point already made by Professor Paul Ansah at a UNESCO-sponsored conference on the Press in Africa held in Namibia in May 1991.

In his paper, 'The Legal and Political Framework for a Free and Pluralistic Press in Africa',[11] Professor Ansah, the distinguished director of the School of Communication Studies at the University of Ghana, argued that of all countries on the continent, only Egypt, Nigeria and South Africa were able to support an independent press of sufficient diversity to ensure that a wide range of views was available to the reading public. All the other countries were either too small or too poor (or, usually, both), and that whatever independent press did emerge would be concentrated in the hands of a narrow financial elite who would effectively operate a monopoly on information. He also argued that there were special conditions within developing countries, 'where information is seen as a social asset whose acquisition should enable people to form intelligent opinions about social issues'; and, further, that governments in such countries had an added responsibility 'to provide people with as broad a range of views as possible to enable them to reach rational conclusions and thus contribute to national development'. In other words, such societies needed both the private and the government press in order to function properly as democracies, and that to simply exchange one for the other would create as many problems as it solved:

> In the light of the foregoing, one would consider as ideal a situation in which the government could operate its own media system while guaranteeing to individuals and other groups the right to establish their own systems and providing the necessary facilities and creating a favourable environment for the private press sector.[12]

Given the record of African governments to date, one might baulk at the notion of these same governments 'creating' the environment for their own opposition, even in these heady days of UNESCO-sponsored seminars; but the ease with which Ansah's argument was politely dismissed by the non-African delegates present at the conference ought to have alerted at least some of them to the hidden ideological agenda behind the conference itself. It is no accident that UNESCO should have discovered the virtues of press freedom at a time when the free-market philosophy is everywhere triumphant, but the ideology of the free market is, precisely, that it is non-ideological, which only makes it more sinister for those on the receiving end.

The Standard is a case in point. 'Tiny' Rowland's primary concern is not the well-being of Kenyan citizens but the well-being of his company. In a continent like Africa, where political patronage has destroyed the institutions of the modern democratic state, it is inconceivable that the newspaper he owns should seek to undermine its own financial viability in the pursuit of an abstract principle, however worthy. It was for this reason alone that corruption, itself both the cause and the consequence of this patronage, became an issue when his business interests were threatened; and why, conversely, any criticism of Malawi, where his business interests were *not* threatened, should be stamped on as thoroughly as possible. One might argue that this is simply a fact of life everywhere, hence the sordid role of *The Observer* in all matters African, except that Kenya, which is wealthier than most countries on the continent (and certainly wealthier than Malawi), can hardly hope to support the diversity of newspapers and magazines – to say nothing of the electronic media – that ensures the response of a *Sunday Times*. Moreover, *The Observer* would never have dared to behave so abominably where a more serious country was concerned, the problem being that more serious countries do not produce dictators like Banda. In other words, an independent press can only serve the wider public interest within the framework of a sophisticated economy. Such economies guarantee the competition which alone limits the excesses of the 'free' market. To imagine otherwise is to confuse private enterprise with monopoly.

As with *The Standard*, so with the *Daily Nation*, which is owned by the Aga Khan; and this monopoly of the private press (in effect, a monopoly on information) is true of nearly all the countries in Africa. With the exception of the aforementioned, there is generally room for perhaps two weighty newspapers, one of which will almost invariably be owned by the government. In Uganda, for instance, the independent *Weekly Topic* is the only realistic rival to the government-owned *New Vision*, but the independence of the former should be treated with some caution, since it is owned by three cabinet ministers. This, in itself, is a comment on the unwillingness of the Ugandan business community to venture into an enterprise which, until recently at least, invariably meant trouble. All the other newspapers – independent, admittedly – are destined to remain poorly produced broadsheets of limited interest for the simple reason that they are unable to generate sufficient revenue to be anything else. The situation is even more dramatic in Sierra Leone. Of the sixteen weekly newspapers, all but two of them – the government-owned (and misnamed) *Daily Mail*, and *We Yone*, the mouthpiece of the former ruling party* – are small-scale, independent publications edited by the proprietors themselves. The market within which they operate is restricted by the low rate of literacy (30 per cent) in what is already a small population (4.5 million). The maximum sales of any of those papers is 4,000, but according to the figures supplied by the proprietors themselves, each would need to sell an additional 1,000 copies in order to break even, let alone make a profit. How was it possible for them to survive? A clue was provided by, ironically enough, the editor of *We Yone*, a man who readily described himself as 'a party man', and who then went on to pour scorn on his colleagues for what he termed their 'spinelessness': 'Look, these people are only interested in blackmailing those who have something to hide. That's why they carry on these private vendettas against businessmen and a few of the less popular politicians. . . . It's just a form of extortion, that's all.'[13]

I had myself already noticed the extent to which suggestion and innuendo appeared to play a disproportionately large part in the articles published in these newspapers, and the way in which promises of future revelations concerning the underhand activities of this or that businessman (usually Lebanese) failed to materialise in the following week's edition. On one occasion, I even witnessed two well-known Lebanese brothers in urgent conversation with one such editor who had just published a front-page story concerning a government contract that hadn't been fulfilled by the brothers in question. The story itself gave little away, but promised further revelations in due course. The following day the intrepid editor was to be seen driving around Freetown in a reconditioned vehicle, and that was the end of the matter. So much, at any rate, for the independent press in Sierra Leone; but if such activities were unusual even within the African context, the bottom line, here as elsewhere, was poverty. Journalists had to make a living. In Sierra Leone, they were merely exploiting a variation of what is widely referred to as 'the brown envelope' syndrome.

In a continent where the average monthly salary is barely enough to feed a family of four for a week, bribery is a way of life. Journalists no less than the police and civil servants are at the mercy of just those sections of society – Lebanese businessmen, say – whom they should otherwise be monitoring in the interests of the society itself. Conversely, those few independent newspapers which attempt to remain true to their vision are guaranteed a short life-span as a consequence of the economic constraints within which they are forced to operate. It isn't necessary to resort to the measures adopted by a President such as Samuel Doe of Liberia, whose solution was to firebomb the offices of awkward publications. A simple court case will do. This was what happened with *The Torch* newspaper in The Gambia, when a libel action was brought against the editor, Sanna Manneh, following an article in which he accused four cabinet ministers of corruption. Three of the ministers promptly took the matter to court, and the editor was duly charged with libel on three counts against each of the plaintiffs. The case lasted from November 1988 to April 1989, and was hailed at the time as 'a landmark in Gambian political, legal and press history'. Manneh was eventually acquitted on two counts, and cautioned and discharged on the third, but the legal expense involved subsequently forced him to cease publication. When I met him, six months after his celebrated 'victory', he was sceptical that he would ever be able to publish again.

Economic constraints also operate in more nebulous ways. It is rarely possible, for instance, for such newspapers to extend their coverage of events in the country much beyond the capital city, which is where they are invariably based. This is made worse by the poor infrastructure that is the definition of a 'developing country', which means, in turn, that it is only governments that are able to ensure that the more remote areas are properly monitored. A case in point was an accident at a makeshift gold-mine near a village in the Mwanza Region of Tanzania sometime between December 1985 and February 1986, and in which thirty men died. The story only came to light through a report from SHIHATA, the government-controlled news agency which was founded in 1976 'to ensure that correct and important information reaches our people and the outside world'. As it turned out, this particular 'correct and important information' proved to be embarrassing to the government because such mining had already been declared illegal, but the subsequent attempt at a cover-up was less important than the fact that the story only emerged through the official media in the first place. Only a government agency had the resources at its disposal to keep a reporter in such a remote region on the off-chance that something might happen there. The few independent newspapers which have since emerged in the wake of the new dispensation are barely able to employ extra staff in the major towns of the country. Put briefly, the problem isn't with SHIHATA as an institution, but with the political ends it has been made to serve.

In the case of Tanzania, these ends were enshrined in the famous 1967 Arusha Declaration 'on socialism and self-reliance'. In the words of a former editor of the government-owned *Daily News*:

> We are striving to create a Tanzanian Press that not only projects the Party line, but reflects the fears, hopes, trust and thinking of all the working people. Our objective is to create a people's Press, one that will hold the will of the people to be paramount.[14]

There is very little left to be said about the familiar sophistry that has gone the way of the Berlin Wall. In the context of Africa, however, the ideology itself was always less important than the overriding sense of nationalism which propelled all governments, whatever their stated positions within the political spectrum, to attempt to break the colonial monopoly on information that is every bit as invidious now as it was at the time of independence thirty years ago; in short, to assert that newly won independence. Kwame Nkrumah, Ghana's first Prime Minister and one of the great African nationalists, put it succinctly when he said: 'The African press has a vital role in the revolution that is sweeping our continent; our newspapers, our broadcasting, our information services, our television must reach out to the masses of our people . . .'.[15]

The fact that Nkrumah was unable to resist what Wole Soyinka, the Nobel laureate, called 'the seductive experiment in authoritarianism'[16] that became a familiar feature of the continent's political landscape, including its treatment of the press, doesn't necessarily detract from the sincerity of his position; in any case, he himself was merely giving expression to a deeper collective desire, which was why euphoric populations, galvanised by the new sense of nationhood, were able to be duped so easily by those who continued to talk in a familiar language. Whose interests are you serving? was, until recently, a legitimate question to ask journalists bent on exposing their shortcomings, especially when the interests in question rarely practised what they preached, at least where Africa was concerned. The distortions of the Western media in all matters African only served to reinforce the nationalist argument at the same time as it reduced the options available to the isolated journalist who remained true to a higher ideal. It is only now, with the continent on the verge of collapse, that the limits of nationalism have become apparent, and that politicians, whatever their claims to the contrary, have been seen for what they are: men and women who seek power as an end in itself. The only check on their excesses is provided by the institutions of the state, of which the government-owned press is as much a part as the law courts and the civil service.

Because the government is – or ought to be – directly responsible to the electorate; the electorate, in turn, reserves the right to withdraw the trust reposed in the government the moment it ceases to discharge its duties:

> That if the [government], in breach of the Laws and Liberties of the People, do betray the Trust reposed in them, and act negligently or arbitrarily and illegally, it is the undoubted Right of the People . . . to call them to Account for the same, and by Convention, Assembly or Force, may proceed against them as Traitors and Betrayers of their Country.[17]

It is the citizens of the country, and not the body of elected ministers, who own the newspapers which, in the present African context, might be best placed to fulfil the primary function of the media in any society: to provide the society with the information it needs to regulate properly its own affairs. One would hardly expect a private press monopolised by a narrow financial elite – foreign or otherwise – to discharge such an obligation. On the other hand, governments themselves can hardly be trusted to regulate themselves in the interests of the society they seek to govern. African governments are even now inclined to imagine that the current agitation for proper democracy (as opposed, that is, to 'African democracy') is simply a passing phase got up by meddling foreigners. 'This year's fashion in Paris,' was the cynical response of the former President of Chad, who obviously thought 'his' people incapable of sophisticated responses towards political institutions that didn't proceed directly – à la President Mobutu of Zaire – from the cock that leaves no hen alone. It is for this reason that Ansah recommends the setting up of an independent Media Trust involving both government appointees and members of interested organisations, for instance Bar Associations, Labour Unions, Womens' Movements and Journalists' Associations. But such Trusts are hardly enough in themselves. More important again is the determination of the people themselves that democracy will work. The government media, no less than the independent newspapers, have a role to play in the process.

*The government of President Joseph Saidu Momoh was overthrown in a military coup in April 1992. The National Provisional Ruling Council, headed by Captain Valentine Strasser, initially promised to hand over power to an elected civilian government as quickly as possible, but appears increasingly reluctant to name a date. In the meantime, a new Decree, 'Prevention of Corruption', has imposed censorship on the press.

Notes

1. Quoted in 'Tiny Rowland Wages a War of Words with Moi', *Sunday Times*, 3 November 1991.
2. Ibid.
3. From a speech to the Malawian parliament in January 1965: quoted in Philip Short, *Banda* (London, 1974), p. 255.

4. Editorial, 'Where Silence Rules: The Suppression of Dissent in Malawi', *Africa Watch*, October 1990, p. 21.
5. P. Short, *Banda*, p. 201.
6. Editorial, 'Ngwazi Happy with Development', *Daily Times*, 1 October 1991.
7. Julie Flint, 'Land of the Funny Peculiar', *The Observer*, 16 June 1991.
8. Ibid.
9. J.Z.U. Tembo, 'Malawi: "Oasis of Achievement" in Desert of the Third World', *The Observer*, 23 June 1991.
10. 'African Despot of Influence Brings *The Observer* to Heel', *The Sunday Times*, 7 July 1991.
11. Paul A.V. Ansah, 'The Political and Legal Framework for a Free and Pluralistic Press in Africa', reprinted as 'Blueprint for Freedom', in *Index on Censorship*, vol. 9 (1991), pp. 3–8.
12. Ibid.
13. A. Maja-Pearce, 'The Press in West Africa', *Index on Censorship*, vol. 6 (1990), p. 56.
14. Quoted in Nkwabi Ng'wanakilala, *Mass Communication and the Development of Socialism in Tanzania* (Dar-es-Salaam, 1981), p. 22.
15. Quoted in K. Nkrumah, *Kwame Nkrumah* (London, 1974), p. 97.
16. Wole Soyinka, 'The Writer in a Modern African State', in Per Wastberg (ed.), *The Writer in Modern Africa* (Uppsala, 1968), p. 15.
17. Daniel Defoe, 'Legion's Memorial', in *Selected Writings of Daniel Defoe*, ed. James T. Boulton (Cambridge, 1975), p. 84.

14 *Post-colonialism and language*

Kwaku Larbi Korang and Stephen Slemon

The question of 'post'-colonialism

Perhaps no term in wide circulation in the fields of literary and cultural studies at present finds itself so hotly contested as the term 'post-colonialism'. This is curious, for 'post-colonialism' works not so much to describe a fixed ideological formation, or a coherent critical perspective, or even a specific moment in historical time. Rather, 'post-colonialism' provides a name for a complex and heterogeneous set of critical and theoretical *debates*, all of them centring on the question of how we are to understand European colonialism as a cultural, historical, and political phenomenon, and how we might interpret what takes place *after* colonialism, and *in reaction* to it, both in those nations and cultures once colonised by Europe and within the metropolitan centres of the Western colonising nations themselves. Since European colonialism occupies at least five hundred years of history, and at its apogee in the late nineteenth century involved the establishment of dominating relations over three-quarters of the Earth's land surface, the 'post-colonial' is clearly an umbrella term which is meant to cover an enormous and remarkably disparate critical territory. Needless to say, the extent to which this term is capable of housing such a long and complex history and such a multifaceted set of critical debates, is itself a subject for heated debate within the general field of 'post-colonial' critical theory.

Part of the problem with 'post-colonialism', of course, stems from the general looseness that characterises the way in which so many political terms are used in literary or cultural criticism. Terms such as 'imperialism', 'colonialism', 'post-colonialism', 'decolonisation', and 'neo-colonialism' have a tendency to attract remarkably divergent, and sometimes voluntary, meanings within critical language, and readers can well be excused for finding themselves genuinely wondering exactly which theory of imperialism a 'post-colonial' critical writer is analysing, to which specific form of colonialism he or she is referring, and which type of post-colonial resistance or reaction to colonialism the post-colonial critic is attempting to examine. In the area of literary and cultural studies, however, most post-colonial critical theorists tend to eschew the specific definitions for these terms that prevail in the political sciences, preferring the more generalist definitions which Edward Said employs in his magisterial *Culture and Imperialism*, where ' "*imperialism*" means the practice, the theory, and the attitudes of a dominating metropolitan centre ruling a distant territory; "*colonialism*", which is almost always a consequence of imperialism, is the implanting of settlements on distant territory'.[1]

Decolonisation, in most post-colonial writing, refers to that historical process by which formerly colonised peoples, having been organised by colonialism into governing units, at last break free of direct colonialist control and achieve self-governing, sovereign status, thus transforming the 'colony' into the 'nation' at a moment of national or 'flag independence'. *Anti-colonialism* refers to the ways in which resistance to foreign administrative control under colonialism has been organised and articulated within the colony; and usually, the term implies a very direct relation between this opposition and the phenomenon of nascent or emerging 'nationalism'. In much (but by no means all) of Africa and the so-called 'Third World', therefore, the moment of 'direct colonialist control' by Europe has now passed, and in one of its many uses the term 'post-colonialism' refers to the period of a specific national history that takes place *after* this moment of direct colonialism has ended.[2] Few students of contemporary international relations, however, would agree with the hypothesis that the historical demise of this strategy of direct European colonialist administration as a means of securing unequal international relations amounts to anything like a genuine 'End of Empire', as the title of a recent Granada Television series in the United Kingdom would have it.[3] Rather, they would argue, the old regulatory practices of direct colonialism have simply been relocated into new modes and forms of imperialist management – the manipulation of 'third world' national economies through the production and administration of 'third world debt', for example. To describe these new modes and forms, Kwame Nkrumah the former President of Ghana, coined the term *neo-*

colonialism, and his definition still holds in most forms of post-colonial critical writing. 'The essence of neo-colonialism,' wrote Nkrumah, 'is that the State which is subject to it is, in theory, independent and has all the outward trappings of international sovereignty. In reality its economic system and thus its political policy is directed from the outside.'[4]

It is at this point – where questions of history and politics become inseparable from questions of culture and from the problems that attend the processes of cultural analysis – that these terms become extremely difficult ones, for each of them begins to name a complex set of *relations* between culture, politics, and representations, and these relations are enormously difficult to discern, let alone articulate. It is at this point, we would argue, that the idea of 'post-colonialism' as a critical field – that is, as a set of propositions, as a set of critical methods, and as a set of intellectual and academic debates – enters into the critical language of empire and its aftermath.

This form of 'post-colonialism' – this set of debates that lie at the intersection between colonial politics and the problems of understanding colonising and colonised 'cultures' – is very different from the 'post-colonialism' that identifies a specific historical period which comes *after* decolonisation. This 'post-colonialism' refers not to a moment in history but rather to a heterogeneous field of critical and intellectual *work* – a set of competing and overlapping strategies for cultural analysis within the framework of European colonisation. Increasingly, this difference between 'post-colonialism' as a temporal term and 'post-colonialism' as a term for a field of intellectual labour is finding itself distinguished at the level of orthography. The term 'post-colonialism' (with a hyphen) is being used to denote the historical period in a former colony that comes *after* the period of direct colonialist control. And the term 'postcolonialism' (without the hyphen) is being used to denote the many analytical strategies and interpretive positions which attempt to read exactly what it is that takes place in culture, politics, and history within and between the many and varied encounters of Europe with its colonial Others.[5]

Any attempt to summarise the *kinds* of intellectual labour that go on within the field of postcolonialism (without the hyphen) is bound to be reductive and misleading. Nonetheless, it is possible to identify, at least at a very blunt level, rather different *objects* of critical attention within postcolonialism – though of course most work, which begins with the analysis of any one of these objects in the first instance, finds itself shading into the others as it proceeds. One mode of postcolonial analysis – a mode often called 'colonial discourse' analysis or theory – takes as its primary object of study the wide range of literary, figurative, and governmental documents that comprise the 'cultural text' of European imperialism, with a view to discovering the ways in which various forms of colonialist governmentality are promulgated and secured through representations, and to discovering the ways in which European self-fashioning is predicated upon an 'othering' of its colonial subjects.[6] Another mode of postcolonial critical work takes as its primary object the ways in which colonised, and formerly colonised, cultures *resist* colonialism and its discourses at the level of cultural representation.[7] A third mode of analysis within post-colonialism examines – to use Frantz Fanon's terms – that 'zone of occult instability' that resides *between* coloniser and colonised, or *within* the complex and overdetermined 'contact zone' of the 'colonial encounter' itself.[8] Each of these modes of postcolonial analysis, of course, needs to be understood as a field for critical debate in and of itself.

But more to the purpose, each of these postcolonial critical modes is in large part comprised of a long-standing and vigorous debate about the cultural politics of *language* and its uses. Partly this is because almost every theory of culture puts language at the centre of debates about power, ideology, subjectivity, and agency; partly this is because the question of language, in the cultures formerly colonised by Europe, is of necessity overdetermined and bound to ongoing tensions between traditionalism and modernity, or between freedom and social determination, in their many guises and articulations. In Africa, each of these modes of critical postcoloniality continues to play a role in cultural and intellectual life, and each addresses a critical endeavour which continues to be played out in debates about language and its uses. We now want to turn to the language of 'Africa' in order to examine some of the ways in which the politics of literary *writing* have been debated within what might loosely be called a postcolonial critical field. At the centre of these debates is the question of what it is, and what it might be, that comprises the idea and the reality of 'Africa', after, and because of, its encounters with European colonialism.

The language of 'Africa'

The term 'Africa' is a colonial tag, one that was imposed upon the continent from the outside through colonialism, and one that now implies a critical endeavour to define a particular idea of collective and consensual being. 'Africa', in other words, is an object of ongoing critical inquiry and knowledge, the subject of a set of overlapping cultural debates taking place at the intersection between 'post-colonial' time and 'postcolonial' meaning; and at the heart of *this* 'Africa' one will find – in sustained and belligerent opposition to the darkness Joseph Conrad thought he might find – a long-standing history of energetic and deeply mindful debates about what a postcolonial 'Africa' might mean.

These debates, from the beginning, have involved not only Africans from the 'home' continent but also diasporic Africans from the Caribbean and the Americas. Edmund Blyden, for example, originally from the Danish West Indies, is widely perceived to be the 'father of African nationalism': his ideas of 'nativism'[9] influenced Casely-Heyford, from the Gold Coast (later Ghana), at the turn of the century, and helped shape the debates over 'Negritude' that took place in the 1930s, involving such figures as Leopold Sedar Senghor of Senegal and Aimé Césaire of Martinique.[10] The debates over nativism and Negritude, in turn, helped shape post-colonial debates about nationalism, traditionalism and modernity, and they continue to echo in contemporary debates over language-use in Africa and over the shape and form of what might comprise an 'African' literary tradition. This means that questions of writing and language-use in Africa have been debated, from the beginning, by a remarkably widespread set of participants, diverse in their politics, historical moment and geographical location, and each responding to differing structures and forms by which Europe imposed its several colonial languages and its differing political forms on 'Africa' and on African peoples. It should not surprise anyone that no single consensus, no monadic definition, for 'Africa', or for African writing, has yet to emerge from this vigorous and enduring history of intellectual debate.

Post-colonial debates about African 'writing' or 'literature' need to be understood as comprising far more than simply a set of debates over the ways in which African oral literatures and indigenous representational forms can be carried into new modalities of expression. In Africa the question of 'writing' is *already* positioned within larger debates about the politics of language use. Because of European colonialism, present-day African nations comprise peoples speaking different languages, and this immediately raises the question of which group, which language, within a national society initiates and controls the means and media for representing a people to itself. During the direct colonial phase of African history, some of the most urgent claims for the recognition of African national status found themselves in a position of social contradiction: first, because they necessarily represented the emerging African nation as being coterminous with a specific social *group* within the 'nation'; and secondly because, as Lewis Nkosi describes it, 'in asserting their right to self-determination Africans had to employ the language of their colonial masters. . . . [T]he rhetoric of political demand they adopted was better understood in Europe among rulers and the common people, than among the African masses for whom, presumably, the demands were being made.[11]

This structure of social contradiction has continued to inform, and vex, post-colonial debates over language and writing in Africa, and a good place to begin examining these debates is with the position taken in June 1962 by a group of African writers using English as their literary language, who met in Kampala to discuss the question of what might comprise and define an 'African' writing in English. These writers achieved a consensus, and a joint resolution – as reported by Ezekiel Mphahlele – that 'it is better for an African writer to think and feel in his own language and then look for an English transliteration approximating the original'.[12] Gabriel Okara put the argument this way:

> As a writer who believes in the utilisation of African ideas, African philosophy and African folk-lore and imagery to the fullest extent possible, I am of the opinion the only way to use them effectively is to translate them almost literally from the African language native to the writer into whatever European language he is using as his medium of expression.[13]

The results of this attempt to 'translate' the syntax of a native language 'almost literally' into English can be seen in Okara's own experimental novel, *The Voice*. The following passage, where the hero of the novel, Okolo, muses on the meaning of an unnamed 'it', is indicative of this attempt to render 'African' philosophy and linguistic structure within a 'European language':

> Is it possible to make your inside so small that nothing else can enter? Are spoken words blown away by the wind? No! Okolo in his inside saw. *It is impossible not to touch another's inside. It is impossible to*

make your inside so small that nothing else can enter. . . . There may be only one meaning in life and everybody is just groping along in their various ways to achieve it like religion – Christians, Moslems, Animists – all trying to reach God in their various ways. What is he himself trying to reach? For him *it* has *no name. Names bring divisions and divisions, strife. So let it be without a name; let it be nameless . . .* [14]

It is worth paying attention to what Okara is trying to achieve in this passage. Okara is after a distinct 'African' style that is capable of expressing a specifically 'African' philosophy, as well as the cadences of his own native Ijaw language, *through* English. He is also attempting to render an idea of 'Africa' as a territory in the *world*: a territory that comes *after* the colonial moment and which remains 'without a name'. In this passage 'it' – Africa – cannot be named purely, since 'it' appears in a philosophy and style of cross-cultural interaction. And when names harden, Okara implies, they impede cross-cultural under-standing.

The Kampala resolution, therefore, is not simply an aesthetic manifesto concerning literary technique. Rather, the Kampala resolution is a commitment to a specific mode of cultural *negotiation* with the colonial legacy at the level of representation, one that seeks to establish an 'African' uniqueness within a 'standard' global language (English) and a 'common' human endeavour ('literature'). It was this aspect of the resolution – its implicit gesture, as it were, towards the rehabilitation of an original 'African' endeavour within the power-laden uniformities of 'standard' English – that provoked the Nigerian critic Obiajunwa Wali into joining the postcolonial debate. The Kampala writers, Wali argued, were in effect betraying 'Africa', playing into the hands of 'Western midwives', because they were promulgating a literary practice which could *only* give birth to an African literature that remained 'a minor appendage in the main stream of European literature'. 'The whole uncritical acceptance of English and French as the inevitable medium for educated African writing,' Wali wrote, 'is misdirected and has no chance of advancing African literature and culture.' Such a literary practice, argued Wali, can only produce 'sterility, uncreativity, and frustration', and comprises nothing less than 'the dead end of African literature'. Instead, Wali insisted, a 'true African literature' *requires* the use of African languages. [15]

In effect, what Wali was asking in this response to the Kampala writers was this: Why were they content, in a politically decolonised

Africa, merely to approximate an African original in their writing? Did not the practice of transliterating African realities into the languages of the colonisers contain the dangerous implication that Africans were only 'free' to be original *within* the limits imposed upon them by their colonialist past? Wasn't their literary practice of attempting to harmonise pre-colonial, colonial, and post-colonial 'Africa' within the framework of a 'world language' really nothing more than a capitulation to European standards disguised under the banner of 'universalism'?

For some writers, however, the problem with Wali's turn to African languages as the *only* appropriate media for the expression of African realities was that – as Chinua Achebe put it – 'there are not many countries in Africa where you could abolish the language of the erstwhile colonial master and still retain the facility for mutual communication'.[16] Wole Soyinka extended this argument to the continental level: the use of English 'creates no conflict whatever,' he declared, 'especially as I want to be able to speak to the Ngugi wa Thiongos [Kenya], the Taban lo Liyongs [Uganda], the Nuruddin Farahs [Somalia]'.[17] Nevertheless, for many of the writers who argued along these lines, the Kampala resolution did seem to imply that a writing approach grounded upon the single, over-arching principle of linguistic transliteration would in fact produce a sub-standard literature, both in African and in European terms. Achebe, who had attended the Kampala conference, later offered a modified position on the Kampala resolution, while at the same time actively avowing the usefulness of languages forced on to Africa through colonialism, by claiming, 'I feel that the English language will be able to carry the weight of my African experience. But it will have to be a new English, still in full communion with its ancestral home but altered to suit its new African surroundings.' Achebe would declare: 'The English language has been given to me and I intend to use it.'[18]

Decolonisation and language

But how was English 'given', and what political residuum does it carry into neo-colonial times? At the same time that Okara was reproducing 'Africa' in his generous, post-independence, 'gift-giving' style of trans-literation, Frantz Fanon, in an essay entitled 'The Pitfalls of National Consciousness', was arguing that the easy transportation of Western liberal humanism into colonial territory amounted to the *giving away* of a cognitive space for freedom, and warning that the establishment of national independence was in no way equivalent to a liberation from imperialist forms of control by the West.[19] One of the most vigorous contemporary voices to apply Fanon's arguments to the level of language-use is Ngugi wa Thiong'o, a Kenyan writer and critic whose book, *Decolonising the Mind: The Politics of Language in African Literature* (1986), considers the ways in which language shapes the political consciousness of its users. Ngugi's argument is that language constitutes a storehouse or 'memory bank' that holds the collective experiences of a people, and as such makes and *re*makes peoples by giving them integrity and direction. The European languages, therefore, were not simply the media through which European imperialism operated during the pre-independence phase of African history, but part and parcel of the violence European colonisers enacted upon the continent. For Ngugi, English, French and Portuguese were more than just languages in Africa: they became *the* languages, and indigenous African languages were actively devalued in relation to them. The colonisers' languages played a formative role, as Ngugi sees it, in remaking African subjects in the image of European speakers, and this has produced an enduring condition of *alienation* in Europhone African elites. Since these elites comprise the very groups charged with the post-colonial task of shaping and directing the new national societies of Africa, African nations *still* find themselves incapable of working meaningfully towards their own best interests, the integral structures of African communities *remain* fractured and compromised, Africa *continues* to be exiled in language and out of place on African soil, and African peoples *remain* bound to a cultural and cognitive structure of dependency which has its economic correlative in neo-colonialist structures of political control.[20]

How then, Ngugi wonders, might literary language work to *renovate* African communities and help turn the corner on neo-colonialist modes of control? Ngugi's answer is that African literary languages must first and foremost be representative of what African communities at large actually speak – languages adapted to place, in tune with, and historically grounded in, indigenous African realities. 'To neglect our languages,' Ngugi asserts in his introduction to *Caitaani Mutharaba-ini*, 'and grab those of foreigners is tantamount to blasphemy. People without their own language are but mere slaves.'[21] Having become one of the most internationally celebrated African writers in English, Ngugi nonetheless follows his own critical logic scrupulously and denounces the whole genre of 'Afro-European (or Euro-African) literature' for its bad faith in calling itself *African* literature.[22] 'This book,' writes Ngugi in *Decolonising the Mind*, '. . . is my farewell to English as a vehicle for any of my writings. From now it is Gikuyu and Kiswahili all the way' (p. xiv).

Networks and affinities

Ngugi's argument has obvious affinities with Wali's rejection of the Kampala resolution in preference of an indigenous and 'true African literature'; but debates over the present and future structure of 'Africa' have always found themselves in negotiation with the *question* of post-colonialism, and at this point it might be useful to consider the counter-arguments of Kwame Anthony Appiah, an African philosopher and literary critic based in the United States of America. Appiah's critical and cultural identity, he tells us, comprises *both* Ghanaian and English 'worlds', and '[i]f my sisters and I were "children of two worlds" ', he writes,

> no one bothered to tell us this; we lived in one world, in two 'extended' families divided by several thousand miles and an allegedly insuperable cultural distance that never, so far as I can recall, puzzled or perplexed us much. . . . I am used to seeing the world as a network of points of affinity.[23]

Appiah thus finds himself rejecting the philosophical position that imagines post-colonial Africa as a state of uncontaminated cultural autonomy. Such a position, Appiah argues, is at heart a nativist one, and so is 'the claim that the African independence requires a literature of one's own' (p. 56). Appiah rejects the basic cultural binarism of 'nativist' positions such as Ngugi's – the establishment of oppositions between 'universalism' and 'particularism', 'inside' and 'outside', 'us' and 'them' (p. 56) – and he argues that such positions make language and literature into a mystique, for they require these constructs to *stand in* for autonomous and pure notions of culture, community, nation and tradition. A nativist critical position, according to Appiah, authorises the critic to say, in effect: we can know, and be at home in, *only* what our language has created. And as Appiah sees it, such a position, falling back as it does on an insular and inward-looking concept of tradition and imagining it to be the source of *all* authentic knowledge and being, is simply not tenable as an intellectual or philosophical stance.

Appiah thus joins the postcolonial debate over African language and literature by questioning the assumptions behind nativism and African cultural autonomy. But like Ngugi, Appiah does not want to lose sight of the ways in which the 'might of the legions of Europe' has been, and is, represented within the colonial languages. Appiah wants *also* to question the intellectual position that sees European languages as 'mere tools; tools that can be cleansed of the accompanying imperialist – and, more specifically, racist – modes of thought', and he recognises that within post-colonial cultural life, the European languages work like 'double agents' and must therefore remain 'perpetually under suspicion' (p. 56).

What results from this double order of critical questioning is a carefully balanced definition of a post-colonial Africa adapted to the widest demands of cultural modernity: a postcoloniality, that is, which makes room for both Okara and Ngugi. At the heart of this definition is a peculiar conception of the postcolonial which Appiah articulates around the structure of *intellectual* work. Intellectuals everywhere, he believes, 'are now caught up – whether as volunteers, draftees, resisters – in a struggle for the articulation of their respective nations'. And everywhere, 'language and literature' appear to be 'central to that articulation' (p. 53). Therefore, Appiah's postcolonial Africa – *his* 'nation' – must strive for a cultural room of its own, but the demand for that cultural room must be cast not in absolute or autonomous terms but, rather, in comparative and relative ones. Appiah's 'Africa' is a necessary party to an international and cross-cultural set of exchanges, and his African 'intellectual' is a product of these cross-cultural exchanges. But since the intellectual struggle to articulate an African nationality appears on the *periphery* of international modernity, that struggle begins to make sense only in, and as a search for, *fair* exchange, equitable dealing, within a global politics. Appiah's African intellectual *knows* that Africa's colonial encounter with Europe comprised *un*fair exchange, and that a language of colonial racism helped produce that sustained structure of unfairness. This intellectual therefore works to revalue 'Africa', and to make that revaluation relevant to *both* African cultures and the world at large. *This* intellectual work, as Appiah formulates it, goes beyond the opposition between the 'local' or 'national' and the 'universal', and enacts an exchange between them. And this *style* of intellectual work reveals itself in the very tension, the double-facedness, within the Euro-African (or Afro-European) literatures that Ngugi denounces as a symptom of bad faith.

Appiah's critique of pure language is, as he puts it, calculated to yield an 'ethical universal', a postcolonial 'humanism' whose literature is 'post-realist', whose politics are 'postnativist', and whose solidarities are '*transnational* rather than . . . *national*' (p. 155). The 'post' in Appiah's 'postcolonialism', then, appears in this respect as a 'space-clearing gesture' (p. 149) – an attempt, in and through a colonially imposed language, to go beyond those hierarchies of self over other, identity over difference, centre over periphery, sovereign over subordinate, that the language of colonialism has imposed and which reproduce themselves in unexamined form within the seemingly autonomous and pure languages of nativism and nationalism.[24] Appiah's critique of pure language is thus meant to 'post' for African critical and cultural practice a space *after* colonialism – a colonialism that appears and reappears in the entrancing binaries of colonialist language, and one that has long held the language of 'Africa' spellbound. As such, his critique recalls the efforts of the great social theorist Mikhail Bakhtin to locate cultural agency in a *dialogics* of language. 'The word in language', Bakhtin wrote,

> is half someone else's. It becomes 'one's own' only when the speaker populates it with his own intention, his own accent, when he appropriates the word, adapting it to his own semantic and expressive intention. Prior to this moment of appropriation, the word does not exist in a neutral and impersonal language . . . but rather it exists in other people's mouths, in other people's contexts, serving other people's intentions: it is from there that one must take the word, and make it one's own.[25]

Language and emergency

Appiah's engagement with the question of language addresses African cultural modernity at a high order of philosophical negotiation, but it needs to be remembered that not all of the voices that contribute to postcolonial debates in Africa are articulated from within, and in response to, a fully 'post-colonial' time. For the writer and critic Njabulo Ndebele, writing about South Africa, the question of post-colonialism and language produces a rather different set of answers than it does for Appiah, for of course in South Africa the formal moment of political decolonisation from white settler male has only just come. Writing under apartheid and – to borrow the white South African writer André Brink's phrase – 'writing in a state of emergency', Ndebele chooses not to reach for transnational terms in quite the way that Appiah does, although both writers share broadly humanistic and ethical concerns. Rather, in a powerful essay entitled 'The English Language and Social Change in South Africa',[26] Ndebele sets out *another* modality of negotiating between the claims of linguistic 'nativism' and those of Europhonic 'universalism'. We will conclude this short chapter on language and postcolonialism in Africa with an examination of his argument.

The corner-stone of Ndebele's position is that English in South Africa, despite its many poses of political innocence, is inevitably the carrier of social perceptions, attitudes and goals that perpetuate unequal relations in race and class, and is functionally bound to social mechanisms for the manufacture of consent to oppression. English works hegemonically in South Africa, Ndebele argues, partly because it is equated with authority – 'education appears to have become synonymous with the acquisition of English' (p. 232) – and partly because it is already positioned within international capitalism as *the* language of corporate globalism. 'English is an international language', Ndebele notes,

> but it is international only in its functionally communicative aspects. For the rest of the time, indigenous languages fulfil the range of needs that English similarly fulfils for its native speakers. From this point of view, the functional acquisition of English in a capitalist society such as ours can further reinforce the instrumentalization of people as units of labor. So it is conceivable that the acquisition of English, precisely because the language has been reduced to being a mere working tool, can actually add to the alienation of the work force.
>
> (pp. 232–3)

Despite this, however, Ndebele wants to recognise that the consolations of linguistic nativism may not fully address the contemporary sensibilities of the urban and 'detribalized' communities in South Africa. Ndebele, therefore, despite his rigorous critique of English in South Africa, is nonetheless prepared to accord English speech and writing a viable place within South African cultural life. In order to negotiate this gap, he attempts to imagine a South African English 'freed from the functional instruction of corporate English', and 'open to the possibility of becoming a new language' (p. 231) – renewed both in vocabulary and in grammatical structure to accord to 'foundations rooted in the experience of the people themselves' (p. 224). Ndebele's position differs from those discussed above, in that it grounds this 'new English' within an *emergent* racial or group sensibility. His position is 'nationalist' to the extent that it seeks an expressivist capacity for language to represent the 'experiences of the people' who use it, but the *authority* for this nationalism is discovered within traditions shaping themselves *in the present*, not ones associated with a fixed and immemorial past. The traditions that are shaping, and will continue to shape, Ndebele's 'new English' are ones that emerge from the experiences of struggle for cultural, linguistic and political survival in a state of emergency; and the orientation of this 'new English' is towards the future: towards what must emerge *beyond* apartheid, in a fully 'post-colonial' political state.

Ndebele's assault on English *as it is* demonstrates his need – in a Bakhtinian act of appropriation – to reshape English into the way it *must be*: a reconstituted language of the future. 'The inherently subversive quest for freedom by the oppressed of South Africa,' he writes, 'is even more evident today where their erstwhile demand merely to be allowed to participate in the various structures of government has clearly given way to an insatiable desire to create: to create comparable structures on the basis of a new human sensibility' (p. 227). For Ndebele, the fulfilment of this quest calls for nothing less than a reshaping of those social forms – such as language – in which power is *already* invested, and in which resistances are already taking shape. For within the field of language, as Ndebele reads it, the struggle for a viable post-apartheid postcolonialism is already taking place.

Ndebele's argument carries the question of language-use squarely into the many debates that now take place about the prospects for genuine social change for Africa – that is, change not only from the colonial past but also from a neo-colonial present. His insistence upon a future-directed orientation to this debate suggests that the remarkable tradition of intellectual engagement with the vexed questions of postcolonialism and language in Africa not only will continue, but will continue to find new voices, new articulations, new modalities of cultural and political negotiation. For, of course, there can be no end to these debates until there emerges some future world order that renders the critical terms of postcolonial studies – terms like colonialism, imperialism, neo-colonialism – genuinely historical ones, with no descriptive purchase on contemporary inter-cultural relations. And as Gabriel Okara has pointed out in the passage earlier in this chapter, a genuinely *post*-colonial world order remains, at present, an idea we only grope towards, a space without a name.

Notes

1. Edward Said, *Culture and Imperialism* (New York, 1993), p. 9, emphasis ours. Said's fairly typical 'post-colonial' definition of imperialism, for example, departs not only from orthodox Marxist definitions, such as Lenin's theory of imperialism as that *specific* stage within capitalism marked by a turn to overseas markets and labour resources in order to counter the effects of the domestic accumulation of capital, but also from a range of quirky uses, such as that given by Lewis S. Feuer in *Imperialism and the Anti-Imperialist Mind* (New Brunswick, Canada, 1989), where 'imperialism' defines that 'progressive' force that causes 'civilisation' to move 'forward'. Useful discussions of the meanings of 'imperialism' and 'colonialism', as they appear within historical and political studies, are given in Anthony Brewer (ed.), *Marxist Theories of Imperialism: A Critical Survey* (London, 1989); Harry Magdoff, *Imperialism: From the Colonial Age to the Present* (New York, 1978); and Wolfgang J. Mommsen, *Theories of Imperialism*, trans. P.S. Falla (Chicago, 1977).

2. See, for example, Partha Chaterjee's *The Nation and its Fragments: Colonial and Postcolonial Histories* (Princeton, NJ, 1993).

3. See Brian Lapping's companion volume to this series, *End of Empire* (New York, 1985).

4. Kwame Nkrumah, in *Neo-colonialism: The Highest Stage of Capitalism* (London, 1974), cited in Kofi Buenor Hadjor, *The Penguin Dictionary of Third World Terms* (Harmondsworth, 1992), p. 215. Ella Shohat, in 'Notes on the "Post-Colonial"', *Social Text*, vols 31/32 (1991), pp. 99–113, argues against the concept of 'post-colonialism' because of the way in which it implicitly 'undermines a critique of contemporary colonialist structures of domination, more available through the repetition and revival of the "neo"' (p. 107).

5. See, for example, the Introduction to Francis Barker, Peter Hulme and Margaret Iversen (eds), *Colonial Discourse/Postcolonial Theory* (Manchester, forthcoming), pp. 3–4; Vijay Mishra and Bob Hodge, 'What is Post(-)colonialism', *Textual Practice*, vol. 5 (1991), pp. 399–414.

6. As yet, there is no single text which sets out a thorough summary of the kinds of work going on within the field of 'colonial discourse' theory. The larger principles of discourse analysis are laid out in Michel Foucault's 'archaeological' texts: *The Order of Things: An Archaeology of the Human Sciences*, trans. A.M. Sheridan Smith (London, 1970), and *The*

Archaeology of Knowledge, trans. A.M. Sheridan Smith (London, 1972). Edward Said's *Orientalism: Western Conceptions of the Orient* (London, 1978), which applies Foucault's theories to the ways in which British and French writers of the eighteenth and nineteenth centuries constructed the 'Orient' as a contradictory field of both desire and knowledge, is often thought to be the ur-text of colonial discourse theory. Robert Young lays out a useful genealogy of this field in terms of Europe's crisis with 'historiography': *White Mythologies: Writing History and the West* (London, 1991). Compelling accounts of the ways in which European colonial discourse has applied itself to sub-Saharan Africa are provided in Christopher L. Miller's *Blank Darkness: Africanist Discourse in French* (Chicago, 1985), his *Theories of Africans: Francophone Literature and Anthropology in Africa* (Chicago, 1990), and in V.Y. Mudimbe's, *The Invention of Africa: Gnosis, Philosophy, and the Order of Knowledge* (Bloomington, IN, 1988).

7. A useful introduction to this form of work is provided by W.D. Ashcroft, Gareth Griffiths and Helen Tiffin in *The Empire Writes Back: The Theory and Practice of Post-Colonial Literature* (London, 1989). These writers advance an argument for comparative studies across 'all the cultures affected by the imperial process from the moment of colonization to the present day' (p. 2). Other work in this field advances the concept of 'minority discourse' as a way of examining how peoples and groups of different places and persuasions – long oppressed into silence and made 'minor' and invisible by various forms of colonial power – find voices with which to carve out their own cultural territory and shape their own self images. See 'Introduction: Toward a Theory of Minority Discourse: What Is To Be Done?', in Abdul JanMohamed and David Lloyd (eds), *The Nature and Context of Minority Discourse* (Oxford, 1990), pp. 1–16. Almost all work in this form of postcolonial criticism has been influenced profoundly by the work of the late Frantz Fanon: see *Black Skins, White Masks*, trans. Charles Markmann (1952; New York, 1967), and *The Wretched of the Earth*, trans. Constance Farrington (Harmondsworth, 1969). Fanon's influence on African political figures, too, is an immense one: see Amilcar Cabral's *Unity and Struggle* (New York, 1979), for example, or Steve Biko's *I Write What I Like*, ed. Aelred Stubbs (London, 1978).

8. Mary Louise Pratt employs the term 'contact zone' in *Imperial Eyes: Travel Writing and Transculturation* (London, 1992); Peter Hulme employs the term 'colonial encounter' in *Colonial Encounters: Europe and the Native Caribbean, 1492–1797* (London, 1986). Work in this third mode of postcolonial analysis attempts to move away from the kind of absolute separation between coloniser and colonised that characterises, for example, Albert Memmi's influential study, *The Colonizer and the*

Colonized, trans. Howard Greenfeld (1957; New York, 1967), and examines the ways in which power and its resistances are both fragmented and distributed across 'Western' and 'non-Western' worlds. Much of the work in this area indexes itself back to the philosophical novels and cultural criticism of the Guyanese writer, Wilson Harris. The most widely quoted critical theorist of this form of postcolonial analysis is Homi K. Bhabha, who argues that historical subjectivity and agency is the product of cross-cultural negotiation and, as such, is always paradoxical and ambivalent in affect and address – 'less than one and double', to quote Bhabha. Postcolonial work in this area comprises a sustained effort at defining a postcoloniality capable of challenging ideas of cultural purity at almost every level. A number of Bhabha's essays are collected in the volume *The Location of Culture* (London, 1994).

9. For a comparative account of nativism in African cultural thought, see Kwame Anthony Appiah, 'Out of Africa: Topologies of Nativism', in his *In My Father's House: Africa in the Philosophy of Culture* (New York, 1992), pp. 47–72.

10. For a useful discussion, see Abiola Irele, *The African Experience in Literature and Ideology* (London, 1981), pp. 67–117.

11. Lewis Nkosi, *Tasks and Masks: Themes and Styles of African Literature* (London, 1981), p. 1.

12. Cited in Obiajuna Wali, 'The Dead End of African Literature?', *Transition*, vol. 4, no. 10 (1963), p. 14.

13. Gabriel Okara, 'African Speech . . . English Words', *Transition*, vol. 4, no. 10 (1963), p. 15.

14. Gabriel Okara, *The Voice* (London, 1964), pp. 110, 112, emphasis ours.

15. O. Wali, 'The Dead End of African Literature?', p. 14.

16. Chinua Achebe, *Morning Yet on Creation Day* (London, 1975), p. 57.

17. John A. Stotesbury, 'Interview with Wole Soyinka at the Second Stockholm Conference for African Writers, April 1986', *Kunapipi*, vol. IX, no. 1 (1987), p. 61.

18. C. Achebe, *Morning Yet on Creation Day*, p. 62. See also the letters that were written in response to Wali's 'The Dead End of African Literature?', in *Transition*, vol. 3, no. 11 (1963), pp. 7–9, and vol. 3, no. 12 (1964), pp. 6–10.

19. In *The Wretched of the Earth*, pp. 119–65.

20. Ngugi wa Thiong'o, *Decolonising the Mind: The Politics of Language in African Literature* (London, 1986), pp. 5–15. A similar argument concerning the divisive nature of European languages within African societies is provided by Lewis Nkosi in *Tasks and Masks*, p. 2ff. Ngugi's stance is shared by the participants in the Colloquium on Black Civilization and Education held in Lagos in 1977. They argued that 'the psycho-physiology of knowledge would confirm a built-in handicap for

any human group who cannot work in their indigenous language form. The standing tragedy of all blacks and Africans wherever they may be is that their tongues have been pulled out and they must speak strange tongues': cited in Chantal Zabus, *The African Palimpsest* (Amsterdam, 1991), pp. 39–40.

21. Cited in Al-Amin Mazrui, 'Ideology' or Pedagogy: The Linguistic Indigenisation of African Literature', *Race and Class*, vol. XXVII, no. 1 (1986), p. 65.

22. Ngugi wa Thiong'o, *Decolonising the Mind*, pp. 26–7, 33n.

23. K.A. Appiah, *In My Father's House*, p. viii. Further page references are given in the text.

24. For a reading of the 'politics of post-colonial narratives', see Simon Gikandi's 'The Politics and Poetics of National Formation: Recent African Writing', in Anna Rutherford (ed.), *From Commonwealth to Post-Colonial* (Sydney, 1992), pp. 377–89.

25. Mikhail Bakhtin, 'Discourse in the Novel', in *The Dialogic Imagination: Four Essays*, trans. Caryl Emerson and Michael Holquist (Austin, TX, 1981), pp. 293–4.

26. Njabulo Ndebele, 'The English Language and Social Change in South Africa', in David Bunn and Jane Taylor (eds), *From South Africa: New Writing Photographs and Art* (Chicago, 1987), pp. 217–35. Further page references are given in the text.

Part III
Selected Documents

1. Countering colonial and neo-colonial hegemony: Frantz Fanon, 'Reciprocal Bases of National Culture and the Fight for Freedom', *The Wretched of the Earth* (London: Penguin, 1967), pp. 190–4.

Colonial domination, because it is total and tends to over-simplify, very soon manages to disrupt in spectacular fashion the cultural life of a conquered people. This cultural obliteration is made possible by the negation of national reality, by new legal relations introduced by the occupying power, by the banishment of the natives and their customs to outlying districts by colonial society, by expropriation, and by the systematic enslaving of men and women.

Three years ago at our first congress I showed that, in the colonial situation, dynamism is replaced fairly quickly by a substantification of the attitudes of the colonizing power. The area of culture is then marked off by fences and signposts. These are in fact so many defence mechanisms of the most elementary type, comparable for more than one good reason to the simple instinct for preservation. The interest of this period for us is that the oppressor does not manage to convince himself of the objective non-existence of the oppressed nation and its culture. Every effort is made to bring the colonized person to admit the inferiority of his culture which has been transformed into instinctive patterns of behaviour, to recognize the unreality of his 'nation', and, in the last extreme, the confused and imperfect character of his own biological structure.

Vis-à-vis this state of affairs, the native's reactions are not unanimous. While the mass of the people maintain intact traditions which are completely different from those of the colonial situation, and the artisan style solidifies into a formalism which is more and more stereotyped, the intellectual throws himself in frenzied fashion into the frantic acquisition of the culture of the occupying power and takes every opportunity of unfavourably criticizing his own national culture, or else takes refuge in setting out and substantiating the claims of that culture in a way that is passionate but rapidly becomes unproductive.

The common nature of these two reactions lies in the fact that they both lead to impossible contradictions. Whether a turncoat or a substantialist the native is ineffectual precisely because the analysis of the colonial situation is not carried out on strict lines. The colonial situation calls a halt to national culture in almost every field. Within the framework of colonial domination there is not and there will never be such phenomena as new cultural departures or changes in the national culture. Here and there valiant attempts are sometimes made to reanimate the cultural dynamic and to give fresh impulses to its themes, its forms and its tonalities. The immediate, palpable and obvious interest of such leaps ahead is nil. But if we follow up the consequences to the very end we see that preparations are being thus made to brush the cobwebs off national consciousness, to question oppression and to open up the struggle for freedom.

A national culture under colonial domination is a contested culture whose destruction is sought in systematic fashion. It very quickly becomes a culture condemned to secrecy. This idea of a clandestine culture is immediately seen in the reactions of the occupying power which interprets attachment to traditions as faithfulness to the spirit of the nation and as a refusal to submit. This persistence in following forms of cultures which are already condemned to extinction is already a demonstration of nationality; but it is a demonstration which is a throw-back to the laws of inertia. There is no taking of the offensive and no redefining of relationships. There is simply a concentration on a hard core of culture which is becoming more and more shrivelled up, inert and empty.

By the time a century or two of exploitation has passed there comes about a veritable emaciation of the stock of national culture. It becomes a set of automatic habits, some traditions of dress and a few broken-down institutions. Little movement can be discerned in such remnants of culture; there is no real creativity and no overflowing life. The poverty of the people, national oppression and the inhibition of culture are one and the same thing. After a century of colonial domination we find a culture which is rigid in the extreme, or rather what we find are the dregs of culture, its mineral strata. The withering away of the reality of the nation and the death-pangs of the national culture are linked to each other in mutual dependence. This is why it is of capital importance to follow the evolution of these relations during the struggle for national freedom. The negation of the native's culture, the contempt for any manifestation of culture whether active or emotional and the placing outside the pale of all specialized branches of organization contribute to breed aggressive patterns of conduct in the native. But these patterns of conduct are of the reflexive type; they are poorly differentiated, anarchic and ineffective. Colonial exploitation, poverty and endemic famine drive the native more and more to open, organized revolt. The necessity for an open and decisive breach is formed progressively and imperceptibly, and comes to be felt by the great majority of the people. Those tensions which hitherto were non-existent come into being. International events, the collapse of whole sections of colonial empires and the contradictions inherent in the colonial system strengthen and uphold the native's combativity while promoting and giving support to national consciousness.

These new-found tensions which are present at all stages in the real nature of colonialism have their repercussions on the cultural plane. In literature, for example, there is relative overproduction. From being a reply on a minor scale to the dominating power, the literature produced by natives becomes differentiated and makes itself into a will to particularism. The intelligentsia, which during the period of repression was essentially a consuming public, now themselves become producers. This literature at first chooses to confine itself to the tragic and poetic style; but later on novels, short stories and essays are attempted. It is as if a kind of internal organization or law of expression existed which wills that poetic expression becomes less frequent in proportion as the objectives and the methods of the struggle for liberation become more precise. Themes are completely altered; in fact, we find less and less of bitter, hopeless recrimination and less also of that violent, resounding, florid writing which on the whole serves to reassure the occupying power. The colonialists have in former times encouraged these modes of expression and made their existence possible. Stinging denunciations, the exposing of distressing conditions and passions which find their outlet in expression are in fact assimilated by the occupying power in a cathartic process. To aid such processes is in a certain sense to avoid their dramatization and to clear the atmosphere.

But such a situation can only be transitory. In fact, the progress of national consciousness among the people modifies and gives precision to the literary utterances of the native intellectual . . .

The contact of the people with the new movement gives rise to a new rhythm of life and to forgotten muscular tensions, and develops the imagination. Every time the storyteller relates a fresh episode to his public, he presides over a real invocation. The existence of a new type of man is revealed to the public. The present is no longer turned in upon itself but spread out for all to see. The storyteller once more gives free rein to his imagination; he makes innovations and he creates a work of art. It even happens that idle characters, which are barely ready for such a transformation – highway robbers or more or less anti-social vagabonds – are taken up and remodelled. The emergence of the imagination and of the creative urge in the songs and epic stories of a colonized country is worth following. The storyteller replies to the expectant people by successive approximations, and makes his way, apparently alone but in fact helped on by his public, towards the seeking out of new patterns, that is to say national patterns. Comedy and farce disappear, or lose their attraction. As for dramatization, it is no longer placed on the plane of the troubled intellectual and his tormented conscience. By losing its characteristics of despair and revolt, the drama becomes part of the common lot of the people and forms part of an action in preparation or already in progress.

2. Writing and gender: Micere Githae Mugo, Interviewed by Adeola James, *In Their Own Voices: African Women Writers Talk* (London: James Currey, 1990), pp. 93–101.

ADEOLA: Would you like to summarize the radical changes that have taken place in your life in these past three or four years?

MICERE: It will be very difficult to pin down the many things that have happened to me during the last three or four years. I think the only thing that I can possibly say is that I have grown a lot in terms of ideological orientation, and my complete commitment to the transition of our African societies, and the so-called Third World, from capitalism to socialism. For one major reason: that we are dealing with a philosophy that agrees that it is wrong for just a few to possess when the majority are dispossessed. What led to my leaving Kenya has to do with the responsibility that I held as Dean of the biggest faculty at the University of Nairobi, the Faculty of Arts, the things that I said, and the confidence colleagues and students had in me, in electing me to such an important position. Can one compromise and act as if one is betraying these very people who have voted one into the position of authority and trust, by acting as if one is a policewoman towards them? Academically and intellectually, they have no freedom, whatever they say is censored. It is very difficult, in Kenyan society, to speak one's mind, especially if one takes a position that is prosocialism. One faces harassment and imprisonment.

I felt, therefore, that with my obvious commitment to this kind of development, it was going to be of no use to find myself behind bars or to have to compromise my position, not being able to speak my mind or write what I think. So I have opted to live outside my country. So long as I live on the African continent, I can carry on the struggle which, essentially, is the same.

ADEOLA: Is it inevitable for the artist who speaks to her people to have to leave her home environment?

MICERE: I don't think it is inevitable, but not to can be quite tricky. The task of the artist, and, indeed, of any of us, who seeks a change that will better the lives of our people, is actually to stay at home and struggle with the people there in order to bring about this change. But I feel that it is adventurist, a way of wanting to be a martyr, which doesn't help anybody, to see a situation in which an artist or teacher, whatever, is obviously going to end up behind bars, and continue to wait for it to happen. I think it is better to go and use your talent somewhere else. The artist has a choice. The one who has decided to speak for her people, the oppressed, and to take sides with them, has got a very, very difficult line of existence indeed, whether one is living at home or outside, because the struggle continues even when one is outside.

As I said earlier, mine was a very conscious choice. I had enough evidence to know that it was going to be very difficult for me to live outside and live free unless I were to shut up and I have a problem with shutting up. When I really believe in something I want to say it. I don't want to compromise. I took this as maybe another tactic that writers and revolutionaries have to learn – to shut their mouths and keep quiet at critical moments, as a strategy.

ADEOLA: Do you think that in Africa, your type of experience has compromised many writers or has even prevented others from becoming writers?

MICERE: What I do know is that if you really have the urge to be a writer, it is very difficult for anything to stop you. Having said that, I must admit that there is a lot of talent among people who cannot read and write today, but of course they cannot sit down and write. Some of them compose and produce in form of orature. So I make the previous statement and then take it back. What I mean by saying that if you have the urge to write nothing can stop you, is that if you do have the facilities and the ability and the skill to write, I think it is very difficult for any one to stop you. As many of us have seen, you lock a man or a woman up in prison and they find a way of collecting bits and pieces and they continue writing. They learn to train their memory to retain a lot of the things that they are composing and later on they put it on paper. It is really not a very difficult thing since you have the images that you are writing about gazing at you full in the face.

ADEOLA: Do you ever wish that you were not charged with this agonizing responsibility to write?

MICERE: It keeps happening to me. I have many things in my mind that I want to write about, many manuscripts that I have started and have not been able to complete. So that I get frustrated, and at such moments I sort of wish I did not have the urge to write. Sometimes, I cannot go to sleep because of this frustration. However, a new kind of person is emerging who is so deeply involved in community affairs and happenings within where I am living that, much as I want to get away from it, I am not successful. I find myself at schools speaking to school children, at colleges in Harare and other places. There is so much to be done that I tell myself, 'Well, you cannot say no to any of these calls because Africa is in a crisis. You don't know what may happen tomorrow. So long as you are doing these things you are, as it were, writing a poem that will never find itself on the pages of a book, but at least it may have touched another person's soul.'

ADEOLA: Do you think writers are different from other people?

MICERE: I want to insist very firmly that writers are not different from other people. They are very ordinary people, like the people in the villages, in the factories, out there, wherever people are. The only advantage, talking about the writer who actually communicates through putting pen to paper – most of us are spoilt brats – is that we have good jobs, good houses, places where we can actually write. We are spoilt because of this image of a writer as an exceptional person, to be treated exceptionally and so on. I want to repeat what Okello Oculi said at a writers' conference, I think it was in Washington D.C. He said, 'In Africa writers cannot afford the luxury of acting like spoilt children. We are ordinary people. Any writer who is not recognized in her or his village by the villagers and ordinary people is not worthy of being called a writer.'

Having said that, I do want to add that a writer has a special talent in that not everybody . . . can actually write. I think you have to have that gift of originality, in terms of being able to give an extra dimension to the world you perceive; in terms of being able to be moved by images, by incidents, by people in such a way that you want to comment about them. Writing is a creative process, therefore I feel that writers should be concerned with the destructive elements and political systems which impede and arrest our people's development. A writer has to develop a special sensitivity and a specified ideological position, in order to be able to show people in which direction the imagination is going.

ADEOLA: I have with me your collection of poems, *Daughter of My People Sing* and your two plays, *The Trial of Dedan Kimathi* (co-author, Ngugi wa Thiong'o) and *The Long Illness of Ex-Chief Kiti*. An obvious theme they all have in common is the call for a meaningful liberation in Africa. Obviously you are disillusioned with our so-called Independence. Is this disillusionment localized or can you see a common trend in our history of failure on this continent?

MICERE: It is not localized. It is a history that is common to all formerly colonized people, most of whom, today, are neo-colonialists, promoting the very same structures as under colonialism. If you do a class analysis, a lot of the black people who are in power present precisely the same ideology of capitalism as the colonizer. This is my quarrel with the present-day African intelligentsia. It is true that I am a member of the petit-bourgeoisie, a very privileged and elite person, because of my job as a university professor. But how can I be happy with my class position when the majority of my people are living in poverty. What arrogance have I to talk of myself as having succeeded?

ADEOLA: As a writer among other writers and other privileged people in Africa do you find a nucleus of serious people who are working for change?

MICERE: Most of our intelligentsia are liberals. We are ready to discuss things and to talk intellectually about issues. But when it really comes to a hard choice in which there is a clear struggle with the people against imperialist and capitalist forces, then we find reasons for escaping. A clear third are outright conservatives. Probably they make two-thirds, who knows? These reaped the fruits of Independence, so they are comfortable, and they feel they deserve to be privileged. Some of them may even rationalize that the workers are poor because they didn't have the brains to go far in their education, they are lazy, and so on.

The writer too has a class position. We have only a very few writers who have chosen to side with the oppressed majority, who have actually taken a clear ideological position in which they are going to use their writing as a weapon in the struggle for liberation. We have another category of humanistic writers, who feel very angry about the sufferings of the majority of our people, but who couch it in a very evasive way, in imagery, in their writing. Then, of course, there are those who tell you, 'I write for myself. I write for pleasure. My writing is my own business. It has nothing to do with politics.' The kind of writer that I have a lot of time and respect for is a writer like the late Alex La Guma. I admire the fact that his writing was not only talking about struggle, but he was really part and parcel of the struggle in South Africa. I admire somebody like Ngugi wa Thiong'o, whose example and position in life has demonstrated his commitment to the struggle of the Kenyan people. I admire somebody like Sembene Ousmane. This kind of writer I want to identify with.

ADEOLA: The examples you have just cited are great African writers who have had no problem being published in spite of their ideological position. Is this the experience of the majority?

MICERE: No, it isn't. I'm very glad you point it out. The thing about western capitalists is that where profit will get into their pockets, they will not let a chance go. So that even when the books of somebody like Ngugi wa Thiong'o were very, very dangerous and nobody dared to touch them, Heinemann went ahead and published them, with all the risks involved, because they knew the books would sell. This is not the case with some of the younger and unknown writers. Some of them have great problems in getting anywhere near a publishing house. The majority of our people, who compose in our tongues and who cannot write, are even worse off. Their materials will first have to find a collector and then go through the publishing house. This is very difficult. That is why I said earlier that a lot of our writers are still unsung. We have not seen them, we have not seen their talents.

ADEOLA: To continue with the question of publishing, I have interviewed several women writers, both well-known and unknown, most of whom complain about the problems they encounter with publishers. Some have been downright discouraged and have stopped writing. Do you have any ideas or suggestions as to what could be done about this problem?

MICERE: The only position I can take on this will be that of someone who is thoroughly committed to socialism as an economic system. Under socialism you could organize your publishing houses as cooperatives, owned by the State, which would ensure that discrimination and repression did not take place. But so long as our publishing houses are owned by western capitalists or their local supporters, our problems will continue. They will go for writers who have big names, who will make money for them.

ADEOLA: I have spoken to some writers here in Zimbabwe and been told that, at present, anybody who writes will have no problem getting published. On the other hand, in places like Kenya and Nigeria, writers are saying that in the 1960's publishers were soliciting for manuscripts, but now it is a different story. Do you think the establishment of writers' cooperatives will guard against these discrepancies? Do you think the time will come when writers in Zimbabwe will experience the same problems as other African writers?

MICERE: One exciting thing about being in Zimbabwe at this particular time is that, because the Government has declared socialism as its policy and has taken a clearly legislated party line, even publishing houses are very, very careful not to thwart any line that the Government has officially committed itself to.

ADEOLA: Do you think the struggle in South Africa is part of the same struggle as yours in Zimbabwe or is it at a different level?

MICERE: The South African struggle is very close to us here in Zimbabwe, and is both impressive and uplifting. A people have said, 'We are moving forward and this is the way the stream is going to flow.' They have taken action against racism, against apartheid, and a lot of them understand that the true enemy, the chief contradiction that they are fighting, is the economic system under capitalism that impoverishes the majority. At a conference I attended in Oslo recently, Ellen Kuzwayo spoke with strength and determination about the struggle. The role of the progressive writer, who has aligned herself with the suffering majority, is to create a consciousness by the kind of poems, novels and drama she writes; to ensure that our people – workers and peasants, old women and men, and children – see themselves in the pages of those books. In bourgeois writing we don't see them, unless as servants, or supportive characters. So we want to give them a central position in our stories, novels, poems and plays, and to give them powerful and authentic voices. So I see this as the role of the writer. But this role is not feasible if we see ourselves as speaking to the people. We can only speak with them and write with them. We are not gurus, translating what they say or what they do.

ADEOLA: In *Daughter of My People Sing*, a beautiful and inspiring collection of poetry, you challenge the youths to struggle to 'make a new earth' . Do you see part of the struggle for a new Africa the struggle to free her womenfolk?

MICERE: Yes, surely. By her class position, the African woman occupies the lowest rung of the ladder. But on top of that, most of the women in Africa have grown up under patriarchy, in which the male principle is promoted and the female principle is repressed. So we are talking about a continent where women face at least two levels of oppression.

ADEOLA: Would you say that on the whole African women writers have confronted seriously the ultimate questions that literature attempts to explore: 'Who are we?', 'Why was I born?', 'What does life mean for me?'

MICERE: I think that our women writers have wrestled with the questions in various ways. But women writers have not gone very far, really, beyond our male counterparts, in analysing the condition of the majority of oppressed women among the workers and peasants. Very often the women who are portrayed are from intellectual circles and the privileged class. So we are still speaking for the minority instead of the majority. My call to African women writers is to find ways and means of reaching the majority of our people, who are women, to speak for them.

ADEOLA: Will it damage the ultimate struggle for a complete social, economic and political liberation of Africa if we focus on singing the song about the oppression of women?

MICERE: There is nothing wrong with singing about women but I think that we must be very careful to define and specify which women we are singing about. I still insist that we must sing and sing and sing again about our mothers out there in the rural areas, in the high density 'suburbs', and their poverty. This song can never be too much because it is the song of Africa. My only quarrel with singing is when we only sing for the well-known women, those who have made it in society, as if they represent the condition of all African women.

ADEOLA: *The Trial of Dedan Kimathi* focuses on the strength of women and their contribution to the liberation struggle in Kenya. Significantly, it is the Woman and the Girl (I am referring to the characters) who instil strength and courage into the Boy. In the same way, Kimathi attributes his strength to his grandmother in these words:

> . . . I was blessed by a blind grandmother. A peasant, a toiler. She imparted her strength, the strength of our people into me. I felt her blind faith, blind strength enter my bones. Fire and light.[1]

What is the purpose of this shift of focus from the great heroic figure of Kimathi to the women?

MICERE: We didn't mean it to be a shift but a kind of fusion, to show that what Kimathi was fighting for was the same thing that a lot of our women were fighting for. Our concern was that whereas, the part that the men played in the struggle has been recorded by historians and biographers, the women on the whole have simply been forgotten. It is as if they were just sitting at the back somewhere and doing nothing. When I was doing the research on *Visions of Africa*, a thesis that was going to deal, among other things, with novels contrasting the colonialist–imperialist view with the vision of the insiders, and those committed to the people, this research revealed a lot of women who had actually served in the Mau-Mau war as generals or lieutenants. Ngugi too had come across similar findings in his research. We even met some women who had worked very closely with Kimathi, and they were responsible for revealing to us the real character of the Kimathi that we depicted in the book, rather than the one presented by the colonialist: a Kimathi full of warmth, a great leader, a person who was really loved and respected. We did not meet anyone, man or woman, who did not love him, though they may have disagreed with some of the ways he carried out this or the other. The women were some of the strongest of the voices that told us what went on during the Mau-Mau war. These voices gave us a vision, so we said the least we could do was to bring them out in the book and bring out this hidden strength. So we did it deliberately.

ADEOLA: Do you believe that each generation builds on a higher level? How do you view our generation in comparison with our mothers'?

MICERE: I will tell you the honest truth. It depends on who we think we are in terms of our class position. I think that the educated who are conservative and the educated who still have not aligned themselves with the impoverished majority of our people, have betrayed the position that our mothers and our fathers found themselves in thirty years ago.

I will tell you a story. There was a woman who witnessed a kind of quarrel, an illiterate woman who saw the educated women quarrelling for high position in the women's organizations. She stood up and made a very moving statement that I took note of. She said, 'Look, I do not have all those high degrees that you people have, but so long as you have them, they are mine. I feel they are as much mine as they are yours.'

You know, the workers and peasants, our mothers and grandmothers, even as we are talking now, have so much faith in us. They believe we went to school in order to learn the secrets of the enemy. Progressive people are fashioning history, pushing history forward, because they can see the sacrifices that were made so that we are where we are today. I think this should be the task of any progressive writer.

ADEOLA: You have done this in *The Trial of Dedan Kimathi*. There are clearly stated challenges in the play. The Woman challenges all women to be involved in the struggle when she says:

The trial of our strength.
Our faith, our hopes, our resolve
The trial of loyalty
Our cause.

(p. 14)

Kimathi's challenge is to all when he tells the Business Executive:

We shall win the war. For, let me tell the fainthearted that this our struggle will continue until we seize back the right and the ability to make ourselves new men and women in our own land.

(p. 45)

It is a unique play, one that takes us close to the theatre of Brecht and plays like *Mother Courage*. It is a theatre of consciousness-raising and encouragement to struggle. What sort of reactions have you got from people concerning the play?

MICERE: When we wrote the play we were very conscious of our positions as lecturers and writers. We were using drama specifically in order to conscientize our people, to review our history with them and theirs with us to be able to answer the questions, 'Where are we?' and 'Where are we heading?'

ADEOLA: Most critics believe that Ngugi's creative talents are to be appreciated more in his fiction than his drama; could one then attribute the success of *The Trial of Dedan Kimathi* largely to you?

MICERE: You are being a typical female critic. Quite a lot of male critics assume that because Ngugi is a famous writer, he is the sole writer and spirit behind *The Trial of Dedan Kimathi*. I don't think that it has occurred to any of them that I have been writing since school under Rebeka Njau, my involvement in drama goes back to the age of eight years [sic]. Those who realize this sing a different tune. Since the book has been published, Ngugi and I have tried to show that it is a collective effort. It is immaterial to say who came up with the idea – we were living through the same problem, the same issues in the struggle. Ngugi mentions this in his latest book, *Decolonising The Mind*.[2] He and I would agree with what those people who broke through the door of the theatre said, that it was their story. We just added poetic licence and dramatic form to it.

Notes

1. Ngugi wa Thiong'o and Micere Githae Mugo, *The Trial of Dedan Kimathi* (London: Heinemann, 1977), p. 36.
2. Ngugi wa Thiong'o: *Decolonising the Mind* (London: James Currey, 1986).

3. The role of the writer: Chinua Achebe, 'The Novelist as Teacher', in Chinua Achebe, *Morning Yet On Creation Day: Essays* (New York: Anchor Press/Doubleday, 1975), pp. 67–73.

Writing of the kind I do is relatively new in my part of the world and it is too soon to try and describe in detail the complex of relationships between us and our readers. However, I think I can safely deal with one aspect of these relationships which is rarely mentioned. Because of our largely European education, our writers may be pardoned if they begin by thinking that the relationship between European writers and their audience will automatically reproduce itself in Africa. We have learned from Europe that a writer or an artist lives on the fringe of society – wearing a beard and a peculiar dress and generally behaving in a strange, unpredictable way. He is in revolt against society, which in turn looks on him with suspicion if not hostility. The last thing society would dream of doing is to put him in charge of anything.

All that is well known, which is why some of us seem too eager for our society to treat us with the same hostility or even behave as though it already does. I am not interested now in what writers expect of society; that is generally contained in their books, or should be. What is not so well documented is what society expects of its writers.

I am assuming, of course, that our writer and his society live in the same place. I realize that a lot has been made of the allegation that African writers have to write for European and American readers because African readers, where they exist at all, are only interested in reading textbooks. I don't know if African writers always have a foreign audience in mind. What I do know is that they don't have to. At least I know that I don't have to. Last year the pattern of sales of *Things Fall Apart* in the cheap paperback edition was as follows: about 800 copies in Britain; 20,000 in Nigeria; and about 2,500 in all other places. The same pattern was true also of *No Longer at Ease*.

Most of my readers are young. They are either in school or college or have only recently left. And many of them look at me as a kind of teacher. Only the other day I received this letter from Northern Nigeria:

> Dear C. Achebe, I do not usually write to authors, no matter how interesting their work is, but I feel I must tell you how much I enjoyed your editions of *Things Fall Apart* and *No Longer at Ease*. I look forward to reading your new edition of *Arrow of God*. Your novels serve as advice to us young. I trust that you will continue to produce as many of this type of book. With friendly greetings and best wishes. Yours sincerely,
>
> I. Buba Yero Mafindi

It is quiet clear what this particular reader expects of me. Nor is there much doubt about another reader in Ghana who wrote me a rather pathetic letter to say that I had neglected to include questions and answers at the end of *Things Fall Apart* and could I make these available to him to insure his success at next year's school certificate examinations. This is what I would call in Nigerian pidgin 'a how-for-do' reader and I hope there are not very many like him. But also in Ghana I met a young woman teacher who immediately took me to task for not making the hero of my *No Longer at Ease* marry the girl he is in love with. I made the kind of vague noises I usually make whenever a wise critic comes along to tell me I should have written a different book to the one I wrote. But my woman teacher was not going to be shaken off so easily. She was in deadly earnest. Did I know, she said, that there were many women in the kind of situation I had described and that I could have served them well if I had shown that it was possible to find one man with enough guts to go against custom?

I don't agree, of course. But this young woman spoke with so much feeling that I couldn't help being a little uneasy at the accusation (for it was indeed a serious accusation) that I had squandered a rare opportunity for education on a whimsical and frivolous exercise. It is important to say at this point that no self-respecting writer will take dictation from his audience. He must remain free to disagree with his society and go into rebellion against it if need be. But I am for choosing my cause very carefully. Why should I start waging war as a Nigerian newspaper editor was doing the other day on the 'soulless efficiency' of Europe's industrial and technological civilization when the very thing my society needs may well be a little technical efficiency?

My thinking on the peculiar needs of different societies was sharpened when not long ago I heard an English pop song, which I think was entitled 'I Ain't Gonna Wash for a Week'. At first I wondered why it should occur to anyone to take such a vow when there were so many much more worthwhile resolutions to make. But later it dawned on me that this singer belonged to the same culture which, in an earlier age of self-satisfaction, had blasphemed and said that cleanliness was next to godliness. So I saw him in a new light – as a kind of divine administrator of vengeance. I make bold to say, however, that his particular offices would not be required in my society because we did not commit the sin of turning hygiene into a god.

Needless to say, we do have our own sins and blasphemies recorded against our name. If I were God, I would regard as the very worst our acceptance – for whatever reason – of racial inferiority. It is too late in the day to get worked up about it or to blame others, much as they may deserve such blame and condemnation. What we need to do is to look back and try to find out where we went wrong, where the rain began to beat us.

Let me give one or two examples of the result of the disaster brought upon the African psyche in the period of subjection to alien races. I remember the shock felt by Christians of my father's generation in my village in the early forties when, for the first time, the local girls' school performed Nigerian dances at the anniversary of the coming of the gospel. Hitherto they had always put on something Christian and civilized which I believe was called the Maypole dance. In those days – when I was growing up – I also remember that it was only the poor benighted heathen who had any use for our local handcraft, e.g., our pottery. Christians and the well-to-do (and they were usually the same people) displayed their tins and other metalware. We never carried waterpots to the stream. I had a small cylindrical biscuit tin suitable to my years, while the older members of our household carried four-gallon kerosene tins.

Today, things have changed a lot, but it would be foolish to pretend that we have fully recovered from the traumatic effects of our first confrontation with Europe. Three or four weeks ago, my wife, who teaches English in a boys' school, asked a pupil why he wrote about winter when he meant the harmattan. He said the other boys would call him a bushman if he did such a thing! Now, you wouldn't have thought, would you, that there was something shameful in your weather? But apparently we do. How can this great blasphemy be purged? I think it is part of my business as a writer to teach that boy that there is nothing disgraceful about the African weather, that the palm tree is a fit subject for poetry.

Here then is an adequate revolution for me to espouse – to help my society regain belief in itself and put away the complexes of the years of denigration and self-abasement. And it is essentially a question of education, in the best sense of that word. Here, I think, my aims and the deepest aspirations of my society meet. For no thinking African can escape the pain of the wound in our soul. You have all heard of the African personality, of African democracy, of the African way to socialism, of negritude, and so on. They are all props we have fashioned at different times to help us get on our feet again. Once we are up, we shan't need any of them any more. But for the moment it is in the nature of things that we may need to counter racism with what Jean-Paul Sartre has called an anti-racist racism, to announce not just that we are as good as the next man but that we are much better.

The writer cannot expect to be excused from the task of re-education and regeneration that must be done. In fact he should march right in front. For he is after all – as Ezekiel Mphahlele says in his *African Image* – the sensitive point of his community. The Ghanaian professor of philosophy, William Abraham, put it this way:

> Just as African scientists undertake to solve some of the scientific problems of Africa, African historians go into the history of Africa, African political scientists concern themselves with the politics of Africa; why should African literary creators be exempted from the services that they themselves recognize as genuine?

I, for one, would not wish to be excused. I would be quite satisfied if my novels (especially the ones I set in the past) did no more than teach my readers that their past – with all its imperfections – was not one long night of savagery from which the first Europeans acting on God's behalf delivered them. Perhaps what I write is applied art as distinct from pure. But who cares? Art is important, but so is education of the kind I have in mind. And I don't see that the two need be mutually antagonistic. In a recent anthology, a Hausa folk tale, having recounted the usual fabulous incidents, ends with these words:

> They all came and they lived happily together. He had several sons and daughters who grew up and helped in raising the standard of education in the country.

As I said elsewhere, if you consider this ending a naive anticlimax, then you cannot know very much about Africa.

4. The Language question: Ngugi wa Thiong'o, 'The Language of African Literature', in Ngugi wa Thiong'o, *Decolonising the Mind: The Politics of Language in African Literature* (London: James Currey, 1981), pp. 4–9.

I

The language of African literature cannot be discussed meaningfully outside the context of those social forces which have made it both an issue demanding our attention and a problem calling for a resolution.

On the one hand is imperialism in its colonial and neo-colonial phases continuously press-ganging the African hand to the plough to turn the soil over, and putting blinkers on him to make him view the path ahead only as determined for him by the master armed with the bible and the sword. In other words, imperialism continues to control the economy, politics, and cultures of Africa. But on the other, and pitted against it, are the ceaseless struggles of African people to liberate their economy, politics and culture from that Euro-American-based stranglehold to usher a new era of true communal self-regulation and self-determination. It is an ever-continuing struggle to seize back their creative initiative in history through a real control of all the means of communal self-definition in time and space. The choice of language and the use to which language is put is central to a people's definition of themselves in relation to their natural and social environment, indeed in relation to the entire universe. Hence language has always been at the heart of the two contending social forces in the Africa of the twentieth century.

The contention started a hundred years ago when in 1884 the capitalist powers of Europe sat in Berlin and carved an entire continent with a multiplicity of peoples, cultures, and languages into different colonies. It seems it is the fate of Africa to have her destiny always decided around conference tables in the metropolises of the western world: her submergence from self-governing communities into colonies was decided in Berlin; her more recent transition into neo-colonies along the same boundaries was negotiated around the same tables in London, Paris, Brussels and Lisbon. The Berlin-drawn division under which Africa is still living was obviously economic and political, despite the claims of bible-wielding diplomats, but it was also cultural. Berlin in 1884 saw the division of Africa into the different languages of the European powers. African countries, as colonies and even today as neo-colonies, came to be defined and to define themselves in terms of the languages of Europe: English-speaking, French-speaking or Portuguese-speaking African countries.

Unfortunately writers who should have been mapping paths out of that linguistic encirclement of their continent also came to be defined and to define themselves in terms of the languages of imperialist imposition. Even at their most radical and pro-African position in their sentiments and articulation of problems they still took it as axiomatic that the renaissance of African cultures lay in the languages of Europe.

I should know!

II

In 1962 I was invited to that historic meeting of African writers at Makerere University College, Kampala, Uganda. The list of participants contained most of the names which have now become the subject of scholarly dissertations in universities all over the world. The title? 'A Conference of African Writers of English Expression'.

I was then a student of English at Makerere, an overseas college of the University of London. The main attraction for me was the certain possibility of meeting Chinua Achebe. I had with me a rough typescript of a novel in progress, *Weep Not, Child*, and I wanted him to read it. In the previous year, 1961, I had completed *The River Between*, my first-ever attempt at a novel, and entered it for a writing competition organised by the East African Literature Bureau. I was keeping in step with the tradition of Peter Abrahams with his output of novels and autobiographies from *Path of Thunder* to *Tell Freedom* and followed by Chinua Achebe with his publication of *Things Fall Apart* in 1959. Or there were their counterparts in French colonies, the generation of Sédar Senghor and David Diop included in the 1947/48 Paris edition of *Anthologie de la nouvelle poésie nègre et malgache de langue francaise*. They all wrote in European languages as was the case with all the participants in that momentous encounter on Makerere hill in Kampala in 1962.

The title of the 'Conference of African Writers of English Expression' automatically excluded those who wrote in African languages. Now on looking back from the self-questioning heights of 1986, I can see this contained absurd anomalies. I, a student, could qualify for the meeting on the basis of only two published short stories, 'The Fig Tree (Mugumo)' in a student journal, *Penpoint*, and 'The Return' in a new journal, *Transition*. But neither Shabaan Robert, then the greatest living East African poet with several works of poetry and prose to his credit in Kiswahili, nor Chief Fagunwa, the great Nigerian writer with several published titles in Yoruba, could possibly qualify.

The discussions on the novel, the short story, poetry, and drama were based on extracts from works in English and hence they excluded the main body of work in Swahili, Zulu, Yoruba, Arabic, Amharic and other African languages. Yet, despite this exclusion of writers and literature in African languages, no sooner were the introductory preliminaries over than this Conference of 'African Writers of English Expression' sat down to the first item on the agenda: 'What is African Literature?'

The debate which followed was animated: Was it literature about Africa or about the African experience? Was it literature written by Africans? What about a non-African who wrote about Africa: did his work qualify as African literature? What if an African set his work in Greenland: did that qualify as African literature? Or were African languages the criteria? OK: what about Arabic, was it not foreign to Africa? What about French and English, which had become African languages? What if a European wrote about Europe in an African language? If . . . if . . . if . . . this or that, except the issue: the domination of our languages and cultures by those of imperialist Europe: in any case there was no Fagunwa or Shabaan Robert or any writer in African languages to bring the conference down from the realms of evasive abstractions. The question was never seriously asked: did what we wrote qualify as African literature? The whole area of literature and audience, and hence of language as a determinant of both the national and class audience, did not really figure: the debate was more about the subject matter and the racial origins and geographical habitation of the writer.

English, like French and Portuguese, was assumed to be the natural language of literary and even political mediation between African people in the same nation and between nations in Africa and other continents. In some instances these European languages were seen as having a capacity to unite African peoples against divisive tendencies inherent in the multiplicity of African languages within the same geographic state. Thus Ezekiel Mphahlele later could write, in a letter to *Transition*, number 11, that English and French have become the common language with which to present a nationalist front against white oppressors, and even 'where the whiteman has already retreated, as in the independent states, these two languages are still a unifying force'. In the literary sphere they were often seen as coming to save African languages against themselves. Writing a foreword to Birago Diop's book *Contes d'Amadou Kosomba* Sédar Senghor commends him for using French to rescue the spirit and style of old African fables and tales. 'However while rendering them into French he renews them with an art which, while it respects the genius of the French language, that language of gentleness and honesty, preserves at the same time all the virtues of the negro-african languages.' English, French and Portuguese had come to our rescue and we accepted the unsolicited gift with gratitude. Thus in 1964, Chinua Achebe, in a speech entitled 'The African Writer and the English Language', said:

> Is it right that a man should abandon his mother tongue for someone else's? It looks like a dreadful betrayal and produces a guilty feeling. But for me there is no other choice. I have been given the language and I intend to use it.[1]

See the paradox: the possibility of using mother-tongues provokes a tone of levity in phrases like 'a dreadful betrayal' and 'a guilty feeling'; but that of foreign languages produces a categorical positive embrace, what Achebe himself, ten years later, was to describe as this 'fatalistic logic of the unassailable position of English in our literature'.[2]

The fact is that all of us who opted for European languages – the conference participants and the generation that followed them accepted that fatalistic logic to a greater or lesser degree. We were guided by it and the only question which preoccupied us was how best to make the borrowed tongues carry the weight of our African experience by, for instance, making them 'prey' on African proverbs and other peculiarities of African speech and folklore. For this task, Achebe (*Things Fall Apart; Arrow of God*), Amos Tutuola (*The Palmwine Drinkard; My Life in the Bush of Ghosts*), and Gabriel Okara (*The Voice*) were often held as providing the three alternative models. The lengths to which we were prepared to go in our mission of enriching foreign languages by injecting Senghorian 'black blood' into their rusty joints, is best exemplified by Gabriel Okara in an article reprinted in *Transition*:

> As a writer who believes in the utilization of African ideas, African philosophy and African folklore and imagery to the fullest extent possible, I am of the opinion the only way to use them effectively is to translate them almost literally from the African language native to the writer into whatever European language he is using as medium of expression. I have endeavoured in my words to keep as close as possible to the vernacular expressions. For, from a word, a group of words, a sentence and even a name in any African language, one can glean the social norms, attitudes and values of a people.
> In order to capture the vivid images of African speech, I had to eschew the habit of expressing my thoughts first in English. It was difficult at first, but I had to learn. I had to study each Ijaw expression I used and

to discover the probable situation in which it was used in order to bring out the nearest meaning in English. I found it a fascinating exercise.[3]

Why, we may ask, should an African writer, or any writer, become so obsessed by taking from his mother-tongue to enrich other tongues? Why should he see it as his particular mission? We never asked ourselves: How can we enrich our languages? How can we 'prey' on the rich humanist and democratic heritage in the struggles of other peoples in other times and other places to enrich our own? Why not have Balzac, Tolstoy, Sholokov, Brecht, Lu Hsun, Pablo Neruda, H.C. Anderson, Kim Chi Ha, Marx, Lenin, Albert Einstein, Galileo, Aeschylus, Aristotle and Plato in African languages? And why not create literary monuments in our own languages? Why in other words should Okara not sweat it out to create in Ijaw, which he acknowledges to have depths of philosophy and a wide range of ideas and experiences? What was our responsibility to the struggles of African peoples? No, these questions were not asked. What seemed to worry us more was this: after all the literary gymnastics of preying on our languages to add life and vigour to English and other foreign languages, would the result be accepted as good English or good French? Will the owner of the language criticise our usage? Here we were more assertive of our rights! Chinua Achebe wrote:

> I feel that the English language will be able to carry the weight of my African experience. But it will have to be a new English, still in full communion with its ancestral home but altered to suit new African surroundings.[4]

Gabriel Okara's position on this was representative of our generation:

> Some may regard this way of writing English as a desecration of the language. This is of course not true. Living languages grow like living things, and English is far from a dead language. There are American, West Indian, Australian, Canadian and New Zealand versions of English. All of them add life and vigour to the language while reflecting their own respective cultures. Why shouldn't there be a Nigerian or West African English which we can use to express our own ideas, thinking and philosophy in our own way?[5]

How did we arrive at this acceptance of 'the fatalistic logic of the unassailable position of English in our literature', in our culture and in our politics? What was the route from the Berlin of 1884 via the Makerere of 1962 to what is still the prevailing and dominant logic a hundred years later? How did we, as African writers, come to be so feeble towards the claims of our languages on us and so aggressive in our claims on other languages, particularly the languages of our colonisation?

Berlin of 1884 was effected through the sword and the bullet. But the night of the sword and the bullet was followed by the morning of the chalk and the blackboard. The physical violence of the battlefield was followed by the psychological violence of the classroom. But where the former was visibly brutal, the latter was visibly gentle, a process best described in Cheikh Hamidou Kane's novel *Ambiguous Adventure* where he talks of the methods of the colonial phase of imperialism as consisting of knowing how to kill with efficiency and to heal with the same art:

> On the Black Continent, one began to understand that their real power resided not at all in the cannons of the first morning but in what followed the cannons. Therefore behind the cannons was the new school. The new school had the nature of both the cannon and the magnet. From the cannon it took the efficiency of a fighting weapon. But better than the cannon it made the conquest permanent. The cannon forces the body and the school fascinates the soul.[6]

In my view language was the most important vehicle through which that power fascinated and held the soul prisoner. The bullet was the means of the physical subjugation. Language was the means of the spiritual subjugation.

Notes

1. The paper is now in Achebe's collection of essays, *Morning Yet On Creation Day*, London: 1975.
2. In the introduction to *Morning Yet On Creation Day* Achebe obviously takes a slightly more critical stance from his 1964 position. The phrase is apt for a whole generation of us African writers.
3. *Transition*, no. 10, September 1963, reprinted from *Dialogues*, Paris.
4. Chinua Achebe, 'The African Writer and the English Language', in *Morning Yet On Creation Day*.
5. Gabriel Okara, *Transition*, no. 10, September 1963.
6. Cheikh Hamidou Kane, *L'Adventure Ambiguë* (English translation: *Ambiguous Adventure*). This passage was translated for me by Bachir Diagne.

Select Bibliography

General post-colonial studies

DICTIONARIES, BIBLIOGRAPHIES AND READERS

Ashcroft, Bill, Gareth Griffiths and Helen Tiffin (eds), *The Post-Colonial Studies Reader* (London: Routledge, 1995).

Benson, Eugene and L.W. Connolly (eds), *The Routledge Encyclopedia of Post Colonial Studies* (London: Routledge, 1994).

Herdeck, Donald E. (ed.), *Three Dynamite Authors: Derek Walcott (Nobel, 1992), Naguib Mahfouz (Nobel, 1988), Wole Soyinka (Nobel, 1986): Ten Bio-Critical Essays* (Colorado Springs: Three Continents Press, 1994).

Lindfors, Bernth and Reinhard Sander (eds), *Twentienth-Century Caribbean and Black African Writers*, vol. 1 (Detroit: Gale Research Inc., 1992).

Lindfors, Bernth and Reinhard Sander (eds), *Twentienth-Century Caribbean and Black African Writers,* vol. 2 (Detroit: Gale Research Inc., 1993).

Patrick Williams and Laura Chrisman (eds), *Colonial Discourse and Post-Colonial Theory: A Reader* (New York: Harvester Wheatsheaf, 1991).

POST-COLONIAL STUDIES

Adam, Ian and Helen Tiffin, *Past the Post: Theorizing Post-colonialism and Post-modernism* (Hemel Hempstead: Harvester Wheatsheaf, 1991).

Ahmad, Aijaz, *In Theory: Classes, Nations, Literatures* (London: Verso, 1992).

Ashcroft, Bill, Gareth Griffiths and Helen Tiffin, *The Empire Writes Back: Theory and Practice in Post-colonial Literatures* (London: Routledge, 1989).

Bhabha, Homi, *The Location of Culture* (London: Routledge, 1994).

Barker, Francis, Peter Hulme and Margaret Iversen (eds), *Colonial Discourse/ Postcolonial Theory* (Manchester: Manchester University Press, 1994).

Davies, Carole Boyce, *Black Women. Writing and Identity Migrations of the Subject* (London: Routledge, 1994).

Fanon, Frantz, *The Wretched of the Earth* (Harmondsworth: Penguin, 1967).

Fanon, Frantz, *Black Skins, White Masks* (London: Pluto Press, 1986).

Fanon, Frantz, *Studies in a Dying Colonialism* (London: Earthscan Publications, 1989).

Gates, Henry Louis (ed.), *Black Literary Theory* (London: Routlege, 1984).

Nasta, Susheila (ed.), *Motherlands: Black Women's Writing from Africa, the Caribbean and South Asia* (London: The Women's Press, 1991).

Ngugi wa Thiong'o, *Homecoming: Essays on African and Caribbean Literature, Culture, and Politics* (London: Heinemann, 1972).

Said, Edward, *Culture and Imperialism* (London: Chatto & Windus, 1993).

Slemon, Stephen and Helen Tiffin, *After Europe* (Coventry and Sydney: Dangaroo Press, 1989).

Spivak, Gayatri Chakravorty, *In Other Worlds: Essays in Cultural Politics* (London: Routledge, 1988).

Tiffin, Chris and Alan Lawson (eds), *Describing Empire: Post-colonialism and Textuality* (London: Routledge, 1994).

Young, Robert, *White Mythologies: Writing History and the West* (London: Routledge, 1990).

Walder, Dennis (ed.), *Literature in the Modern World: Critical Essays and Documents* (Oxford: Oxford University Press in Association with the Open University, 1990).

General studies of African writing

DICTIONARIES, BIBLIOGRAPHIES AND READERS

Besterman, Theodore, *A World Bibliography of African Bibliographies* (Oxford: Blackwell, 1975).

Bullwinkle, Davis, *African Women: A General Bibliography, 1976–1985* (New York: Greenwood Press, 1989).

Eastbrook, David, *Africana Book Reviews, 1985–1945: An Index to Books Reviewed in Selected English-Language Publications* (Boston, MA: G.K. Hall, 1979).

Jahn, Janheinz, *A Bibliography of Neo-African Literature from Africa, America and the Caribbean* (London: Andre Deutsch, 1965).

Jahn, Jahnheinz and Clauss Dressler, *A Bibliography of Creative African Writing* (New York: Krauss Thompson, 1973).

James, Adeola (ed.), *In their Own Voices: African Women Writers Talk* (London: James Currey, 1990).

Klein, Leonard (ed.), *African Literatures in the Twentieth Century* (Harpenden, Herts, England: Oldcastle Books, 1988).

Lindfors, Bernth, *Black African Literature in English: A Guide to Information Sources, 1936–1976* (London: Hans Zell, 1979).

Lindfors, Bernth, *Black African Literature in English, 1977–1981* (London: Hans Zell, 1985).

Lindfors, Bernth, *Black African Literature in English, 1982–1986* (London: Hans Zell, 1989).

Nichols, Lee, *African Writers at the Microphone* (Washington, DC: Three Continents Press, 1984).

Wilkinson, Jane (ed.), *Talking with African Writers: Interviews with African Poets, Playwrights and Novelists* (London: James Currey, 1992).

Zell, Hans, Caroline Bundy and Virginia Coulon (eds), *A New Reader's Guide to African Literature*. Revised edition (London: Heinemann, 1983).

STUDIES OF AFRICAN WRITING

Amadiume, Ifi, *Male Daughters, Female Husbands: Gender and Sex in an African Society* (London: Zed Books, 1987).

Amuta, Chidi, *The Theory of African Literature: Implications for Practical Criticism* (London: Zed Books, 1989).

Anozie, Sunday, *Structural Models and African Poetics: Towards a Pragmatic Theory of Literature* (London: Routledge and Kegan Paul, 1981).

Appia L, Kwame Anthony, *In my Father's House* (London: Methuen, 1992).

Arnold, Stephen, *African Literature Studies: The Present State* (Washington, DC: Three Continents Press, 1985).

Bjornson, Richard, *The African Quest for Identity: A Cameroonian Writing and the National Experience* (Bloomington, IN: Indiana University Press, 1991).

Brown, Lloyd, *Women Writers in Black Africa* (Trenton, CT: Greenwood Press, 1981).

Chinua, Achebe, *Morning Yet On Creation Day: Essays* (London: Heinemann, 1975).

Chinua, Achebe, *Hopes and Impediments: Selected Essays, 1965–87* (London: Heinemann, 1988).

Chinweizu, Onwuchekwa Jemie and Ihechukwa Madubuike, *Toward the Decolonization of African Literature: African Fiction and Poetry and Other Critics* (London: Kegan Paul International, 1985).

Chinweizu, Onwuchekwa Jemie and Ihechukwa Madubuike, *Anatomy of Female Power: A Masculinist Dissection of Matriarchy* (Lagos: Pero Press, 1990).

Cook, David, *African Literature: A Critical View* (London: Longman, 1977).

Cooper, Brenda, *To Lay These Secrets Open: Evaluating African Literature* (Cape Town: David Philip, 1992).

Dathorne, Oscar, *African Literature in the Twentieth Century* (Minneapolis: University of Minnesota Press, 1975).

Davies, Carole Boyce and Anne Adams Graves (eds), *Ngambika: Studies of Women in African Literature* (Trenton, NJ: Africa World Press, 1994).

Diop, Cheikh Anta, *The African Origins of Civilisation: Myth or Reality* (Westport, CT, Laurence Hill, 1974).

Diop, Cheikh Anta, *Civilisation or Barbarism* (Chicago: Laurence Hill, 1991).

Duerden, Dennis and Cosmo Pieterse (eds), *African Writers Talking* (London: Heinemann, 1972).

Egejuru, Phanuel Akubueze, *Black Writers, White Audience: A Critical Approach to African Literature* (New York: Exposition Press, 1978).

February, Vernon, *And Bid Him Sing: Essays in Literature and Cultural Domination* (London: Kegan Paul, 1988).

Finnegan, Ruth, *Oral Literature in Africa* (Oxford: Clarendon Press, 1970).

Gakwandi, Shatto, *The Novel and Contemporary Experience in Africa* (London: Heinemann, 1977).

Gérard, Albert S., *African Language Literatures: An Introduction to the Literary History of Sub-Saharan Africa* (London: Longman, 1981).

Gikandi, Simon, *Reading the African Novel* (London: James Currey, 1987).

Griffiths, Gareth, *A Double Exile: African and West Indian Writing Between Two Cultures* (London: Boyars, 1978).

Gugelberger, George (ed.), *Marxism and African Literature* (London: James Currey, 1985).

Gugler, Joseph, Hans-Jurgen Lusebrink and Jurgen Martin, *Literary Theory and African Literature/Theorie literaire et litterature Africaine* (Munster: Beitrage zur Afrikforschung, 1994).

Gurnah, Abdulrazak (ed.), *Essays On African Writing: A Revaluation*, Vol. 1 (London: Heinemann, 1993).

Gurnah, Abdulrazak (ed.), *Essays On African Writing: A Revaluation: Contemporary Literature*, Vol. 2 (London: Heinemann, 1995).

Irele, Abiola, *The African Experience in Language and Ideology* (Bloomington, IN: Indiana University Press, 1990).

Harrow, Kenneth, *Thresholds of Change in African Literature: The Emergence of a Tradition* (London: James Currey, 1993).

Heywood, Christopher (ed.), *Perspectives on African Literature* (London: Heinemann, 1971).

JanMohamed, Abdul R., *Manichean Aesthetics: The Politics of Literature in Colonial Africa* (Amherst, MA: University of Massachusetts, 1983).

Jeyifo, Biodun, *The Truthful Lie: Essays in a Sociology of African Literature* (London: New Beacon Books, 1985).

Kerr, David, *African Popular Theatre: From Pre-colonial Times to the Present Day* (London: James Currey, 1995).

Killam, G.D., *African Writers on African Writing* (Evanston, IL: Northwestern University Press, 1973).

Larson, Charles R., *The Emergence of African Fiction* (Bloomington, IN: University of Indiana Press, 1972).

Lazarus, Neil, *Resistance in Postcolonial African Fiction* (New Haven, CT: Yale University Press, 1990).

Miller, Christopher, *Blank Darkness: Africanist Discourses in French* (Chicago: University of Chicago Press, 1985).

Miller, Christopher, *Theories of Africans: Francophone Literature and Anthropology in Africa* (Chicago and London: University of Chicago Press, 1990).

Moore, Gerald, *Twelve African Writers* (London: Hutchinson University Library, 1980).

Mphahlele, Ezekiel, *The African Image* (London: Faber and Faber, 1974).

Mudimbe, V.Y., *The Invention of Africa: Gnosis, Philosophy, and the Order of Knowledge* (Bloomington, IN: Indiana University Press, 1988).

Mugo, Michere, *Visions of Africa* (Nairobi: East African Literature Bureau, 1978).

Mutiso, Gideon-Cyrus, *Socio-Political Thought in African Literature* (London: Macmillan, 1974).

Ngara, Emmanuel, *Art and Ideology in the African Novel: A Study of the Influence of Marxism on African Writing* (London: Heinemann, 1985).

Ngugi wa Thiong'o, *Writers in Politics: Essays* (London: Heinemann, 1981).

Ngugi wa Thiong'o, *Decolonising the Mind: The Politics of Language in African Literature* (London: James Currey, 1986).

Ngugi wa Thiong'o, *Moving the Centre: The Struggle for Cultural Feedoms* (London: James Currey, 1993).

Nkosi, Lewis, *Tasks and Masks: Themes and Styles of African Literature* (London: Longman, 1981).

Nkosi, Lewis, *Home and Exile and other Selections* (London: Longman, 1983).

Obiechina, Emmanuel, *An African Popular Literature: A Study of Onitsha Market Literature* (Cambridge: Cambridge University Press, 1973).

Okpewho, Isidore, *Myth in Africa: A Study of its Aesthetic and Cultural Relevance* (Cambridge: Cambridge University Press, 1983).

Okpewho, Isidore, *The Oral Performance in Africa* (Ibadan: Spectrum Books, 1990).

Olney, James, *Tell Me Africa: An Approach to African Literature* (Princeton, NJ: Princeton University Press, 1973).

Owomoyela, Oyekan, *A History of Twentieth-century Literatures in English* (Lincoln, NB: University of Nebraska Press, 1993).

Palmer, Eustace, *An Introduction to the African Novel* (London: Heinemann, 1972).

Palmer, Eustace, *The Growth of the African Novel* (London: Heinemann, 1979).

Pieterse, Cosmo and Donald Munro, *Protest and Conflict in African Literature* (London: Heinemann, 1969).

Rao, A. Ramakrishna and C.R. Visweswara (eds), *The Indian Response to African Writing* (New Delhi: Prestige, 1993).

Schipper, Mineke, *Beyond Boundaries: African Literature and Literary Theory* (London: Allison and Busby, 1989).

Soyinka, Wole, *Myth, Literature and the African World* (Cambridge: Cambridge University Press, 1976).

Soyinka, Wole, *Art, Dialogue and Outrage: Essays on Literature and Culture* (Ibadan: New Horn Press, 1988).

Stratton, Florence, *Contemporary African Literature and the Politics of Gender* (London: Routledge, 1994).

Taiwo, Oladele, *Female Novelists of Modern Africa* (London: Macmillan, 1984).

Udenta, Udenta, *Revolutionary Aesthetics and the African Literary Process* (Enugu, Nigeria: Fourth Dimension Press, 1993).

Wanjala, Chris, *Standpoints on African Literature* (Nairobi: East African Literature Bureau, 1973).

Wastberg, Per (ed.), *The Writer in Modern Africa* (Uppsala: Scandanavian Institute of African Studies, 1968).

Wauthier, Claude, *The Literature and Thought of Modern Africa*. Trans. Shirley Kay (London: Heinemann, 1978).

Zabus, Chantal, *The African Palimpsest* (Amsterdam: Rodopi, 1991).

Zirimu, Pio and Andrew Gurr (eds), *Black Aesthetics: Papers from the Colloquium Held at the University of Nairobi, June 1971* (Nairobi: East African Literature Bureau, 1973).

Studies of North African writing

Allen, Roger M., *The Arabic Novel: An Historical and Critical Introduction* (Manchester: Manchester University Press, 1982).

Amin, Samir, *The Maghreb in the Modern world: Algeria, Tunisia, Morocco* (Harmondsworth: Penguin, 1970).

Aresu, Bernard, *Counterhegemonic Discourse from the Maghreb: The Poetics of Kateb's Fiction* (Tubingen: Gunter Narr, 1993).

Badawi, M.M., *A Critical Introduction to Modern Arabic Poetry* (Cambridge: Cambridge University Press, 1975).

Baghli, Anmed, *Aspects of Algerian Cultural Policy* (Paris: UNESCO, 1978).

Cachia, Pierre, *An Overview of Modern Arabic Literature* (Edinburgh: University of Edinburgh Press, 1990).

Kaye, Jacqueline (ed.), *Maghreb: New Writing from North Africa* (York: Talus Editors and University of York, 1992).

Kaye, Jacqueline and Abdelhamid Zoubir, *The Ambiguous Compromise:*

Language, Literature and National Identity in Algeria and Morocco (London: Routledge, 1990).

Lazreg, Marnia, *The Eloquence of Silence: Algerian Women in Question* (New York: Routledge, 1994).

Lorcin, Patricia M., *Imperial Identities: Stereotyping, Prejudice and Race in Colonial Algeria* (London: I.B. Tauris, 1995).

Monego, Joan, *Maghrebian Literature in French* (Boston, MA: Twayne Publishers, 1984).

Mortimer, Mildred, *Assie Djebar* (Philadelphia: Celfin Editions, 1988).

Ortzen, Len, *North African Writing* (London: Heinemann, 1970).

Ostle, R.C. (ed.), *Studies in Modern Arabic Literature* (Warminster: Aris Phillips, 1975).

Woodhull, Winifred, *Transfigurations of the Maghreb: Feminism, Decolonization, and Literatures* (Minneapolis: University of Minnesota Press, 1993).

West Africa

DICTIONARIES, BIBLIOGRAPHIES AND READERS

Baldwin, Claudia, *Nigerian Literature: A Bibliography of Criticism, 1952–1976* (Boston, MA: G.K. Hall, 1980).

Gibbs, James, Ketu Katrak and Henry Louis Gates, *Wole Soyinka: A Bibliography of Primary and Secondary Sources* (Westport, CT: Greenwood Press, 1986).

Yemi Ogunbiyi (ed.), *Perspectives on Nigerian Literature: 1700 to the Present, Vol. 1: Selections from the Guardian Literature* (Lagos: Guardian Books Nigeria Limited, 1988).

Yemi Ogunbiyi (ed.), *Perspectives on Nigerian Literature: 1700 to the Present, Vol. 2: Selections from the Guardian Literature* (Lagos: Guardian Books Nigeria Limited, 1988).

STUDIES OF WEST AFRICAN WRITING

Achebe, Chinua, *Nigerian Essays* (Ibadan: Heinemann, 1988).

Blair, Dorothy Sarah, *African Literature in French: A History of Creative Writing in French from West Africa and Equatorial Africa* (Cambridge: Cambridge University Press, 1976).

Dunton, Chris, *Make Man Talk True: Nigerian Drama in English since 1970* (London: Hans Zell, 1992).

Fraser, Robert, *The Novels of Ayi Kwei Armah: A Study in Polemical Fiction* (London: Heinemann, 1980).

Fraser, Robert, *West African Poetry: A Critical History* (Cambridge: Cambridge University Press, 1986).

Gikandi, Simon, *Reading Chinua Achebe: Language and Ideology in Fiction* (London: James Currey, 1991).

Innes, C.L., *Chinua Achebe* (Cambridge: Cambridge University Press, 1990).

Jones, Eldred Durosimi, *The Writing of Wole Soyinka* (London: Heinemann, 1983).

Killam, Douglas, *The Writings of Chinua Achebe* (London: Heinemann, 1977).

King, Adele, *The Writings of Camara Laye* (London: Heinemann, 1980).

Maja-Pearce, Adewale, *A Mask is Dancing: Nigerian Novelists of the Eighties* (London: Hans Zell, 1992).

Mezu, Sebastian, *The Poetry of Leopold Sedar Senghor* (London: Heinemann, 1973).

Mortimer, Mildred, *Journeys Through the French African Novel* (Portsmouth: Heinemann, 1990).

Ngate, Jonathan, *Francophone African Fiction: Reading a Literary Tradition* (Trentog, NJ: African World Press, 1988).

Obiechina, Emmanuel, *Culture, Tradition, and Society in the West African Novel* (Cambridge: Cambridge University Press, 1975).

Omotoso, Kole, *Achebe or Soyinka? A Reinterpretation and a Study in Contrasts* (London: Hans Zell, 1992).

Petersen, Kirsten Holst and Anna Rutherford, *Chinua Achebe: A Celebration* (Oxford: Heinemann, 1991).

Roscoe, Adrian, *Mother is Gold: A Study in West African Literature* (Cambridge: Cambridge University Press, 1971).

Senghor, Leopold Sedar, *Prose and Poetry*. Selected and trans. John Reed and Clive Wake (London: Oxford University Press, 1965).

Taiwo, Oladele, *An Introduction to West African Literature* (Walton-on-Thames: Nelson, 1967).

Wren, Robert, *Achebe's World: The Historical and Cultural Context of the Novels of Chinua Achebe* (London: Longman, 1981).

Wright, Derek, *Wole Soyinka Revisted* (New York: Twayne, 1993).

Yoder, Carroll, *White Shadows: A Dialectical View of the French African Novel* (Washington, DC: Three Continents Press, 1990).

East and Central Africa

DICTIONARIES, BIBLIOGRAPHIES AND READERS

Lindfors, Bernth, *Kulankula: Interviews with Writers from Malawi and Lesotho* (Bayreuth: Universtat Bayreuth, 1989).

Molnos, Angela, *Sources for the Study of East African Cultures and Development* (Nairobi: East African Research Information Centre, 1968).

Pichanik, J., A.J. Channells, and L.B. Rix, *Rhodesian Literature in English: A Bibliography (1890–1974)* (Gweru: Mambo Press, 1977).

Zimbabwe National Bibliography (Harare: National Archives of Zimbabwe, 1987).

STUDIES OF EAST AND CENTRAL AFRICAN WRITING

Chimombo, Steve, *Malawian Oral Literature* (Zomba: Centre for Social Research, University of Malawi, 1988).

Cook, David, *In Black and White: Writings from East Africa with Broadcast Discussions and Commentary* (Nairobi: East African Literature Bureau, 1976).

Cook, David and Michael Okenimkpe, *Ngugi wa Thiong'o: An Exploration of his Writings* (London: Heineman, 1993).

Gurr, Andrew and Angus Calder (eds), *Writers in East Africa* (Nairobi: East African Literature Bureau, 1974).

Heron, G.A., *The Poetry of Okot p'Bitek* (London: Heinemann, 1976).

Johansson, Lars, *In the Shadow of Neo-colonialism: Meja Mwangi's Novels, 1973–1990* (Stockholm: Almqvist and Wiksell International, 1992).

Kahari, George, *The Search for Zimbabwean Identity: An Introduction to the Zimbabwean Novel* (Gweru: Mambo Press, 1980).

Kahari, George, *The Rise of the Shona Novel: A Study in Development, 1890–1984* (Gweru: Mambo Press, 1989).

Killam, G. Douglas (ed.), *The Writing of East and Central Africa* (London: Heineman, 1984).

Killam, G. Douglas, *An Introduction to the Writings of Ngugi* (London: Heinemann, 1990).

Krog, E.W. (ed.), *African Literature in Rhodesia: National Creative Writers Conference, Ranche House College* (Gweru: Mambo Press, 1966).

Lo Liyong, Taban, *The Last Word: Cultural Synthesism* (Nairobi: East African Publishing House, 1969).

Lo Liyong, Taban, *Another Last Word* (Nairobi: Heinemann Kenya, 1990).

Maughan-Brown, David, *Land, Freedom and Fiction: History and Ideology in Kenya* (London: Zed Books, 1985).

Mcloughlin, T.O. and F.R. Mhonyera, *Insights: Criticism of Zimbabwean and Other Poetry* (Gweru: Mambo Press, 1984).

Ngara, Emmanuel and Anne Morrison (eds), *Literature, Language and the Nation* (Harare: Association of University Teachers of Literature and Language in association with Baobab, 1989).

p'Bitek, Okot, *Africa's Cultural Revolution* (Nairobi: Macmillan, 1973).

Roscoe, Adrian, *Uhuru's Fire: African Literature East to South* (Cambridge: Cambridge University Press, 1977).

Roscoe, Adrian and Mpalive-Hangson Msiska, *The Quiet Chameleon: Modern Poetry from Central Africa* (London: Hans Zell, 1992).

Schild, Ursula, *The East African Experience: Essays on English and Kiswahili Literature* (Berlin: Dietrich Reimer Verlag, 1980).

Smith, Angela, *East African Writing in English* (London: Macmillan, 1989).

Veit-Wild, Flora, *A Survey of Zimbabwean Writers: Educational and Literary Careers* (Bayreuth: Bayreuth University, 1992).

Veit-Wild, Flora, *Teachers, Preachers, Non-Believers: A Social History of Zimbabwean Literature* (London: Hans Zell, 1992).

Wanjala, Chris, *The Season of Harvest: A Literary Discussion* (Nairobi: Kenya Literature Bureau, 1978).

Wanjala, Chris, *For Home and Freedom* (Nairobi: Kenya Literature Bureau, 1980).

Wild, Flora, *Patterns of Poetry in Zimbabwe* (Gweru: Mambo Press, 1988).

Zimunya, Musaemura, *Those Years of Drought and Hunger: The Birth of African Fiction in English in Zimbabwe* (Gweru: Mambo Press, 1982).

Southern Africa

DICTIONARIES AND BIBLIOGRAPHIES

Adey, David, *Companion to South African English Literature* (Craighall, South Africa: Ad Donker, 1986).

Goddard, Kevin, *J.M. Coetzee: A Bibliography* (Grahamstown: National English Literary Museum, 1990).

Gorman, G., *The South African Novel in English since 1950: An Information and Resource Guide* (Boston, MA: G.K. Hall, 1978).

Musiker, Reuben, *South African Bibliography: A Survey of Bibliographies of Bibliographical Work* (London: Crosby Lockwood and Son, 1970).

Read, John, *Athol Fugard: A Bibliography* (Grahamstown: National English Literary Museum, 1991).

Strauss, Julie, *A Select Index to South African Literature in English, 1990* (Grahamstown: National English Literary Museum, 1991).

Switzer, Les, *The Black Press in South Africa and Lesotho: A Descriptive Bibliographic Guide to African, Coloured and Indian Newspapers and Magazines, 1830–1976* (Boston, MA: G.K. Hall, 1979).

Woodson, Dorothy, *Drum: An Index to Africa's Leading Magazine, 1951–1965* (Madison, WI: African Studies Programme, University of Wisconsin, Madison, 1988).

Wyley, Chantelle and Theo du Plessis, *Language and Politics in South Africa since 1976* (Durban: E.G. Malherbe Library, 1990).

STUDIES OF SOUTH AFRICAN WRITING

Abrahams, Cecil (ed.), *The Tragic Life: Bessie Head and Literature in Southern Africa* (Trenton, NJ: Africa World Press, 1990).

Barnett, Ursula, *A Vision of Order: A Study of Black South African Literature in English (1914–1980)* (London: Sinclair Brown, 1983).

Boehmer, Elleke, Laura Chrisman and Kenneth Parker (eds), *Altered State?: Writing and South Africa* (Coventry and Sydney: Dangaroo Press, 1994).

Bunn, David and Jane Taylor (eds), *From South Africa: New Writing, Photographs, and Art* (Chicago: Chicago University Press, 1987).

Chapman, Michael, *Southern African Literatures* (London: Longman, 1995).

Davis, Geoffrey (ed.), *Southern African Writing: Voyages and Explorations* (Amsterdam: Rodopi, 1994).

February, Vernon, *Mind Your Colour: The 'Coloured' Stereotype in South African Literature* (London: Kegan Paul 1981).

Gray, Stephen, *Southern African Literature: An Introduction* (New York: Barnes and Noble, 1979).

Heywood, Christopher, *Aspects of South African Literature* (London: Heinemann, 1976).

Horn, Peter, *Writing My Reading: Essays on Literary Politics in South Africa* (Amsterdam: Rodopi, 1994).

Parker, Ken (ed.), *The South African Novel in English: Essays in Criticism and Society* (London: Macmillan, 1978).

Shava, P., *A People's Voice: Black South African Writing in the Twentieth Century* (Harare: Baobab, 1989).

Watts, Jane, *Black Writers from South Africa: Towards a Discourse of Liberation* (New York: St. Martin's Press, 1989).

White, Landeg and Tim Couzens, *Literature and Society in South Africa* (London: Longman, 1984).

Index

ETHICS, EVIL, AND FICTION